D1075196

Outline of Comparative Literature

By the same author:

Spiritualismus und Sensualismus in der englischen Barocklyrik. Wien, 1932.

Werden und Wachsen der U.S.A. in 300 Jahren. Politische und literarische Charakterköpfe von Virginia Dare bis Franklin D. Roosevelt. Bern, 1939.

Dante's Fame Abroad, 1350—1850. The Influence of Dante Alighieri on the Poets and Scholars of Spain, France, England, Germany, Switzerland, and the United States. Rome, 1950.

Textbooks

Die Schweiz. Philadelphia, 1938.

Kurze Geschichte des deutschen Volkes. New York, 1938.

The American Short Story. Bern, 1940.

In Collaboration

An Outline-History of German Literature, by Werner P. Friederich, with the Collaboration of Philip A. Shelley and Oskar Seidlin. New York, 1948.

Bibliography of Comparative Literature, by Fernand Baldensperger and Werner P. Friederich. Chapel Hill, N. C., 1950.

UNIVERSITY OF NORTH CAROLINA PRESS

Outline of Comparative Literature

from Dante Alighieri to Eugene O'Neill

by

Werner P. Friederich

with the collaboration of

DAVID HENRY MALONE

Chapel Hill   1954

Printed in U.S.A. by
The Orange Printshop
Chapel Hill, North Carolina

UNIVERSITY OF NORTH CAROLINA
STUDIES IN COMPARATIVE LITERATURE

1. and 2: out of print.
3. R. C. Simonini, Jr. Italian Scholarship in Renaissance England, 1952. Pp. 125. Cloth $3.50.
4. Frank G. Ryder: George Ticknor's The Sorrows of Young Werter. Edited with Introduction and Critical Analysis. 1952. Pp. XXXII and 108. Cloth $3.50.
5. Helmut A. Hatzfeld: A Critical Bibliography of the New Stylistics Applied to the Romance Literatures, 1900-1952. 1953. Pp. XXII and 302. Cloth $6.-
6. Yearbook of Comparative and General Literature, I. 1952. Pp. VIII and 148. Paper $3.50.
7. Yearbook of Comparative and General Literature, II. 1953. Pp. X and 164. Paper $3.50.
8. Nan C. Carpenter: Rabelais and Music. 1954. Pp, XIII and 149. Cloth $4.25; Paper $3.50.
9. Yearbook of Comparative and General Literature, III. 1954. Pp. 196. Paper $3.50.
10. Charles E. Passage: Dostoevski the Adapter. A Study in Dostoevski's Use of the Tales of Hoffmann. 1954. Pp. X and 205. Cloth $4.50. Paper $3.50.
11. Werner P. Friederich and David H. Malone: Outline of Comparative Literature from Dante Alighieri to Eugene O'Neill. 1954. Pp. XII and 451. Halfbound $6.-

European Sales through Librairie E. Droz
8 Rue Verdaine, Geneva, Switzerland

Table of Contents

Preface

It seemed thoroughly worthwhile to write this book, for in many ways it endeavors to sketch quite a new view of the panorama of Western literature. The most serious rival of the present work is Paul van Tieghem's "Histoire littéraire de l'Europe et de l'Amérique de la Renaissance à nos jours" (Paris, 1946); yet even that highly informative outline points only to the fascinating parallelisms in the development of literary genres and does not actually dwell on the constant give and take and the deeply inspiring interrelationship between the literatures of various nationalities. It was this constant flow of forms and ideas across national borders and the dissemination of cultural values among neighboring countries which seemed most deserving of presentation, for only such a presentation of modern literature is able to show the essential oneness of Western culture and the stultifying shortsightedness of political or literary nationalism. The very arrangement of the various chapters was conceived in a manner to underscore modern man's lasting indebtedness to the various national and racial strains of Europe.

A work of this scope called for a greater condensation than we were able to give. A judicious selectiveness was successful only when it came to choosing the poets that served as emitters, for it was quite natural that only the very greatest authors and the most significant national contributions should become the subjects of closer scrutiny. Matters became much more difficult in the selection of receivers, for among the poets influenced by Dante, Shakespeare, Cervantes, Voltaire, Goethe, Tolstoy, Whitman, or Ibsen were often minor but interesting writers who could not be excluded. And when it came to other modes of investigation essential for Comparative Literature, the barriers of selectiveness seemed all but to break down, for in the field of intermediaries (translators, travellers, diplomats, refugees) and of thematology (the scores of persons treating the same particularly attractive theme across the barriers of time or space—or, for that matter, adapting similar literary genres as their mode of expression) a multitude of lesser lights had to be included, partly because the work of certain translators and other intermediaries is unusually significant in the history of international literature, and partly because a brief enumera-

tion even of admittedly lesser lights attested to the attractiveness of themes like Caesar, Joan of Arc, or the Alps, or of genres like the sonnet or the apprenticeship novel. All this was part of our task, and minor writers—so easily omissible in the histories of national literatures—could not be treated too cavalierly in an outline of the main currents of Western literature in which minor figures, intermediaries rather than poets, often play an amazingly important role. For this reason, too, we hesitate to call our book an "Introduction" into Comparative Literature, for a beginner, looking for initial guidance, will be helped only by our general discussions of trends and by our restricting ourselves to really significant emitters among the world's great poets. But as soon as he goes beyond that into the problem of receivers, intermediaries, themes, and genres, he will be caught in a real plethora of names and hints which may well perplex him— though that aspect should be quite stimulating and far from perplexing to the advanced student of international literature. We are naturally aware of the fact that the vast field of Comparative Literature covers many more problems than the ones emphasized in this outline—but we thought that the book introduced enough new material in its present form and that weightier questions of aesthetic or philosophical interpretation and coordination would best be left to graduate seminars.

It should be emphasized that in spite of our somewhat unusual mode of presenting our material we do not for one moment wish to belittle the creative genius of the great poets discussed in the following chapters. After the publication of hundreds of pettily nationalistic histories of individual literatures in which various foreign sources of a poet are never even alluded to (because the reader should be made to believe that great national poets created every single incident and idea out of their own divine and unfathomable minds), it seemed bitterly necessary and long overdue indeed to write a new history of literature in which these foreign obligations—graciously given and, in most cases, graciously received—should be properly underscored. To point to the many and rich stimulations from abroad received by a Milton or a Goethe does not in the least mean that these two poets should be called mere imitators of Italy or of France; it simply means to set the record straight and to show that even the greatest among our poets have borrowed, and borrowed gladly, from values given by other lands. In the words of a witty Frenchman: we all feed on others, though we must properly digest what we thus receive. Even the lion is nothing but assimilated mutton.

Among the colleagues at North Carolina to whom we are indebted for careful readings and profitable suggestions are Mrs. Mary Pettis Sanford for stylistic, Mr. Jacques Hardré for French, and Mr. John E. Keller for Spanish matters, and Mr. Albert Suskin for the chapter on Antiquity. And we gratefully acknowledge the assistance given us by a grant from the Alumni Annual Giving Program of the University of North Carolina which was appropriated by the University Research Council. The grant helped to make possible the publication of this book.

W.P.F.
D.H.M.

INTRODUCTION

This book would be extended far beyond its envisaged scope if Antiquity, Christianity, and the Middle Ages were fully included. Ancient oriental influences upon the Mediterranean world or the exact nature of Greek contributions to Roman letters would seem to be quite beyond the pale of students interested essentially in modern literature. Yet, since the study of the interrelations of modern national literatures would be unthinkable without at least a brief consideration of their great and lasting indebtedness to Antiquity, the Orient and the formative centuries of Christianity, it has been deemed best to discuss this indebtedness up through the sixteenth century in these introductory pages. Such a preliminary treatment will allow us, in our later chapter on the Renaissance, to concentrate almost exclusively upon the great contributions of Italy—though in our outline of the international importance of Italian Humanism we naturally shall have ample occasion to come back to the Graeco-Roman inheritance of Modern Europe, just as later, when discussing the reverberations of the German Reformation, we shall refer again to some of the earlier Christian and Hebrew influences.

A. THE CLASSICAL REVIVAL.

Thematology

Some of the literary manifestations of the myths and legends of Antiquity came down to us mainly in the epic and the dramatic literature of Greece and Rome and can, therefore, not be assigned to Homer or Aeschylus or Ovid alone. Space permits us to show the significance and to outline the ramifications and the international reverberations of only one of these cycles.

The STORY OF TROY, after having passed on from Homer, Aeschylus, Sophocles, and Euripides to Romans like Virgil and Seneca, lived on in the Middle Ages through two fabulous accounts, one the *Ephemeridos Belli Troiani (Diary of the Trojan War)* by the pro-Greek Dictys of Crete, and the other, the clumsy *De excidio Troiae historia (The History of the Destruction of Troy)*, by the pro-Trojan Dares the Phrygian. Both versions influenced the important epic *Le Roman de Troie* (ca.

1160) by Benoît de Sainte-Maure, through whom the tale of
Troy was really made known in Europe. Sainte-Maure inspired
Guido delle Colonne's *Historia destructionis Troiae* (*The Story
of the Destruction of Troy*, 1287) which, in 1464, was rendered
from Latin into French by Raoul Lefèvre under the title of *Le
recueil des hystoires de Troie* and of which an English translation, *The Recuyell of the Historyes of Troye* by William Caxton,
was finished in 1471 and printed three years later. Sainte-Maure
also inspired Boccaccio's *Filostrato* which, in turn, supplied the
basis for Chaucer's beautiful epic on *Troilus and Criseyde*.
Among later English adaptations of the tale of Troy should be
mentioned *The Legend of Troy* by John Barbour, *The Troy Book*
(1420) by Lydgate and, of course, Shakespeare's drama *Troilus
and Cressida*, which drew from Chaucer as well as from Caxton.
Among the German translations and adaptations, mention should
be made of *Das Liet von Troye* (ca. 1200) by Herbort von Fritz-
lar, *Der Trojanerkrieg* (ca. 1287) by Konrad von Würzburg, and
Das Buoch von Troja by Hans Mair. Various translations of
Benoît as well as of Guido delle Colonne existed also in medieval
Spanish literature, noteworthily in the encyclopedic *General
Estoria* of King Alfonso the Wise and in the translation of
Guido's *Crónica troyana* by the famous Pero López de Ayala.
A particularly interesting phenomenon was the generally pro-
Trojan bias displayed by these late medieval authors: not only
were the Romans, according to Virgil, descendants of Aeneas
and of Troy, but Geoffrey of Monmouth claimed the same ances-
try for King Arthur, and in Ronsard's *Franciade* (1572), the hero
Francus, the founder of France, was in reality Astyanax, the
son of Hector. The same bias can be found in *Illustrations des
Gaules et singularitez de Troie* by Jean Lemaire des Belges
(1509).

Individual figures and problems belonging to the vast Trojan
cycle were singled out and treated poetically as the centuries
went by: thus the episode of Troilus (Boccaccio, Chaucer), of
Ulysses (Dante, Bermudez), of Aeneas (Wace, Marie de France,
Heinrich von Veldeke), and of Dido (Chaucer, Dolce, Jodelle,
Gager, Virués, Marlowe, Frischlin)—not to speak of such post-
Renaissance treatments as Racine's *Iphigénie*, Goethe's Helen
of Troy (in *Faust*) or O'Neill's *Mourning Becomes Electra*. The
comparatist may wish to investigate, with regard to a particular
modern version, whether it came from Homer, from the *Oresteia-*

trilogy of Aeschylus, from Sophocles (*Ajax, Electra, Philoc-tetes*), from Euripides (*Andromache, Hecuba, Trojan Women, Electra, Iphigenia in Aulis, Iphigenia in Tauris, Helen, Orestes*), from Virgil or from Seneca (*Trojan Women, Thyestes, Agamem-non*)—or he may wish to examine the fascinatingly new inter-pretations which Renaissance authors often gave to material drawn from Antiquity, such as we find, *e.g.*, in Dante's descrip-tion of Ulysses' last quest and of his death in *Inferno* XXVI. In addition to such source studies, also critical comparisons of the kinship between characters and themes in ancient and modern literature have often been made: for instance between Clytemnestra and Lady Macbeth, Clytemnestra and Mary Stuart, Orestes and Hamlet, and so on.

Foremost among other Greek themes deriving either from epic cycles or from the dramatic versions of the Golden Age is the story of Thebes. It was treated by Aeschylus (*Seven Against Thebes*), Sophocles (*Antigone, Oedipus Rex, Oedipus at Colonus*), Seneca (*Oedipus*) and Statius (*Thebais*). The Middle French *Roman de Thèbes*, based largely upon Statius, was translated into English in John Lydgate's *Story of Thebes* (ca. 1420). Many of the Theban heroes and tales (Oedipus, Antigone) were treated poetically, especially from the seven-teenth century on (Vondel, Zamora, Rotrou, Racine, Dryden, Voltaire, Alfieri, Hasenclever). Other cycles and themes of special significance after the Renaissance are the following: the cycle of the Argonauts, the story of Medea and Jason (as treated from Euripides, Ovid, and Seneca to Corneille, Rojas Zorrilla, and Grillparzer); the problem of Prometheus (from Hesiod and Aeschylus to Calderón, Goethe, and Shelley), Al-cestis (Euripides, Wieland), Amor and Psyche (Apuleius, Cor-neille), Phaedra and Hippolytus (Euripides, Seneca, Garnier, Racine), Hero and Leander (Boscán, Marlowe, Chapman, Brac-ciolini, Leigh Hunt, Grillparzer—and comparable to Romeo and Juliet), and so on.

The Epic

The tremendous influence of HOMER, not only on the Greek dramatists, but also on such Romans as Livius Andronicus (who around 220 B. C. was the first to render the *Odyssey* into Latin), Ennius, and, above all, Virgil, makes it difficult to decide just what during the Renaissance and after was due to Homer's influence and what to Virgil's. From the Middle Ages until the eighteenth century the Roman poet tended to overshadow Homer, so that the Greek poet began to occupy his deserved place in the esteem of the moderns only after about 1700. But even before approaching the problem of Homer's influence during the Middle Ages, we must bear in mind that the schism of the Greek Orthodox Church from the Church of Rome in 1054 and the ensuing deep cultural rift made practically impossible the knowledge of ancient Greek language, literature, and philosophy in Western Europe. In fact, at the height of the Middle Ages it was more likely for scholars to know Hebrew or Arabic than Greek. Among the few who, between Boethius and Boccaccio, preserved some knowledge of Greek, we might mention John Scotus Eriugena, Roger Bacon, and the important translator Robert Grosseteste. In Petrarca's *Trionfi* there are far more allusions to Greek authors than there are in Dante's *Divine Comedy*—and Boccaccio again knew more Greek than Petrarca. It was Boccaccio's tutor, Leontius Pilatus, who, after the Trojan versions of Dares, Dictys and Benoît de Sainte-Maure, again provided first-hand information about Homer by translating his two epics into wooden Latin prose. His work was easily surpassed by the Latin version of the *Odyssey* made by Lorenzo Valla (1474).

Beginning with the Renaissance revival of the Greek language, the number of translators of Homer, and other Greek authors, became so great that we will refer only to those men who established reputations as authors in their own right or who translated classical works so frequently or with so much skill that their translations contributed significantly to modern literature. Thus, we should mention in connection with Homer the Spanish poet and translator Juan de Mena (*Iliad*, 1440), the Hugues Salel-Amadis Jamyn translation of the *Iliad* in France (1545-80), the significant version of Lodovico Dolce in Italy (*Odyssey*, 1573), and the George Chapman renderings of the *Iliad* and the *Odyssey* in England (1598-1616). These modern versions of the Homeric poems, along with the translations of other Greek and Roman classics, certainly enriched the vocabulary, the style, and the thought of the various European countries, establishing new stylistic patterns which, with Greek and Latin neologisms, gradually became thoroughly native, and furnishing some of the tools with which the new literature of

Europe was created. That the humanists themselves were aware of the importance of their task is indicated, for instance, in Dolet's essay *De la manière de bien traduire d'une langue en aultre (About the Manner of Translating Well from one Language into Another,* 1540), and by similar philological treatises such as Henri Estienne's *Traité de la conformité du langage français avec le grec* (1565).

The problem of VIRGIL'S indebtedness to Homer indicates that Roman authors might perhaps more accurately be called Graeco-Roman authors, though in spite of the overhelming Greek influences upon Rome, a good case, no doubt, could and should be made for Roman originality, too. The importance of the influence of the *Aeneid* during the Middle Ages is best demonstrated by *Waltharius manufortis (Walther with the Strong Hand),* a Latin epic on Germanic lore written around 930 by the monk Ekkehard in the monastery of St. Gall, and again by the *Eneit* of Heinrich von Veldeke (ca. 1185), the first example of a courtly epic in Germany. More important than the occasional medieval interpretation of Virgil as a sorcerer was the concept of his being considered one of the wisest men of Antiquity—one of the roles assigned to him in Dante's *Divina Commedia.* Virgil's influence upon Dante was certainly great, inferior only to that of Dante's devout Catholicism and that of his love for Beatrice. Through his intense admiration of Virgil Dante in his great epic also created the perfect synthesis between pagan Antiquity and the Christian Middle Ages, and he combined, in one work, an *Inferno* that was predominantly Virgilian (and for which he could find a model in *Odyssey* XI and in *Aeneid* VI) with a *Paradiso* that was predominantly Catholic. Virgil was only slightly less influential on Petrarca, who, even though he borrowed his subject matter from Livy, wrote his *Africa* in almost slavish imitation of the epic technique of Virgil and of Virgil's disciple Statius. Also Boccaccio's *Teseide* (ca. 1341), medieval though it may be in many aspects, was thoroughly Virgilian in its technique; it was the first conscious attempt to recreate the Virgilian epic in a modern vernacular tongue.

Later, with the Renaissance gradually developing into Classicism, the imitations of Virgil became more and more faithful to the spirit of the *Aeneid,* and the patriotic Virgilian epic and its emulation by modern poets came to be considered one of the loftiest and noblest forms of poetry. Hence the immense influence of the *Aeneid* upon *L'Italia liberata de' Goti (Italy Liberated from the Goths,* 1547) by Gian Giorgio Trissino, an epic which intensified the increasingly neo-classical tendencies of the Renaissance.   Ronsard in his ill-fated *La Franciade* (1572) claimed to imitate Homer more than Virgil; yet the opposite was true, and in his patriotic intention to trace all national greatness back to noble Trojan ancestors he certainly tried to achieve for France what Virgil had achieved for ancient Rome.   The same mixture of patriotism and stylistic refinement—both of them so typical of the budding nationalism and Neo-Classicism of the Renaissance—we find in Spain in *La Araucana* (1569) by Don Alonso de Ercilla y Zúñiga, an epic about the Spanish conquest of Chile so inspiring that it was one of the few books in the possession of Don Quijote which was not burnt by his well-meaning friends.   To this class belongs also Lope de Vega's epic *La Dragontea,* which concerns the deadly feud between the Spanish and the English sea-power (the latter represented by Sir Francis Drake).   In Portugal, finally, the imitation of Virgil produced one of the finest masterpieces of the entire Renaissance, *Os Lusiadas* (1572) by Luis de Camoens, on the circumnavigation of the Cape of Good Hope and the finding of India by Vasco da Gama—again an epic exquisitely classical and pagan in inspiration, with Christian elements peacefully co-existing with this Virgilian mood.   Even the "irregular" epic poets of the Renaissance who did not succumb to the increasingly neo-classical trends of these Virgil-imitations, were deeply influenced by the *Aeneid* (Chaucer, Ariosto, du Bartas, Spenser).   It is no exaggeration to say that the impact of Virgil upon the epic writers constitutes one of the most important aspects of sixteenth and seventeenth century literature.

Among the translations of the *Aeneid,* mention should be made of the important first Spanish version by Don Enrique de Aragón, Señor de Villena in 1428.   Among the French translators was Octovien de Saint-Gelais; among the Italians were the well-known Lodovico Dolce (1568) and Annibale Caro (1581); and among the English were Gavin Douglas (1513) and Henry Howard, Earl of Surrey (published in 1557).   The version by Douglas constituted the first scholarly translation into English of a classical work, and Surrey's version is particularly important because it utilizes blank verse for the first time in English literature.

Two minor Roman influences on the epic are represented by Lucan and Statius. LUCAN was influential on Dante and Chaucer; Marlowe translated the first book of his *Pharsalia*. The fact that Lucan had been a Roman born in Spain made him particularly attractive to Spanish patriots like Ercilla, who imitated him in his *Araucana*. From Lucan's baneful tendency towards baroque artificiality of language, the Spaniards, beginning with Juan de Mena's *Laberinto* in the fifteenth century, inherited certain stylistic tendencies which came to the fore with Góngora. The influence of STATIUS, author of the *Thebaid*, is noticeable in Boccaccio's *Teseide*, in Chaucer and in Ariosto; Dante thought of him as a Christian poet and therefore gave him a rather prominent place in the *Divina Commedia*.

In conclusion, a word might be said about what, at best, can be mere comparisons of the poems of Homer and Virgil with certain medieval epics. A comparison of *Beowulf* with the Homeric epics opens up interesting vistas into the important tribal, geographical, martial and poetic differences in early Greek and Germanic epic literature. Similar comparisons are possible also for the *Nibelungenlied* and *Gudrun*; the former epic, the tale of how a woman (Kriemhild) caused war and the subsequent extirpation of an entire people, has often been called the German *Iliad*, while *Gudrun* with its atmosphere of seas and ships and its emphasis upon a woman's loyalty towards her long-absent mate can be likened to the *Odyssey*. The problem of actual influences has been brought up with regard to the possible indebtedness of *Beowulf* or *La Chanson de Roland* to Virgil's *Aeneid*, but it seems safer to proceed quite circumspectly in such matters.

The Drama

The drama shows much more clearly than any other literary form how very dependent upon classical literature the authors of the Renaissance were. In no European country was there any mature drama until authors began to imitate the models they found in the re-discovered corpus of classical literature. These imitations of classical models were, to be sure, adapted to local and contemporary taste and furthermore often pushed out of classical shape by the pressure of the native tradition, but in every country the drama acquired its modern character primarily as a result of the imitation of Greek and Roman models, especially the Roman. The cause of the Renaissance drama in France was also immensely furthered when the Parliament of Paris, in 1548, forbade the continued performance of medieval mystery-plays. Since the development of the modern drama and the comparative study of its growth is so very dependent upon the imitation of classical models, the influence of classical drama on the modern will be re-emphasized in most subsequent chapters and periods. At this point, however, it might be useful to point out the broad lines of classical imitation.

While, with regard to the tragedy, AESCHYLUS had to wait for the age of Racine and Goethe to be duly appreciated, SOPHO-CLES and, even more, EURIPIDES achieved some significance during the Renaissance, though their influence unfortunately could not compare with that of their disciple Seneca, whose works became of paramount importance throughout the Renaissance and the Baroque. In Italy, Luigi Alamanni translated Sopho-cles' *Antigone* in 1533, and the influence of the Sophoclean technique upon Italian dramatists can be seen, among other examples, in Tasso's *Il Re Torrismondo* (1574). In France, Lazare de Baïf translated *Electra* (1537), and his son Jean-Antoine de Baïf, *Antigone* (1573). Though Roman influences upon the Elizabethan theatre prevailed over Greek influences, Sophocles and Shakespeare have often been compared, from Lessing and Herder down to the present time. Euripides, who in style and mentality was far more modern, dramatic, emancipated, and popular than his two Greek predecessors, was translated into Italian by Lodovico Dolce (ca. 1550). Among his French translators was the famous Jacques Amyot (*Hecuba*, 1544), and in 1566 George Gascoigne translated Dolce's version of *The Phoenician Woman* into English under the title of *Jocasta*. The knowledge of Greek dramas was facilitated also by the Latin translations made by Erasmus (who translated *Iphigenia in Aulis* and *Hecuba*) and by the great Scot humanist, George Buchanan (1544).

It was, however, the Roman SENECA who became the most important dramatist of the Renaissance, not only because of the topics actually treated and repeated by him, but also because of the technique of blood and thunder evidenced in these tragedies. Seneca's plays may have been mere cabinet dramas or dramas written for the private stage of Emperor Nero; with their emphasis on ghosts and corpses, revenge and bombast, and pathos and stoicism, they reflected well the atrocities of the Roman arena under Nero. Such appalling models, plus the record of ever so many criminal and monstrous events in contemporary Italian, English and French history, could not but push the Renaissance playwrights ever more deeply into the horror and gore of Seneca-imitations. The earliest dramatic poem to be written under the impact of Seneca was *Eccerinis* by Alberto Mussato (1314), about the criminal life of Ezzelino da Romano. Foremost among the Italian translators of Seneca's plays was again Lodovico Dolce (1560). Our later chapter on the growth of neo-classical tragedy will indicate that Seneca's influence extended in Italy from Poliziano's *Orfeo* (1471) through Trissino's *Sofonisba* (1515) to Cinthio's *Orbecche* (1541), Aretino's *Horatia* (1546) and beyond; in France from Jodelle (*Cléopâtre captive*, 1552), Jean de la Taille and Garnier into the seventeenth century; in England from Norton and Sackville's *Gorboduc* (1561), Kyd's *Spanish Tragedy*, and Shakespeare's *Titus Andronicus* up to the Jacobean playwrights; in Portugal and Spain it can be noticed in Ferreira, Virués and Cervantes; and in Germany it assumed its latest and perhaps worst forms in Lohenstein.

The double aspect of Seneca's influence as a stoic philosopher (his *Letters,* for instance, achieved great circulation through the excellent edition provided by Erasmus) and as a dramatist can be seen especially in two of his greatest disciples, Shakespeare and Montaigne, both of whom were also heavily indebted to Plutarch. Seneca's stoicism was an integral part of Montaigne's philosophy of life, and with regard to Shakespeare it may be asserted that the hopeless pessimism of many of his tragedies and the gloomy fatalism of their heroes are greatly tinged with a Senecan attitude indeed. Thanks to Seneca's influence, Shakespeare's tragedies were far more inspired by ancient Rome than by ancient Greece. Only Racine and Boileau were later able to stop the baneful influence of Seneca's dramatic technique and, by so doing, to transform neo-classical gore into classical dignity. We might add that it would be worthwhile for a comparatist to investigate once and for all the significance of the fact that Seneca (and also Lucan) was born in Spain, for it can be maintained that there is a necessary correlation between the naturalism of Seneca and the famous naturalism of Spanish literature, for instance of the picaresque novels—just as there

may be a connection between the bombast of Lucan's style and
the famous Spanish trend towards baroque turgidity of style as
evidenced, for instance, in Góngora.

In the field of the comedy ARISTOPHANES, though exceedingly influential on PLAUTUS and TERENCE, was hardly
known during the Renaissance. In spite of the basic significance
of Aristophanes, Romans, Italians and Frenchmen did not dare
to follow his political comedies, which were potentially dangerous in times of rising governmental absolutism (think of Molière's self-imposed restrictions in the Paris of Louis XIV, where
no political lampooning would have been tolerated), but preferred the far more harmlessly satirical and social comedies of
Menander (of whom today, however, nothing but fragments are
preserved). In the tenth century the German nun Roswitha
von Gandersheim tried to emulate Terence in her own six
Latin playlets (*Paphnutius, Abraham,* etc.), while at the same
time christianizing his often licentious plots. From Petrarca
on, the fame of Plautus and Terence kept growing in leaps
and bounds, with humanists of the type of Poggio particularly successful in the search for long-lost manuscripts of their
plays. They were translated with increasing frequency, beginning in Germany with Albrecht von Eyb in the fifteenth
century and continuing with Sebastian Brant and Jakob Locher.
Plautus' *Amphitryon* was rendered into Portuguese by Camoens
around 1545; Spanish versions of both *Amphitryon* and the
Menaechmi by Juan de Timoneda were made in 1559. Terence
was translated into Spanish in 1577 by Pedro Simón Abril who,
together with Ronsard in France, deserves to be mentioned also
for having been among the very first to translate a play by
Aristophanes (*Plutus*). In France Jean-Antoine de Baïf in
1567 rendered Plautus' *Miles Gloriosus* into French under the
title of *L'Héros.* Plautus and Terence were imitated widely in
the comedies written both in Latin and in the vernacular languages of the Renaissance, as indicated for instance by the
plays of Wimpfeling (*Stylpho,* 1470), Reuchlin (*Henno,* 1498)
and Hans Sachs in Germany. Shakespeare's *Comedy of Errors*
is indebted both to the *Menaechmi* and to the *Amphitryon* of
Plautus. Among other imitators in this period were Heywood
in England, Torres Naharro in Spain, and, most important of
all, Ariosto in Italy.

The court of Ferrara may indeed be called the cradle of Renaissance comedy; an Italian translation of the *Menaechmi* was performed there as early as 1486. It was due to Ariosto's swiftly-moving imitations of the two Romans in his own plays that the Italian Renaissance comedy came to dominate in Western Europe, with the plots of the *Amphitryon,* the *Captives,* the *Braggart Soldier,* the *Menaechmi* or again of the *Eunuch* and the *Woman of Andros* reshuffled and reformulated over and over again. Ariosto began this trend with his *La Cassaria (The Coffer)* in 1508; his *I Suppositi* of 1509 was translated into French in 1545; the English version by Gascoigne in 1566, called *The Supposes* (a better translation would have been *The Masqueraders*) became the first English neo-classical comedy. Among Ariosto's imitators mention should be made of *La Calandria* by the Cardinal Bibbiena (a clever mixture of Boccaccio and of Plautus), the famous *Mandragola* (*Mandrake,* 1513) by Machiavelli in Italy, and *Cornelia* (an adaptation of Ariosto's *Negromante*) by Juan de Timoneda in Spain (1559). Through intermediaries like Larivey, these Italian imitations of the Latin adaptations of a genre essentially developed by Aristophanes and Menander later spread into France.

Perhaps even more interesting to study than the influence of classical comedy upon the form of Renaissance comedy are the contributions which Plautus and Terence made in basic plots and character types. The stock characters which the Italian commedia dell'arte supplied to European comedy seem to have stepped right out of Plautus and Terence: the bragging soldier, the clever valet, the dull pedant, or the scheming mother. And some of the comic situations which the two Romans exploited seemed never to lose their humor for the Renaissance audience: mistaken identity involving identical twins, the resoluteness of two young lovers to defeat the amorous appetite of an old suitor, and so on.

From the broader point of view of the evolution of modern drama any of the studies of specific influences which have been suggested lead to the realization that the classical plays, both tragedies and comedies, helped to impose the modern form on the drama of Western Europe. Any investigation of the development of the native dramas in Italy, France or England must therefore include a thorough examination of the effect of Seneca or Terence on the dramatic forms and techniques. However native the great Elizabethan tragedies may seem in spirit, the five-act form, the metrical dialogue, and even many of the tragic plots show that the tap root of English tragedy grew through classical Antiquity. But while native traditions caused England and Spain to move ever further away from classical form, it should be emphasized that France and Italy moved more and more toward the strictest kind of imitation of classical models and precepts. Adhering to the reforms and strictures imposed by the critics, French dramatists, toward the middle of the seventeenth century, were determined to turn away from the excesses of the Senecan horror and the imitation of the irregular Spanish *comedias,* and finally attempted to write trage-dies which were more strictly classical than those of the classical authors themselves. The same dependence on classical tradition can be seen in the comedy of most countries. But the proper place for a detailed examination of this development will be our chapters on the baroque and classical periods.

Philosophy

The preceding references to the philosophical and dramatic writings of Seneca have given us a chance to speak of STOICISM, one of the three great philosophical movements to come down to us from Antiquity. Zeno, the father of Stoicism, had a profound influence not only on Seneca, Epictetus, and Marcus Aurelius (who wrote his works in Greek) but, through them, on the en-tire Middle Ages and the Renaissance, from St. Augustine and Maimonides down through Montaigne—with Stoicism at times blending with medieval Christian fervor, then again uniting in a strange combination with Renaissance Epicureanism. It re-mains for us to discuss the other two great philosophical move-ments in some detail, Neo-Platonism and Epicureanism, for they contributed considerably to the history of the world's great ideas.

NEO-PLATONISM, as it developed during the Renaissance, must be studied not merely as a product of humanist scholarship, but as a fusion of genuine interest in Plato and his disciple Plotinus on the one hand with Christian attitudes inherited from the Middle Ages on the other. Platonic ideas were transmitted through the Middle Ages by such men as St. Augustine and Thomas Aquinas, but they began to emerge again in a relatively pure form only with Petrarca, whose sonnets expressed neo-Platonic ideas and attitudes somewhat divorced from, but not uninfluenced by, Christianity. However, Petrarca showed no exclusive or systematic interest in Platonic thought as such. It was only in the fifteenth century that Neo-Platonism became the conscious philosophy of a group of humanist scholars centered around Bessarion in Rome (where he wrote, for instance, his *In calumniatores Platonis*, 1469) and, even more, around the new Academy in Florence. Cardinal Bessarion was one of the most important single intermediaries between the doomed East Roman Empire of Byzantium and Renaissance Italy and a guiding spirit in the tragically futile attempts at a belated rapprochement between the Greek Orthodox and the Roman Catholic Church. Marsilio Ficino and Pico della Mirandola were among the outstanding scholar-teachers at the Florentine Academy, but it was especially the former who led the work of reviving (*Theologia platonica*, 1478), translating (1482) and spreading the philosophy of Plato. Although the products of the scholarly labors of men like Ficino and Pico may seem to be of only indirect literary interest, the extent and very great importance of their activities is a constantly fruitful area for study, for their work helped to give the strongly neo-Platonic flavor to much of what was said and written during the sixteenth century. Indeed, it would be difficult to say where their direct influence stopped, since the Neo-Platonism *e.g.* of Wordsworth can be traced back through Coleridge to Ficino's Latin translations of various neo-Platonic authors. Pico's influence on Hutten's friend Willibald Pirckheimer in Germany and the fact that Thomas More, in 1510, translated the *Life of Picus, Earl of Mirandula* by the latter's nephew, are other indications of the international importance of these Italian neo-Platonists. Among the French translators of Plato one should mention Bonaventure des Périers, the unfortunate Etienne Dolet, who, in 1546, was burnt because of heresies inspired by Plato and Luther, and, above all, Loys Le Roy.

The comparatist will be interested in following this spread of neo-Platonic ideas and sentiments from the humanist scholars into literature proper. This study will take him to every European country and every form of literature. Neo-Platonism contributed above all to the special color and texture of Renaissance lyric poetry, from Michelangelo and Bembo to Sidney and Shakespeare, and from Garcilaso de la Vega and Ronsard to Camoens in Portugal and Kochanowski in Poland. It can be studied as it contributed to the intellectual fabric of the Renaissance epic in such authors as Tasso and Spenser. The neo-Platonic conception of love can likewise be examined in virtually every other kind of literary and semi-literary form, from the drama to the courtesy book. The beautiful definition of neo-Platonic love contained in Bembo's *Asolani* (1505) and, even more, in the fourth book of Castiglione's *Cortegiano* had an almost inexhaustible influence in literature all over Europe. This conception of love expressed by Castiglione, a blend of Neo-Platonism, Petrarchism, and the medieval conventions of courtly love, can be traced into the twentieth century. Of very great importance were also the *Dialoghi d'amore* by the exiled Spanish Jew León Hebreo (1535), which, translated into French by Ponthus de Thyard, influenced not only Marguerite de Navarre, one of the noblest personifications of Neo-Platonism during the Renaissance, but also the entire Pléiade. The popularity and spread of various neo-Platonic ideas during the Renaissance were such that virtually no aspect of Renaissance literary and intellectual activity was untouched in some way by them.

EPICUREANISM was another of the products of the humanist movement which, transmitted from Epicurus through Lucretius, Ovid, Horace and others, helped to color much of Renaissance literature and thought. Although ideas and attitudes close to Epicureanism occurred in literature as early as Boccaccio and Petrarca, it was Lorenzo Valla who made the first systematic and compelling statement on Epicurean philosophy in his dialogue *De voluptate (On Pleasure*, 1431). After Valla, Epicureanism, like Neo-Platonism, was absorbed into Renaissance thought and became one of the fundamental and controlling concepts of many of the writers and thinkers of the period. Lyric poetry as early as Bembo and Aretino reflected neo-Epicurean attitudes, but these attitudes received their most delicate and charming embodiment in the *carpe diem* lyrics of such poets as Ronsard in France and Herrick in England. Indeed, the spontaneous and zestful enthusiasm for living in this world that is so characteristic of Renaissance writing can be viewed as the product of revived Epicureanism. Perhaps the most obvious example of a full-bodied disciple of the new Epicureanism was Rabelais, whose *Gargantua* and *Pantagruel* sparkle with a more than Epicurean lust for life. The program for the education of Gargantua and the rules of conduct for the *Abbaye de Thélème* constituted militant re-statements of Epicurean doctrines which were certainly in opposition to the ascetic Christian traditions of the Middle Ages. That Epicureanism helped to shape the Renaissance character and the Renaissance concept of the good life is fairly obvious, especially in the comedies and the amorous verses of that time, but its spread into other areas of thought and writing is no less important, even though it may be subtler. Even Renaissance political writing can be seen to have been influenced by Epicureanism, for Machiavelli's *Principe* might be considered as an application of Epicurean philosophy to the state as a whole. And Thomas More in the second book of his *Utopia* explained that the strength of the Utopian politic rested upon an Epicurean concept of the nature and purpose of human life. The essential sanity of understanding in the satire of Erasmus' *Praise of Folly* is likewise derived in part from the author's sympathy with Epicureanism.

Late in the sixteenth century the robust Epicureanism of the earlier Renaissance came under attack from the stricter morality of rising Puritanism. The frequently prudish rejection of Epicureanism is, however, an indication of the enormous popularity of the philosophy. The conflict between Epicureanism and strict morality can best be seen in such a work as the *Faerie Queene,* in which Spenser's use of the gracefully Epicurean episodes from Ariosto show that despite his essential Puritanism he could not escape the impact of Epicureanism. And in Montaigne's *Essais,* Epicureanism constituted one of the principal threads of thought, though after the violence and bloodshed of the religious upheavals the concept of happiness was altered from the robust and physical pleasure-seeking of Rabelais to the subtle, contemplative pleasures of the inner man. As Epicureanism and Protestant morality became ever more violently opposed in the seventeenth century, the fresh and natural ideas concerning human enjoyment were frequently lost in the guilt-ridden concept of pleasure during the Baroque Period—a concept which mixed the questionable desires of satisfying sheer appetite and of tasting forbidden fruit. The seventeenth century tradition of libertinism (for instance in the Epicurus-interpreter Gassendi) was but a jaded heritage of Renaissance Epicureanism.

The Historians

Greek and Roman historians from Herodotus to Suetonius became important for content and form as well as for thematological topics with which they supplied modern European literature. Among the Renaissance translators of HERODOTUS were the two Italians Boiardo and Lorenzo Valla, the former rendering him into Italian, the latter into Latin. In 1535, Hieronymus Boner, one of the most prolific German translators of the classics, translated Herodotus into German. THUCYDIDES served as a model to Sallust; he was rendered into Latin by Valla and, as happened so often during the Renaissance, this Latin version, more often than the Greek original, then served as a basis for further renderings into modern European tongues. Among other translators of Thucydides were Claude de Seyssel in France (1520), H. Boner in Germany (1533), and Diego Gracián in Spain (1564). XENOPHON's *Anabasis* was translated essentially by the same group of men: Seyssel, Boner, and Gracián. We shall have occasion to refer to Xenophon's *Education of Cyrus* in connection with the state-novels; it was translated, among others, by Philemon Holland, one of the most significant translators of Elizabethan England.

The influence of CAESAR as historian was far less important than the influence of Caesar as statesman because, for centuries to come, he provided a fascinatingly heroic figure for accounts and tragedies to be written about, for or against him, from Plutarch to Muret, Grévin, and Shakespeare and from Voltaire to Shaw. Among the earliest French books on Caesar's life was *Li hystoire de Julius Caesar* by Jehan de Tuim, who used Lucan as his principal source. *Li fet des Romains compilé ensemble de Saluste et de Suétoine et de Lucan* (*The Deeds of the Romans compiled from Sallust, Suetonius and Lucan*, ca. 1250) by an unknown author is likewise not so much a history of Rome as a biography of Caesar. Among the English translators of Caesar's *Commentaries* were W. Rastell and Arthur Golding (1565).

SALLUST was known to St. Augustine as well as to Dante; together with Caesar, Lucan, and Suetonius he was translated into French (ca. 1370) for King Charles V who, together with his favorite scholar and translator, Nicole Oresme, certainly was one of the earliest French forerunners of the Renaissance. Among Sallust's English translations mention should be made of the *Jugurthan War* by Alexander Barclay (1523). LIVY, an emulator of Xenophon, was used by Plutarch and Petrarca, and was translated into French by Petrarca's friend Bersuire and into Spanish by the well-known early humanist Pero López de Ayala. In Italy, Livy influenced Machiavelli (*Discorsi sopra la prima deca di Tito Livio,*) and in Spain especially Juan de Mariana (*Historiae de rebus Hispaniae libri XXX,* 1592) ; in England he was translated by Philemon Holland. TACITUS was studied by Boccaccio; among his disciples were Machiavelli in Italy and Hurtado de Mendoza, author of *La Guerra de Granada,* in Spain. Finally, SUETONIUS influenced Eginhard's *Vita Karoli magni (Life of Charlemagne)* in the ninth century and Geoffrey of Monmouth's *Historia regum Britanniae (History of the British Kings)* in the twelfth; his *Lives of the Caesars,* translated into English by Philemon Holland, were consulted by Shakespeare as well as by Racine.

Of the late Greek historians PLUTARCH was far more important than either Josephus or Polybius. He may be called one of the most important single influences on the European Renaissance, for his *Parallel Lives* conveyed to the readers of that period an impressive and unforgettable picture of the heroic greatness and the political acumen of Greek and Roman Antiquity. Plutarch was translated into Latin by Guarino early in the fifteenth century; among his German translators we must again name H. Boner (1541), and among his French translators there was especially Jacques Amyot (1559), whose version was at once masterful and famous as one of the greatest examples of French Renaissance translations. Plutarch was well-known to Rabelais, Ronsard, Jodelle and Etienne de la Boëtie; in Amyot's version he was the favorite author of Montaigne and one of the chief architects of Montaigne's philosophy of life. In England, Amyot's version of the *Parallel Lives* was translated by Lord North (1579) ; Queen Elizabeth also translated from Plutarch, and Bacon was thoroughly familiar with him. Through Amyot-North, Plutarch became one of the chief classical sources of inspiration for Shakespeare, whose tragedies derived from him (*Julius Caesar, Coriolanus, Antony and Cleopatra,* and *Timon of Athens*) afford a most convincing example of how such Renaissance dramas, which sometimes incorporated Plutarch's text almost word for word, were able to enrich the intellectual life of the Renaissance and to spark the genius of its greatest poets. Also Plutarch's *Moral Essays* were frequently consulted:

Budé translated them into Latin, Amyot into French (1572), and Philemon Holland into English (1603).

The world of heroic figures described by these Roman and Greek historians included—besides the topic of Caesar, mentioned above—the tragedy of Brutus and (to recall two of the favorite heroines especially among the neo-classical tragedy-writers) the stories of Cleopatra as treated by Chaucer, Cesari, Jodelle, Garnier, and Shakespeare, and of the fiercely anti-Roman schemer Sophonisbe as described by Petrarca, Galeotto del Carretto, Trissino, Mellin de Saint-Gelais, and Montchrestien (to give only a few examples before 1600). Livy's account of the rape of Lucrece inspired retellings and poetic treatments from St. Augustine through Coluccio Salutati, Lydgate and Shakespeare to Alfieri. Also the heroic figure of Alexander the Great should be included here, as Lambert le Tort and Alexandre de Bernay represented it in the Middle Ages in their well-known *Roman d'Alexandre,* and Gautier de Châtillon in his *Alexandreis.* The metre of the *Roman d'Alexandre,* the rhymed hexameter, thenceforth was known as the Alexandrine metre and as such became the great classical metre of French literature. Around 1130 the Priest Lamprecht translated *Le Roman d'Alexandre* into German and, in doing so, laid new stress on the exotic influences from the Orient which just then were being discovered by the Crusaders. *El libro de Alexandre,* very well known in medieval Spain, was influential, among others, on Juan Ruiz, the Archpriest of Hita. Among Renaissance dramatists treating the story of Alexander, mention should be made of Jean de la Taille (*La mort d'Alexandre,* 1561) and Alexandre Hardy.

Lyric and Narrative Poetry

Though important, the influence of Greek and Latin lyricists upon Renaissance poetry was not quite so revolutionary as, for example, the influence of Antiquity upon the drama. In the field of lyric poetry the Middle Ages, from the troubadours in the Provence to the *dolce stil nuovo* in Italy, had developed its own traditions, so that the impact of the *Greek Anthology,* of Pindar, Horace, or Catullus did not strike the Renaissance poets as a completely revolutionary novelty. Nevertheless, the influence of Greece and Rome naturally encouraged a distinct trend towards dignity, nobility, and smoothness which differentiated

Renaissance lyricism considerably from the homespun and didactic atmosphere of certain late medieval poetry which had
prevailed in Europe as late as the middle of the sixteenth century (Hans Sachs) ; and folk-poetry now distinctly became art-
poetry.

SAPPHO's influence, though considerable on Catullus, Horace, and Ovid, was relatively insignificant in the Renaissance;
Luis de León may be mentioned as one of her disciples.   The
same might be said of ANACREON, the inspirer of Horace and
Ovid; yet though most of his works are lost, the discovery, in
the *Greek Anthology,* of pseudo-anacreontic poems by Henri
Estienne in 1552, called forth a rich vogue of imitations.   And
so the bard of wine, women and song became quite an important
medium for the rich sensuousness and Epicureanism so typical
of the entire Renaissance, from the Pléiade in the sixteenth century up to and beyond Robert Herrick in the seventeenth century.   The entire *Anthologia graeca* was for the first time published by Estienne in 1566.

The most important among the three Greek lyricists was
PINDAR; his *Odes* were for the first time edited by the famous
Aldus in Venice in 1513.   His metre, language and thought,
to be sure, were often obscure and difficult to fathom; yet in
his festive poems he conveyed a mood of exaltation, nobility, and
patriotism which could not fail to enflame the Renaissance poets.
Among the Italians Luigi Alamanni was perhaps the first to
emulate him; in Spain, Luis de León studied and partly translated him while detained by the Inquisition.   But his greatest
disciple was Ronsard in France, who in his Pindaric odes glorifying, for instance, royal and political events, may be said to
have become the founder of classical elevated poetry in modern
Europe.   Less important were the Pindar-imitations of du Bellay and of the Italian Ronsard-imitator Chiabrera; only England,
in the seventeenth century, was to produce another great creator
of the Pindaric ode: Milton.   It has sometimes been maintained
that the elevated mood, the lyrical tenor, and the musical accom-
paniment of the Pindaric odes contributed to the growth of the
opera, and in a sense supplied one of its constituent parts.

VIRGIL as a lyrical author was appreciated early; Petrarca—
one of the most important stimulators of lyrical poetry in the
whole of Europe—emulated his *Bucolics* in his own twelve Latin
Eclogues.   Among the translators of Virgil's *Bucolics* and

Georgics, we can name Juan del Encina and Luis de León on the Iberian peninsula, Clément Marot in France, and George Turberville in England. Of particular importance was, of course, Virgil's famous fourth Eclogue which, some enthusiastic readers held, made him a prophet of the birth of Jesus, a Christian before Christ, comparable to John the Baptist—and it may indeed be that before composing it Virgil had read some of the messianic writings of the early Hebrews. As for CATULLUS, he influenced particularly Ronsard and such neo-Latin poets as Johannes Secundus and Scaliger; the prevailing Epicureanism of his mood made him especially attractive to Renaissance lyricists.

Yet it was HORACE who achieved the greatest fame among the Romans, just as Pindar had been most richly emulated among the Greeks. The Middle Ages seemed to prefer his moral works, his *Satires* and *Letters,* over his lyrical poems; Dante, for instance, spoke of him as a satirist. Petrarca, Landino, and Poliziano were among the first to be enthusiastic about him; Bernardo Tasso translated his *Odes* (1531) and Dolce his *Letters* (1549) and his *Satires* (1559). With Horace there began the trend towards classical polish, and his *Odes* called forth a beautifully rich vogue of finely chiselled imitations, especially in the Spain of Garcilaso de la Vega, Luis de León, and the majestic Fernando de Herrera. In France, Péletier du Mans began with his translations and imitations in 1547; Ronsard followed him, perhaps gladly forsaking the exaltation of his previous model Pindar for the somewhat simpler classicism of form and Epicureanism of thought of Horace. Among other French imitators might be named Vauquelin de la Fresnaye and Habert, the latter the translator of his *Satires.* Horace's Portuguese disciples included Ferreira and Camoens; among those in England were Harvey, Jonson, and Herrick.

OVID, more prominent for his narrative than for his lyric poetry and, together with Horace, the greatest poet of ancient Rome, supplied the Renaissance authors with an immense fund of allusions and with a softly sensuous quality of versification which, in turn, produced some of the finest and mellowest works of the Renaissance. His constant emphasis on love—romantic love as in Dante and Spenser, as well as cynical and erotic love, such as was prevalent, for instance, among the anti-Petrarchists —made him a popular poet from Jean de Meung and Boccaccio up to Ariosto and Shakespeare, and of all the countries France seems most thoroughly to have taken to him. He was known throughout the Middle Ages, from St. Augustine to Chrétien de Troyes (whose translation of the *Ars amandi* is today lost), and he exerted a very great influence upon the second and larger part of the *Roman de la Rose* which was written by Jean de Meung (1277). Considerably more flippant and satirical than his rather idealistic collaborator Guillaume de Lorris, Jean de Meung, in his endless and at times realistic discussions of love, profited greatly from the worldly wisdom of Ovid, though he was influenced, too, by the occasional misogyny of the satirist Juvenal. The *Romance of the Rose* was, at least in part, translated by Chaucer; yet even aside from this, Ovid was the classical author Chaucer knew best, and in their attitude towards life and love and in their facility and clarity of style there is indeed a great resemblance between the two poets. Echoes of the *Metamorphoses* can be found in the *Book of the Duchess* and in the *House of Fame*; echoes of the *Heroides*, in the *Legend of Good Women* and again in the *House of Fame*. In Italy, Dante in the *Divina Commedia* had more than one hundred references to Ovid—another proof of the latter's great significance in medieval intellectual life. More important than Ovid's influence upon Frenchmen like Machaut and Germans like Heinrich von Morungen is the very deep impact he left upon one of the most significant books of medieval Spain, *El libro de Buen Amor (The Book of Good Love)*, by Juan Ruiz, the Archpriest of Hita, written towards the middle of the fourteenth century. A French paraphrase of the *Metamorphoses* was made by Bersuire in the same fourteenth century; William Caxton published it in English in 1480.

Among the translations of the *Metamorphoses* in the sixteenth century we must name the German version by H. Boner (1534), the French version by Habert (1562) and, above all, the English translation by Arthur Golding (1565), which was used by Shakespeare. As in the case of Plutarch, so also in the case of Ovid, Montaigne and Shakespeare could be counted among his greatest admirers; Montaigne devoured the *Metamorphoses* even as a small boy, and Shakespeare felt Ovid's influence to an even greater extent than he did the influence of Seneca and Plutarch, with the rich world of Ovid's fables being mirrored in *Venus and Adonis, The Rape of Lucrece*, and *Romeo and Juliet*.

Another English work to reflect the rich texture of the *Metamorphoses* was Spenser's *Faerie Queene*. Among the English translators of Ovid's *Heroides* must be named George Turberville; Marlowe translated the *Amores*. Of the episodes contained in the *Metamorphoses* (Jason and Medea, Philemon and Baucis, Orpheus, and others) especially two should be singled out: the tale of the rape of Philomela is echoed in Shakespeare's *Titus Andronicus,* and the originally Babylonian story of Pyramus and Thisbe (which may be compared to the stories of Aucassin and Nicolette or of Romeo and Juliet) led from Ovid to Boccaccio (*Fiammetta*), Chaucer (*The Legend of Good Women*), and Gower (*Confessio Amantis*) to Shakespeare's *Midsummer Night's Dream* and, beyond, to Gryphius' *Peter Squentz.*

Two further minor forms deserve passing mention: the satire and the epigram. Following Lucilius, often called the creator of the satire, the genre was perfected by Martial, Juvenal, and, above all, the late Greek poet LUCIAN—and for once in the Renaissance (as already with Plutarch) it was a Greek author rather than a Roman who was most widely acclaimed. The *Dialogues* of Lucian were enormously popular during the Renaissance, especially in Germany where, between 1450 and 1550, he was honored by more than ten translators. Humanists like Aeneas Sylvius Piccolomini in Italy and Reuchlin in Germany appreciated him keenly. Echoes of Lucian can be heard in *The Praise of Folly* by Erasmus of Rotterdam, in *Das Gesprächbüchlein (Book of Dialogues)* by Ulrich von Hutten, and in the *Utopia* by Thomas More. Marot imitated him in France, and Lucian was about the only Greek whom Rabelais knew really well. Among his English translators were W. Rastell and Sir Thomas Elyot. JUVENAL, known to Dante, was emulated only later in the Renaissance and contributed mainly to the neoclassical satire of the seventeenth and eighteenth centuries.

The epigram of the Renaissance derived primarily from the *Greek Anthology* and from MARTIAL. Although epigrams were composed by such earlier Renaissance authors as Buchanan and More, it was notably John Owen who did most to re-establish the genre. His ten books of epigrams (the first published in 1606) contained about 1500 epigrams, which had considerable influence on such seventeenth century Germans as Paul Fleming, Georg Rudolf Weckherlin, Andreas Gryphius, Daniel Georg Morhof, and especially on Friedrich von Logau, the greatest German epigrammatist of that century.

The Novel

Like the other Renaissance literary forms, the typical Renaissance novel was a combination of native tradition and classical imitation. Four types of novels can be distinguished, and three of these types can be studied for their classical antecedents, because the chivalric, pastoral and state novels are all derived in one way or another from classical forms. Only the picaresque novel is uniquely modern—yet even it has certain similarities with the debunking *Feast of Trimalchio* by the famous prose-satirist Petronius (who was also the author of the scathing tale of the *Widow of Ephesus*, the prototype of all later pilloryings of unfaithful widows).

In their dependence upon the conventions of disguises, mistaken identities, lovers separated, and infants kidnapped by pirates, both the chivalric and the pastoral novels of the type of the *Amadis* and of Sannazaro's *Arcadia* remind one of the *Golden Ass* of Apuleius, the *Aethiopica* of Heliodorus, and the *Babyloniaca* of Iamblichus. Apuleius was rendered into Italian by Boiardo; among the English translations the one by Thomas Adlington (1566) is still very readable. The *Aethiopica* was translated into French by Jacques Amyot (1548). Although the chivalric novel often borrowed plot situations and even characters from the Greek novel, it is the Renaissance pastoral novel which most dramatically illustrates the dependence even of prose writers upon classical inspiration. Pastorals derived in part not only from similar elements in Theocritus and Virgil, but also from the Greek novel and from such Greek pastorals as *Daphnis and Chloe* by Longus. This latter was translated into Italian by Annibale Caro and into French again by Jacques Amyot (1559). The Greek novel was influential on Renaissance prose fiction, and in addition it supplied the plot for some Renaissance dramas. The anonymous *Apollonius of Tyre*, for example, is the ultimate source for Shakespeare's *Pericles*.

The state novels or political novels, in spite of their many differences, can roughly be subdivided into two big groups: either they outline and elaborate on the ideal state, the best form of government, the most sensible social institutions—in which case they go back to Plato's *Republic* (not a novel, of course, but rather a political treatise, much like Cicero's subsequent *De re publica*); or they visualize and describe in great detail the ideal education to be given to a young prince in order to make sure that he will turn into the best of all possible monarchs—and in that case they will tend to go back to Xenophon's *Education of Cyrus*. Aristophanes' *Clouds* added satirical variations to the same theme in the field of the drama and St. Augustine with his *Civitas Dei (The City of God)* shifted the accent to the religious possibilities of such a vision, as did John of Salisbury with his twelfth-century mirror for princes, *Polycraticus*. Humanism encouraged this type of political speculation, as evidenced by Thomas More's *Utopia* (1516), perhaps the most famous single work of this genre, and by Elyot's *Governor* (1531). Erasmus in his *Handbook of a Christian Soldier* (1516) reverted again to the religious attributes of a good ruler, whereas Guevara in his important *Clock of Princes or Golden Book of Marcus Aurelius* (1528) strove for an ideal emperor-husband combination. If it were not for his amazing appearance and personality, one might think that also Rabelais' *Gargantua* was a citizen of Plato's imaginary Republic when one studies the kind of education he received in order to become a philosopher-king. However different they may be in their mentality, Castiglione's *Courtier* and Machiavelli's *Prince* can perhaps also be brought together under this one denominator, the one striving for cultural perfection, the other outlining the ideal of a ruthless general and amoral diplomat. With Campanella's *La città del sole (The City of the Sun,* 1602) and Bacon's *New Atlantis* (1627), this type of vision, enhanced by transatlantic discoveries of new continents and ensuing new political possibilities, led over into the age of the Baroque.

Literary Criticism

All of the more specific influences of the humanist movement on literature might be subsumed under the single heading of Neo-Classicism, for the study of the specific influences of Greek and Roman literature upon the literatures of fifteenth and sixteenth century Europe is the study of the Renaissance attempt to write in imitation of classical literature. At first this imitation was highly conscious, but it became ever more modified by native traditions and by the demands of contemporary taste (which was often medieval and anti-classical), so that the Renaissance author was increasingly compelled to adapt his originally classical form to his own language and audience. As authors in all of the European countries found their own audience and developed their own styles, they became ever more independent of their classical models.

But even as these authors were asserting their independence, the scholar-critics were crystallizing a body of literary theory which demanded the closest kind of imitation of classical models. This conflict between the native traditions and the classical standards became most violent in the distortions of the baroque period, and the conflict, at least in France, was finally resolved in favor of the critics, with the triumph of modern Classicism around 1660. In studying the evolution of Neo-Classicism during the Renaissance, through the Baroque, and into the mature Classicism of the late seventeenth century, the student will need to examine not only the specific influences of classical models on later authors (as we have done in the preceding pages), but also the development of the literary criticism which usually opposed contemporary violations of classical principles.

Literary criticism in Antiquity really began with Plato when he put poets on the defensive by banning them from his imaginary republic. With the notable exception of Aristotle, most of the important literary criticism of Antiquity and of the Renaissance was written in a somewhat defensive tone, as if Plato's dismissal of the poets had placed an indelible blot on their profession. From Plato to Quintilian, literary criticism flourished in both Greece and Rome, and the product of this flourishing was the body of theories concerning literature which the Renaissance scholars later froze into the doctrine of Neo-Classicism. Despite the abundant remarks of men like Cicero, Quintilian, and even Longinus, it was Aristotle and Horace who almost alone provided the bulk of the critical ideas for the Renaissance. Cicero and Quintilian had been concerned with oratory rather than with imaginative literature, and Longinus was virtually unknown until Boileau rescued him from oblivion in 1674—even though the great Aristotle-editor Robortello had published Longinus' *Peri Hypsous (On the Sublime)* as early as 1554.

The revival of ARISTOTLE's *Poetics* and the reinterpretation of Horace's *Ars poetica* contained in his *Epistle to the Pisos* (which was never really unknown during the Middle Ages) provided the Renaissance critics with a theory of the nature of poetry and with a justification of poetry which they could use to combat the scholastic prejudice against it that had developed during the Middle Ages. Once they had begun formulating their critical doctrines and realized that poetry no longer needed any justification, they commenced applying these doctrines to the literature which was being written by their contemporaries. As their ideas became ever more widely and thoroughly understood, the practicing authors and public began to use them in the creation and evaluation of current writing. It is particularly interesting to study the process by which the native ingenuity and originality which flourished so beautifully during the Renaissance gradually came to be snuffed out by the new strictures of the classical rules taken over from Aristotle and Horace by the humanist scholar-critics. In doing so we will have to follow the growth of the popularity of Aristotelian and Horatian doctrines and the subtle changes which the Renaissance critics made in their interpretations of these doctrines.

With regard to the translators of Aristotle: some of his works reached Western Europe early through Averroes and Maimonides, Arabic and Jewish intermediaries in twelfth century Spain. Later, William of Moerbeke translated his *Ethics* and *Politics* into Latin, and it was this Latin version which Nicolas Oresme rendered into French in the days of Charles V (1371). Moerbeke's translation supplied St. Thomas Aquinas and Dante with their entire ethical and physical concept of Aristotelian philosophy and thus it cannot be overestimated in its supreme significance for the whole structure of medieval Catholic thought. The *Comparatio Platonis et Aristotelis* by George of Trapezunt (1464) deserves special mention because it was one of the first basic confrontations of the two Greek philosophers. Among the sixteenth century translators of Aristotle might again be mentioned Loys le Roy (1568), the translator of Plato. To turn especially to his *Poetics*: it was first revived at the very end of the fifteenth century, when Giorgio Valla (the cousin of Lorenzo) made a Latin translation in 1498. However, this translation and the publication of the Greek text in 1508 seem to have had little influence, except possibly on the development of the drama. It was really only Robortello's translation of, and commentary to, the *Poetics* (1548) that established its influence as one of the principal factors in the formulation of Renaissance criticism. Its echoes can be found as early as Trissino, the last books of whose own *Poetics* (1529-62) are little more than a paraphrase of Aristotle. It is debatable whether Trissino's own attempts in neo-classical tragedy (*Sofonisba,* 1515) and epic (*L'Italia liberata de' Goti,* 1547) were influenced only by Horace or also by Aristotle. Trissino's dramatic efforts were continued by Rucellai who used a neo-classical frame not only in such Greek-inspired tragedies as *Oreste* (1525), but even in his dramatization of *Rosmunda,* a medieval tale of horror in Lombardy (which was later treated also in *Morir pensando matar* by Rojas Zorrilla and in Alfieri's *Rosmunda*). Also Tasso's tragedy *Il Re Torrismondo* of 1574 followed the neo-classical pattern.

Following the path marked out by Robortello and Trissino, a whole host of Renaissance critics took over Aristotelian concepts of poetry, froze them into rigid doctrines, and applied these doctrines to the literature they read as if they were laws. Vida, Cinthio, Daniello, Minturno and Castelvetro in Italy, Scaliger and Jean de la Taille in France and Heinsius (author, for instance, of *De tragoediae constitutione,* 1611) in Holland were a few of the more important Renaissance critics who contributed to the formulation of neo-Aristotelian rules for the drama. It was probably Castelvetro (who spent considerable time in Vienna) in his *Poetics* of 1570 who first formulated the absolute rule concerning the three unities which was later to figure so prominently in the *Querelle du Cid* and which became the key-stone of neo-classical dramatic theory. But it was Scaliger who gave theoretical justification for the cardinal principle of Neo-Classicism, the imitation of the Ancients. His *Poetices libri VII* (1561) combined ideas from Aristotle and Horace to form a complete poetics for the Renaissance.

While Aristotle contributed most of the principal theories which ultimately governed the drama, HORACE provided most of the ideas which constituted the foundation for neo-classical insistence upon form, decorum, *bienséance,* restraint and polish. His *Ars poetica* was studied and not only published in Latin but frequently translated into the modern vernacular—for instance into Italian by Dolce in 1535 (and paraphrased by Robortello in 1548) and into French by Péletier du Mans in 1544. Horatian critical theories had as much influence on Vida, Daniello, Cinthio, Castelvetro, Minturno and Scaliger as did the Aristotelian, and sometimes more. Two basic works to intensify the trend towards neo-classical poetry in France were the *Défense et illustration de la langue française* (*Defense and Glorification of the French Language,* 1549) by Joachim du Bellay and the *Abrégé de l'art poétique français* (*Short Treatise on French Poetic Art,* 1565) by Pierre de Ronsard. In Italy, the trend towards neo-classical decorum was accentuated by Bembo's efforts on behalf of linguistic (Florentine) purity in literature and, above all, by the founding of the Accademia della Crusca in Florence in 1582. Perhaps the most ingratiating influence which Horace had was that of his urbane and unpretentious tone, which can best be detected in the finest piece of Renaissance criticism: Sidney's *Apologie for Poetry* of 1595 (which, incidentally, attempted to refute the old Platonic attack on the poets). Sidney's critical treatise has little that is original except its charm and wit, its ideas being essentially Horatian and Aristotelian, apparently having been borrowed largely from Minturno's *De Arte poetica* of 1563.

From the middle of the sixteenth century to the middle of the eighteenth century European literary criticism never strayed far from Aristotle and Horace. Any list of important critics during this two hundred year period is a list of critics who were almost totally in the debt of these two men. By the early part of the seventeenth century the ideas of Aristotle and Horace had become a virtual code of law governing literature, as can be seen if one examines the critical writings of Ben Jonson and Martin Opitz, or the *Sentiments de l'Académie sur le Cid.* The famous criticism of European classical authors themselves, such as Corneille, Boileau, Pope, Luzán, Gottsched, Dr. Johnson, and even the seemingly revolutionary Lessing, was but the natural produce of the humanist codification of classical literary theory.

Other Greek and Roman Contributions

Though old Oriental literatures indicate that AESOP was by no means the only creator of animal-tales, his *Fables* proved to be exceedingly influential not only upon ancient Rome (Phaedrus, Horace), but also upon the entire Middle Ages and the Renaissance—as indicated by Dante and Valla, Marie de France, Lydgate, the translators Ulrich Boner, Heinrich Steinhöwel and Luther in Switzerland and Germany, and the occasional parallelism with the Reynard the Fox stories of the Lowlands. But Aesop had to wait until the seventeenth century until he found a great emulator worthy of mention.

While the influence of the *Characters* by THEOPHRASTUS likewise had to wait until the seventeenth century to be fully appreciated, the *Idyls* of THEOCRITUS—as we have already seen in the case of the novel—contributed much to encourage the Renaissance predilection for pastoral literature. Theocritus' influence on the rustic poetry of Virgil is especially marked; though Theocritus is usually identified with Alexandria, both he and Virgil glorified mostly the countryside of Sicily. Theocritus was translated into Italian by Annibale Caro; his *Idyls* and Virgil's *Bucolics* influenced Italian authors like Battista Mantuanus. Spaniards like Garcilaso de la Vega, Frenchmen like Clément Marot and Ronsard, and above all Englishmen of the type of Spenser (*The Shepherd's Calendar*, 1579). It was Virgil who was the discoverer of Arcadia—a name which, from Sannazaro's *Arcadia* (1480, printed in 1501) on, was given a new popularity in sixteenth century Europe. From this classical inheritance the pastoral spread in all directions: not only into the novel, but also into the drama (Poliziano, Castiglione, Tasso—and also Shakespeare's comedies are full of pastoral elements), the elegiac (Spenser), the autobiographical, and occasionally the anti-ecclesiastical poem (Milton). Because of its musical, mellow, and yet spectacular qualities the pastoral poem is often called another forerunner of the opera.

Among the orators of Antiquity DEMOSTHENES was less widely acclaimed by the Renaissance than Cicero. Among the former's German and French translators were H. Boner (1540) and Loys le Roy (1551), respectively, while an English version of the *Olynthiacs* by T. Wilson (1570) is noteworthy because, *mutatis mutandis*, it was transformed into an attack against Philip of Spain. But CICERO became one of the most significant single inspirers of the entire Renaissance; it was indeed the renewal, mainly through Petrarca, of the stylistic perfection, the intellectual astuteness, and the classical culture of this orator, philosopher, and statesman that constituted such an integral part of European Humanism, with Cicero serving as one of the great spearheads of the entire movement. It was the absence or the presence of the polish, the accuracy, and the elegance of the Ciceronian language that marked the great divide between medieval and Renaissance Latin. Even before Petrarca, Cicero exerted a profound influence upon St. Augustine, Boethius, and Thomas Aquinas and upon Lupus of Ferrières, one of the great translators and transmitters of ancient literature during the Middle Ages. Echoes of Cicero's *Somnium Scipionis* (*The Dream of Scipio*) can be found in Dante's *Divina Commedia* as well as in Chaucer's *Parliament of Fowls*. Coluccio Salutati, chancellor of Florence, became one of the most impeccable Ciceronians, and Brunetto Latini began to translate various speeches of Cicero into Italian. *On Friendship (Laelius)* and *On Old Age (Cato maior)* were rendered into French in 1418 by Laurent de Premierfait, the well-known translator of Boccaccio; Caxton printed the English translations in 1481. In the sixteenth century especially men like Rabelais, Montaigne and Shakespeare felt Cicero's influence; Etienne Dolet translated his *Letters* and also his *Tusculan Discussions* (1543). Erasmus' well-known attack upon shallow Ciceronians and Scaliger's spirited defence of Cicero constitute another interesting aspect of this problem.

Two late Roman and early Christian writers should be mentioned here, too: ST. AUGUSTINE and Boethius, for their influence throughout the Middle Ages and up into modern times has been very considerable indeed. St. Augustine, noted for his theological depth in discussing the problems of sin and divine grace, and famous both for his soul-searching *Confessions* and his utopian *Civitas Dei (The City of God)*, left distinct traces in the works of Alfred the Great of England, Dante, Chaucer, Huss in Bohemia, Luther in Germany, and Luis Vives in Spain. BOETHIUS, one of the last to know Greek before darkness fell over Europe, endeavored to translate Plato and Aristotle and others in order to save them from oblivion. His *De consolatione philosophiae (On the Comforts of Philosophy)*, one of the most important single books of the entire Middle Ages, was written in incarceration, shortly before his execution in 524 by Theoderic the Great. In anticipating his death—the death of one of the last truly cultured Romans at the hands of a barbarian usurper, so deeply symbolic for sixth century European history in general—Boethius conceived of Philosophy as a comforter as great as St. Mary or Beatrice had been or were to be to others. Besides being inspired by Cicero's *Somnium Scipionis*, he emulated, above all, Plato's beautiful description in *Phaedo* of how Socrates had awaited death. In the Middle Ages Boethius was translated by Alfred the Great of England (ca. 900), the monk Notker Labeo in St. Gall, Switzerland (ca. 1000), Jean de Meung, Chaucer, and by the early Spanish humanist Pero López de Ayala—and all these men, through their translations, imposed upon their as yet unwieldy vernacular tongues a philosophical prose, a richer vocabulary, and a certain fluency not known before their time. Among sixteenth century readers, emulators, or translators of Boethius we might mention Lorenzo de' Medici, Spenser, and Queen Elizabeth.

Neo-Latin Literature

While we will assign a brief discussion of European Humanism to our chapter on Italian Contributions (for Italy was certainly most instrumental in stimulating the awakening interest in classical Antiquity), we should, at this point, still say a few words about neo-Latin literature. The Renaissance produced a great body of works written in Latin which deserves to be studied for itself, for the influence of Antiquity which it reveals, for the impact it had on vernacular literature, and for the function it may have served as an intermediary between classical literature and modern Europe. This rich field, for reasons that are quite evident, is unfortunately far too neglected and should yield many new and fascinating results. In approaching it, the comparatist should distinguish between more or less philological works undertaken by humanistically trained editors of old texts, and the "original" works of neo-classical and imitative character in which other humanists strove to emulate their Greek and Roman models.

Petrarca's *Africa* (ca. 1340) may be said to mark the beginning of this new phase of activity, though it is, of course, quite difficult to draw an exact line between medieval and Renaissance Latin literature. As the vogue for writing originally in Latin increased, works in almost every genre were being written. Didactic literature ranged from Fracastoro's famous poem on *Syphilis* (1530) to Dedekind's notorious satire *Grobianus* (1552). Important authors of neo-Latin comedies were Wimpfeling (*Stylpho,* 1480), Reuchlin (*Henno,* 1497), and Naogeorgus in Germany, Macropedius in Holland, and, as an interesting example of the influence also of folk-literature upon neo-Latin literature, Connibertus, who, in his *Veterator* (1512), provided a humanist adaptation of the well-known farce of *Maître Pierre Pathelin* of 1485. In the field of the tragedy, *Eccerinis* by Mussato in 1314 chronologically certainly occupies the very first place. Among topics of interest to a comparatist we might mention *Richard III* by Thomas Legge (1579) and *Stuarta tragoedia* by Roulerius of Lille (1593), the first dramatic treatment of the tragic death of Mary Stuart. More frequent, however, were tragedies on classical topics, from the *Achilleid* by Mussato in fourteenth century Italy to *Julius Caesar* by Muret in France (1544), and from Erasmus' rendering of *Hecuba* to tragedies like *The Return of Ulysses, Meleager,* and *Dido* (1593) by William Gager in England. It is, however, in the field of the biblical tragedy that neo-Latin literature produced a particularly rich harvest: our next chapter on religious influences will make that clear.

Prose literature—apart from practically the complete works of Erasmus of Rotterdam—ranged all the way from the *Facetiae* of Poggio and the interesting tale of *Euryalus and Lucretia,* or *De duobus amantibus (About Two Lovers)* by Aeneas Sylvius Piccolomini (1444) to the *Utopia* by Thomas More and the well-known political and pastoral novel of adventure, *Argenis,* by John Barclay (1616). In a larger sense, however, neo-Latin prose literature included whatever scientific, historical, moral, philosophical, theological, pedagogical, and juridical works may have been written, from Leonardo Bruni, Ficino, Valla, Copernicus, Vesalius, Vives and Calvin to Bacon, Comenius, Spinoza and Leibniz. More to the point with regard to their relationship to literature proper were the many neo-classical *Poetics* written in Latin, from Robortello and Minturno in Italy to Scaliger in France and Heinsius and Vossius in Holland. Nor should we forget the great mass of pamphleteering during this sixteenth century of strife, such as represented especially by Ulrich von Hutten, author of *Nemo (Nobody), Julius Exclusus (Pope Julius Excluded from Paradise),* and, in part, the *Epistolae obscurorum virorum (Letters of Obscure Men,* 1516).

In the field of lyric poetry all types and genres were cultivated. Religious lyrics extended from Pontanus and Vida in Italy to Buchanan in Scotland and France and to Grotius in Holland. Bucolic poetry was represented chiefly by Battista Mantuanus in Italy. Occasional poetry appeared with Petrarca, Pontanus, and Ariosto and, in Germany, with Petrus Lotichius Secundus, Eobanus Hessus, Ulrich von Hutten and Paulus Melissus; while love-lyrics, reaching a kind of perfection in the *Basia (Kisses,* 1535) of Johannes Secundus, were composed by Conrad Celtis in Germany, Poliziano in Italy, Baïf and Belleau in France, and dozens of others. It is particularly in connection with this lyric poetry that we make the interesting discovery that in its neo-classical trend towards stylistic perfection and elegant polish, neo-Latin literature was about one century ahead of the vernacular literature. It achieved a Renaissance smoothness of form generations before that same smoothness and artificiality could be seen in individual French, English, or Spanish works. And this Renaissance cult of form apparent in Latin writings, especially in lyric poetry, was later carried to absurdity in stylistic extravaganzas, conceits, and metrical acrobatics, commonly called Baroque, as early as the sixteenth century, whereas the same stylistic excesses again appeared in the vernacular tongues only one hundred years later.

In conclusion, we must emphasize that many works in vernacular tongues achieved great international fame only because they were translated into Latin, thus becoming part of the great and cosmopolitan body of neo-Latin literature: for example, tales from Boccaccio's *Decamerone*, Ariosto's *Orlando*, Tasso's *Aminta*; likewise the Spanish *Celestina*, the Flemish *Reynard the Fox*, the German *Till Eulenspiegel*, and many others.

B. SOME BIBLICAL CONTRIBUTIONS

Greek and Roman literature and philosophy are with us to stay; very much of what is best and finest in Western civilization can always be traced to Antiquity. The same does not hold true with regard to Greek and Roman religion, for Christianity has so completely impregnated Western civilization in general and literature in particular that it would be quite impossible (and carrying much too far the principle of Comparative Literature in the study of "Near Eastern" "influences" upon the Western World) to ascertain in detail the Christian elements in modern literature—unless they should happen to concern such striking instances as the influence of the Bible, for example, upon Milton, Goethe, Chateaubriand, Manzoni, Emerson, or Tolstoy. We can, therefore, be rather brief in this chapter because we cannot afford even to approach the immensely complex problem of Christianity in literature. Instead, we shall merely sketch some leading religious trends and biblical topics in literature and then return to some of them later, when discussing the German Reformation. Religious problems, during the Middle Ages, were so closely connected with theology anyhow that we must beware of disregarding the border-line between the two.

The comparatist with a predilection for religious problems might accept the pleasantly challenging task of investigating just how many or how few Christian concepts can be found in early Greek, Hebrew, and Roman writers—for instance, in Virgil's famous fourth eclogue or in the amazingly Christian character of "pious" Aeneas. Horace, Martial, Tacitus, and, of course, Seneca, Marcus Aurelius, and Epictetus and, among the late Greeks, also Lucian, Plutarch and Plotinus, might be well worth investigating from this angle. In the field of thematology attention might be given to the late Roman Lactantius, author, among other things, of *De ave phoenice,* and the first to transmit and to use in a Christian sense the concept of the bird Phoenix which Herodotus had probably found in ancient Egypt and which was meant to signify the death and resurrection of Christ—a Latin poem which was among the very first to be translated into Anglo-Saxon poetry.

During the Middle Ages we can turn to distinctly religious writers and works such as Caedmon and Cynewulf in England

and the *Heliand,* an anonymous ninth century adaptation and popularization of the life of Christ, made for pagan North Germany.   Bede, that Herodotus of oldest pagan and earliest Christian England (from Caesar to 731 A.D.) in his *Ecclesiastical History of England* offers an interesting example of the gradual amalgamation of the pagan and Christian forces.   A particularly rich field for comparative investigations can be found in the almost inexhaustible mass of saints' lives and legends that spread from country to country, of the type of St. Alexis, St. Brandan, or Barlaam and Josaphat.   Among these, the *Legenda aurea (The Golden Legends)* and their destinies from the hagiographer and archbishop of Genoa Jacopo da Voragine (ca. 1290) through Caxton up to Lope de Vega, one of their most prolific users, should be particularly interesting. At the peak of the Middle Ages, the forbidding structure of Scholasticism and the blending of Aristotelianism with Christianity into a firm and solid dogma under St. Thomas Aquinas might perhaps be too exclusively theological to concern us here. Instead, we should turn our attention to Dante and his perfect synthesis of medieval Christianity with Virgilian Antiquity in the *Divina Commedia*—or again we might marvel at the way in which Wolfram von Eschenbach in his *Parzival* gave a deep Christian meaning to the current Arthurian romances, and a wondrously religious symbolism to the quest of the Grail.

With the dawn of the Renaissance, however, as humanists from Boccaccio to Valla prove, Christianity often was almost completely eliminated and replaced by an Ovidian concept of life. That was exemplified, for instance, by the Roman Academy which had to be closed in 1468 because of its outspokenly pagan tendencies—though other humanists (such as Ficino in his *De christiana religione* of 1474) remained loyal to the Church. This innate loyalty to the traditional Church became even more evident with the coming of the Reformation, when great intellectual leaders like Reuchlin, Erasmus and More refused to join Luther against Rome.

Christian Themes in Neo-Latin and Vernacular Literature.

More pertinent than the study of the Christian ethic in literature would be a study of Christian themes in modern literature, especially where these themes are treated in a style and form imitative of pagan literature.   From the Anglo-Saxon

Judith up to the Jesuit works of the seventeenth century, biblical themes were immensely popular, especially in the drama. Generally speaking, the medieval theatre and the Catholic plays of the sixteenth century concentrated mostly on the life of Christ, derived from the *New Testament,* while the Protestant dramas of the Reformation as well as the humanistic and neo-Latin plays depended more upon the characters and stories drawn from the *Old Testament.* The tragedy of Adam was treated by Macropedius (1552) as well as by Grotius (1601) ; the latter version had a distinct influence on Vondel's *Lucifer,* as well as on Milton's *Paradise Lost.* The story of Abraham was dramatized by Théodore de Bèze in his *Abraham sacrifiant* (1550), while the tale of the chaste Joseph, easily comparable, for instance, to Seneca's Hippolytus, was treated, among others, by Macropedius in Utrecht (1544). Lotichius wrote a *Job* (1542) ; Burkard Waldis is noted, above all, because of his drama about *Der verlorene Sohn (The Prodigal Son,* 1526). Naogeorgus in *Hamanus* (1543) took up the story of Esther, while in his *Jeremiah* (1551) he converted the prophet into a fiery Lutheran preacher. The story of Judith was dramatized both by Hans Sachs in Germany (1551) and by du Bartas in France (1573). The pathetic tale of Jephtha has always been one of the most appealing themes in literature, resembling, in a way, the story of Agamemnon's sacrifice of Iphigenia. In the sixteenth century it was treated not only by Hans Sachs (1555), but especially by Buchanan (*Jephthes sive votum,* 1542), who thereby produced the first tragedy written north of the Alps that was distinctly Senecan. The Swabian Nikodemus Frischlin was one of the most prolific dramatists in the second half of the century, both in Latin and in German; among the biblical dramas of this "Christian Terence" may be named *Rebecca, Ruth,* and *Susanna* (1577). The story of the slander of Susanna was particularly popular among the German Protestants as also indicated, among several others, by the version of Paul Rebhun (1535). Frischlin, incidentally, deserves credit, too, for having been a pioneer in the effort to dramatize the stories also of medieval Christian heroines, as *e.g.* in his *Hildegardis magna* of 1585. Of the various tragedies treating John the Baptist, the version by Buchanan (*Baptistes sive calumnia,* 1540) is especially significant because it excoriated in reality the execution of Thomas More by a new Herod, Henry VIII. During his exile in Basel

John Foxe was one of the few Protestants to write a play about Christ himself (*Christus triumphans*, 1556). Even Judas Iscariot did not escape dramatic treatment, for example in the tragedy by Naogeorgus in 1552. Neo-Latin authors produced some worthwhile works also in the field of the biblical epic: for instance Sannazaro with his *De Partu Virginis* (*The Motherhood of the Virgin*, 1526) and Vida, a forerunner of Milton and Klopstock, with his *Christiad* (1535). To these various biblical themes may be added other problems worth investigating, such as the descriptions of Heaven and Hell or of figures such as Satan, supplied by pagans like Homer and Virgil and by Christians like Caedmon, Dante, Vondel or Milton.

C. OTHER ORIENTAL INFLUENCES

Of two great literary influences which made themselves felt
from the Middle Ages on, the Celtic and the Mahometan, the first
can be discussed somewhat later, in connection with the *Amadis*
and then again in connection with Ossian; but the Mahometan
should be brought in right here. In trying to restrict ourselves to
a few general remarks about a very great political and cultural
impact which approached Europe from the Bosporus and from
Sicily as well as from Morocco, we shall do well to distinguish
three different phases: the earliest Mahometan onslaughts in
the days of the Carolingians, the Crusades, and the coming of the
Turks.

The first phase, culminating in the beginning of the conquest
of Spain in 711, the decisive battle of Tours and Poitiers in 732,
and later in the constant warfare of rulers like Charlemagne
against the hordes of infidels, inspired above all the *chansons
de geste* of France and much that is finest in early Spanish
literature. A striking example of the former is, of course, *La
chanson de Roland,* which reflects well the crude and martial
atmosphere of warfare between the Crescent and the Cross and
the spirit of racial and religious intolerance that animated these
early fighters for Christ. Later, after the age of the Crusades
had added the mellowness of tolerance and after the Renaissance
had contributed its love for flippant satire, the Carolingian cycle
of France with all its doughty heroes and martial manners
passed over into Italian literature—and the examples of Boiardo's *Orlando innamorato* (1487 ff.) and, above all, of Ariosto's
Orlando furioso indicate from what angle of wolfish amorousness
the skeptical Italians viewed the proud world of medieval
thanes—of those peers of France who formerly had been the
very mainstay of Emperor and Church, but who now were smit-
ten with the charms of nubile Angelica to the point of interrupt-
ing the entire war. This transformation of Old French *chansons
de geste* in the hands of nimble-witted and satirical Italian Renaissance poets cannot but be a great source of interest and of
delight to the reader investigating it.

Moorish Spain

More serious and more stately were the Mahometan influences
in Spain, where the Moors remained well over 700 years and

where they left an indelible imprint on Spanish culture even into our own days. It would seem that Spanish comparatists would never tire of investigating ever anew this fascinating problem of Hispano-Mahometan literary relations from 711 till beyond 1492, which Spaniards are by far best qualified to study; and, in doing so, they might examine the Mahometan influences not only upon Spain, but through Spain also on Provençal lyrical poetry. The noblest work reflecting the constant struggle between Christian and Arab is, of course, *El cantar de mio Cid,* (1140) about Don Rodrigo de Bivar, who in the eleventh century had become the greatest champion of Spanish Christendom in the great task of *reconquista*—and the baroque chapter will show that the many popular martial ballads about this patriotic hero were later dramatized by Guillén de Castro, from whence they spread into the rest of Europe. Nor was the entire intercourse between Spaniard and Arab restricted to warfare alone, for Arabic Spain (think of Sevilla, Granada, Cordova, Toledo) served as a great intermediary for transmitting into Central Europe the knowledge of Greek culture which the Arabs had been quick to absorb after overrunning such centers of Greek culture as Alexandria; and the Arab Averroes and the Jew Maimonides (and also the Mallorcan Raimundo Lulio) distinguished themselves particularly in such tasks.

Oriental influences are particularly evident in *El Conde Lucanor* (1335) by Juan Manuel, whose fluently written short stories, in many ways comparable to Boccaccio's *Decamerone,* may have influenced both Chaucer and Shakespeare (*The Taming of the Shrew*). Also the works of the Archpriest of Hita and of the humanist López de Ayala, as well as the famous proverbs of the Spanish Jew Sem Tob are full of oriental wisdom. Among the most beautiful literary results of this borderland co-existence of Spanish and Mahometan cultures is *La historia del Abencerraje y de la hermosa Jarifa (The Story of Abencerraje and of Beautiful Jarifa),* one of the very finest representatives of that typically Spanish genre, the Moorish tale. The colorful and exotic atmosphere of this pathetic love story contributed to its being repeated quite often, from the *Diana* of Montemayor to *El remedio en la desdicha (The Remedy in Misfortune)* by Lope de Vega, and to its being translated into most European tongues, foremost among the translations being the romantic French version by Chateaubriand (1807). A mixture of history and fantasy as well as a real treasure-house for Mahometan-Spanish lore is also the famous *Historia de los bandos de Zegries y Abencerrajes o Guerras civiles de Granada* (*The Civil Wars of Granada*, 1588 ff.) by Ginés Pérez de Hita, while *La Guerra de Granada* by Diego Hurtado de Mendoza (printed in 1627) deals with the later and even more pathetic theme of the persecutions of the defeated Moors from 1568 to 1571.

The Crusades

In the second phase of oriental influences, the Christians rather than the Mahometans were the aggressors: it was the age of the Crusades and of a constantly growing intimate contact with the Orient. These oriental influences were reflected in many fields of literature, from the anonymous epic *Le Pèlerinage de Charlemagne,* the Crusade poems of the Provence, and the accounts of the chronicler Villehardouin (*La conquête de Constantinople,* ca. 1210) up to Tasso's epic on *La Gerusalemme liberata* (*Jerusalem Delivered,* 1575) and the *History of the Holy War* by the Puritan Thomas Fuller (1643). The gradually increasing tolerance for the Mahometans and the Christian respect for their culture can best be seen in the way in which Wolfram von Eschenbach rendered more modern and human the old and fanatical French *chanson de geste* about *Willehalm* (ca. 1215). Half-orientalized monarchs of the caliber of Frederick II in Palermo (who may be considered one of the first great Renaissance-types) contributed to this atmosphere of fairly tolerant cosmopolitanism—and in the same breath one should mention the general Christian respect for Sultan Saladin, who later was to become an idol of the political thinkers of the eighteenth century.

Mahometan influences spread all over medieval literature, from the significant oriental sources in Dante's *Divina Commedia* to the Arthurian Romances; epics like *Le Roman d'Alexandre* even pointed farther East, towards Persia and India, while the famous Marco Polo brought back early news from China, and Camoens from India. Fantastic oriental adventures and exaggerations—results, in part, of the tall tales of returning crusaders—filled even epics such as the one on *Herzog Ernst von Schwaben* (*Duke Ernest of Swabia,* ca. 1170), whose hero in truth had never left his native Germany. The important role of Venice, the queen of Eastern Mediterranean trade, in transmitting the physical as well as cultural wealth of the Orient, should be particularly underscored. Also the humanists soon began to busy themselves with Oriental studies: the first Arabic book was printed in Fano in 1514; the first Latin translation of the Koran (investigated by Nicolaus von Cues as early as the middle of the fifteenth century) appeared in Basel in 1543; and the first professorship of Arabic at the Collège de France was established in 1587.

A third wave of oriental influences, the repercussions, in European literature, of the coming of the Turks, will be treated in the baroque chapter.

I. THE RENAISSANCE

A. GENERAL OBSERVATIONS

No period in European literature offers more exciting and more exacting problems for the student of Comparative Literature than does the Renaissance. By its very nature, the Renaissance was a period of intellectual cosmopolitanism and at the same time of growing political nationalism. On the one hand, humanist scholars belonged to an international community of learned men who spoke an international language and who shared in, and were infected with, an international enthusiasm for rediscovering the culture of ancient Greece and Rome. On the other hand, the various linguistic and ethnic groups of Europe became aware, as they never before had been aware, of their unique political identity, with the result that, politically and culturally, they struggled to establish themselves as proud and powerful autonomous nations. These opposing trends had an inevitable effect upon literature. The rich profusion of literary forms, styles, sentiments and themes of Antiquity became the common property of the international community. But in each individual country these international forms, styles, sentiments and themes were modified by the increasingly assertive national tastes and biases. Thus, for the comparatist, the Renaissance poses a super-abundance of fascinating and even baffling problems in every field. Indeed, students of the Renaissance, whether they be students of English, French, Spanish, or German literature, cannot avoid becoming internationalists. For, even should they vainly attempt to study a single nation's literature apart from what was being done contemporaneously in other countries, they would immediately be confronted with the problem of measuring the length of the shadow cast upon their nation's literature by ancient Greece and Rome and by contemporary Italy.

In the complex tapestry of inter-relations which is the Renaissance we will at the start have to determine how and why this particular period can and should be studied as a relatively unique and distinct phenomenon in the whole course of European history. Scholarly works dealing with the period have investigated and must continue to investigate not only the scope and the literary values of this great movement, but, at times, the question of whether or not there really was such a thing as a Renaissance. There exists a moderate number of apologists for the Middle Ages who insist that the Middle Ages (except, perhaps, for the seventh century) were not really as dark and ignorant an era as is sometimes held and that it is therefore ill-advised to speak of a renascence of literature and learning if literature and learning, in truth, were never quite dead. To support this contention, these apologists point to the Carolingian Renaissance of the ninth century, to the Ottonian Renaissance of the tenth century, and, above all, to the great cultural activity which extended from the England of Richard Lionheart in the late twelfth century to the Italy and Germany of Frederick II and the France of Saint Louis in the thirteenth century—not to speak of the wealth of the two greatest centers of medieval literature, Iceland and the Provence. Yet even if we should admit that there is some truth in these assertions, it is still reasonable to insist that of all these movements the period from the fourteenth to the sixteenth century was by far the greatest with regard to the influx of the literary, philosophical, and artistic values of Antiquity and that it, therefore, more than any other era, is the era which can with the most accuracy be called *the* Renaissance.

The duration of the Renaissance is likewise still a moot question. Did it begin before Petrarca (for instance, with Saint Francis of Assisi or with Dante) or after Petrarca? Did it begin with the fall of Constantinople, the invention of book-printing, the birth of Luther, or the French invasion of Italy? Although the year 1350 is too early a date to set for England, France, and Germany, it would seem appropriate for Italy as marking the period when the two great Italian leaders of the Renaissance, Petrarca and Boccaccio, flourished. If the question of the beginning of the Renaissance is difficult to answer, the question of its ending is even more complicated. There are many scholars who insist that everything up to Corneille and through Milton should be included in the Renaissance, regardless of the fact that the Counter-Reformation cleft such a tremendous hiatus into this over-extended period. Probably we can safely say that the Renaissance proper came to an end sometime in the sixteenth century and that the era from 1550 to 1650 would much better be called the age of the Counter-Renaissance, of the Counter-Reformation, or of the Baroque. At any rate, the old habit of more or less identifying the sixteenth century with the Renaissance (a habit justified, perhaps, in France and England, but most certainly not in Italy, Spain, and Germany) has long been discarded; the Renaissance came to an end when the spirit of free intellectual investigation and of unrestrained artistic expression was muzzled and when religious fanaticism and ecclesiastical and dynastic absolutism destroyed the proud individualism and self-reliant emancipation of that Golden Age. Subject to more qualified investigations it might be suggested that this great change occurred in Italy in 1530 with the fall of Florence, the last Italian city-republic; in Spain in 1556, when the austere Philip II replaced his father Charles V; in France in 1572, when the St. Bartholomew's Massacre intensified the horrors of religious persecution; in England in 1603, when the glorious age of Elizabeth was replaced by the inherently troublesome Stuart dynasty; and in Germany in 1618, when the outbreak of the Thirty Years' War put an end to the bourgeois prosperity of the preceding century.

The definition of the term Renaissance causes a good many difficulties, too, especially if, as is often done, we use Burckhardt's famous book on the Italian Renaissance as a measuring rod—for although the amoral and gigantic traits of the Renaissance Italians can, here and there, be found in France and England, they are not easy to find in the two leaders of European Christianity, Spain and Germany. Also if we take as a criterion the impact of the pagan philosophy of life of Antiquity and the neo-classical concept of artistic perfection, there is no doubt that Italy and France were most truly and Spain and Germany least truly representative of the Renaissance, while England, as so often in her intellectual history, occupied a middle position, clinging to her own native medieval traditions while at the same time absorbing the new intellectual and artistic wealth emanating from Italy. Sixteenth-century Spain was so completely imbued with an old-fashioned Catholic ardor and with medieval, realistic, and irregular literary traditions (as exemplified best in the picaresque novel and the irregular *comedia*), and sixteenth-century Germany in her crudely realistic literature was so completely absorbed in the world-shaking task of the Reformation, that (it is often asserted) neither country really experienced a Renaissance. Germany, according to this opinion, knew only a Reformation and Spain went from the Middle Ages straight into the Baroque—although the very real existence of at least some of the Renaissance ideals can be traced in these two countries, too.

A discussion of the Renaissance involves not only the question of how completely the various countries had broken with the traditional values of the Middle Ages, specifically with the Christian ideals and the unclassical style; it also involves a constant re-examination of the relationship of the Renaissance with the two succeeding movements, Baroque and Classicism. The three periods can be conceived of as thesis, antithesis, and synthesis, for it was only the Classicism of France after 1660 which succeeded in uniting, into one harmonious masterpiece (*e.g.* Racine's *Andromaque*) the pagan mythology of Antiquity and the Christian fervor of the Middle Ages, those two opposing views of life which authors of the Renaissance and the Baroque respectively had vainly tried to reconcile in their art. The three movements can be considered as thesis, antithesis, and synthesis also because the excessive Renaissance preoccupation with perfection and smoothness of form and the baroque preponderance of deeply problematical thought could harmoniously be joined together only in the Classical Age after 1660.

A vast and likewise still largely untilled field for study is that of the relationship between the literature of the Renaissance and other areas of human endeavor such as history, art, philosophy, and the sciences. Many scholars might be reluctant to approach this borderland between literature and something else; the comparatist, however, is better equipped to explore this region, not only because he naturally opposes narrow classifications, but also because he can judge the repercussions of these outside influences upon literature as a whole, and not just upon a small national slice of that vast concept that is called literature. How did Italian communal life in the fourteenth century or the splendor of the aristocratic courts in the sixteenth century contribute to the shaping of the ideals of the Italian and, therefore, European Renaissance? What were the literary consequences of the fall of Constantinople? Of the unification of Spain? Of the French descent into Italy? Of Luther's Reformation? Of the Church-Council of Trent? These are questions which transgress into the field of history. And of the writers themselves: what was the attitude of men like Machiavelli and Bodin towards history, and how did poets from Dante to

Shakespeare treat history in their own poems and dramas? To turn to another problem: What effects did the flourishing of Renaissance music have upon the great vogue of sonnetteering? What justification is there in comparing Shakespeare to Bach or Händel? Why and how were Shakespeare's dramas set to music by Haydn, Mendelssohn, Verdi, Debussy? How did the rebirth of art, particularly of sculpture and painting, affect the Petrarchists in their endless descriptions of female beauty? To what extent did philosophers like Roger Bacon, Nicolaus von Cues, or Giordano Bruno represent the new spirit of their age? Such questions are addressed to a comparatist with a keen additional interest in art and philosophy. Students with a liking for sciences might wish to answer questions about the tremendous literary repercussions of Gutenberg's invention in Germany and Italy; of the discovery of new continents on the Spanish or the English mentality; of the influence of astronomy upon the works of Marlowe or Lope de Vega. No doubt much more could be learned about the depressing effect of Copernicus' *De revolutionibus orbium coelestium (Concerning the Revolutions of Heavenly Spheres)* of 1543 upon the attitudes and literature of the next one hundred years, for Copernicus' discovery that our world is not the center of all things contributed enormously to the change from the expansive optimism of the Renaissance to the despairing pessimism of the Baroque.

B. THE CONTRIBUTIONS OF ITALY

The immense influence of Italy on the aesthetic rebirth of Western civilization is so supreme and absolutely uncontested that Italy in every way, in literature as well as in the arts, is to be considered the undisputed intellectual leader of the Renaissance period. In these brief pages, of course, we cannot dream of giving anything but the sketchiest outline of her manifold influences abroad—and though the Pléiade or the Elizabethans might vie with her poets, and though German Humanism was almost as rich in its output as Italian Humanism, no foreign country inspired by her quite managed to equal her in cultural wealth.

The Italian Renaissance lasted, roughly speaking, from the first half of the fourteenth century to the first half of the sixteenth century. The student of this period will do well to distinguish between the two great waves that emanated from Italy: the first wave of the so-called *Trecento* (or fourteenth century), issuing from the three great Florentines (or ex-Florentines) Dante, Petrarca, and Boccaccio—and the second wave of the so-called *Cinquecento* (or sixteenth century), issuing not only from the continued greatness of Florence (Poliziano, Machiavelli), but also from Ferrera (Ariosto, Tasso,) Urbino (Castiglione), Naples (Pontano, Sannazaro) and other cities like Venice (Bembo) and Rome (Caro, Aretino). The student of this age will also want to examine all the factors that contributed to the slow development of the Italian Renaissance: the court of Frederick II (1215-50), the last Hohenstaufen, in Palermo; the beginnings of vernacular Italian literature shortly before Dante; the influence of the Provence upon the Sicilian and the Florentine poets; the emancipatory effects of the great schism in the Catholic Church in the fourteenth century; the ephemeral efforts of Cola di Rienzo, aiming at a political renascence of Rome; the supreme importance of old Roman traditions and of new Greek influences; the steadily growing leadership of Florence under the Medicis; the significance of the Byzantine refugees. He will then scrutinize also the first beginnings of the influence of these new Italian trends abroad: in the Bohemian Humanism under Charles IV around 1350; in the England of Chaucer and the Duke Humphrey of Gloucester; in the Spain of Pero López de Ayala, king Juan II, and Santillana; and in the France of

Christine de Pisan, Charles d'Orléans, and Charles VIII, who with his descent into Italy in 1494 really opened up the peninsula to foreign invasions.

Even more fascinating, perhaps, is the not easily solved problem of the date of the end of the Italian Renaissance, possibly indicated by the battle of Pavia which eliminated France and made Spanish power supreme (1525), the sack of Rome (1527), the fall of Florence (1530), the founding of the Jesuits by Loyola (1534), the compilation of a regular *Index of Forbidden Books* (1543 ff.), the Church Council of Trent (1545-63), the spreading of the Inquisition from Spain (where it had been established in 1473) all over Western Europe. Any of these dates might mark the end of the Golden Age of Italy of which the unfortunate Tasso and Bruno were the last flickering and vanishing lights. Abroad, the end was indicated by the vilifications of Italy by such English Puritans as Roger Ascham (*The Schoolmaster*, 1570); by the professional Rome-haters among the German Lutherans; by the attacks, in France, both on Catherine de' Medici and on the italianization of the French language (as evidenced, for instance, in Henri Estienne's *Deux dialogues du nouveau langage français italianisé* of 1578 and *De la précellence du langage français* of 1579); or by the anti-Italian tenor in the Spanish poems of Cristóbal de Castillejo (*Contra los que dejan los metros castellanos y siguen los italianos*).

We need not be one-sided adherents of Burckhardt to admit freely that the Renaissance was, above all, the time of great, titanic, emancipated men and women who stood beyond good and evil and who made history. Petrarca's accounts in his *De viris illustribus (About Illustrious Men)* and Boccaccio's accounts in his *De claris mulieribus (About Famous Women)* had indicated the attitude and the trend, and in the early sixteenth century the Hispano-Germany of Charles V, the France of Francis I, the England of Henry VIII, and the Turkey of Solyman the Magnificent epitomized what they meant. The same holds true for women who stepped out from behind the often colorless anonymity of the Middle Ages; in the midst of a Renaissance full of power and perversity they assumed true political or intellectual leadership before the Baroque again relegated them into their subordinate, sex-circumscribed role: Isabella in Spain; Marguerite de Navarre and Catherine de' Medici in France;

Ann Boleyn, Elizabeth, Mary Stuart in England. Italy, of course, had the richest representation of men and women of immense *virtù*, great in culture, in genius, in political acumen, or in dastardliness, from Dante through Lorenzo de' Medici, Cesare Borgia, Lucrezia Borgia, Julius II, Catherine Sforza and Michelangelo to Leo X and Clement VII. The student of great men, of bold history-making leaders, will certainly find the richest field during the Renaissance; and the unsurpassed role of outstanding women is especially well worth closer investigation. Renaissance chroniclers from the *Claros varones de Castilla* (*Famous Men of Castile*, 1486) by Hernando del Pulgar to the *Vies des dames galantes* and the *Vies des dames illustres* by Brantôme in France one hundred years later were well aware of their significance and colorfulness.

In examining this Golden Age of the Italian Renaissance and its monumental influence abroad, we realize, of course, that from the viewpoint of Comparative Literature, intermediaries occupied a particularly important place in the ever wider spreading of Italian culture and ideals all over Western Europe. We will discuss them here in some detail, though in later chapters we will not be able to give them quite so much space.

First among these intermediaries were travellers from abroad who became completely steeped in the cultural wealth Italy had to offer them: Spaniards like the humanists Nebrija and the Valdés brothers, the dramatist Torres Naharro, the pastoral writer Montemayor, the lyric poet Garcilaso de la Vega; Portuguese poets like Sâ de Miranda; Frenchmen like Lefèvre d'-Etaples, Rabelais, du Bellay, Montaigne; Englishmen like Chaucer, Colet, Linacre, Wyatt, Surrey; Teutons like Erasmus, Pirckheimer, Hutten—though some of these visitors, notable among them Luther and Roger Ascham, went home with a distinctly anti-Italian animosity. Among the Italophile Englishmen we should perhaps single out William Thomas, who is very important because he was the first to write a *Historie of Italie* (1549) and a grammar of its language (*Principal Rules of the Italian Grammer*, 1550). Some comparatists might even wish to investigate again the pleasant fable that Shakespeare had travelled in Italy; others might concentrate on foreigners who for some reason or other stayed on in Italy—for instance, the notorious and originally Spanish Borgia family; the Catalan poet Garreth, who in Italy went under the name of Cariteo; the

expelled Spanish Jew Judá Abrabanel, who under the name of
León Hebreo became such an outstanding transmitter of Neo-
Platonism.

Italians going abroad as merchants, diplomats, artists, visitors, or refugees likewise exerted a tremendous influence.   In
Germany Petrarca and Cola di Rienzo had, in a way, contributed to the growth of Bohemian Humanism at the Imperial
Court in Prague; a century later the learned cleric Aeneas Sylvius Piccolomini, the later Pope Pius II, was for years in the
service of the Habsburgs in Vienna and as such was the most
important representative north of the Alps during a period when
Humanism, after the tragedy of the Hussite Wars, was all but
extinguished and needed to be kindled anew.   In England reference should be made, above all, to Polydorus Vergilius, the friend
of the Oxford humanists, a historian of no mean achievements,
whose *Anglicae Historiae Libri XXVI* appeared in Basel in
1534—and then especially to one of the greatest intermediaries
of the entire Renaissance, Giovanni (or John) Florio.   Florio,
son of an Italian preacher exiled for his Protestant leanings,
was tutor of Italian and French at Oxford and later Italian
reader for Queen Ann, wife of James I.   His Italian-English dialogues written for potential travellers appeared in his *First
Fruites* of 1578 and his *Second Fruites* of 1591; but they were
surpassed by his great Italian dictionary, *A World of Words*
(1598).

Not only did France know how to attract artists like Leonardo
da Vinci and Benvenuto Cellini—she gave shelter also to refugee
scholars and poets like Luigi Alamanni or to men like Jacopo
Corbinelli, the editor in Paris of the *editio princeps* of Dante's
De Vulgari Eloquentia (1577), who had come to France in the
retinue of Catherine de' Medici.   Catherine herself, who in 1533
became the wife of Henry II and subsequently the mother of the
last three Valois kings, was certainly another great representative of Italian culture abroad.   Many of the refugee scholars,
like Florio in England, earned a living also as teachers of Italian,
acquainting foreign aristocrats and courtiers especially with the
beauties of the language and literature of Italy.   Different was
the case of Jules César Scaliger: he was a physician and inhabi-
tant of Agen in Southern France and one of the important formu-
lators of Neo-Classicism.   A native Italian, he claimed to be the
heir and descendant of the unfortunate della Scala family in

Verona which, centuries before, had granted a shelter to Dante. With regard to Frenchmen residing in Italy we might point to Clément Marot, for a while a religious refugee in Turin and Ferrara, or to Lazare de Baïf, French ambassador in Venice; and among French women in Italy the brilliant court of Renée de France at Ferrara should be especially noted.

As to Spain, Italy's relations were particularly close with Catalonia, not only because of geographical proximity which encouraged trade, but because Sicily and, from 1442 on, also Naples belonged to the kings of Aragón. Among influential Italians there reference can be made to Bernat Metge, who was said to be a descendant of the Medicis and who, in his *Sompni,* was one of the first Catalan imitators of Dante's *Inferno.* Francisco Imperial, another early imitator of Dante, was the son of a Genoese merchant who had settled in Sevilla. Very important also was the Venetian ambassador Navagero, who in a persuasive conversation converted Boscán, a native Catalan (and with Boscán the rest of Spain) to the cause of Petrarchism. Another Italian diplomat in Spain was the noted historian Guicciardini, while the important Spanish poet and historian Hurtado de Mendoza was ambassador in Venice.

Translators constitute another big group of intermediaries which no true comparatist can afford to overlook. We anticipate some of the bigger names: Pero López de Ayala, the translator of Boccaccio's *De casibus virorum clarorum* (*About the Lives of Famous Men,* ca. 1400); Villena, who translated Dante's *Divina Commedia* into Castilian (1428), and Febrer, who translated it into Catalan (1429); Boscán, the translator of Castiglione (1534), and Hierónimo de Urrea, the translator of Ariosto (1549)—all significant apostles of Italian culture in Spain. In France we can point to Laurent de Premierfait, the translator both of Boccaccio's *De casibus virorum clarorum* (which Lydgate later used for his English version of *The Falls of Princes*) and of the *Decamerone*—though the later *Decamerone* translation by Le Maçon was far superior; to Boaistuau and Belleforest, the translators of Boccaccio and Bandello; to Ponthus de Thyard, the translator of the *Dialoghi d'amore* by León Hebreo; to the versatile Gabriel Chappuys, the translator, among many other authors, of Castiglione and Ariosto; to Gentillet, the misrepresenter of Machiavelli. Germany had a humbler crowd in such translators as Heinrich Steinhöwel and Nikolaus von Wyle and in adaptors like Hans Sachs; but Tudor England had a brilliant group with Painter, Fenton, Whetstone, and other translators of Italian (and French) *novelle*; with Sir John Harington, the translator of Ariosto; Sir Thomas Hoby, English ambassador to France, the translator of Castiglione; and with Bartholomew Young, the translator of Boccaccio's *Fiammetta* and of Stefano Guazzo's *Civil Conversation*.

Among royal courts serving as intermediaries of Italian culture mention must be made, above all, of the courts of Francis I of France at Fontainebleau (at times seemingly an Italian rather than a French residence) and of his sister, Marguerite of Navarre, one of the greatest patrons of Italian art, the friend of poetesses like Vittoria Colonna and Gaspara Stampa, the protectress of poets, scholars, and refugees. Of almost equally great importance for Eastern Europe was King Matthias Corvinus of Hungary who, around 1480, made Budapest the Danubian center of Italian Humanism. Also the court of the Spanish viceroys in Naples deserves to be mentioned as a very important bridge connecting Italian and Spanish culture, with literary, political, and social influences constantly flowing in both directions. Turning to other intermediaries, the comparatist might wish to investigate the importance of cities—for instance, the significance of Lyons for spreading Italian culture into sixteenth century France, or of Nürnberg for spreading it into seventeenth century Germany.

Our subsequent pages will show what a wealth of genres and themes Italian Renaissance literature from Dante to Machiavelli contributed to European literature. Here we might also refer to a few particularly picturesque or bloody events in Italian history that fascinated foreign poets and tempted them to treat the subjects poetically: the fall of the Viscontis (Chaucer's *Monk's Tale*); the conspiracy by Marino Faliero against Venice (Byron, Swinburne); the tragedy of yet another doge of Venice (Byron's *The Two Foscaris*); the Medicis (Massinger's *The Great Duke of Florence*, Diego Jiménez de Enciso's *Los Medicis de Florencia*, Musset's *Lorenzaccio*, Paul Ernst's *Der Tod des Cosimo*); the lives of the Borgias (Nathaniel Lee's *Caesar Borgia*, Hugo's *Lucrèce Borgia*, C. F. Meyer's *Angela Borgia*); the battle of Pavia (C. F. Meyer's *Die Versuchung des Pescara*); the sack of Rome (Alfonso de Valdés' *Diálogo en que particularmente se tratan las cosas acaecidas en Roma el año de 1527*, and

Juan de la Cueva's *El saco de Roma*) ; the imposing figure of
Michelangelo (Hebbel, Ruskin) ; the conspiracy of Fiesco of
Genoa in 1547 (Schiller's tragedy of 1782, imitated by Ancelot
in France in 1824) ; the murder of Isabella de' Medici by her
husband Orsini at the instigation of his mistress Vittoria Ac-
coramboni (Webster's *The White Devil,* Stendhal's *Histoire de
Vittoria Accoramboni,* Tieck's *Vittoria Accorambona*) ; the story
of incest and murder among the Cencis (Shelley, G. B. Niccolini,
Stendhal, Hawthorne) ; the burning of Giordano Bruno (Kolbenheyer's *Heroische Leidenschaften*), and so on. For many
European authors, especially the dramatists from Massinger's
Duke of Milan and Webster's *Duchess of Malfi* through Lessing's
Emilia Galotti up to the French romanticists, Italy commonly
served as an ideal background for heinious deeds and dastardly
crimes. To turn to somewhat more wholesome possibilities, the
comparatist interested in Italian thematology might also study
the poetic treatment of the city of Rome from Virgil through
Petrarca and du Bellay to Goethe and beyond, the portrayal of
Venice as we find it reflected in Bodin, Shakespeare, Ben Jonson,
and Manzoni, or the attitude towards Florence from Dante to
Ricarda Huch.

Dante

Dante Alighieri (1265-1321), the first great Italian to be considered among the contributors to modern literature, has often
been called a dreamer of vanished utopias, a typically medieval
visionary, and his *Divina Commedia* the last great Gothic ca-
thedral. Yet it is true, too, that in his *Vita Nuova* he was one of
the first keenly sensitive modern men; that his *Divina Commedia*
is a masterpiece of classical concision and linguistic perfection;
that his character represents the typical *uomo universale* of
the Renaissance, indicating the tremendous *virtù* in the love
and the hates of a man equally well versed as a poet, a diplomat,
a lover, a patriot, a soldier, and a courtier—and that in his *De
Monarchia* he was certainly one of the first modern men to advocate a complete separation of church and state. Dante's fame in
Italy, while great with Boccaccio, Michelangelo, and Machiavelli,
began to decline with Petrarca and the humanists, and his works,
written in the vernacular, and occasionally anti-Popish, were
disregarded while the learned humanists, the verisimilitude-
preaching neo-classicists, and the heresy-searching Jesuits ruled

supreme. His real rehabilitation as one of the world's great poets began only in the second half of the eighteenth century.

Chaucer in England was one of the first foreigners to know and to imitate him; he retold the episode of Ugolino in the *Monk's Tale,* and there are striking parallels between the *Divina Commedia* and the *House of Fame.* Furthermore, in his *Complaint to his Lady,* Chaucer was the first to introduce Dante's *terza rima* into English literature. In view of the fact, however, that Dante's *Vita Nuova* was first printed only in 1576, he had no direct influence upon the Elizabethan lyricists. In France he was first made known by Christine de Pisan around 1400; a hundred years later Jean Lemaire de Belges became the first French poet to use the *terza rima*—but in the sixteenth century Dante was really emulated only by Marguerite de Navarre (*e.g.* in *Les Prisons* and *Le Navire*) because the poets of the Pléiade, like their Italian contemporaries, had little use for his medieval allegory. Fifteenth century Spain was enthusiastic about imitating Dante's great epic (Metge's *Sompni* and Fra Rocaberti's *Comedia de Gloria de Amor* in Catalonia; Imperial's *Decir de las Siete Virtudes,* Santillana's *Infierno de los Enamorados,* Mena's *Laberinto* and Padilla's *Los doce triunfos de los doce apóstoles* in fifteenth-century Castile) ; indeed he was translated into Castilian by Villena in 1428 and into Catalan by Febrer (the first Spaniard to use the *terza rima*) in 1429, almost a century before he was rendered into French (by Bergaigne and others) and more than three centuries before he was rendered into German and English. But from the moment that the Inquisition began to find fault with his works, he was completely dropped by the ardently Catholic Spaniards. Germany and Switzerland, finally, knew him only as a theologian, an enemy of many popes, a possible forerunner of Luther; and they hailed his *De Monarchia,* which was first printed in Latin and in a German translation in Basel in 1559.

In the seventeenth century of French Classicism, the nadir of Dante's fame abroad, the *Inferno* was emulated by one solitary Spaniard, Francisco de Quevedo y Villegas, in *Los Sueños* (*The Visions,* 1627) ; and the *Paradiso* served as a source, above all, for Milton (who was as like Dante as Chaucer had been unlike him) in his *Paradise Lost* of 1667. The two epics of Dante and Milton have been the objects of frequent and fascinating comparisons. In connection with Dante's visions, the student in-

terested in thematology might also wish to investigate the dream
or vision in literature as represented by Cicero's *Somnium
Scipionis,* Dante, Chaucer's *House of Fame,* Sir David Lindsay's
Dream or Quevedo's *Sueños*—or the concept of Fortune in Dante's
Inferno, in Boccaccio's *De casibus virorum illustrium,* in Chaucer, or in Juan de Mena's *Laberinto.* Another thematological
investigation worth making might be Dante's treatment of the
emperor, both in the *Divina Commedia* and in *De Monarchia* and
its contrast, for instance, with Shakespeare's or Lope de Vega's
treatment of the king.

Even though critics of the type of Voltaire, Bettinelli (*Lettere
virgiliane,* 1757), and even Louis Racine, the admirer of Milton,
continued to belittle Dante among the neo-classicists of Europe,
the pre-romanticists at last brought about a true renascence of
Dante-appreciation. Baretti and Gaspare Gozzi in Italy, Bodmer
in Switzerland, and Meinhard in Germany spearheaded the
movement; a first German translation of the *Divina Commedia*
by L. Bachenschwanz appeared in 1767-69. Gerstenberg combined a Dantesque theme with allegedly Shakespearian technique in his tragedy *Ugolino* (1768)—a dramatic theme treated
again by Bodmer, Hahn, Böhlendorff, and others. In England
Reynolds' powerful picture of Ugolino (1773) was followed by a
first translation of the *Divina Commedia* by H. Boyd (1785),
soon to be surpassed by the famous translation of H. F. Cary
(1805 ff.). More important than early French biographies of
Dante and the significant translation of the *Inferno* by Rivarol
(1783) were the pioneer efforts of Chateaubriand in France,
Mme de Staël in Switzerland, and, especially, A. W. Schlegel in
Germany to prepare the ground for the immense Dante enthusiasm of the Romantic Age which became evident among great
scholars (Witte in Germany, Ozanam in France), royal translators (Philalethes, *i.e.* King John of Saxony), and enthusiastic
poets (Shelley's *Epipsychidion,* Goethe's *Faust II,* Tennyson's
In Memoriam, and Browning's *Sordello* and *One Word More*)
who emulated him. Now at last the story of Francesca became
as popular as the story of Ugolino, the Dante who hated was
reinterpreted as a Dante who could also be tender and delicate—
as in Hunt's *Story of Rimini,* in Byron's *Francesca da Rimini,* or
in the dramas by Boker in America and Heyse in Germany.
Mme de Staël, Byron, and Victor Hugo, defiant exiles themselves,
vied with Dante's noble haughtiness. Italians abroad, from

Foscolo to Mazzini, contributed to his rising fame—not the least important among them the Rossettis, in spite of the elder Rossetti's fantastic effusions in his *Sullo spirito antipapale che produsse la Riforma* (*On the Anti-papal Spirit which Produced the Reformation*, 1832). Theologians (La Mennais, Church Goeschel) got hold of Dante; philosophers praised (Hegel) or scorned him (Schopenhauer); artists (Blake, Ingres, Delacroix, Doré) and composers (Liszt, Tchaikovsky) were inspired by him.

Americans did not stay behind in all this; on the contrary, the stern Protestant Brahmins of New England were strangely attracted to the stern Catholic exile from Florence: Emerson was the first to translate *La Vita Nuova* into English (1842); Lowell's essay on Dante appeared in 1859; Longfellow's great translation of the *Divina Commedia* (and his six marvellous sonnets on Dante) were finished in 1865; Norton's translations of both the *Vita Nuova* and the *Commedia* appeared in 1867 and 1892 respectively. The great international celebrations of the six hundredth anniversary of Dante's birth witnessed, among other things, the founding of the first Dante Society outside of Italy: the *Deutsche Dante Gesellschaft* of 1865. In our own twentieth century Dante has become a true world classic of the sort that provides new inspiration to each succeeding age and demands constant revaluation and reinterpretation. One might almost say that no single poet of the past has exerted a more profound overall influence on the symbolist poets of our century, from Rilke and George in Germany to Eliot, Pound, and the imagists in England and America.

Petrarchism

While the fame of Dante had to wait until the age of Romanticism before it was fully and unreservedly acknowledged abroad, Francesco Petrarca (1304-74) and his Petrarchism were an almost immediate and complete success in all of Western Europe. Petrarca's immense influence upon posterity was of a twofold nature: as the father of Humanism he was second to no one, and as the perfecter of the Italian sonnet and the worshipper of Laura he created a subtle and analytical type of love-poetry which, permeated later with Neo-Platonism, became the generally accepted model for the lyric poetry of the sixteenth century. Of Petrarca's importance as the fountainhead of European Humanism we shall speak below, but even apart from this

his influence on lyrical poetry alone is great enough to mark him
as one of the most significant writers of all time. He not only
created a convention for love poetry, but contributed tremendously to the style, imagery, and sensibility of all Renaissance
lyricism.

Petrarca's influence upon the love poetry of the Renaissance
can be traced in Italy from Serafino dall' Aquila and Cariteo to
Michelangelo and Bembo. The most important collection, by
far, of Petrarchist and Bembist lyrics to spread the new fashion
and technique abroad was the anthology *Rime diverse di molti
eccellentissimi auttori nuovamente raccolte*, 1545, which its
compiler, Lodovico Domenichi, dedicated to Hurtado de Mendoza.
Petrarchism in Spain may be said to have begun in the fifteenth
century with the Marqués de Santillana (*Sonetos fechos al
itálico modo*) and with Auzias March, the greatest lyrical poet
of Catalonia; but it received a new impetus with Juan Boscán
and the exquisite Garcilaso de la Vega early in the sixteenth
century, from whence it spread to Fernando de Herrera "el
divino" and Luis de León and other poets of the Golden Century
of Spanish literature. In Portugal, Italian influences in general
and Petrarchism in particular encouraged the flowering of the
finest age of Portuguese literature, with poets like Sâ de Miranda,
Ferreira, and Camoens distinguishing themselves in the Petrarchizing vein. French Petrarchism, beginning with Marot
and such Lyonese poets as Maurice Scève and Louise Labé, and
combining Petrarca's subtlety of thought with Bembo's purist
polish of form, reached its apex around 1550 with the French
Pléiade, with the poems to *Marie*, to *Cassandre*, or to *Hélène* by
Ronsard and with *L'Olive, Les Regrets*, and *Les Antiquitez de
Rome* by Du Bellay; it began to decline with the excessive glitter
and artificiality of poets like Desportes. Wyatt and Surrey are
commonly hailed as having begun the Italianizing and Petrarchizing trends in English literature; their chief poems, addressed,
among others, to Ann Boleyn and Geraldine respectively, appeared posthumously, in Tottel's *Miscellany* of 1557. But it was,
of course, in the Age of Elizabeth that English Petrarchism
produced its finest results—in Shakespeare's *Sonnets*, in Sidney's *Astrophel and Stella*, in Spenser's *Amoretti*, and in a multitude of minor English Petrarchists.

The almost stiflingly pervasive influence of Petrarca on lyric
poetry can best be realized by studying the Petrarchan stylistic

devices which are apparent in lyric poetry of all kinds in all
of the countries touched by the Italian Renaissance. Notable
among these stylistic devices is the conceit, the use of metaphor
which exploits all of its logical possibilities. In the lyrics of
Bembo, Garcilaso de la Vega, Ronsard, Spenser—in short, in
almost any lyric one might pick up at random from the whole of
the Renaissance—the reader will find love compared to a storm
at sea, to a burning fire, or to a petrifying cold, and the portrait
of Dante's Beatrice or of Petrarca's Laura, of a passionate,
cold, or angelic mistress, will reappear in a score of Delias,
Dianas, Phyllises, Cynthias or Fidessas. Indeed, the Petrarchan
texture of imagery can also be found in much of the dramatic
poetry of the period, as for example the plays of Shakespeare
or of Alexandre Hardy. Not only Petrarca's sonnets to Laura
in life and in death but also his *Trionfi* were frequently imitated
—as indicated, for instance, by the *Triunfos divinos* of Lope de
Vega (1625).

The impact of Petrarchism was so great that even its decline
is deserving of study, for after a hundred years of writing in the
Petrarchan tradition poets often reacted violently to these conventions. This reaction can be studied in two areas: the reaction in poetic style, and the reaction in the attitude toward love.
The stylistic reaction took different forms. There were poets
like Donne, Marino, and Góngora, who extended the conceit to
include many new terms which intensified the complex, intricate,
and often obscure writing of the Baroque Period. But there
were also those like Berni, Tassoni, Jonson, and Malherbe, who
either parodied the Petrarchan style for ironic effects or reacted
against the artificiality of the Petrarchan conventions, turning
to a simpler, more rational, and more classical style, and often
insisting not only that the stylistic excesses of Petrarchism be
purged from poetry, but also that much of the subtle eroticism
that had been expressed through the Petrarchan conventions be
deleted.

Equally rewarding in any investigation of the gradual decline
of Petrarchism is the study of the changing attitudes toward
love. Poets found it hard to remain in the attitude of prostrate
and unselfish adoration without proceeding either to religious
sublimation (Santa Teresa, Tansillo, Crashaw—Dante had earlier indicated this quality of love in his *Vita Nuova*, and Malipiero
in his *Il Petrarca spirituale* of 1536 had slanted the sonnets to

Laura in a similar fashion), or, far more often, descending into
sensualism which could no longer be satisfied with unselfish and
distant pining and which gave glittering and detailed catalogues
of the charms (and even the blemishes) of a mistress for emphatically passionate reasons (Berni, du Bellay's *Poète courtisan*,
Desportes, Donne, Carew, Suckling, Lohenstein, Hofmannswaldau). The rise of Puritanism on the one hand and of rationalism, libertinism, and a cynical type of galanterie, which
evaluated womanhood exclusively for its sexual potentialities, on
the other hand, in the early seventeenth century likewise contributed to the downfall of the romantic (though often hypo-
critical) idealism of Petrarchism.

Though dethroned during much of the seventeenth and eighteenth centuries (but never as forgotten as Dante had been),
Petrarca came to the fore again with the age of Pre-Romanticism
and Romanticism proper, which devoted so much of its inspiration to love poetry. But the great age of Petrarca-enthusiasm
had nonetheless died with the Renaissance. Among the few examples of later Petrarca influences we can mention Johann
Nikolaus Meinhard's *Versuche über den Charakter und die
Werke der besten italiänischen Dichter (Attempts at the Character and the Works of the Best Italian Poets)* of 1763; though
still somewhat pedestrian and rationalistic, this German did
much to engender a better appreciation not only of Petrarca, but
of all great poets of the *trecento* and the *cinquecento*. We might
also mention Immermann's tragedy, *Petrarca* (1822), but more
important is the belated but beautiful evolution of German son-
net-writing which achieved its finest form in August Graf von
Platen and other poets of the nineteenth century. In England
Henry Boyd, the translator of Dante, also rendered into English
in 1807 *The Triumphs of Petrarch*. Shelley in his *Triumph of
Life* (1822) was likewise inspired by the *Trionfi*, while the discreetly passionate *Sonnets from the Portuguese* by Elizabeth
Barrett Browning echo Petrarca and Camoens both in form and
in thought (1850). Particularly significant were *The Imaginary
Conversations* by Walter Savage Landor (1824 ff.), which emphasized the hostility Petrarca felt towards Dante and which
indicate the preference Landor had for the former. Of a like
mind was Alphonse de Lamartine in his *Cours familier de littérature* of 1857, for like a belated neo-classicist Lamartine

hailed Petrarca's classical perfection of form and opposed it to Dante's medieval mysticism.

Humanism.

Though Humanism naturally owes its primary inspiration to classical Antiquity, the reawakening of Greek and Latin culture was to such a great extent due to the stimulus received from Italy that we most logically discuss it under the heading of Italian contributions in general and, in view of Petrarca's unparalleled significance as the father of the entire movement, under the heading of Petrarca in particular.

The growth of Humanism can be understood as a predominantly scholarly and academic movement which not only revived the actual texts of Latin and Greek authors, but also led to the new appraisals and interpretations of these texts that brought them back to life for the readers and students of the period. And then growing out of the new appraisals of the literature of Antiquity came exciting new ideas that spread over all of Europe and helped to give a particular character to the writing and attitudes of the Renaissance. It is therefore evident that Humanism has several meanings as the term may be applied to this period. Its narrower meaning encompasses that scholarly movement which revived, re-studied, and re-evaluated the writings of Antiquity. The study of the primarily scholarly work of humanists in this category, from Petrarca and Boccaccio through Reuchlin and Erasmus, can be a profitable one, but the student will probably be more interested in examining the effects which this revival of ancient learning had upon Renaissance literature. In its larger sense Humanism means that attitude toward life which believes that the most interesting things in life are the human things, that the human being has a measure of divinity within himself and, therefore, a large measure of dignity, and that the beginning of wisdom lies in the understanding of man. Most of the humanist scholars were humanists in both senses, for in their scholarly examination of the wisdom of Antiquity they rediscovered the richness of the world around them and of the human values implicit in that world. Because of the breadth of these interests the humanist movement was an enormously complex one, which profoundly affected not only literature, but science, philosophy, political thought, and virtually every other aspect of human life. The comparatist will be interested in examining the relationship between Humanism and these other areas of experience, but he will need to focus his study on the more specific relationships between Humanism and literature, because, in thought as well as in form, practically every piece of literature of the Renaissance period was conditioned, if only indirectly, by Humanism.

After these brief introductory remarks it remains for us to point even more briefly to some of the great humanists who were most instrumental in transmitting the literary and philosophical values of Antiquity to the modern world. While Erasmus of Rotterdam in the sixteenth century is commonly hailed as the greatest of all humanists, PETRARCA in the fourteenth century must certainly be given credit for being the initiator of the entire movement, the first truly modern European. He was famous for the fluency and the Ciceronian perfection of his *Epistolae (Letters)*, which he addressed to the leading scholars and princes of his day, for his accounts, in *De viris illustribus (Of Illustrious Men)*, of the destinies of the great men of Antiquity, for the anecdotes and opinions of famous men contained in *De rebus memorandis (Of Memorable Things)*, and for what he considered his most ambitious work, his Latin epic *Africa* on Scipio Africanus the Elder, modelled after Virgil's *Aeneid*. Nor should we forget his Christian works, such as *De contemptu mundi (About the Contempt of the World)* and *De vita solitaria (About Solitary Life)*, which were influenced by a good deal of pagen stoicism—or his early efforts on behalf of Greek literature, especially on behalf of Plato. His own enormous achievements made him one of the most widely respected men of his age, and the respect which he earned for himself inspired others to emulate him. No specific piece of humanist writing of Petrarca's is of quite so much importance as his correspondence, which he collected himself. This body of letters created the concept of the ideal humanist man which inspired so many later students—and in this vision of the modern man who patterns his life after the lives of great men of Antiquity, the all-pervading influence of Cicero is particularly striking. This ideal is fully developed in the whole body of Petrarca's correspondence; perhaps no heritage which he handed to the Renaissance is of greater importance than this one.

In his endeavors Petrarca was closely followed by BOCCACCIO, who continued his presentation of Antiquity in his *De casi-*

bus virorum illustrium (About the Stories of Illustrious Men), *De claris mulieribus (About Famous Women)*, and *De Genealogiis Deorum (About the Genealogy of the Gods)*. Also Boccaccio's *Vita di Dante (Life of Dante)* and his *Commento sopra la (Divina) Commedia (Commentary on the Divine Comedy)* can be put down as early scholarly works of budding Humanism. Later in the fourteenth and fifteenth centuries, with Salutati and others, came important discoveries of old manuscripts and an increasing influx of Greek teachers (Leontius Pilatus, Manuel Chrysoloras, Georgios Gemistos Plethon, Cardinal Bessarion), to be followed by Leonardo Bruni, Ficino, Poggio, Valla, and others whose works and translations we cannot enumerate—though the comparatist might wish to investigate, for instance, the ramifications of Ficino's Neo-Platonism or the story of the gradual exposing of the hoax of the so-called Donation of Constantine, which, doubted ever since Walther von der Vogelweide and Dante, was finally undertaken by the essentially anti-Christian and pro-pagan Valla. No discussion of Italian Humanism should cmit reference to the founding of the Vatican Library in Rome under Pope Nicolas V in 1475 and of the famous Medici Library in Florence; nor dare we forget the Aldus Manutius family in Venice, which more than anybody else put Gutenberg's invention of book-printing into the service of scholarship (1490 ff.). This famous family of editors published the first and, from a philological viewpoint, the finest texts of many Greek and Roman classics, so that Venice soon surpassed Basel or the Estienne family in Paris as providers of the best scholarly texts possible. The first Greek book was printed in Milan in 1476, a Greek grammar by Constantine Lascaris.

In Germany, especial reference should be made to the beginnings of Humanism—the so-called Bohemian Humanism—under Charles IV, whose court in Prague was visited by Petrarca and Cola di Rienzo; to the founding of the first German university there in 1348; and later to such remarkable works as *Der Ackermann und der Tod (The Plowman and Death*, ca. 1400) by the humanist Johannes von Saaz, a first declaration of man's spirit of rebelliousness against the omnipotence of Death. After the Hussite War had destroyed Bohemian Humanism, the fifteenth century brought important Italo-German intermediaries like Aeneas Sylvius Piccolomini (the later Pope Pius II) and minor translators like Heinrich Steinhöwel (Aesop, Boccaccio) and

Albrecht von Eyb (Plautus). The Golden Age of German Humanism lasted from about 1480 till about 1540; it was marked by men like Jakob Wimpfeling, a historian who liberated the universities from the yoke of Scholasticism; Sebastian Brant, lawyer and author of *Das Narrenschiff* (*The Ship of Fools*, 1494); and, especially, Johann Reuchlin and Ulrich von Hutten, the greatest Germans of them all; and Philip Melanchthon, the famous friend of Luther, because of his educational efforts often called the *praeceptor Germaniae*. Wimpfeling's academic program was deeply symbolic of the whole trend of the Renaissance, in which the scholastic traditions even of the oldest European universities (Salerno, Bologna, Paris, Oxford, Cambridge, Montpellier, Salamanca, Prague, Cracow, Vienna, Heidelberg, etc.) were gradually being replaced by the far more modern and vital curricula of the humanists.

In connection with REUCHLIN a word should be said, too, about the importance of the Hebrew influences coming in with the humanists. The comparatist might wish to look into the problem of the attitude of various writers towards the Jews, from Aristotle, Tacitus, and St. Augustine up to Dante and Luther, their expulsion from Spain in 1492, and the alleged anti-Semitism in Chaucer, Montaigne, and Shakespeare. Within the field of Humanism, the revival of Hebrew studies deserves special treatment for itself because it resulted in a new kind of biblical influence on literature. This revival of biblical studies was naturally given added impetus by the cataclysmic Protestant Revolt and, therefore, cannot be divorced from the influence which emerging Protestantism had on Humanism and on literature itself. The first Hebrew book was printed in Reggio in 1475, and among the many European scholars turning to Hebrew studies (Gianozzo Manetti in Italy and others) we wish to point especially to Johann Reuchlin, because he became the center of an ugly anti-Semitic quarrel in which reactionary scholasticists tried to deal a fatal blow to the heretically progressive and liberal humanists in general. Though attacked by reactionary groups and condemned by the Pope, Reuchlin in his studies of Hebrew religion and literature was warmly supported by most intellectual leaders of Europe (Erasmus, More, Luther, Hutten, and others) whose testimonies in his behalf and in behalf of Humanism he published under the title of *Epistolae clarorum virorum* (*Letters of Famous Men*, 1514). Later Ulrich von HUT-

TEN and others ridiculed the position of the scholasticists even more by publishing, in the anonymous *Epistolae obscurorum virorum* (*Letters of Obscure Men,* 1516), bigoted attacks on Reuchlin, supposedly written by ignorant enemies of Humanism who debased Reuchlin with such poor arguments, propounded in such miserable Latin, that all readers would instinctively feel repelled by them and side with Reuchlin. The *Letters of Obscure Men* are significant because they represent the most important satire of that age, and also because they indicate the final victory of Humanism over Scholasticism.

Some aspects of the great international significance of ERASMUS OF ROTTERDAM will be discussed later, in connection with a brief outline of Dutch contributions. Erasmus can be called a Hollander only in a limited sense, for at that time the Netherlands were still part of the Holy Roman Empire, and in between his frequent travels to England, France, and Italy he seemed to prefer to reside in Basel, Switzerland, where he spent the greatest number of years. He was certainly the most illustrious of all humanists—the leader of Europe's intelligentsia, the friend of popes and princes, the first great European, the unwilling umpire between Catholicism and Protestantism, the enemy of Luther's radicalism, the author of the *Adages,* the restorer of the philologically correct Greek text of the *New Testament* (1516), and the author of the famous satire *Enkomium Moriae* (*The Praise of Folly,* 1508) and the *Enchiridion militis christiani* (*Handbook of a Christian Soldier,* 1517) in which he searched for the quintessence of religion and of moral law. The immense prestige of Erasmus all over Europe was unchallenged.

The real development of English commercial and intellectual relations with Italy had to wait till the end of the Hundred Years' War with France. After that we can point to patrons of the new learning like Duke Humphrey of Gloucester, the supporter of Lydgate in England and of Leonardo Bruni in Italy; to Italians like Aeneas Sylvius Piccolomini, Poggio, Polydore Vergil, and Castiglione travelling to England; and above all to Linacre (the friend of Poliziano and the Medicis), Grocyn, and Colet, who studied in Italy and who through their international friendships increasingly drew London, Oxford, and Cambridge into the orbit of continental Humanism. They were followed by Thomas Elyot, a frequent translator from the Greek, the author of the first English-Latin dictionary (1538) and of *The Governor,* a treatise

on education and politics which netted him an ambassadorship
to Charles V. Most important among all English humanists was,
of course, THOMAS MORE, scholar, lawyer, statesman, and conservative Christian, the author of *Utopia* (1516), the great
friend of Erasmus, and a victim of the despotism of Henry VIII,
whose life and death inspired the Spaniard Herrera to write his
biography. After the execution of More in 1535, English Humanism at Oxford and elsewhere began to decline—and with
Roger Ascham's bigoted Puritanism Italy ceased to be a source
of inspiration, though men like Florio strove to maintain close
relations with foreign cultures and to fight back at the increasingly perverted interpretations of Catholic Italy. Outstanding
among the later humanists delving into the treasures of Antiquity was Philemon Holland, the translator of Livy, Pliny, Plutarch, Suetonius, and Xenophon.

Castilian Humanism, after promising beginnings by Pero
López de Ayala, the chronicler of Spanish history and the translator of Livy, Boethius, Guido delle Colonne, and Boccaccio, began to flourish at the court of Juan II of Castile with the brilliant
figure of the Marquis of Santillana and lesser lights and translators like Villena, while among the Catalan humanists Rodericus
Zamorensis with his *Historia Hispanica* and his *De arte, disci-
plina et modo alendi et erudiendi pueros (About the Ways and
Means of Bringing Up and Teaching Children)* gave expression
to the historical, patriotic, and pedagogical preoccupation of
many humanists. Antonio de NEBRIJA, the greatest Spanish
humanist, excelled in philology (*Dictionarium latino-hispanicum,
Introductiones latinae, Gramatica castellana*—published significantly in 1492, when Columbus' discoveries made Spanish a
world language), as well as in law *(Lexicon juris civilis)*, archeo-
ology *(Antigüedades de España)*, and pedagogy *(De liberis edu-
candis)*. Second only to Nebrija and even greater in international fame was Juan Luis VIVES, a professor both at Louvain
and at Oxford, a member of the court of Catherine of Aragón in
London, an ardent Christian *(De veritate fidei christianae)*, and
also a philologist *(Exercitatio linguae latinae)* and a pedagogue
(De institutione feminae christianae, 1524). A typical inter-
twining of the new learning with increasingly anti-Catholic
leanings can be found also in Alfonso and Juan de Valdés—the
former author of the satirical *Diálogo de Mercurio y Carón*

(1530), the latter of *El Diálogo de la doctrina cristiana* (1529) and *Las Ciento diez consideraciones divinas* (Basel, 1550).

In France, the line between humanist scholars and humanistically trained poets can be less easily drawn than, for instance, in Germany, where most poets were not humanists, but continued to write in a predominantly popular, unscholarly, and medieval vein. The literature of the entire French sixteenth century is permeated with a humanistic atmosphere and polish which was quite unthinkable in the Germany of Hans Sachs. Therefore, rather than refer to humanist-poets like Ronsard and to patrons of the new learning like Marguerite de Navarre, we mention only two scholars: Guillaume BUDÉ and Lefèvre d'Etaples. Budé achieved honors under King Francis I, and through his influence upon that monarch he may be considered the founder not only of the Collège de France, but also of the royal library at Fontaine-bleau, which, transferred to Paris, later became the Bibliothèque nationale. As a painstaking philologist, Budé was a French pioneer in the task of exploring the literature of Antiquity; among his best known works mention might be made of his *Commentarii Linguae Graecae* (1529) and of his important *De transitu hellenismi ad christianismum* (*Concerning the Transition from Hellenism to Christianity*, 1534). LEFÈVRE D'-ETAPLES, on the other hand, like Grocyn, Erasmus, Vives, or Valdés before or after him, tended to emphasize the religious preoccupation and the biblical studies of ever so many humanists; indeed, like the unfortunate Etienne Dolet, he even portrayed a certain trend towards Protestantism. He is noted for his *In Aristotelis Ethicen Introductio* (1501) and for his translation of the gospels into French (1523) which appeared even a few years before the monumental German Bible translation by Luther.

Boccaccio.

In approaching the study of the contributions of Giovanni Boccaccio (1313-1375) to European literature, one is confronted with a prodigious variety of innovations. Because Boccaccio was the first to develop many of the literary genres which became widely adopted in Italy and elsewhere, the examination of his influence is intimately bound with a study of many other authors who served sometimes as intermediaries between Boccaccio and the future and who occasionally contributed something to the tradition themselves. It becomes necessary, then, to present Boccaccio somewhat differently from the way in which we presented the more personal influences of Dante and Petrarca. As the father of the modern short story or *novella,* of the Renaissance romanesque epic, and of the Renaissance pastoral, Boccaccio can be used as the starting point for a study of the spread of these genres through Renaissance literature.

But even before looking at the development of these genres out of models provided by Boccaccio, we should sketch the direct influence of his works and themes. As in the case of Petrarca, we have already discussed Boccaccio's significant contributions to Humanism, and these alone would assure him an important place in the history of Renaissance culture. Probably even more important, however, was his contribution to literature directly through some individual tales and themes of his *Decamerone.* Although he had been preceded in the kind of short stories which he included in his own frame-story in ancient India, in the Arabic tales, in the Greek novels, in the French *fabliaux,* and in the Spain of Juan Manuel and the Archpriest of Hita, and although he did not really "invent" a great number of his stories but merely recorded them through the medium of his own narrative artistry, Boccaccio in effect created a virtually new type of literature and several of his tales were later used over and over again as plots for dramas and poems.

Three stories in particular became quickly popular all over Europe: the tale of the friendship between Titus and Gisippus (X. 8), treated for instance (to mention only English examples) in Sir Thomas Elyot's *The Governor* (1531) ; the bloody narrative of father, suitor, and daughter, Tancred, Guiscard, and Ghismonda (IV. 1), translated into Latin by Leonardo Bruni and presented in dramatic form by Wilmot (1591) and in a poem by Dryden; and the story of patient Griseldis (X. 10), of which Petrarca thought well enough to translate it into Latin and which Chaucer (ignoring the true authorship) translated from Petrarca's Latin into English as his *Clerk's Tale.* Griseldis, among many other European versions ranging from Hans Sachs to Gerhart Hauptmann, was also presented in dramatic form by Chettle and Dekker (1603) and by Friedrich Halm, a militant Young German, who in 1835 used it as the basis of a social drama advocating women's rights. These are but three of the more popular themes which came from the *Decamerone*; only a few of the longer and more serious stories were not used by later authors. Lope de Vega's *El halcon de Federico (The Falcon of Frederick)* was based on the ninth story of the fifth day which Paul Heyse almost five hundred years later used as the model for the perfect *Novelle,* and Lope's *El anzuelo de Fenisa* was also derived from the *Decamerone.* The study of themes taken from Boccaccio during the sixteenth century of Hans Sachs and up into the seventeenth century particularly of La Fontaine's verse retellings is rich enough, but does not come close to exhausting his thematological contributions. Lessing, for example, found the source for his wonderful parable of the three rings (contained in his *Nathan der Weise,* 1779) in the third story of the first day, and Keats re-told the fifth story of the fourth day in his *Isabella, or the Pot of Basil.* Sometimes the problem of Boccaccio's contribution is not so easily solved, as for instance in the famous Spanish story of *Los Amantes de Teruel* (as treated, for example, in the epic by Yagüe de Salas of 1616 and in the dramas by Tirso de Molina, Pérez de Montalbán, and the romanticist Hartzenbusch). Here the comparatist might ask whether an old Spanish legend of love and death influenced Boccaccio in his eighth story of the fourth day or whether he, rather, contributed by founding and localising it in a Spanish community.

The universal popularity and influence of these tales has tended to overshadow Boccaccio's very great contribution of themes drawn from his other, lesser known works. His Latin works, for example, were translated and widely known considerably ahead of his Italian works. Christine de Pisan in France (around 1400) and Lord Morley in sixteenth-century England translated *De claris mulieribus.* John Gower rendered into English *De genealogiis deorum,* a work which also served as a frequent source both for Chaucer and Spenser. *De casibus virorum illustrium* reached England through the French translation by Laurent de Premierfait; it was adapted in Lydgate's *The Falls of Princes* (1438) and also served as a model for Sackville's *Mirror for Magistrates* (1559). The influence of Boccaccio on Chaucer alone provides one of the richest fields for Anglo-Italian studies. For example, Chaucer's *Knight's Tale* is based on the *Teseide,* his *Troilus and Criseyde* on the *Filostrato,* while his *Monk's Tale* and *Legend of Good Women* are indebted to *De casibus virorum illustrium* and *De claris mulieri-*

bus respectively. One of Spain's accomplished story-tellers at the end of the fifteenth century, Juan de Flores, was distinctly indebted to yet another work of Boccaccio, for his *Grimalte y Gradissa* (1495) was in truth an imitation and continuation of *Fiammetta*. On the other hand, however, Flores also repaid some of his debts to Italy, for an echo of his *Historia de Grisel y Mirabella* can be found, for instance, in Ariosto's *Orlando furioso*. These two tales by Flores enjoyed an immense popularity; they were translated into all Western European languages and were even published in several bilingual, trilingual, and quadrilingual editions.

There is a surfeit of other kinds of problems growing out of Boccaccio's enormous international influence, aside from those having to do with individual works and themes. Thus, his *Corbaccio* gives the comparatist a chance to look into the significant problem of late medieval anti-feminism, which was quite universal in Europe, even though the French have claimed it as their own by calling it a result of their "esprit gaulois." Boccaccio's work can be studied in conjunction with the *Libro de Buen Amor* by the Archpriest of Hita; the *Corbacho o Reprobación del amor mundano* (*The Whip, or the Rejection of Earthly Love*, 1438) by Alfonso Martinez, Archpriest of Talavera; or such later works as *Les quinze joies de mariage* (*The Fifteen Joys of Wedlock*), the sarcastic product of Antoine de la Salle. Especially in Spain a veritable war for and against ladies broke out, with Juan Rodríguez del Padrón (*Triunfo de las doñas*), Mosen Diego de Valera (*Defensa de virtuosas mujeres*), and Don Alvaro de Luna (*Libro de las claras e virtuosas mujeres*) pitted against whatever conscious or unconscious misogynist imitators Boccaccio might have had in Spain. Echoes of the same sort of conflict can be found even in the sixteenth century, in the England of Elyot's *Defense of Good Women* (1545) and Dekker's *Bachelor's Banquet* (1603) no less than in the Spain of Fray Luis de León's *La perfecta casada* (1583) or the Italy of Dolce's *Della istituzions delle donne* (1547). Such a problem as this is merely one of a countless number which can be found in Boccaccio and which can lead the investigator down to the modern age in studies of the indebtedness to Boccaccio of men like Dryden, Landor, and Tennyson in England; Longfellow in America; Mirabeau, Musset, and Anatole France in France;

and Bürger, Wieland, Schnitzler, and Oskar Maria Graf in Germany and Austria.

After these direct contributions of works and themes we now turn to the three genres initiated by him which were of considerable importance in the Renaissance: the short story, the romanesque epic, and the pastoral.

The *Decamerone* (ca. 1350), with its frame structure and its great variety of narrative moods and techniques, spawned almost as many imitators as did the sonnets of Petrarca. In Italy alone such authors as Franco Sacchetti, Giovanni da Firenze, Giovanni Sercambi, Masuccio dei Guardati, Luigi da Porto, Giraldi Cinthio, and, above all, Matteo Bandello followed in the footsteps of Boccaccio. In Spain, *El Conde Lucanor* by Don Juan Manuel and *El Libro de Buen Amor* (in verse rather than in prose) by Juan Ruiz, the Archpriest of Hita, written probably a few years before the *Decamerone,* afford interesting insights into parallel developments, techniques, sources and "Zeitgeist." The first Spanish translation of the *Decamerone* was made in 1496, and definite Italian influences can be seen in the short stories of Juan de Timoneda (*Patrañuelo,* 1578) and in the *Novelas ejemplares* by Cervantes, as well as the short stories which were included in his *Don Quijote.* Since Italy and Spain produced the finest narrative prose of the Renaissance, a comparison of the differences in styles, attitudes, and backgrounds of the Italian *novella* and the Spanish *novela* offers another pleasant task to the comparatist. In Germany, translators like Heinrich Steinhöwel and Nicolaus von Wyle in the fifteenth century prepared the way for imitators like Hans Sachs in the sixteenth century. The German predilection for small collections of short stories of a didactic and amusing character (as evidenced, for instance, in Johannes Pauli's *Schimpf und Ernst* of 1522 and Jörg Wickram's *Rollwagenbüchlein* of 1555) can at least in part be explained by the popularity of the Italian genre. In France the *Decamerone* was translated by Laurent de Premierfait early in the fifteenth century; but his version was easily surpassed by the one by Antoine Le Maçon in 1545 which went through sixteen new editions before the end of the century. The Italian type short story was then cultivated in such works as *Les cent nouvelles Nouvelles* (*The One Hundred New Tales,* 1462) by Antoine de la Salle, the *Nouvelles recréations et joyeux devis* by Bonaventure des Périers, and especially the important *Heptam-*

éron by Marguerite de Navarre (1558). England was, of course, first given a short story collection in the *Canterbury Tales*, though Chaucer, strangely enough, seems to have known practically all the works of Boccaccio with the exception of the *Decamerone* and therefore is commonly assumed to have been inspired by Sercambi for his frame-technique rather than by Boccaccio himself. William Painter's significant *Palace of Pleasure* (1566-67) anthologized translations of short stories from several authors, mainly from Boccaccio, Bandello, and Marguerite de Navarre; his work became a treasure-house of dramatic plots and incidents of inestimable value for the Elizabethan dramatists. Although individual tales from Boccaccio had thus been translated, retold, and dramatized throughout the Tudor period, the first complete English translation of the *Decamerone* did not actually appear until 1620.

In the further development of the Renaissance short story the widely translated tales by Aeneas Sylvius Piccolomini (*Historia duorum amantium*) in Italy and by Juan de Flores in Spain were quite important, but of more special interest are Matteo Bandello (*Novelle,* 1554) and Giraldi Cinthio (*Hecatommithi,* 1565), for they were important aside from their contributions to the genre established by Boccaccio. Bandello, internationally known through the French translations of Boaistuau (1559) and Belleforest (1568) and the above-mentioned *Palace of Pleasure,* if anything, even surpassed Boccaccio in the dramatic and realistic punch of his tales; and Cinthio is especially notable for having provided Shakespeare with the plot of *Othello.* The story of *Romeo and Juliet,* which came to Shakespeare through the *novella* of Bandello, offers an especially fine problem in thematology. It can perhaps be traced back to the *Ephesiaca* of Xenophon of Ephesus and the *Babyloniaca* of Iamblichus, down into the Italian stories of Masuccio (1476), da Porto (1530), and Bandello (1554), and into the French of Boaistuau (1559) and the English of Arthur Brookes (1562) and Painter, from whom Shakespeare received the story. In Spain Lope de Vega treated Bandello's version in his drama *Castelvines y Montescos,* as did Rojas Zorrilla in *Los bandos de Verona.* Modified and modernized, the story can be found again in late nineteenth century Switzerland in Keller's *Romeo und Julia auf dem Dorfe (A Village Romeo and Juliet).* This sketch of the history of the *Romeo and Juliet* theme merely suggests the possibilities of thematological studies alone which pivot on the Renaissance short story ultimately derived from Boccaccio.

In addition to virtually creating the Renaissance short story, Boccaccio with his *Teseide* and his *Filostrato* likewise deserves credit as a pioneer in the development of the romanesque epic. The romanesque epic, in contrast to the more determinedly neoclassical and patriotic Virgilian epics of the type of Camoens' *Lusiads,* allowed far more colorful descriptions of medieval chivalrous and amorous episodes, and it led from Boccaccio not only to more or less faithful adaptations (such as in Chaucer's abovementioned *Knight's Tale* and *Troilus and Criseyde*), but also to new creations such as Ariosto's *Orlando furioso* and Spenser's *Faerie Queene.* Although Boccaccio may be credited as a pioneer in the development of this genre, it was really the fifteenth century Florentine humanist poet, Luigi Pulci, who deserves most of the honor. His *Morgante Maggiore* (1483) marked the change from the medieval glorification of the chivalric legends to the sattiric, quixotic, and sensuous treatment so typical of many Renaissance poets. In his treatment of the Roland story he became much more interested in the giant Morgante than in Orlando who subdued him and made him his comrade in arms. The burlesque and satiric elements in the poem can be traced into Ariosto and Rabelais, while the sensuosity can be found in Boiardo and later in Spenser. Spenser's *Faerie Queene,* although quite romanesque and therefore suggestive of Boccaccio and Ariosto, also made use of the neo-classical epic and especially of the mythological-allegorical tradition of Ovid which continued through the Middle Ages from the *Roman de la Rose* down to Marino. Although the romanesque epic seemed to wither away during the seventeenth century and be supplanted by the religious and patriotic neoclassical epic, it did make permanent contributions to later European literature. For example, the *ottava rima,* used by Boccaccio, transmitted by Pulci, Ariosto, and Tasso, and encountered, in a modified form, in the so-called Spenserian stanza of the *Faerie Queene,* was revived by Wieland in Germany and by Byron in England. Byron in particular was drawn to Pulci, translated passages from his epic, and adapted his satiric method to his own uses.

As if Boccaccio's contributions to European literature as a story teller, humanist, and encyclopedic collector of legends and themes, and as the founder of the modern short story and romanesque epic were not enough, he also became the first Renaissance author to revive the pastoral. Here Boccaccio's *Ameto* and *Ninfale Fiesolano* are important because they revived what in a way may be said to go back to the Greek novel (Longus' *Daphnis and Chloe,* for example) and to the pastoral poetry of Theocritus and Virgil. The vogue of the pastoral, in the novel as well as in the drama, lasted considerably longer even than the vogue of Petrarchism, with which the pastoral literature had much in common. Although a typical product of the Renaissance, it represented an ideal form of escape literature during and after the horrors of the Thirty Years' War in the seventeenth century, and it lasted on—sometime in a somewhat parodied form as in *Le berger extravagant* (*The Extravagant Shepherd,* 1627) by Charles Sorel—ever more graceful and Epicurean, into the eighteenth century of the Rococo (for instance, the *Pastorals* of Ambrose "Namby Pamby" Philips in 1709) until the French Revolution put a cruel end to the fool's paradise that had been the *Ancien Régime.*

Notable among the successors of Boccaccio in the field of the pastoral novel are Sannazaro with his *Arcadia* (1480), Jorge de Montemayor with his *Diana enamorada* (1550), Sidney with his *Arcadia* (1580), Cervantes with *Galatea* (1585), and Lope de Vega with his *Arcadia* (1598). In the early seventeenth century the pastoral novel, mixed with gallant-heroic elements, reached the apex of its popularity with the *Astrée* of Honoré d'Urfé in France (1607-27). In Germany, the pastoral tradition was reflected in Opitz (author of *Die Schäferei von der Nimfen Hercinie,* 1630) and the so-called Pegnitz Shepherds in Nürnberg (Harsdörffer, Claj and others). Montemayor's *Diana* was especially popular during the Renaissance: it was translated into French in 1578 and imitated in Belleforest's *Pastorale amoureuse* of 1569, while among its English and German translators we can name Bartholomew Young (1598) and Harsdörffer (1646), respectively. Second in importance was Sidney's *Arcadia*: it was translated into French three times before 1625, and an early German translation of 1629 was reworked by Opitz in 1638.

The pastoral drama, on the other hand, foreshadowed by Poliziano's *Orfeo* (1471) and the eclogues of Juan del Encina as well as by Castiglione's *Tirsi* (1506), began with Tasso's *Aminta* (1573) and Guarini's elaborate *Pastor fido* (*The Faithful Shepherd,* 1590) in Italy. From there it spread rapidly into the

England of Lyly's *Galathea* (1584), Fletcher's *The Faithful Shepherdess* (1609), and Ben Jonson's *The Melancholy Shepherd*; the Holland of Hooft's *Granida* 1615) ; and the France of Mairet's *Sylvie,* and it lasted well beyond the Germany of young Goethe's *Die Laune des Verliebten* (*The Wayward Lover,* 1768). Even more important from an international point of view than *Aminta* (translated into French in 1584, into Latin in 1585, and so on) was *Il pastor fido*: it went through twenty Italian editions in the first twelve years and, all in all, through fifty French, eighteen German (among them Hofmannswaldau's in 1678), and fifteen English translations (among them Sir Richard Fanshawe's in 1648). The influence of the pastoral drama on other types of plays is apparent in many authors, such as Lope de Vega, Shakespeare, and Hardy, while the mellow lyricism of the pastoral's mood and its artificial and picturesque settings make it a forerunner of opera and ballet alike. The whole problem of the pastoral tradition includes, of course, also the pastoral lyric poetry which we have discussed earlier.

Ariosto

Lodovico Ariosto (1474-1533) was by far the most brilliant artistic representative of the Italian Renaissance and all it stood for, and as such free of the moral scruples of the Christian Middle Ages that preceded him as well as of the fussy considerations of Neo-Classicism that followed him. His honest, homespun, and interestingly autobiographical *Satire* (1512) were imitated, for instance, by Vauquelin de la Fresnaye in France; and his comedies, translated or emulated by men like Gascoigne in England, Jodelle in France, and Torres Naharro in Spain, contributed to the spread of neo-classical principles in playwriting. But it was above all his epic, *Orlando furioso* (*Mad Roland,* 1516-32), one of the finest masterpieces of the Renaissance, which represents Ariosto as the peak of Italian glory in literature. Ariosto's classical indebtedness can be seen in his picturesque and alluring figures of lady warriors as well as of enchantresses; they lead from Homer's Circe and Virgil's Camilla and Penthesilea through Boiardo's Marfisa and Ariosto's Bradamante straight into Tasso's Armida and Spenser's Britomart. Colorful, sensuous, melodious, fantastic, gently ironic, he excelled in lively episodes rather than in narrative coherence—and lyric poets from Ronsard and du Bellay to Des-

portes and La Fontaine made great use of the many picturesque
scenes and episodes contained in his poem, just as did dramatists
like Garnier in his famous *Bradamante,* du Ryer in his excellent
Alcionée (1637), Mairet in his *Le Roland Furieux* (1638), and
writers of libretti like Quinault in his opera *Orlando furioso*
(1685).

Orlando furioso was translated into Spanish by Hierónimo
de Urrea (1549), into French by Gabriel Chappuys (1576),
and into German by Diederich von dem Werder (1636). The
brilliant translation into English by Sir John Harington and
the extensive use made of the epic in the *Faerie Queene*—a
strange case of indebtedness to the epicurean Ariosto of the
essentially Puritan Spenser—attest to the popularity of this
work in Elizabethan England. Shakespeare was probably also
familiar with the epic: in his *Much Ado About Nothing* he borrowed from Ariosto the famous episode of the foul slander of
Ginevra (though he might have found it in Bandello and Whetstone, too). English interest in this type of Italian literature
is attested also by Robert Tofte's translation of Boiardo's *Orlando innamorato* in 1598. In Spain, adaptations like *La her-
mosura de Angélica (The Beauty of Angelica)* by Lope de Vega,
Las Lagrimas de Angélica (The Tears of Angelica) by Bara-
hona de Soto, *Angélica y Medoro* by Góngora, *Los celos de
Rodamonte (The Jealousy of Rodamonte)* by Rojas Zorrilla,
the burlesque poem *Las locuras de Orlando el enamorado (The
Madness of Enamored Orlando,* 1635) by Quevedo, the well-
known epic *Bernardo o Victoria de Roncesvalles* by Bernardo de
Balbuena, and *comedias* by many minor dramatists indicate
the intensity of Ariosto's influence. Cervantes' *Don Quijote*
was completely conceived in the anti-chivalric and gently sarcastic spirit of the *Orlando*; together, these two works did most
to undo some of the craze for the chivalric novels of the type of
Amadis.

The quarrel, around 1600, between the supporters of Ariosto
and the supporters of Tasso, was in many ways a forerunner of
the Quarrel between the Ancients and the Moderns one hundred
years later, for at stake was the issue of the free and unencum-
bered creativeness of Ariosto's Renaissance versus the restrictions (as evident in Tasso) of neo-classical criticism and religious orthodoxy. Although Ariosto's fame, in the seventeenth
and eighteenth centuries, may have receded somewhat if com-

pared to the far more regular and more devoutly Christian Tasso, he never ceased playing an important role. In France, La Calprenède wrote yet another tragicomedy on *Bradamante* (1636), as did Thomas Corneille in 1695. Cyrano de Bergerac in his *L'autre monde ou les états et empires de la Lune* (*The Other World, or the States and the Empires of the Moon,* 1657) may have been influenced by Astolpho's trip to the moon, and La Fontaine, in his *Nouvelles en vers tirées de Boccace et de l'Arioste* (1665) put into fluent French verse not only the naughty adventures of Giocondo (which Boileau even considered worthy of a laudatory *Dissertation critique sur l'aventure de Joconde,* 1669), but also *La coupe enchantée* (*The Magic Cup*), which likewise deals with the delicate problem of woman's loyalty. In the eighteenth century it was especially Voltaire (in spite of some initial hostility) and Wieland who became the great admirers and reawakeners of Ariosto, for these enlighteners, in their struggle against the orthodoxy of the preceding baroque century, realized how thoroughly akin they were to the men of the Renaissance who had likewise striven to liberate man physically as well as mentally from the yoke of orthodox oppression. This identity with a more or less Epicurean philosophy of life was more important to the neo-classical enlighteners than Ariosto's "regrettable" irregularity and incoherence of epic presentation; hence the zest with which the Frenchman Voltaire imitated him on practically every page of *La pucelle d'Orléans* (*The Maid of Orleans*) and with which the German Wieland emulated him, his mentality, his metre and his colorful sensuousness in his own beautiful epic *Oberon* (1780). Among later Ariosto-enthusiasts may be mentioned Delille in France, Byron in England, Heinse and Goethe in Germany, Sismondi in Switzerland.

Castiglione and Machiavelli

The contrast in the works and the quality of the influence abroad of Baldassare Castiglione (1478-1529) and Niccolò Machiavelli (1469-1527) gives us a chance to visualize the inspiring gamut of Italian Renaissance thought, which ran from the noblest idealism, the most exalted formulation of culture, courtliness, and love in the former to the most ruthlessly detached kind of realism and political opportunism in the latter. Castiglione's *Cortegiano* (*The Courtier,* 1528) is significant not only for its embodiment of Renaissance idealism, but for its enormous popularity and, as a consequence, its influence on later authors. After its publication it went through more than forty editions in Italy alone during the sixteenth century, and among the many translations into foreign languages were those of Boscán into Spanish (1539), Hoby into English (1561), and Chappuys into French. It inspired many imitations, one of which was the *Galateo* by Giovanni della Casa in 1558, which Robert Peterson translated as *Galateo of Manners and Behaviour* (1576), and Dantisco as *Galateo español* (1582), and which is concerned with the middle class rather than the aristocracy. Another imitation, *Della civil conversazione* by Stefano Guazzo (1574), was translated into English by George Pettie (first three books, 1581) and Bartholomew Young (fourth book, 1586). An indication of the popularity of the courtesy books in general and of Castiglione's urbane book in particular might, perhaps, be gleaned from the fact that the Spanish Inquisition banned it in 1576 and placed it on the Index in 1590.

Castiglione deserves most of the credit for formulating the ideals of gentlemanly conduct so perfectly typified, for instance, in the gallant figures of Garcilaso de la Vega in Spain and Sir Philip Sidney in England. We have already mentioned the importance of Castiglione as one of the main transmitters and representatives of Neo-Platonism; his *Cortegiano* became, there-fore, the great guide-book not only of etiquette but of an entire moral code deeply rooted in ancient culture. Not only can the ideals expressed in the *Cortegiano* be found reflected in Renaissance literature, but even the characters who participate in the dialogue can be found mirrored in some of the dramas—as, for example, Lady Emilia Pia and Lord Gaspar Pallavicino, who seem quite close to Beatrice and Benedick in Shakespeare's *Much Ado About Nothing*. The whole ideal of man embodied in the *Courtier* can also be studied in other Shakespearian dramatic characters such as Hamlet and Romeo. Many of the basic patterns of *El Héroe* (1630) by Gracián were likewise modelled after Castiglione's concepts. Indeed, a comparatist should find it enthralling to absorb the entire atmosphere of the *Cortegiano*, an Italian *uomo universale* with his neo-Platonic, humanist background, and then to compare this ideal with, say, the *honnête homme* of seventeenth century France (Molière) or the concept of a *gentleman* in eighteenth century England (Lord Chesterfield).

Machiavelli's *Principe* (*The Prince*, 1531), on the other hand, was the book of a despairing patriot who, not guided by any moral considerations whatever, sketched the most efficacious way for a prince to acquire, maintain, and enlarge his power until he might some day unite the whole of Italy and free it of all the barbarians that had invaded this garden of Europe. By the very choice of its probable prototype, the criminal Cesare Borgia, *The Prince* lent itself to an ever-widening flood of moral indignation and one-sided interpretation and thus contributed much to the rising tide of abuse heaped by ungrateful Europe upon a country which, but a few decades before, had been hailed as the undisputed leader in modern culture. Machiavelli's admirably keen, rational intellect, as exhibited also in his other works on history (*Istorie fiorentine*, 1525) and warfare (*Arte della guerra*, 1521), was completely overlooked by these zealots —and the Protestant abomination of the Papal and Spanish domination of the unhappy peninsula added its share in this increasing tendency to represent Machiavelli as the very incarnation of diabolical infamy. The French Huguenot Gentillet, through the misrepresentations of the Machiavellian *Prince* contained in his *Discours sur les moyens de bien gouverner* (*Discourse on the Ways of Good Government*, 1576), was largely responsible for this frenzied abhorrence, and the great villains of dramatic literature, from Marlowe's *Jew of Malta* and Shakespeare's Iago up to Lessing's Marinelli (in *Emilia Galotti*) and similar characters in Victor Hugo's romantic melodramas were all personifications of this alleged Italian perfidiousness. In England, Gentillet's biased excerpts became known in 1602, long before *The Prince* was actually translated (1640). Spanish refutations of Machiavelli can be seen in *Las empresas politicas o Idea de un principe politico-cristiano* by Saavedra Fajardo (1640) and in *El Héroe* by Gracián. In his political thinking, however, Machiavelli contributed positive values to La Boëtie and Bodin, who in turn were very important as forerunners of the political enlighteners of seventeenth century England and eighteenth century France. In Germany, his influence extended from Fischart through Frederick the Great (who is noted for his unconvincing *Anti-Machiavel*), Herder, and Goethe to Fichte, Hegel, and Nietzsche; in England, from Raleigh, Bacon, and

Jonson to Milton, Hobbes, and Bolingbroke; in France it can be seen in Montesquieu, Voltaire, and Napoleon. To this day moralists consider it necessary to heap abuse upon a Machiavelli whom they probably have never read; his alleged influence is blamed for much of what was most objectionable in the Spain of Philip II, the France of Louis XIV, and the Italy of Mussolini.

These were among the major contributions of Italy to the European Renaissance: the achievements of Dante, Petrarca, Boccaccio, Ariosto, Castiglione, and Machiavelli, and the rich new modes of literary expression—the sonnet, the *novella* and frame-story, the romanesque epic, and the pastoral novel and drama. These contributions should be added to the invaluable humanistic contributions that came in the wake of the revival of classical Antiquity, such as the formulation of literary criticism and the creation of neo-classical forms and doctrines.

But the student should not assume that this bare outline of Italian contributions to Western culture exhausts the possibilities for investigation during the Renaissance period. There are innumerable problems solved and unsolved, involving such lesser figures as, for example, Pulci, Boiardo, Bembo, and Guicciardini. There is Lorenzo de' Medici and his poetry and the supremely important problem of Medici influences in general, from Cosimo the Elder to Popes Leo X and Clement VII and to Catherine de' Medici (wife of Henry II) and Marie de' Medici (wife of Henry IV) in France; there is Luigi Alamanni and the question of the Italian refugees (or *fuorusciti*) abroad; there is Michelangelo, who for men like Sir Joshua Reynolds became a spearhead of Pre-Romanticism and whose beautiful sonnets were translated, among others, by Rainer Maria Rilke; and there is Benvenuto Cellini, the prophet of a full and unbridled life, whose autobiography (1559—published in 1728) was rendered into German by Goethe. Aretino brings up the type of the yellow journalist in the Italian Renaissance; while with the "maccaronesque" Folengo and the "bernesque" Berni, we approach the questions of Rabelaisian style and of parody. Tansillo's *Le lagrime di San Pietro* (*The Tears of Saint Peter*) bring up the problem of the blending of the Petrarchan style with the religious ardor of the Baroque; among the translators and imitators of this amazingly popular poem were the Spaniard Boléa y Castro (1578), the Englishman Robert Southwell (*St. Peter's Complaint*, 1595), and the Frenchman Malherbe. These and many other Italians indicate the complex problems of the relationship between literary forms, sentiments, and styles as evolved in Italy and as developed in other countries where contact with Italy helped to bring to life what we know as modern culture.

C. OTHER LITERATURES

Comparative Literature at times brings about a rather startling re-evaluation of literary reputations. Since it concentrates
upon great international trends and contributions, it emphasizes
many emitters, intermediaries, and receivers that might be
neglected in ordinary histories of national literatures—while,
on the other hand, it often tends to relegate to a rather subordinate position great poets who occupy leading places in their own
national literatures but who, for some strange reason, did not
really ever become significant from an international point of
view. If, in this chapter, we have very little to say about great
figures like Ronsard or Spenser, we should underscore at once
that we do not want to diminish their glory or belittle their very
real poetic genius and original contribution by merely dwelling
on the former's indebtedness to Petrarca and the latter's to
Ariosto; rather we have little to say about these men because
Spenser really remained practically unknown outside of England
and because Ronsard's occasional influence among the English
sonneteers, the poets of Holland, or Weckherlin, Opitz, and others
in Germany was so completely tied up with Petrarchism that his
importance abroad can hardly be studied by itself. That Ronsard and Spenser received and used a heritage handed to them
largely by Italy in no way reflects on their poetic merit; indeed,
they can be regarded in some ways as the culmination of the
Renaissance tradition. But for this very reason we need not
dwell upon them, or others like them, in a book which is devoted
to the tracing of the sources of that tradition and its spread to
its culminating points. During the Renaissance it was for Italy
to lead, to assume supreme importance—and for the other nations, the moment to play the great role on the European stage of
cultural interchange came later, when the cue was given for
them to appear, to act, and to disappear. All that does not mean
that we do not pay homage to the genius of Ronsard and Spenser; it simply means that despite the greatness of many of their
earlier poets, the leadership of France had to wait till the seventeenth and the leadership of England till the eighteenth century.

The Protestant Revolt.

There is such a very great difference between Castiglione,
the elegant courtier of Urbino, and Hans Sachs, the humble
shoemaker of Nürnberg, that we may well marvel that both men

really belonged to that same sixteenth century. Yet though Italy
gave to the world an aesthetic Renaissance, Germany, no less
important, gave us a religious Renaissance—and the comparatist
will at once be intrigued by the differences between these typically Italian and typically German contributions, by the relationship
of Renaissance and Reformation, by the exquisite refinement of
art and manners in one nation and the deep-surging wrestling
with religious problems (formulated in literary and semi-literary
works that were clumsily and heavily didactic, late medieval,
realistic, earthy and blunt) in the other nation. The question immediately arises, even far more than in the case of Spain,
whether Germany really did have a Renaissance—for though
she was the leader in the Reformation and also in the scientific
rebirth of that age (Berthold Schwarz, Regiomontanus, Paracelsus, Vesalius, and others) and second only to Italy in the
wealth of her humanistic (Johannes von Neumarkt, Wimpfeling,
Celtis, Brant, Reuchlin, Hutten, Melanchthon) as well as her
neo-Latin endeavors (Eobanus Hessus, Lotichius, Melissus, Naogeorgus, Frischlin), her literature after 1500 certainly did not
change one iota towards neo-classical or courtly elegance, but
remained, like the mentality of the sturdy burghers writing it,
naturalistic and homespun. Let the Italian Petrarchists swoon
over the perfection of a glittering sonnet; German Catholics like
Thomas Murner and Protestants like Johann Fischart, moulding
the polemical missiles to be hurled at each other, had more important things to tend to.

It can not be the task of the average comparatist to investigate the tenuous borderlands between theology proper and literature; nevertheless, the great figure of Martin LUTHER (1483-
1546) will persuade him to investigate the ramifications of the
Reformation at least in their larger outlines. He will search for
the roots of this movement not, perhaps, from Pelagius on, but
among the German mystics from Meister Eckhart in 1300 to
Thomas à Kempis in 1450, among Wyclif in England, Huss in
Bohemia, Savonarola in Italy—and he will follow the spreading
of the rebellion against Rome from Luther (1517 ff.) to Zwingli
in German Switzerland, Calvin in French Switzerland, the Huguenots in France, the Puritans in England and America, and
the Lutherans in Scandinavia.

From these partly historical and partly theological matters
he will turn to more distinctly literary problems like the transla-

tions and editions of the Bible, from St. Jerome's Vulgate and
Wulfila's Gothic version in the fourth century to the efforts of
Wyclif and the Lollards in fourteenth century England, the
various translations in fifteenth century Germany, and the great
collection of oldest biblical texts in Spain, commonly called *La
Políglota complutense* (1517) and published under the general
editorship of the Cardinal Cisneros. Then there was Reuchlin's
painstaking work in establishing the correct Hebrew text of the
Old Testament and Erasmus' parallel effort in establishing the
correct Greek text of the *New Testament*; Luther's own monumental translation (1522-34) ; the translations of the psalms
into Latin verse by Buchanan and into French by Marot and
Théodore de Bèze and, above all, the translation of the gospels
by Lefèvre d'Etaples; the endeavors by Tyndale (1525) and
Coverdale (1535) in England, the Geneva Bible (1560), and the
King James Version (1611) ; the *Bay Psalm Book* (1640—the first
book printed in Puritan America), and so on.

Other problems arise in connection with Luther, for instance
the significance and the international reverberations of his great
programmatic essays, especially those between 1517 and 1520:
the *Ninety-Five Theses* against the sale of indulgences, *An den
christlichen Adel deutscher Nation (To the Christian Nobility
of the German Nation), Von der babylonischen Gefangenschaft
der Kirche (On the Babylonian Captivity of the Church)*, and
*Von der Freiheit eines Christenmenschen (On the Liberty of a
Christian)*. These essays made many great enemies for Luther,
among the first of which was Thomas Murner, author of the
bitter satire *Von dem grossen lutherischen Narren (Of the Great
Lutheran Fool*, 1522)—while Hans Sachs hailed him in *Die
Wittenbergische Nachtigall (The Nightingale from Wittenberg*,
1523). Another problem can be found in the beginnings of the
Protestant church hymns of the type of *Ein' feste Burg ist unser
Gott (A Mighty Fortress is Our God)*, which from Luther spread
especially into the German seventeenth century (Gerhardt, Rist,
Gryphius, Fleming) and from thence into Scandinavian, English
and American hymn books.

Second in importance only to Luther was Jean CALVIN
(1509-64) in Geneva, whose *Institution de la religion chrétienne*,
first published in Latin (Basel, 1536), then in French (Strassburg, 1541), was one of the masterpieces of French sixteenth
century prose which exerted an international influence on Hugue-

nots and Puritans comparable to Luther's great and fundamental pamphlets. The increasing fanaticism of the age became evident in Calvin's execution of Michel Servet in 1553, as also in the ugly quarrel between Luther and Erasmus, the leaders of the Reformation and of Humanism, respectively, which reached what might be called an anti-climax in 1524 with the publication of *De libero arbitrio* (*On Free Will*) by the latter and *De servo arbitrio* (*On Bound Will*) by the former. But the scholar can point to more conciliatory attitudes, too, in the persons of Huldreich Zwingli, the moderate and gentle reformer of Zürich, and Philip Melanchthon, the friend of Luther and often called the diplomat of the Reformation.

The different reactions of princely courts might also be considered in this connection: for instance, the brash and early attack on Luther by the youthful Henry VIII of England; the tolerant atmosphere of Ferrara, where Rabelais went and where Marot and Calvin found a temporary shelter; or the secret sympathy of Marguerite de Navarre, the sister of Francis I of France, for the cause of Protestantism, and the warm-hearted protection she granted to many a persecuted refugee. There are studies investigating the influence of the Bible upon Erasmus, Marlowe, Spenser, Shakespeare, and Spaniards like Luis de León and Herrera, or the experiences of religious refugees like the elder Florio in England or John Foxe in Switzerland; but even more interesting than these would be the fathoming of grave religious conflicts in wavering heretics, from Marot and Dolet in France to Giordano Bruno in Italy, and from the expatriated Spaniard Juan de Valdés in Naples to the expatriated Scotsman George Buchanan in France and Portugal. Restless wanderers and persecuted seekers of truth like George Buchanan or Bernardino Ochino may well serve as symbols of these troubled times; the latter, formerly a powerful Franciscan orator, was initiated into the teachings of Erasmus and Luther by Juan de Valdés and became an Italian refugee in Geneva and London, and after 1553 again in Switzerland and later in Poland and Moravia. A study of minor figures like Théodore de Bèze in Geneva and John Knox in Scotland and of the later Protestant influences from Penn and Wesley to New England Unitarianism would round out the picture of the international repercussions of the movement started by Luther.

Other German Contributions

Two minor German contributions to European Renaissance literature were *The Ship of Fools* and *Grobianus*. Sebastian Brant, a humanist at Basel and later in the Alsace, wrote *Das Narrenschiff* (1494) in the typical satirical vein of the sixteenth century; it was one of the few works written by a German humanist in the vernacular tongue. Another humanist, Jakob Locher, translated it into Latin, and this Latin *Navis stultitiae* then served as a basis not only for the first French translation of 1497, but also for the well-known English version by Alexander Barclay which was one of the first German books ever to be translated into English (1509) and which had a distinct influence on the early English Renaissance poet, John Skelton. Considerably coarser in its satirical crudeness was Dedekind's Latin *Grobianus* (1549), for we might say that it was a book on courtly manners in reverse, depicting the most uncouth character with the most loathsome lack of table manners and social grace imaginable, who in his foulness was, if possible, even surpassed by his female companion, the utterly repulsive Grobiana. This book was translated into German by Kaspar Scheit (1551) and then into most Western European tongues, and, especially if contrasted with the delicate gracefulness of Castiglione's *Courtier*, it tended to convey abroad for generations to come the somewhat unjust impression that the Germans were gross drunkards—though translations like Dekker's *School of Slovenrie* (1605) could amply draw from national English sources too. In connection with Dekker we might refer also to the German origin of his *Old Fortunatus* (1606)—an old German tale of a fateful purse which affects the destinies of its successive owners, a tale often lending itself to descriptions of exotic adventures and Faustian implications. Already Hans Sachs, in 1553, had dramatized the story of a man at first favored, and later disowned, by Fortune.

Hans Sachs, in many ways the most typical representative of solid German sixteenth century burgherdom, was hailed by Goethe in his *Hans Sachsens poetische Sendung (Hans Sachs' Poetic Mission)* and eulogized by Wagner in *Die Meistersinger*; but he is not a subject for comparative investigations (except as an imitator of Boccaccio and others), for he was hardly known abroad. The meistersingers, of which Hans Sachs was such a typical representative, deserve our attention only because their very mediocre efforts were another early attempt to force the vividly pulsating popular literature into the straitjacket of neo-classicizing rules and regulations—though the results of the meistersingers were particularly deplorable in view of the primitiveness of the German language and versification around 1500.

In the field of thematology one German contribution of that time is of utmost significance across all borders of time and space: the publication, in Frankfurt, in 1587, of the first (anonymous) chapbook or *Volksbuch* on DR. FAUST and its almost immediate translation into foreign tongues (French 1589, English 1590, Dutch, 1592, and so forth). Faust can certainly be considered a great symbol of his century, a typical product of the Renaissance—for he was an individual craving for emancipation; a rebel against gods and human restrictions, as Prometheus and Icarus had earlier been; a man unafraid to enter into a pact with the devil, as Cyprianus of Adana and Tannhäuser and, it was whispered, Gregory VII and Roger Bacon had been. Within a very few years Christopher Marlowe had dramatized the story of Dr. Faust. Not only will the comparatist be anxious to contrast the didactically Lutheran German original with Marlowe's titanic exemplification of empire-building Elizabethan activism, but he will also want to follow the story through the seventeenth century with its many German reworkings and addenda, with Marlowe's popular play in Germany represented by wayfaring English Comedians, and with the development of puppet-plays on the same topic. Especially fascinating is *El mágico prodigioso* (*The Mighty Magician*) by the great Spanish dramatist Calderón, an independent treatment of another Faustian theme which, however, in the hands of a Catholic, did not end in despair and hell-fire, but in a grandiose Catholic spectacle of God's mercy towards the sinning and yet repentant Cypriano who died as a Christian martyr. A similarly Faustian story from Portugal is represented in the Spanish play *El esclavo del demonio* (*The Slave of the Demon*, 1612) by Mira de Améscua. A Dutch drama by F. Groen (*The Descent to Hell of Dr. Joan Faustus*, 1690) was published in 1731.

In Germany, it was Lessing who in his lost version first had the intention of ennobling the hitherto very vulgar desires of Faust and of making a seeker of truth rather than a base craver of pleasure out of him, a man worthy to be snatched away from the devils and allowed to enter paradise—and Goethe's immortal drama (1808 and 1831) then, of course, gave to Faust an idealism, a noble humanitarian goal, and to his mating with Helen of Troy a deeply significant symbolism which the Faust of 1587 had never known. Nor will the scholar stop his investigation of Faust with Goethe; he will search on for the Faustian traits in the new versions by Klinger, Müller (1778), Grabbe, Heine, and Lenau; the story of *Peter Schlemihl* by Chamisso (1814—with twelve translations into French alone) ; Byron's *Manfred* (1817) ; *Les sept cordes de la lyre* by George Sand (1839) ; *El Diablo mundo* by Espronceda (1840) ; *La commedia del secolo* by P. de Virgiliis (1840) ; the *Tragedy of Man* by the Hungarian Madach; *El drama universal* (1860) and also *El licenciado Torralba* (1892) by Campoamor; the opera by Gounod; the *Freischütz* by Weber; the *Peer Gynt* by Ibsen; the *Paracelsus* of Browning and of Kolbenheyer; *Mon Faust* by Valéry, and the recent novel by Thomas Mann.

Although the Faust legend was Germany's major contribution to European literary themes, she handed on to future Europe a few other topics which had been developing during the Middle Ages and which then became part of European folklore: for example, the stories of *Till Eulenspiegel* and of the *Schildbürger*. The exploits of Till Eulenspiegel in a way make him the human counterpart to Reynard the Fox; the gay pranks of this tricky scoundrel, conceived as a symbol of the peasants' animosity against city-people, are today preserved both in Low German (1500) and in High German (1515) versions, though the earliest tales must have originated in the Low German districts around Lübeck in the fourteenth century. Foreign translations (English 1516, French 1532) and various German reworkings from Murner and Fischart to the drama by Wedekind, the poem by Hauptmann, and the tone poem by Richard Strauss—and foreign retellings like the popular French version by De Coster (1867)— indicate the continued popularity of a Till whose pranks (an early example of the tall tales of Münchhausen and Paul Bunyan) were gradually retold in most Western European languages. The gay stories about the stupidity of the burghers of Schilda, as collected and told in another folk-book or chapbook of the sixteenth century, indicate the ever-present late medieval love of satire—the satire in this case being directed against small-town folk. Wieland's urbane eighteenth century satire *Die Abderiten* (*The People of Abdera*, 1774) supplied a classical

Greek counter-piece to the stupidity of the late medieval German *Schildbürger*.

Spain

Spain had her greatest moment during the Baroque, to be treated in our next chapter—but we wish to refer here to two great contributions of hers important in the history of Comparative Literature of the Renaissance: the *Amadis* and the *Celestina*. These works, like Castiglione's *Courtier* and Machiavelli's *Prince*, show the whole gamut of Spain's literary wealth, for the *Amadis*, pointing to the past, to the Middle Ages, was as fairy-like and fantastic and idealistic as possible, while the *Celestina*, pointing to the future, to the picaresque novels of the seventeenth and eighteenth centuries and the malodorous Naturalism of the late nineteenth and early twentieth centuries, was as hardboiled, realistic, and cynical as any modern muck-raker.

In its original background, the AMADIS DE GAULA is connected with the idealistic world of medieval chivalry and adventure which is so typical of the Celtic or the Breton cycle; and though first written on the Iberian peninsula, its name *de Gaula* seems to connect it either with France or Wales, while many of its heroes and adventures link it with different parts of England. The Portuguese Vasco de Lobeira in the fourteenth century is said to have been the first to assemble these adventurous tales; however, the version which we possess today and which was published in 1508, is by the Spaniard Rodríguez de Montalvo. In far less ironical a manner than Ariosto in his *Orlando furioso*, the *Amadis* episodes tell us of the ideal, chaste, and persevering love of Amadis and Oriane, of the many cruel separations, the kidnappings by monsters, the valiant struggles with giants, the supernatural events, the fairy-like and miraculous atmosphere, the knightly deeds of courage and gallantry, the disguises and mistaken identities customary in such environments, and the loyalty and final reunion of these lovers. A vast compilation of all the medieval chivalrous adventures imaginable has here been assembled before our eyes, comparable indeed to similar efforts in other countries, the *Morte d'Arthur* by Thomas Malory in England (ca. 1470), and the *Volksbücher vom sterbenden Rittertum (Chapbooks of Dying Knighthood)* in Germany—prosaic retellings among the late-medieval sober burghers of the wondrous deeds of yore.

The men and women of the Renaissance from Francis I of France to Elizabeth of England, though hardened and somewhat cynical in the difficult art of living, enjoyed these fantastic tales immensely. The *Amadis* translation by Herberay des Essarts (1540-48) in France was a great success, and Johann Fischart introduced it into Germany; among the English translations was the one by Arthur Munday (1595). Reference should also be made to the many Amadis imitations such as the *Amadis de Grecia* by Feliciano de Silva (1514) and the *Palmerin da Inglaterra* by Francisco de Moraes (1544). The *Amadis* was a great success in Italy (as evidenced, for instance, in *Amadigi* [1560], an epic by Bernardo Tasso, in Dolce's *Il Palmerino* of 1560 and the *Primaleone* of 1562) as well as in England, and it may well have contributed to the idealized and romantic atmosphere of the *Faerie Queene*. Throughout the seventeenth century of d'Urfé and Quinault-Lulli and even into the eighteenth century of Wieland's *Der neue Amadis,* this important work, in novels, plays, operas and ballets, helped to create an escape literature of pleasantly idealistic make-believe and fantasy. The great enemies of the *Amadis* and *Palmerin* romances were, of course, Ariosto's *Orlando* and Cervantes' *Don Quijote*; yet not even Cervantes' ironical debunking could kill off the trend, and *Amadis* lived on, in heroic novels and heroic plays, well into the Age of Rationalism.

However popular the *Amadis* was during the Renaissance and Baroque, the CELESTINA had a much more profound and permanent influence on Spanish literature and through it on the future literature of Europe. This dialogue novel, written in acts instead of chapters, is the story of the two star-crossed lovers Calixto and Melibea, whose idealistic romantic love leads them to their destruction in a world of cynicism, deceit, knavery, and intrigue. The novel was published by Fernando de Rojas in sixteen acts in 1499 and enlarged to twenty-two acts in 1526. It serves in Spanish literature, if not in all of Western literature, as the matrix of all realistic trends, for there evolved out of it not only the Spanish *comedia* (in part), but also the picaresque novel. The most remarkable quality of the *Celestina* is its duality of tone: its two lovers seem to belong to the age which read chivalric and pastoral novels and narrative poems about noble knights and romantic loves, but its most dramatic characters, particularly the meretricious old hag Celestina and the venal

servants and prostitutes around her, are presented with a naturalistic intensity that is deeply impressive. These lower
characters make up a sordid and cynical world which in its
unscrupulous deceit seems to constitute a bold attack on the
artificial world found in most of the rest of the literature of the
age. The figure of Celestina, the greedy old woman serving as
a procuress and go-between, has become a standard in European
thematology; an echo of her may be found in the nurse in
Romeo and Juliet and in Goethe's description of Frau Martha
in *Faust*. Before the end of the sixteenth century there were
more than fifty Spanish editions, thirteen Italian (1514 ff.), and
seven French (1526 ff.) translations of the book. A German
version appeared in Hamburg as early as 1520, and ten years
later there appeared an English version which may be considered
one of the first English comedies. The best-known of all English translations of *Celestina or Calixto and Malibea* was printed
in 1631: *The Spanish Bawd* by James Mabbe.

France

France had a long line of poets and writers susceptible to
Italian influences, from Christine de Pisan and Charles d'Orléans
up through Marot and the seven members of the *Pléiade* (Ronsard, du Bellay, Baïf, Remi Belleau, Dorat, Ponthus de Thyard,
and Jodelle) to Desportes, Voiture, Chapelain, and the men beyond. Comparatists might wish to investigate particularly men
like Jean Lemaire de Belges, who in his famous *Concorde des
deux Langages* (1513) tried to establish a running parallelism
between Italian and French culture and literature, not exactly
to the disadvantage of the latter—or they might wish to look
into such great Italian cultural centers in France serving as
intermediaries between the two nations as Fontainebleau, the
seat of the Valois kings, and Lyon, the great commercial center
on the road to Italy, the home of italianizing Lyonese poets such
as Maurice Scève and Louise Labé (whom Rilke translated into
German), the city in which was printed the first Italian edition
of Dante's *Divine Comedy* to be published in France (1547).
France naturally also contributed to the literary themes of the
Renaissance and later periods: the lives of Catherine de' Medici
and her weak son, Charles IX, for instance, and the St. Bartholomew's Day Massacre which they may have instigated, have
never ceased to fire the imagination of authors from Marlowe

(*The Massacre of Paris,* 1592) and Lee (*The Duke of Guise,* 1683) down to Mérimée and Conrad Ferdinand Meyer (*Das Amulett.*)

We have already explained why, from a comparatist's viewpoint, the poets of the Pléiade are not quite as significant as the Graeco-Latin or Italian authors who inspired them. In connection with du Bellay's *Défense et Illustration de la langue française* (*Defense and Glorification of the French Language,* 1549) it has always been interesting to notice the striking similarities in structure and thought between it and Dante's *De vulgari eloquentia*—though it is proven that Speroni rather than Dante influenced du Bellay in the composition of this significant programmatic essay. Ronsard's lyrical genius was so great that he passed on his essentially petrarchizing vein not only to Englishmen like Sidney, Dutchmen like Huygens, or Germans like Weckherlin and Paulus Melissus, but even to an Italian poet, Chiabrera, to whom he gave that which he himself had originally received from Italy. Indeed, since the literary Renaissance began a little earlier in France than it did in England, the France of the mid-sixteenth century can be studied as something of an intermediary between Italy and England. Viewed from this angle, such problems as the relationship between Marot, Ronsard, du Bellay and Desportes and Wyatt, Surrey, Sidney, and the Cavalier poets—or again the relationship between Belleforest, Painter, and Shakespeare or Amyot, North, and Shakespeare—assume an interest and importance of their own. Spenser's *Complaints* of 1591, for instance, contained translations both from Petrarca and from du Bellay. One can go further and examine the influence the Pléiade had in encouraging the naturally developing Neo-Classicism in other countries. For example, it might be interesting to study the effect it had upon the formation of the English Areopagus or upon the neo-classical development initiated by Opitz in Germany. Also interesting are the English visitors and diplomats in France (Hoby, Bacon) or the influence of French Huguenots like Hubert Languet on Sidney; but even more important is the gradual emerging of the first grammars and dictionaries: Palsgrave's *Esclarcissement de la langue françoyse* of 1530 was followed by Claudius Hollyband (*The French Schoolmaster,* 1573) and by Cotgrave's *Dictionary of the French and English Tongues* (1611).

However, apart from these minor influences and apart from the before-mentioned Calvin, it was really only Rabelais and Montaigne that contributed distinctly French values to the literature abroad.   François RABELAIS (1494-1553), one of the strangest mixtures of the earthiness of the Middle Ages and the new learning of the Renaissance, was a scholar, an idealist, a utopian, who, however, in his *Gargantua* (1535) and *Pantagruel* (1533) imposed not the slightest restraint either upon his style or his fantasy, upon his manifold physical appetites, or upon his spiritual aspirations.   In the case of this somewhat coarser Ariosto, whose *Abbaye de Thélème* might well be classed among the utopian visions of that time, it is perhaps not the question of influences abroad which is most fascinating—his being translated into German by Fischart (1575) and into English by Urquhart (1653) and Motteux; his effect upon Shakespeare, Swift, Sterne and Joyce in England, Cervantes in Spain, Reuter (*Schelmuffsky*, 1696) in Germany, or Washington Irving in America.   Probably even more intriguing is the whole question of Rabelais' style: his love of the grotesque and the incongruous, of gigantic fantasies, his stylistic twists and neological somersaults, which clearly seem to announce the dawn of many baroque aberrations.   Rabelais' entire style is a challenge to the investigator of international literature: it showed itself earlier in the burlesque epic *Der Ring* by the Swiss Heinrich von Wittenweiler (ca. 1425); it certainly blossomed forth in hitherto unimagined forcefulness in Pulci's *Morgante* and the maccaronesque style of Folengo; and after Rabelais and his German translator Fischart we find it again, with a slight shift of accent, in the burlesque twists of Berni—and we might wish to follow all these threads because we have come to agree with Victor Hugo that the grotesque is indeed an essential part of literature.

Michel de MONTAIGNE (1533-92), the epitome of Renaissance philosophy, was a man who, after many waves of new facts and experiences had flooded Europe for more than a century, brought the age to an end with a vague note of skepticism and a philosophy of life that kept a happy balance between Epicureanism and Stoicism.   His *Essais* (1580-95) abound with brilliant pages that deal not only with big questions of Religion, Peace or War, but with fine probings into the character and the physical and spiritual makeup of man in general and of Montaigne in particular.   With him there began the famous French trend towards subtle psychological analysis which later reached its finest perfection in the age of Racine. His *Essays* became known in England especially through the noted translation by John Florio (1603) and later by the version of Charles Cotton, and in eighteenth century Germany through the version of J. J. C. Bode. But Montaigne's popularity and influences in England went considerably beyond any limited kind of literary influence. His contemplative skepticism and searching self-analysis are deeply reflected in Shakespeare, and his richly informal prose style contributed to the prose of men like Sir Thomas Browne. Of an entirely different kind of interest is the study of Montaigne not only as a thinker, but as the important creator of the modern informal essay—and that leads us especially to an examination of the adaptation of Montaigne's essay style by Sir Francis Bacon. And since Montaigne is a truly modern man who is forever fresh and stimulating, his reputation through the centuries in Spain (Cervantes), England (Shaftesbury, Browning), Germany (Goethe, Nietzsche), and America (Emerson) always deserves intense study.

Portugal

Portugal experienced her brief golden age of literature during this Italy-dominated Renaissance with the Petrarchistic lyrical poetry of Ferreira (often called the du Bellay of Portugal), Sâ de Miranda, and Luis de CAMOENS (1524-80), and with the latter's beautiful epic poem *Os Lusiadas* (*The Lusiads, i. e. The Portuguese*, 1572). It is a Virgil- and Ariosto-inspired glorification of Vasco da Gama's circumnavigation of Africa, the first distinctly neo-classical epic in Europe and one of the finest epic masterpieces of the entire Renaissance. In the seventeenth century Camoens was applauded by the Spaniard Manuel Faria e Sousa (*Las Lusiadas de Luis de Camoens comentadas*, 1639) and translated by Sir Richard Fanshawe (1655), onetime English ambassador to Portugal and Spain. However, the merits of Portugal's greatest poet had little chance of being acknowledged during the subsequent centuries when French classical taste ruled over Europe. He was criticized by Rapin, among others, in his *Réflexions sur l'éloquence et la poétique* (1674) and by Voltaire, who in his *Essai sur la poésie épique* referred to the *Lusiads* only in order to praise all the more the neo-classical artificiality of his own *Henriade*. It was only during the romantic period that Camoens' masterpiece received the literary evaluation it so richly deserves, when the English pre-romantic translator, William Julius Mickle, gave the poem his attention (providing his translation of 1776 with a richly anti-Voltairian commentary) and, above all, when the epic was discovered by the German romanticists, foremost among them Friedrich Schlegel. From then on the fame of Camoens—like the fame of many other great masters hitherto scorned by the French classical parnassus (Dante, Shakespeare, Calderón)—was definitely and lastingly established on an international scale. In his beautiful poem about *Camoens* (1825), the Portuguese romanticist Almeida Garrett used his unhappy life as a symbol of all poets' lives in an unfeeling world. Among modern admirers of Camoens we should name Sir Richard Burton, author of a *Life of Camoens* as well as of a new translation of the *Lusiads.* We might also point to Camoens as one of the first modern and superb depictors of the sea—a field in which his descriptions might be compared with those found in Homer, in *Beowulf* or in *Gudrun.*

In the field of thematology Portugal gave to Europe especially the pathetic story of INEZ DE CASTRO, as treated, for instance, in Ferreira's tragedy by the same name (1558). It is the story of a noble heroine who must be murdered for reasons of state so that the unsuspecting young king may then be induced to contract some politically advantageous marriage—the story of a woman's despair and a king's wrath and revenge which will remind the comparatist immediately of the German tale of the forcefully disrupted marriage of Agnes Bernauer to the duke of Bavaria, as treated, for instance, in Hebbel's tragedy of the same name (1850). The story of Inez de Castro also constitutes one of the most touching episodes in Camoens' *Lusiads.* In Spain, Pero López de Ayala had been one of the first to refer to it in *La Crónica del Rey Don Pedro*; Fray Jerónimo Bermúdez adapted Ferreira's version in two tragedies, *Nise lastimosa* and *Nise laureada* (1577); Juan Suárez de Alarcón retold the story in a poem *La infanta coronada* (1606), and Mexía de la Cerda, in his *Tragedia de Doña Inés de Castro* (1612). Best known among these Spanish adaptations is probably the tragedy *Reinar después de morir* (*To Rule after Death*) by Luis Vélez de Guevara, in which, however, the tragic doom of the heroine is emphasized far more than the rule of a corpse on the throne. In

English literature reference can be made to the stilted retelling of the story of *Agnes de Castro* by Aphra Behn, while among the French versions the neo-classical tragedy by Houdart de la Motte (1723) should be mentioned, which was parodied by Ramón de la Cruz (*Inesilla la de Pinto*). In 1826, Houdart de la Motte's version was translated into Spanish by Bréton de los Herreros. Among other treatments of the theme of Inez de Castro, mention might be made of the Dutch version by Feith (1793), the Portuguese version by Eugenio de Castro (1900) and of the modern French work *La Reine Morte* (*The Dead Queen*) by Montherlant (1947).

Finally, one should not forget certain authors like Juan del Encina, Sâ de Miranda, Gil Vicente, and especially Jorge de Montemayor who, though they were bi-lingual and achieved great triumphs in their Spanish works, were nevertheless Portuguese by birth and thus, like Lobeira for the *Amadis* and Camoens for the *Lusiads*, representatives of more or less distinctly Portuguese literary contributions.

England

English literature, in spite of the greatness of the Elizabethans, had little to contribute to Europe during the period under discussion, for it was the role of the Mediterranean countries to give and to influence, first Italy, then Spain, then France—and the great English poets, Shakespeare in the sixteenth and Milton in the seventeenth century, had to wait until the eighteenth century of the great European movement called Pre-Romanticism to be fully appreciated and to be considered leading figures. Men like Chaucer, Spenser, and even Sidney were hardly known abroad; a minor work, Greene's *Pandosto* (1588) was actually the first English novel to become translated and known in France (1615). However, in our next chapter on the Baroque, we shall speak of the first repercussions abroad of the Elizabethan drama.

Although English literature contributed little, England herself supplied considerable material for literature. The great English explorers and traders of the Elizabethan age led the way in the opening of the new lands; they were foremost in writing accounts of voyages—as evidenced, for instance, in *The Principal Navigations and Discoveries of the English Nation* by Richard Hakluyt (1589)—and so they indirectly provided exotic new materials for literature. Of more direct interest, however, were the men whom that colorful Age of the Tudors produced—and, even more important, the women—whose fortunes and misfortunes were to be re-created imaginatively many times in the future. The struggle of Henry VIII against Catherine of Aragón and the Church of Rome was depicted in a *comedia* by Calderón, *La Cisma de Inglaterra* (*The Schism of England*). The pathetic story of Ann Boleyn supplied more than one plot for drama (H. H. Milman in England, 1826, and G. H. Boker and M. Anderson in America) as did the stories of Mary Tudor (Victor Hugo), Catherine Howard (Dumas père), and Jane Gray (Rowe, Wieland). The tragic tale of Mary Stuart became particularly popular: she was bitterly attacked by Buchanan as early as 1571 and her life and death struggle with Elizabeth (1587) inspired the poem *La Corona trágica* by Lope de Vega (1627) and the dramas by Montchrestien, Vondel, Juan Bautista Diamante, Voltaire, Alfieri, Schiller, Swinburne and Björnson, to mention only a few examples. Also the half-legendary romance between Elizabeth and Essex and his subsequent execution in 1601 can be found in the drama and fiction of France (La Calprenède, Thomas Corneille, Boyer), Spain (Coello y Ochoa's *Dar la vida por su dama o el Conde de Sex.* 1638), and England (Henry Brooke, 1750). The deeds of the bold freebooter Sir Francis Drake were narrated in Lope's epic *La Dragontea* (1598), and the dramatist Marlowe became the theme of a play by Wildenbruch (1884). Thus, Renaissance England did contribute materials for the literature of other nations, even though her literature itself was not widely known on the continent for another two hundred years.

The Lowlands

Dutch literature will be somewhat more fully treated in the baroque chapter, for during the Renaissance proper there was only the leading figure of Desiderius ERASMUS OF ROTTERDAM (1467-1536), the prince of scholars, the leader among progressive and enlightened thinkers. In spite of his opposition to Luther, Erasmus was suspected by the orthodox party and investigated by the Inquisition, and some of his works were later put on the *Index librorum prohibitorum*. Although we have already mentioned something of the importance of Erasmus in European Humanism, perhaps his greatest contribution to all of Europe and to all the future was his own person, which, even more than Petrarca's, came to symbolize the ideal of Humanism and which even today signifies tolerance, understanding, and internationalism of the finest sort. To the student interested in literature from an international point of view no man can be more attractive than Erasmus, who numbered among his friends the great men of all lands. That he wrote in Latin primarily may place him somewhat outside the stream of vernacular modern literature (though his works were translated almost immediately), but the force of his point of view, the depth and understanding of his intelligence, and the urbanity and wit of his style make him a man whom every nation should be proud to claim. And the extent of his influence in Spain (Valdés), England (More), France (Rabelais), Germany (Hutten), and Switzerland (Zwingli) as well as in Italy, Portugal, and Hungary indicates that he was both a citizen of the world and a citizen of many nations.

In the field of thematology, a medieval yet ever popular story might perhaps best be assigned to the Lowlands, particularly to Flanders: the story of REYNARD THE FOX. The comparatist with a predilection for folklore will enjoy delving into the many fables about the smartness or the dumbness of certain animals, from the days of Aesop up through the tales about *B'rer Rabbit* by Joel Chandler Harris. From Flanders the story of Reynard the Fox spread with equal ease eastward into Germany and southward into France. *Ecbasis Captivi* (*The Flight of the Prisoner*), written by a Lothringian monk around 940, was the first example of a beast epic in which the fox figured prominently. In the twelfth century reference can be made to the Latin *Isengrimus* by Nivard from Ghent and also to the German version by Heinrich der Glichezäre, an Alsatian monk. In France the *Roman de Renart* grew into a mighty epic, a symbol at times of political intrigues; in Holland the version by Heinrich von Alkmar should be particularly noted. A Flemish version (*Reinaert de Vos*) was printed in 1487, a Low German version (*Reynke de Vos*) in Lübeck in 1498—and it was this latter version which Gottsched, in 1752, translated into pedestrian High German prose and which Goethe used in 1794 in shaping his masterfully classical and Homeric epic *Reineke Fuchs*.

In looking back over the Renaissance, we see that any comparative study of the period must begin in Italy, that before that study can proceed even in Italy it must probe the revival of classical Greek and Roman literature to understand the development of modern literature; and that the study of the Renaissance period as a whole is in large part the study of the spread of Italian ideas, inspirations, forms, and styles into the other countries of Europe. Once the Italian-inspired new kind of writing began to take hold in the native soil of another country, it quickly adapted itself to its new environment; but in a very real sense the seeds of most of what we call modern literature were germinated in Italian soil and blown from there over the whole of the Western World.

II. THE BAROQUE

A. GENERAL OBSERVATIONS

The very definition of the term Baroque, used for the period formerly known as the Late Renaissance, calls for a constantly new examination and re-evaluation, for it stands to reason, for instance, that a very real abyss separates the titanic aspirations of Marlowe from the mystical pilgrimage of Bunyan's Christian; the joyous outcry of Hutten that it is a delight to be alive from the resigned reply of *Vanitas, vanitatum vanitas* of a Gryphius; the pleasantly Epicurean *Abbaye de Thélème* of Rabelais from the soul-searching *Pensées* of Pascal; the pagan gracefulness of an Ariosto from the Catholic fervor of a Calderón. The entirely new atmosphere of the first half of the seventeenth century, during which the sensualism of the Renaissance reeled under the hammer-blows of a re-awakened spiritualism caused by the Counter-Reformation, can be observed by the comparatist in its European entirety, though different degrees of accent and intensity can, of course, be noticed among Catholic and Protestant nations. The Baroque, initiated perhaps by the founding of the order of the Jesuits and intensified during the Church Council of Trent (1545-63), represents a last flickering up of the spirit of the Middle Ages in its futile attempt to stem the tide of modern godlessness that had started with the Renaissance. Yet what was a Counter-Reformation among the Catholics, became, *mutatis mutandis*, a Counter-Renaissance among the Protestants, too, because Lutherans, Huguenots, and Puritans, as well as the Jesuits and the Inquisition of Catholic Italy, Spain, and Portugal, rose up against what seemed the moral disintegration of the Renaissance and tried to put the clock back, as it were. Political factors supported this essentially religious drive of forcing man back into servitude and of transforming the proud self-reliance and emancipation of the Renaissance man into abject and trembling submission to the wrathfully aroused Church, for the rise of royal absolution coincided with the Age of the Baroque. From the Guerra de las Comunidades in Spain in 1521, the Peasant War in Germany in 1524-25, and the fall of Florence in 1530 to the increasing arrogance of the Stuarts in England and the smashing of the Fronde in France in 1652-53, the last flickerings of popular liberty were gradually being stamped out. Ecclesi-

astical and worldy princes ruled supreme again where, only a
few decades before, the Renaissance had seemed to establish
freedom for ever.

Seen from the angle of the progress of human freedom, however, the Baroque marked really only a last road-block in the path
of freer human development—and what had been started by
Roger Bacon, Valla, and Luther could not for long be stopped by
Loyola, Philip II, or Cromwell. Time was marching on and
Francis Bacon in England, Descartes in France, and Leibniz in
Germany continued what the Renaissance had begun. The Age
of Rationalism, indeed of skepticism, which they initiated, put
an end to the baroque frenzy and established, in the second half
of the seventeenth century, the Age of Classicism and, two
generations later, the Age of Enlightenment. Thus swings
the pendulum from one extreme to another, and the student of
human thought will be tempted to group together the Middle
Ages (1300), the Baroque (1600), and Romanticism (1800) as
being the conservative antipodes of that other far more progressive group consisting of the Renaissance (1500), the Age of
Classicism, Rationalism, and Enlightenment (1700), and the
Age of Realism and Liberalism (1880), though such parallelisms
and contrasts are necessarily somewhat superficial.

Also with regard to literary style we note that the neo-classical
beginnings of the Renaissance were momentarily upset by a
new cacophonic turgidity of language caused by that sudden and
heavy impact of thunderings about hellfire and damnation upon
what had been an essentially serene Renaissance mentality;
but, even though the style of the Baroque at times seemed to
revert to the artless naturalism of the Middle Ages, Italo-French
neo-classical principles managed to survive and to achieve supremacy in 1660, after the Baroque had come to an end.

Many different names have been given to this period of intellectual, emotional, and stylistic upheaval—and the comparatist, if he does not like the little-used term of Counter-Renaissance, may borrow a term from the political historians (Counter-
Reformation), or the art historians (Baroque) ; or he may be
satisfied with local terms such as Marinism, *concettism*, or
secentism in Italy; Gongorism, *conceptism*, or *culteranism* in
Spain; Euphuism or Metaphysical Poetry in England; or
préciosité in France. For the student of international literature, however, one single term is preferable—and the term

Baroque, borrowed from Spanish jewellers and indicating rough, uncouth, unpolished stones, applied to the history of Fine Arts especially by Wölfflin in Zürich and from thence transferred into the realm of German, Italian and Spanish (but less into French and English) literature, is most generally accepted.

In our previous chapter we have noted the dates of the end of the Renaissance and, consequently, the beginnings of the Baroque; here we might add a few suggestions with regard to the end of that period. France, the most classical minded of the nations concerned and one who had been most unwilling to condone the literary irregularities that had prevailed under Henri IV and Louis XIII, ended the Baroque and established the reign of Classicism first: if not with the founding of the French Academy in 1634-35, or with the founding of what is commonly called the School of 1660, then, at the latest, with the appearance of Racine's *Andromaque* (1667) or Boileau's *Art poétique* in 1674. To choose the equally convenient date of 1660, the end of the Cromwellian Commonwealth and the restoration of the Stuarts, would perhaps be somewhat misleading for England, for there are scholars who insist that baroque characteristics (*e.g.* the heroic tragedy) prevailed in England throughout the age of Dryden, too, and that only the Silver Age of Queen Ann and Alexander Pope initiated true Neo-Classicism in England. The last two decades of the seventeenth century marked the end of the Baroque in Spain and Germany: Calderón died in 1681; and in Germany, the religious excesses of what was called the First Silesian School and the Senecan excesses of the Second Silesian School were more or less exhausted in the last years of the century, giving way to the neo-classical dictatorship of Gottsched in 1730. In Italy, finally, the Roman Academy of the Arcadians (1690 ff.) with its innumerable branches in provincial towns marks a somewhat indistinct transition from the Baroque to the Rococo.

Borderland-problems are abundant during the Baroque between literature and some other form of cultural and historical activity. Especially close are the ties between religion and literature proper, and the comparatist might wish to investigate whether the Baroque, in spite of its essentially Catholic origins, did not produce more deeply felt poetry among the Protestants (Donne, Gryphius), who, doubly hard hit by the Counter-Reformation, found this period an extremely shattering experience, than among the relatively self-assured Catholics. He might investigate the literary output of various religious schools of thought: of the *renaissance catholique* and the Jansenists in France; the Lutherans, Calvinists, and Anglicans; the beginnings of Pietism, Quakerism, and Methodism. He might turn his attention especially to the great revival of Mysticism (Santa Teresa, Böhme) which endeavored to be above the strife and hatred of religious wars—wars whose horrors we find mirrored in literature from Ronsard (*Discours des misères de ce temps,* 1562) to Grimmelshausen (*Simplizissimus,* 1669). The comparatist might wish to study also the effect which the religious revival had upon the development of some specific literary genre, for example, oratory (Donne, Abraham a Santa Clara, Bossuet); the novel as exemplified by Camus in France and Bunyan in England; the epic, as handled by Tasso, du Bartas, Fletcher, Heywood and Milton; the flourishing martyr-tragedies; or devotional poetry itself (Luis de León, Herbert, Gerhardt). Or he might turn to purely historical investigations and find out how far and why the Baroque is more or less identical with the Age of the Counter-Reformation in Church History and with the growing Age of Absolutism in political history.

A confrontation with Philosophy, Fine Arts, Music, or Sciences affords equally splendid opportunities. The field ranges from philosophy proper to the burning pantheistic faith of Giordano Bruno in Italy and Spinoza in Holland—and to the shattering discoveries of Copernikus in Poland, Kepler in Germany, Tycho Brahe in Denmark, Galileo in Italy, and Newton in England, which, as intimated already in the last chapter, may have contributed much to undermine the demi-godly pride of Renaissance man. The term Baroque, borrowed from Fine Arts, will naturally lead to many comparisons between art and literature, the disappearance of Renaissance simplicity and serenity in favor of dynamic upheavals, passionate crescendos, *fortissimo* effects— the portrayal of an heroically unhappy and uprooted humanity which seemingly had nothing to cling to except religious ardor. In both fields there is an apparent weakness of artistic means to express this frenzy in its proper intensity, so that in distorted limbs, brooding colors, cacophonic sounds, and bloated accumulations of superlatives in sculpture, painting, music, and literature—as well as in the lines, the pillars, and the duplications of architecture—everything had to be said at least twice or thrice and still did not produce the effect it was meant to have. This vaster concept of the field of Baroque would include a study of the mysticism of Jakob Böhme, the music from Bach to Händel, the sculpture of Bernini, the paintings of El Greco and Murillo, the architectural wealth of "baroque" cities like Prague or Salzburg.

Particularly fascinating is the Janus-faced countenance of this period—for since man was no longer a proud demi-god but a reed in the wind, a miserably wailing sinner, a crushed being at the mercy of the merciless powers that be, a less than nothing more than likely destined to eternal damnation and hell-fire, a good number of individuals and scores of poets and thinkers around 1600, instead of beating their breasts and reforming while it was still time, resolved (by a *non sequitur* that is not so hard to understand) to live on in sensual delights, since most likely they were beyond all hope anyway. Hence the strange fact that the Baroque produced the most piously and pitiously religious literature and the most erotic and uninhibited type of poetry at the same time. The unpleasant connotation of the word Baroque derives not only from the fact that it is a heavy literature, overladen, cumbersome, produced in the dark abysses of struggling human souls amidst a thousand pains and out-cries, so that no aesthetic consideration mattered because of the very weight of the problem experienced—but perhaps even more from the fact that much of it was an immense compilation of studied lasciviousness and bombast. We might well say that the gay, carefree, and naughty sensualism of the Renaissance which had been so enjoyable in Boccaccio, Chaucer, and Ariosto now definitely came to an end and that among the slippery poetasters at the courts of luxurious and absolutistic princelings there was written for the first time what we might distinctly call pornography. The growing age of rationalism, skepticism. libertinism and *galanterie* contributed to this trend—we need only refer to the veiled voluptuousness of Desportes in France, Marino in Italy, the Cavalier Poets like Carew, Suckling, Roches-ter in England, or the unsavory members of the Second Silesian School (Lohenstein, Hofmannswaldau) in Germany. Hence the stark and striking contrast between the disciples of Christ and the disciples of Venus, the deterioration of that which had been good in the hands of Ariosto and Rabelais into just the opposite in the hands of the Restoration dramatists in the seventeenth century and the crowd around the *Encyclopédie* in the eighteenth.

And most interesting for our purpose (and most baroque indeed) were the poets who, because of the shattered peace and harmony of their souls, were both these things at the same time —supreme among them John Donne, a Dean of St. Paul's with a very rebellious flesh. No wonder that the Baroque also indicated the end of genuine Petrarchism, for a detailed enumeration of womanly charms now served entirely different purposes, and prostrate adoration as an end in itself was no longer fashionable. No wonder either that one of the most popularly beloved heroines of the Baroque was Maria Magdalena (such as treated, for instance, in the poem by Crashaw, the plays by Andreini and Vélez de Guevara, and the epic by Desmarets de Saint-Sorlin), for she was a saint and a harlot at the same time, a symbol of the deep inner dissension of that entire period—and also that Solomon's *Song of Songs* became translated and rewritten with scores of glitteringly erotic insinuations.

The bombast of the Baroque was also encouraged by other political and religious developments, for only with splendor and pomp could princes convince their impoverished and war-stricken subjects of the greatness of their god-willed absolutistic regimes—and untold splendor, pomp, and luxury, in churches and in archiepiscopal palaces as well as in gorgeously staged Jesuit plays, served the Catholic Church likewise to convince its faithful ones of its eternal power, and to attract the souls even of Protestants and bring them back into the fold of the Church. It certainly was a period of crassest extremes: the potentates had never been so powerful, and the poor never so crushed; the wicked had never been so thoroughly wicked and the good never so exaltedly religious. Out of the splendor of luxury-loving courts and Jesuit performances was also born the opera, that most typically baroque and overladen *mixtum compositum* of all imaginable arts.

If we look for the one literary genre, not sensual, yet not completely religious either, which most perfectly gave expression to this entire period, we would probably find that it was the martyr tragedy—for it dwelled on the greatness of religion, the mercifulness of God, the staunch steadfastness of the exalted hero or heroine; yet it afforded the author an opportunity to display, too, some of the worst excesses of Senecan horror and tortures, crude eroticism, bombast and other superlativisms so dear to this mentally unbalanced generation. A student of fine aesthetic perfection and supreme delicacy in literature will never turn to the Baroque, for he will not find what he is after; if however, beneath bloated extravaganzas and repulsive hideousness, he is eager to behold the naked soul of a praying, suffering, and sinning generation, then the Baroque will give him one of the most richly rewarding insights into the history of man's thoughts. The martyr-tragedy displayed all these characteristics, and hence its very great success and popularity—though, of course, as a drama it tended to be rather static and undramatic because a true martyr, in spite of all ghastly tortures and glittering temptations, could never be made to stray from the straight and narrow path of virtue and steadfastness, and his painfully slow death was therefore a preconcluded affair from the very first act on. Its macabre atmosphere of death and religious exaltation had been prepared in the sixteenth century, not only by the growing influence of Seneca and vernacular tragedies like *Abraham sacrifiant* by Théodore de Bèze and *Les Juives* by Robert Garnier (the latter imitated by Vondel in his *Destroyed Jerusalem*, 1620) but, above all, by the religious tragedies of the neo-Latinists (Buchanan's *Jephtha*, Heinsius' *Herodes infanticida*), which in turn inspired great and typically baroque Jesuit spectacles on similar subjects. Indeed it might be said that the vogue of martyr-tragedies was so very powerful that even translations of classical dramas were rewritten and reinterpreted in that sense: thus, for instance, the two translations by Martin Opitz of Sophocles' *Antigone* (a perfect martyr for a noble cause) and Seneca's *Trojan Women* (a pathetic reflection of the horrors of the Thirty Years' War then raging in Germany).

Spain, the great intellectual leader of the Baroque, produced martyr plays among many of the fifty-odd saints' lives dramatized by Lope de Vega, and especially in the Faustian story of *El mágico prodigioso* (*The Mighty Magician*, 1637) by Calderón, and again in *El príncipe constante* (*The Constant Prince*, 1629), in which Don Fernando of Portugal preferred to die at the hands of the Moors rather than give up his faith. Massinger and Dekker in England wrote *The Virgin Martyr* (1620) which, besides including vulgar jesters, had the indelicacy of showing how the saintly heroine was thrown into a brothel—the same as in Corneille's later *Théodore, vierge et martyre* (1645), an aesthetic aberration which the increasingly classical French took very much amiss. Most famous, of course, among the French martyr-plays was Corneille's *Polyeucte* (1643)—and by the very fact that he wrote them, Corneille indicates that like Joost van den Vondel in Holland (author of the martyr-tragedy *The Maidens,* 1639), he was a somewhat transitional figure, still considerably baroque in his vigorous language and not yet completely classical in Racine's sense of that word. Also Desfontaines' (1644) and Rotrou's (1645) versions of *Saint Genest* deserve to be mentioned here; the latter is a fascinating play within a play in which a Roman actor, cast to play the role of a doomed Christian martyr, suddenly becomes a Christian himself. We must refer, too, to Germany's greatest dramatist of the seventeenth century, Andreas Gryphius, author of such martyr plays as *Katharina von Georgien* (1666) and *Felicitas,* which combined saintliness and horror and in which the worst excesses of Senecan naturalism somehow were made to serve the greater glory of God. The Roman tragedy *Papinianus* shows us a martyr who died because of his political integrity rather than because of religious implications—and in *Carolus Stuardus* the devoutly pro-royalist Gryphius in a somewhat unfelicitous manner conceived of Charles I of England as a martyr for a god-willed cause. These tragedies, especially those by Vondel and Gryphius, give us a chance to point also to the very lyrical, religious and philosophical character of their choruses—and the comparatist with a predilection for that kind of problem might wish to investigate the gradual extinction of the Greek and Roman chorus and to point to the reasons for its occasional re-emergence (*e.g.* in Racine's *Athalie,* in Metastasio's operas, or in Schiller's *Braut von Messina*).

B. THE CONTRIBUTIONS OF SPAIN.

The Golden Age of Spanish literature coincided with the Baroque, with the Counter-Reformation. It was not only a time when Philip II was the right-hand man of the Church of Rome, the self-appointed St. George to slay the dragon of heresy—as is proved by his struggle against the Netherlands, the victory over the Turks at Lepanto, and especially the attempted invasion of England—but also a time when Spanish letters reached their finest and most truly national expression. The literature of this age was a literature strongly permeated with a deeply and sincerely Catholic outlook on life, as indicated from the time of the Spanish mystics in the sixteenth century to the death of Calderón at the end of the seventeenth century—and in spite of strong undercurrents against aristocracy and the growing corruption of Spain, it was likewise permeated with an equally sincere loyalty to the king and to national traditions. Stylistically, the *Siglo de Oro* distinguishes itself especially by its staunch refusal to be drawn into the sphere of neo-classical doctrines and courtly refinement (except, to some extent, for Calderón). The two greatest contributions of Spain to European literature were great largely because they were so typically Spanish, with a flavor of late medieval naturalism uninfluenced by what the Italian and the French disciples of Aristotle were trying to achieve: the irregular Spanish *comedia* and the earthy Spanish picaresque novel. A third typical contribution of Spain we have discussed under Islamic influences; it was the Moorish tale of the type of the *Abencerraje*.

The duration of the Spanish Golden Century differs according to the viewpoints of various critics: it might be said to have lasted during the reign of Philip II, Philip III and Philip IV (1556-1665) ; or again it may be said to have begun with the birth of Cervantes (1547) and to have ended with the death of Lope de Vega (1635). Calderón lived somewhat beyond the peak of the Golden Age, just as Tasso lived beyond the apex of the Italian Renaissance. Scholars with an eye for well-fitting dates might enjoy the neat succession of literary hegemonies arrived at if the end of the Golden Age of Spain is indicated at the time of Lope's death in 1635 and the beginning of the Classical Period of France is said to have started with Corneille's *Cid* in 1636.

Turning to intermediaries, we can say far less with regard to Spain than with regard to Italy—for whereas Italy, the garden of Europe, the mother of the Renaissance, the center of Catholicism, was flooded by visitors, scholars, and pilgrims who, upon returning home, served in turn as intermediaries of Italian culture abroad, Spain, on the contrary, except for diplomats, was hardly ever visited by foreigners, and the greatness of Spanish culture became known abroad through conquering soldiers and fanatical priests—not, by definition, the most ideal transmitters of what the *Siglo de Oro* had to offer. Foreign accounts ranged all the way from the reports by Guicciardini, who was Italian ambassador in early sixteenth century Spain, to the much-disputed *Relation du voyage d'Espagne* (1679—printed in 1691) and the *Mémoires de la cour d'Espagne* by the Comtesse d'Aulnoy late in the seventeenth century—but they were rare and far between.

From a political and cultural viewpoint Spain left her heaviest imprint upon territories and nations she occupied during her Golden Age: Central and South America, Portugal, the Netherlands, Italy. Volumes have been, and will continue to be, written about the *hispanidad* of Spanish America, about the immense indebtedness of Mexico, Peru, or the Argentine to the Spanish motherland. In Ercilla's *Araucana,* Spanish literature produced its first great masterpiece dealing with the conquest of American territories; in Ruiz de Alarcón, a Mexican by birth, it had its first American author to contribute to its wealth of dramas. An important book to appear on the subject of Spanish expansion was the widely translated *Destruyción de las Indias* by Bartolomé de las Casas (1552), which dwelled not only on the greatness, but even more on the unspeakable atrocities of the Christian conquest of America and which, in the hands of the Protestant haters of Spain, contributed to the establishment of the so-called Black Legend of Spanish colonization.

Spanish cultural centers in the Netherlands and in Italy were Antwerp and Naples respectively, where the printing presses were busy turning out Spanish books. Spanish *comedias* became popular in the Netherlands from 1614 on, in spite of the war then raging between the two nations. Alessandro Tassoni and Trajano Boccalini were leaders among the Italian poets opposing Spanish domination, the former in his *Filippiche contro gli Spagnuoli (Philippica against the Spaniards,* 1614) ; the lat-

ter in *Pietra del paragone politico* (*The Political Testing-Stone*).
It was only with Austria that Spanish relations were affably
normal, because of the fact that Juana la Loca's marriage to
Philip the Handsome in 1496 had acquired the throne of Spain
for the House of Austria; and since the division of the Empire by
Charles V in 1556, related branches of the Habsburgs were ruling
both in Vienna and in Madrid. To the comparatist, this close
affinity between Spain and Austria is quite fascinating; though
the Spanish influence upon Vienna at first was purely military,
religious, and to a lesser extent social and linguistic, it belatedly
became literary, too, especially in the course of the nineteenth
century.

As to France and England, relations, both political and cultural, were strained at best, as was unavoidable in a period of
military clashes which ended with the destruction of Spanish
seapower by the English in 1588 and of Spanish landpower by
the French in 1659. Cultural influences came in through sea-
ports such as Nantes and Rouen (the latter quite significantly the
home-town of Corneille) and London; in spite of the strained
political relations, Frenchmen from Hardy to Molière and de la
Rochefoucauld, and Englishmen from Kyd and Donne to Dryden
and Pepys, could not avoid the impact of Spanish literary influences. This impact in France was intensified by the marriage of
Spanish princesses to both Louis XIII (to Ann of Austria, 1615)
and Louis XIV (to Maria Teresa of Austria, 1660). A special
embassy to Madrid and a similarly planned marriage of the later
Charles I of England ended in failure.

Among the characters and historical events which Spain
contributed to the thematology of Europe, there were the Moorish wars, repercussions of which we find in Peele's *Battle of
Alcazar* (1594) and especially in Dryden's *Conquest of Granada;*
trans-atlantic conquests (Kotzebue's *Pizarro*); the ubiquitous
Inquisition (Hugo's *Torquemada*); and seventeenth century
conspiracies and intrigues (Weise's *Masaniello* and *Olivares,* and
Hugo's *Ruy Blas*). Particularly important was the Armada—
a subject dear to English writers in times of foreign danger—
and, most of all, the story of the mysterious death of Don Carlos
at the hands of his own father, Philip II, a tale of royal tyranny
treated for the first time by the Spaniards Diego Jiménez de
Enciso (*El Príncipe don Carlos*) and José de Cañizares. One
has often seen certain parallelisms of this plot with Euripides'

Hippolytus and Racine's *Phèdre*; at times the prince's plight has also been compared to that of Hamlet. Among the first foreigners to use the theme were Brantôme and Saint Réal (1673) ; it was treated dramatically especially in Thomas Otway's *Don Carlos, Prince of Spain* (1676), in Schiller's beautiful drama *Don Carlos* (1787), in Alfieri's tragedy *Felipe,* and also in Verdi's opera.

The Picaresque Novel.

The Spanish picaresque novel is usually said to have begun with *Lazarillo de Tormes* in 1554, an anonymous, fragmentary, yet highly informative little tale—though one might argue that already the Flemish story of *Reynard the Fox* and the German adventures of *Till Eulenspiegel* had provided heroes who made a living by outsmarting their contemporaries, and though, as we have noted, the *Celestina* had earlier reflected the sordid atmosphere typical of all picaresque tales. Such tales are possible and convincing only in a period of national and moral disintegration such as the one provided by the Spanish seventeenth and the French eighteenth centuries, which announced the day when the last shall indeed be the first, and the first, the last. As we have pointed out in connection with *La Celestina,* this type of novel certainly contributed a completely new and revolutionary trend in European literature, a trend which turned its back on the heroic, the religious, and the fairy-like models of the past in order to turn its attention to the proletarian misery and the hard-boiled cynicism of the future. *Lazarillo* was first translated into French in 1561 and into English in 1576.

Most famous among the Spanish picaresque novels was *La vida del Pícaro Guzmán del Alfarache* by Mateo Alemán (1599 ff.), who, as his novel indicates rather convincingly, seems to have been an observing traveller in Italy and who later emigrated to Mexico. This book, so depressing in its fatalism and cynicism and yet again so moral in its didacticism and so colorful in its individual episodes and interpolated Moorish, Neapolitan, and Sevillan tales, was a quick international success, being translated into French by Gabriel Chappuys in 1600, by Chapelain in 1619, and again by Le Sage in 1732. It was translated into German in 1615 and had a profound influence upon Grimmelshausen; and in 1630 it was rendered into English by James Mabbe, the translator of the *Celestina.* Other novels of this

type were *La Pícara Justina* by Francisco López de Ubeda
(1605), the unsavory life of a female picaro with many broad
and realistic folk-scenes; *La vida del escudero Marcos de
Obregón* by Vicente Espinel (1618) which inspired especially
Le Sage; and, finally, *El Buscón (The Scoundrel)*, the story of
Pablo de Segovia as told by Francisco de Quevedo y Villegas
(1626), one of the leading moralists and satirists of his time—
a work noted for its misanthropy, its irony, and its bitter humor.
It often happened that the detailed account of how these gutter-
born urchins worked their way up through a corrupt society
until they themselves achieved some semblance of power or
respectability and a hard-boiled philosophy of life tended to
approach the level of personal memoirs and autobiographies on
the part of the author.

In addition to the rather special cases of *Till Eulenspiegel* and
the unsavory *Grobianus,* Germany's most famous "picaresque"
tale, there was the life of *Simplizissimus* by Hans Jakob Chris-
toffel von Grimmelschausen (1669). In this most important German novel of the entire seventeenth century, however, the author,
through the criminal career of his hero during the Thirty Years'
War, wanted to preach, above all, the baroque message of the
omnipotence of God and the vanity of all human ambitions. England had an early example of a picaresque tale in Nashe's *Jack
Wilton* (1594) and a faint echo, with another religious twist,
in Bunyan's *Pilgrim's Progress*; however, it was especially in
the eighteenth century that this type of novel began to prevail,
with such examples as Defoe's *Moll Flanders* (1721) and Fielding's *History of Jonathan Wild the Great* (1743).   There are
indeed many traits in the famous realistic novels of Defoe,
Fielding, and Smollett—such as stark descriptions of slums and
human vices, contrite sinners, adventurous voyagers, and found-
lings struggling for their rightful place in society—which remind us of the picaresque technique of Spain; and other works
like Gay's *Beggar's Opera* (1728), fundamentally a satire of the
fantasticalities of the Italian opera, contributed to the increasing
preoccupation with the unsavory atmosphere of jail-birds and
prostitutes.

As to France, Scarron with his five *Nouvelles tragicomiques*
and Julien Sorel with his *Françion* proved to be seventeenth century imitators of the picaresque Spanish trend, and in their
minutely detailed and realistic descriptions especially of the low-

er strata of population they were distinct forerunners of Zola. The greatest French masterpiece of that genre was, however, *L'Histoire de Gil Blas de Santillane* (1715-35), which the author, Le Sage, by telling a supposedly Spanish tale, transformed into a devastating criticism of eighteenth century France and into a dangerously debunking book which prepared the ground for the French Revolution. In Spain, Isla hastened to write a work against Le Sage which in its very title explains its patriotic and anti-French purpose: *Adición a las aventuras de Gil Blas robadas a España y adoptadas en Francia por Lesage, restituídas a su patria y a su lengua nativa por un español celoso que no sufre se burlen de su nación* (1787). Among the Englishmen most influenced by Le Sage's *Gil Blas* was Smollett, who in 1749 translated the novel into English and whose own *Roderick Random* imitated *Gil Blas*. In 1751 Edward Moore published a comedy, *Gil Blas*. No less significant were the two provocative dramas which Beaumarchais wrote about a *picaro* called Figaro: *Le barbier de Séville* (1775) and *Le mariage de Figaro* (1781), for they too, written and, in spite of the censorship, performed on the eve of the French Revolution, reflected only too well the ominous fermentation among the masses which finally led to the storming of the Bastille. *Le mariage de Figaro* was adapted by Thomas Holcroft in *The Follies of the Day* (1784). Indeed, picaresque traits, the misery of mistreated children growing up in slums and hardened by the daily struggle for life, or again the hypocrisy of the parvenus and the satire of snobbery, can be found well into the nineteenth century of Dickens' *Oliver Twist*, Thackeray's *Vanity Fair* and Mark Twain's *Huckleberry Finn*.

Cervantes.

In his twelve *Novelas ejemplares* (1613), notably in the *Coloquio de los perros* (*Colloquy of the Dogs*), Miguel de Cervantes Saavedra (1547-1616) used ample traits of picaresque realism and social criticism; but it is, of course, his famous *Don Quijote* (1605-15), one of the finest novels in world literature and a splendid presentation of the idealism and the folly (and, in the person of Sancho Panza, of the native shrewdness and earthiness) of Spain which had the greatest effect upon European literature as a whole. It united in one work all the trends of the Spanish novel at that time: the *Amadis*, the *Celestina*, the picaresque, and the pastoral elements; and in its realistic

implications we might call it not only a healthy reaction against
the excesses of the fantastic tales of chivalry but, in a way, an
incarnation of the exalted Spanish spirit of idealism which under
Philip II set out to fight all possible wind-mills, in spite of the
woeful inadequacies of strength actually backing up such efforts.

The influence of the various works of Cervantes all over
Europe was and remains considerable. His *Exemplary Novels*
served to inspire English translators, dramatists, and novelists
from Mabbe and Fletcher up through Fielding. Especially noteworthy for our purposes is *La española inglese* (*The English
Spanishwoman*) with its imagined descriptions of the English
court and its reflection of Anglo-Spanish relations; while *La
Gitanilla* (*The Gypsy*) is also very significant, not only because
it at long last brought into European literature, in a romantic
and colorful fashion, the important aspects of gypsies and gypsy-
life, but also because continuations of this new racial contribution can be found up into the nineteenth century of Victor
Hugo's Esmeralda (in *Notre Dame de Paris*) and Mérimée's
Carmen.

But it was, of course, *Don Quijote* which evoked the greatest
and most lasting echo: it was shipped by the hundreds into the
Spanish American colonies, and within a few years after its
publication it was translated into most European languages,
e.g. into English by Shelton (1612 ff.), into French from 1614 on,
and into German under the title of *Junker Harnisch aus Flecken-
land* (1621). The name of Shakespeare brings up not only
occasional comparisons between Don Quijote and Hamlet or
Don Quijote and Falstaff, but the far weightier problem of
whether Shakespeare had ever read that novel. More important
than the fact that Fletcher likewise ridiculed knight-errantry
in *The Knight of the Burning Pestle* is the significant imitation
of Cervantes in Samuel Butler's *Hudibras* (1663-68), a bitter
satire of the Restoration period against Hudibras and his companion Rollo and the spirit of Puritanism, hypocrisy, and intolerance represented by them. In the eighteenth century we
find Cervantes influences upon Holberg in Denmark; Le Sage and
Voltaire in France; Smollett, Fielding (*Don Quixote in England*,
1734), Charlotte Lennox (*The Female Quixote*, 1752), Richard
Graves (*The Spiritual Quixote*, 1773), and others in England.
In Portugal it was even transformed into an opera (*Vida do
grande Dom Quixote e do gorde Sancho Pança*, 1733). Es-

pecially significant is Wieland's novel, *Don Silvio von Rosalva* (1764) with its revealing sub-title "The Victory of Reason over Exaltation"—for Wieland wrote this imitation of *Don Quijote* in order to indicate that he was cured of the pietistic leaning acquired during his stay in Bodmer's Zürich and that he had become an urbane and skeptical rationalist instead. With regard to Goethe, there appear occasional comparisons between the national characteristics of Don Quijote and of Faust. Kleist's newly realistic style was greatly indebted to Cervantes. In the field of translations especially those of Tieck (*Don Quijote*, 1799) and Eichendorff deserve to be mentioned, for German Romanticism was passionately interested in Spanish literature. In the course of the nineteenth century one can find many types of "quixotic" characters: in Dickens' *Pickwickiers*, in Daudet's *Tartarin de Tarascon*, indeed even in Flaubert's *Mme. Bovary*, in Anatole France, and in Dostoevski. Nor should Gustave Doré's illustrations of the novel be forgotten. Echoes of Cervantes seem to be particularly frequent also in American literature: Cooper was indebted to him in his *Mercedes of Castile*, Melville in his *Moby Dick*—and of course, Mark Twain, his greatest imitator, whose Tom Sawyer and Huckleberry Finn occasionally greatly resemble Don Quijote and Sancho Panza.

Spanish Mysticism.

Although we have referred to mysticism previously, for instance in connection with Plotinus and again in connection with Meister Eckhard and Thomas à Kempis (*De imitatione Christi*, first printed in 1483) in medieval Germany, mysticism in the Spain of the Counter-Reformation broke forth with such intensity that we may well call it a new great Spanish contribution and a typical trait of baroque literature. Fray Luis de Granada, Santa Teresa de Jesús, Fray Luis de León, and San Juan de la Cruz were among the foremost Spanish mystics who together with militant Jesuits of the type of Ignacio de Loyola (*Ejercicios espirituales*, 1548) and militant kings like Philip II gave to this Spain-inspired period of European culture the religious intensity for which the Baroque is famous. Fray Luis de Granada was especially noted for his *Guia de pecadores* (*Guide of Sinners*, 1556); among his translations was *Contemptus mundi, o Imitación de Cristo*, from Thomas à Kempis. Santa Teresa's *Libro de su vida* (*Book of Her Life*, 1588) has often been compared to the *Confessions* of St. Augustine; rather than an autobiography, it is almost exclusively an examination of personal religious problems and doctrinary matters. For the edification of nuns (she founded no less than seventeen convents) she also wrote *El camino de perfección* (*The Road to Perfection*, 1585). Poems about her like *La amazona cristiana* by Bartolomé Segura (1619) indicate the very high esteem in which she was held at home. Fray Luis de León is best known for his *Los Nombres de Cristo* (*The Names of Christ*, 1583), *La perfecta casada* (*The Perfect Wife*), and, above all, his prose-translation of *El Cantar de los Cantares* (*The Song of Songs*, 1561). But it is mainly as lyrical poets that these mystics, the ardent Santa Teresa, the exquisite Luis de León, and the ceaselessly searching San Juan de la Cruz (*Obras espirituales que encaminan a un alma a la perfecta unión con Dios*—among them *Noche oscura del alma* and *Cántico espiritual*), succeeded best in expressing their fervent longings. Among them and especially among their followers the wish for a *unio mystica* became at times so intense that this union of the human soul with Christ, of the bride with the bridegroom, was often referred to in barely veiled sexual terms. The popularity of the *Song of Songs* likewise made it very tempting to apply the subtle and glittering language of Petrarchism to express the mystical ecstasy.

We have stated elsewhere how a great religious reawakening, at least in part under the influence of these Spaniards, was characteristic of the entire Baroque Period. In France, where many of the lyrical poems of Marguerite de Navarre had prepared the ground and where the works of Santa Teresa, for instance, went through three different translations before 1644, we can refer to the *renaissance catholique* that set in with St. François de Sales (*Traité de l'amour de Dieu*, 1616) and that showed its effects also in the Jansenism of Port Royal and the Quietism of Mme. Guyon. In England, there was the religious poetry of Donne and Herbert, the mysticism of Vaughan and Traherne, and above all the works of Crashaw, which reflected well the intensity of their Spanish models. Religious exaltation was no less fervent in war-ridden Germany: there were the poems of Protestants like Gryphius and Gerhardt, and of Catholics like Friedrich von Spee—and especially there was the mysticism of Angelus Silesius (*Der cherubinische Wandersmann*, 1657, and *Die heilige Seelenlust*) and Jakob Böhme, the famous cobbler of Breslau, the "philosopher" of mysticism (*Aurora, oder die Morgenröte im Aufgang,* 1612). Böhme, in turn, exerted a great influence upon English and American Puritans, from Milton down to our own days. Nor should we forget the beginnings of German Pietism, which extended from the seventeenth century of Spener and Francke into the eighteenth century of Zinzendorf and Goethe's *Wilhelm Meister.*

The Spanish Comedia.

The Spanish *comedia,* like the Elizabethan drama, was especially important as a glorious example of free creative writing (as opposed to the increasing predominance of rules in French Classicism)—but in itself, because of the completeness of the victory of French Classicism, it did not exert a very considerable immediate influence upon the rest of Europe, and came to be appreciated only after the defeat of Classicism by Romanticism. Apart from the question of early Portuguese influences by Juan del Encina, Gil Vicente, and others upon the early development of the Spanish *comedia,* the student in Comparative Literature might wish to investigate the great affinity between Baroque and Romanticism, the similarities of dramatic technique, for instance, between Lope de Vega and Victor Hugo; or he might juxtapose those two great contemporaries, Lope de Vega and Shakespeare, in all their similarities (in spite of the Catholic Spanish background of the one and the Protestant English background of the other) and contrast them with Racine, that finest incarnation of French classical restraint and verisimilitude. The technique of the Spanish *comedia*—its three acts, its lack of unities, its quick piling up of action upon action, its facile dialogue and variegated metre, its predilection for national, historical or religious topics, its kaleidoscopic colorfulness, its combination of comedy and tragedy, of fine lyricism and coarse realism—may well be investigated as against the background of classical theory. The influence of this genre upon pre-classical Frenchmen like Alexandre Hardy and Corneille and upon English Restoration dramas of the type of Dryden's *Spanish Friar* (1681) may also be worth following up. In general it can be said that these foreign imitators dropped the serious aspects of the Spanish *comedias* and dwelled on the laughter and the intrigues alone, such as they existed above all in the cloak and dagger dramas (*comedias de capa y espada*) of Spain.

Among the minor Spanish dramatists we can point to Ruiz de Alarcón, whose *La verdad sospechosa* (*Suspected Truth*, 1619) inspired Pierre Corneille's outstanding comedy, *Le Menteur* and Goldoni's *Il Bugiardo* (*The Liar*). There is a possibility that Alarcón's *El examen de maridos* (*The Test of Husbands*) was based upon the same Italian source as Shakespeare's *Merchant of Venice*. Francisco de Rojas Zorrilla, famous especially for his *Del rey abajo, ninguno* (*Below the King, Nobody*), was imitated quite frequently: thus his *No hay ser padre siendo Rey* (*Being King, One Cannot Be a Father*) inspired Rotrou's *Venceslas*, and his *Casarse por vengarse* (*To Marry for Vengeance*, 1636) influenced Le Sage's tale, *Le mariage de vengeance*. Rojas Zorrilla's *comedia* of manners, *Obligados y ofendidos* (*Indebted and Offended*), was particularly influential in France, for it inspired Scarron's *L'écolier de Salamanque*, Boisrobert's *Le généreux ennemi*, and Thomas Corneille's *Les illustres ennemis*; and it supplied Le Sage with an episode in *Le diable boîteux* (*The Limping Devil*) which, in turn, was reflected in Beaumarchais' *Eugénie*. Finally, *Entre bobos anda el juego, don Lucas del Cigarral* (*The Game among Fools*) supplied Scarron's *Don Japhet d' Arménie*. Of Agustín Moreto y Cavana, only one play is of importance with regard to its international repercussions: his *El desdén con el desdén* (*Disdain against Disdain*) inspired Racine's *La princesse d'Elide* and Gozzi's *La principessa filosofa*. Fernando de Zárate y Castronovo's *La presumida y la hermosa* (*The Conceited and the Pretty Damsel*), a satire against the conceits of the baroque style, influenced Molière's *Femmes savantes*— though Molière's best parody in this field is usually considered to be his *Les précieuses ridicules*.

Lope de Vega.

In contrast, for instance, to Rojas Zorrilla, the influence abroad of the *comedias* of Lope de Vega (1562-1635), the world's most prolific and Spain's greatest dramatist, was not very considerable. The comparatist might investigate the sources of his very many biblical and hagiographic plays; he might pay attention to dramas inspired by the history of Germany (*La Imperial de Otón*—the story of Ottokar of Bohemia which was treated also by Grillparzer), or Russia (*El gran Duque de Moscovia*—the

story of the false Demetrius which Jesuits may have brought
to Spain) ; or he might explore the themes supplied not only by
Boccaccio (*El halcón de Federico*), but also by other Italian
novelists such as Bandello (*El castigo sin venganza, La difunta
pleiteada*) and Giraldi Cinthio (*El piadoso Veneciano*). We
have mentioned elsewhere his version of the Romeo and Juliet
(*Castelvines y Montescos*) and of the Abencerraje themes (*El
remedio en la desdicha*).

With regard to Lope's fame abroad, we must, of course, assume that his *comedias* formed a very substantial part of the
repertoires of any Spanish comedians travelling through Italy,
Austria, the Lowlands, or, up to a certain time, France. Nonetheless, it is disappointing to notice that in the seventeenth
century we can indicate a definite influence in only one case:
his *Lo fingido verdadero* (*The Feigned Truth*) inspired Rotrou's
famous martyr-tragedy, *Saint Genest*. Incidental borrowings
from Lope can be found also in Hardy, Boisrobert, Scudéry,
and Scarron. The best known imitator of Lope was the Dutchman Rodenburg (*The Duchess Celia,* 1617, and other plays),
who is also noted for his dramatic borrowings from Ariosto
(*Rodomont and Isabella,* 1618). Only during the age of German Romanticism did Lope become internationally as famous
as he had long deserved to become—with the Schlegels and Uhland, his re-appreciators, with Grillparzer, his imitator, and with
Zedlitz and Schack, the translators of *La Estrella de Sevilla*
(*The Star of Sevilla*) and of *Fuente Ovejuna* (*The Sheepwell*)
respectively. Plays such as *La Fuente Ovejuna* or *Peribañez,*
which deal with popular uprisings or revenge against tyrannical
aristocrats, are enjoying a striking popularity in modern Russia. Lope's love of the Spanish peasant and the portrayal of
the latter's childlike faith in the integrity of the king and his
instinctive enmity towards local aristocrats, who are mostly represented as despotic and immoral characters, would be quite
a fascinating thematological topic, especially if compared, for
instance, with the treatment of peasantry in the nineteenth century regional novels.

The Cid.

The Cid, together with Don Quijote and Don Juan, belongs
to the three greatest themes Spain gave to world literature.
Don Rodrigo de Bivar, the Spanish national hero of the eleventh

century, the champion of Christendom who distinguished himself in the early phases of the reconquest of Spain from the
Moors and whom the Arabs called Sidi, Lord or Master, formed
the theme of one of the earliest works in Spanish literature,
El cantar del mio Cid (1140), which shows a distinct influence
of the technique of the French *chansons de geste*, especially the
Song of Roland, whom the Cid resembles in several traits. The
many ballads eulogizing and embellishing the Cid's prowess were
finally dramatized in two *comedias* by Guillén de Castro in 1618.
It is one of the school-examples for comparatists to see how
Corneille made use of Guillén de Castro's *Mocedades del Cid* (*The
Youth of Cid*) in his own famous tragi-comedy of the *Cid* (1636),
how he cut down to a minimum the vast historical background of
the original, eliminated various episodes so dear to Spanish
naturalism (the leper, the assassination of the king, etc.), concentrated the action on the Cid alone and on his love for Chimène,
forced the whole drama into the strait-jacket of the three
unities, and emphasized psychological inner struggles about
the conflict of duty and love rather than heroic outer events—for
such a comparison reveals in a nut-shell, as it were, the basic
differences not only between Baroque and Classicism, but also
between the Spanish and the French national mentality and
literary taste. The story also inspired several minor French
authors to inferior imitations, such as Chevreau (*La suite et le
mariage du Cid*) and Desfontaines (*La vraie suite du Cid*,
1637). Another well-known Spanish version of this topic was
the drama *El honrador de su padre* (*He Who Honors his Father*,
1659) by Juan Bautista Diamante. Corneille's *Cid* is an outstanding example of how even French Classicism, for all its
self-sufficiency, was greatly enriched by Spanish literature.
We shall see in our next chapter that this drama was frequently
translated into foreign tongues and that it introduced into England and Germany a striking example of the famous Spanish
sense of honor and duty.

With the coming of Pre-Romanticism, however, men were
anxious to return again to the balladesque colorfulness of the
medieval original and to disregard the somewhat distorted picture Corneille had given to this story by streamlining it and
envisaging the Cid's adventurous life from its amorous angles
alone. Herder's felicitous German translation of the various
ballads about the Cid were strung together into a coherent epic

form and fulfilled this new desire; his *Der Cid nach spanischen Romanzen besungen* appeared posthumously, in 1805, at a time when the love of the German romanticists for Spain was about to reach its peak. French romantic versions include *Le Cid, romances espagnoles imitées en romances françaises* by Creuze de Lesser (1814) and *Le Cid d' Andalousie* by P. A. Lebrun (1825). In Spain, Scott's historical novels inspired fictions like *La conquista de Valencia por el Cid* by K. Vayo (1831). Among later works, Zorrilla's *La leyenda del Cid* (1882) is especially noteworthy.

Don Juan.

The character of the great and promiscuous lover Don Juan, such as created by Tirso de Molina in his *El burlador de Sevilla y convidado de piedra* (*The Mocker of Sevilla and the Guest of Stone*, 1630)—a little Renaissance titan all by himself and ever so much more plausible if seen against the background of the hot Latin temperament and the Mediterranean sky, set off, as it were, against the ascetic dogma of the Catholic Church—was sure to evoke a great European echo, though in Northern countries the passionate sensualism of the Spaniard was apt to degenerate into viciousness and shameless depravity, as, for instance, in Thomas Shadwell's *The Libertine* (1675). Minor Spanish versions of this theme were those by Alonso de Córdoba Maldonado (*La venganza en el sepulcro*) and Antonio de Zamora (*El convidado de piedra*). With his emphasis on atheism Molière, in his *Don Juan ou le festin de pierre* (reworked by Thomas Corneille in 1677) gave his hero a twist for the worse and made him, for his brazen immorality, fully deservant of his punishment in hell. A Dutch version by Adrian Pels appeared in 1699 (*The Supper of Don Pedro's Guest*). Traces of Don Juan can be found in the villainous seducers of the eighteenth century, for instance in Lovelace of Richardson's *Clarissa Harlowe* (1748), in certain aspects of garb and technique in Goethe's Mephistopheles, and also in Tieck's *William Lovell* (1795). In the field of the opera reference should be made to Mozart's famous *Don Giovanni*, with the libretto written by Lorenzo da Ponte. With regard to Italy, one might also note the striking parallelisms between Don Juan and Casanova.

The Romantic Age used Don Juan either to applaud the great romantic and somewhat cynical hero, as Byron did (1818 ff.), or

to bemoan him, as the Hungaro-German Lenau did, as a restless
wanderer, a melancholy seeker of happiness (1836). One of the
most fascinating combinations was envisaged by the mediocre
German dramatist Christian Grabbe when he, in his *Don Juan
und Faust* (1829), put together as companions the seeker of the
flesh and the seeker of the spirit. Other German versions include
those by E. T. A. Hoffmann (in his *Fantasiestücke* of 1814) and
by Karl von Holtei (1834). A very popular modern rendering,
and one of the greatest successes of the romantic drama in
Spain as well as abroad, was the *Don Juan Tenorio* by José
Zorrilla (1844). French Romanticism and post-Romanticism
was to a rather amazing extent imbued with a love of things
Spanish; it is, therefore, no wonder that we find echoes of Don
Juan from Mérimée (*Les âmes du Purgatoire*, 1834) and Dumas
(*Don Juan de Maraña*—translated back into Spanish by García
Gutierrez), Baudelaire, Blaze de Bury, and Flaubert, up to Ros-
tand and Lenormand (*L'homme et ses fantômes*, 1924). In
Russia the theme was treated both by Pushkin and by Alexis
Tolstoy (1862). Among our contemporaries, the dream-sequence
on *Don Juan in Hell* contained in Shaw's *Man and Superman*
(1901) enjoys a particularly great popularity.

A second play by Tirso de Molina which is of interest especially to those scholars well versed in the religious problem of
predestination versus free will and which deserved a greater
echo abroad than, for instance, the appreciative words bestowed
upon it by George Sand, is *El condenado por desconfiado* (*Condemned because of Lack of Faith*, 1635), one of the most fearless
plays written during this notoriously Church-dominated era.
The same problem forms the basis also of Vondel's poem *Decre-
tum horribile, or The Horror of Desolation* (1630).

Calderón.

Considering the caliber of Pedro Calderón de la Barca (1600-
81), the scope of his influence abroad is as disappointing as it
was in the case of Lope de Vega. His rabid Spanish sense of
honor (for instance in matrimonial tragedies inspired by jealousy, such as *El médico de su honra* and *El pintor de su des-
honra*) and his often stilted and baroque stylistic aberrations
have never made him quite as popular as the quick and warm-
hearted, the colorful and flashy Lope de Vega had been. It was
above all the works of Calderón which best expressed the Catho-

lic ardor which was so typical of baroque literature and so characteristic a contribution of the Spanish *Siglo de Oro: La devoción de la Cruz* (*The Devotion of the Cross,* 1633), *El mágico prodigioso* (*The Mighty Magician,* 1637), *Los dos amantes del Cielo* (*The Two Lovers of Heaven*), *El príncipe constante* (*The Constant Prince*), *La cisma de Inglaterra* (*The Schism in England*—in which Ann Boleyn resembles the Jewess of Toledo), and so forth. Of especially great significance is his *La vida es sueño* (*Life is a Dream,* 1635), a deeply philosophical *comedia* which preached well the baroque gospel of the vanity of life and ambition and the illusiveness of power. A similar story (though with a shallower message) can be found in Weise's *Vom niederländischen Bauer* (*Of the Dutch Peasant*). *La vida es sueño* was translated into German by Schreyvogel in 1816; it also had a considerable influence upon the thought (but not the plot) of Grillparzer's *Der Traum ein Leben* (*The Dream a Life,* 1834)—and in the twentieth century Hugo von Hofmannsthal in his *Der Turm* (*The Tower*) gave it a strange political twist by alluding to rulers isolated from their subjects not through imprisonment (as in Calderón) but through exile (as the Habsburgs were exiled after 1918). We have already spoken of the great predilection of Austrians for Spanish literature: it can also be seen in Hofmannsthal's *Grosses Weltheater,* which was taken from Calderón's *El gran teatro del mundo* (*The Great Theatre of the World.*)

In seventeenth century England George Digby, Earl of Bristol, translated three of Calderón's plays, among them *Elvira, or The Worst is not always True* (*No siempre lo peor es cierto*), and Corneille used his *En esta vida todo es verdad y todo es mentira* (*In this Life all is Truth and all is Lie*) for his own *Héraclius*. But as in everything else it was European Romanticism which brought about a great re-appreciation of Spanish literature in general and of Calderón in particular. In Germany, Goethe recognized the parallelisms between his *Faust* and *El mágico prodigioso*; he also frequently staged *El príncipe constante* in his Weimar theatre. A. W. Schlegel was one of the most enthusiastic admirers of Calderón and translated his best dramas into German (1803 ff.). Other German translators were Eichendorff, Rückert, and Gries (1815)—and even Wagner felt the influence of his religious ardor. In England Shelley, in 1821, translated from *The Mighty Magician* and hailed Calderón

as one of the greatest. In *The Spanish Drama* of 1846 George
Henry Lewes gave a running comparison of Lope and Calderón
and made them better known in England than they had ever
been before. Among Calderón's later translators we should
name Edward Fitzgerald, author of *Six Dramas from Calderón*
(1853), to which he later added two more, *La vida es sueño* and
El mágico prodigioso (1865). Elsewhere in Europe the growing
fame of Calderón extended from the France of Mérimée and the
Poland of Slowacki (the imitator of *The Constant Prince*, 1844)
to the symbolists at the turn of the century.

Minor Spanish Contributions

In Spanish thematology we must mention a historical Spanish
tale which was treated by Lope de Vega and many other Spaniards, but which, in the hands of the Austrian Grillparzer, resulted in a masterpiece which is quite superior to its Spanish
models: namely *Die Jüdin von Toledo* (THE JEWESS OF TO-
LEDO). Lope dealt with the consuming passion of Alfonso
VIII (ca. 1160) for the seductive Jewess in his *Las paces de los
Reyes y judía de Toledo* (*The Peace of Kings and the Jewess of
Toledo*); other treatments of that medieval story can be found
in the poem *Raquel* by Luis de Ulloa y Pereira (1650) and in the
dramas *Las desgraciada Raquel* by Mira de Amescua and *La
judia de Toledo* by Diamante (1670). In the eighteenth century,
García de la Huerta forced this story of a king's love and the
necessity for the courtiers to have the Jewess murdered for reasons of state into the framework of a neo-classical tragedy (*La
Raquel*, 1778). Grillparzer's beautiful tragedy is quite noteworthy because of its fine analysis of the struggle in the king's
breast between duty and love, and of his resolve to conquer himself and to return to his English queen.

Other Spanish contributions during the *Siglo de Oro*, though
perhaps of minor character, deserve nevertheless to be mentioned here. There is especially *El libro llamado Relox de Principes*
(*The Book called the Clock of Princes*, 1529), which is also
known under the title of *El libro áureo del emperador Marco Au-
relio* (*The Golden Book of the Emperor Marcus Aurelius*) by
Fray Antonio de GUEVARA. With its philosophical and
political wisdom and moderation and its plea against corruption
and for the dignity of man, it is not only one of the most popular
state-novels of the Renaissance and the Baroque, mirroring the

picture of a truly ideal monarch, but also one of the first works
in Spanish literature to indicate the coming vogue of baroque
style. Among the Frenchmen influenced by this work were Herberay des Essarts (who translated it in 1555), Montaigne, Brantôme, and La Fontaine; in Italy an early translation of Guevara
(1544) went through more than twenty editions. Lord Berners,
the translator of Froissart (1523), rendered *The Clock of Princes* into English in 1532, and Lord North in 1587. It is often argued that these versions, with their influence on Lyly and others,
brought to England the first seeds of baroque phraseology. Only
Fénelon's *Télémaque* at the end of the seventeenth century
managed to supersede the very real popularity of this work.

Although he had no immediate influence abroad, GÓNGORA
deserves to be included here as the chief propagator of that
euphuistic, excessively elegant, obscure and conceited style which
is generally known as Gongorism or *culteranism*. The similarity
of the baroque phenomena occurring almost simultaneously in
various countries—the Marinism of Italy, the Euphuism or
metaphysical poetry of England, the *Schwulstliteratur* of Germany, the *préciosité* of France—offers seeming support to the
adherents of the *Zeitgeist* theory of literary genesis and suggests that the Baroque Age had a homogeneity that would be
overlooked by the student who merely concentrated on the differences between, say, the Spanish and English drama on the one
hand and the Italian and French on the other. The problem of a
possible Spanish influence upon England, to which we alluded in
connection with Guevara, becomes especially interesting when
it is recalled that the father of English metaphysical poetry,
John Donne, participated in the 1596 campaign against Spain
and spent some time with Essex in the Azores. At any rate, the
examination of the different national brands of baroque literature provides an intriguing demonstration of the essential oneness of European letters as well as a fascinating study of poetic
cross-fertilization. It might finally be observed that Góngora
enjoyed something of a renascence during the late nineteenth
century, at the very time when symbolist poetry was developing
in France—a poetry that resembled the lyric poetry of the Baroque Age in more ways than one.

Among the satirical writers of seventeenth century Spain,
mention should be made of Luis VÉLEZ DE GUEVARA, who,
as we have seen, was not only a fairly significant dramatist, but

also the author of *El diablo cojuelo* (*The Limping Devil*, 1641).
This was an acid and moralizing work mirroring the gradual de-
moralization of Spain; by use of a technical trick the hero, Don
Cleofás, was allowed to observe intimate scenes in the houses of
Madrid, the roofs of which had been removed by his servant, the
Limping Devil. In the eighteenth century, when France began
to reach a similar state of disintegration, this naturalistic novel
with ever so many picaresque traits was imitated and enlarged
by Le Sage in his *Le diable boîteux* (1707). Of a similarly satirical tenor were the works of Francisco de QUEVEDO Y VIL-
LEGAS, whose *Sueños* (*Visions*, 1627) of human viciousness,
as we have seen, had been inspired by Dante's *Inferno*—and
these *Visions*, in turn, served as a basis for *Die Gesichte Philan-
ders von Sittewald* (*The Visions of Philander von Sittewald*,
1642) by Hans Michael Moscherosch, in which the German lashed out against the human follies and degradations during the
Thirty Years' War. In France, Quevedo's *Sueños* were even
more popular than his *El Buscón;* they were translated from
1633 on, and in England from 1666 on.

The Jesuit Baltasar GRACIÁN, the last Spaniard to be mentioned here, in his anti-Machiavellian *El Héroe* (1637) followed
in the footsteps of Antonio de Guevara in sketching the picture
of an ideal prince who distinguished himself especially through
his constant emphasis on reason and sheer will-power—a portrait of man which was translated into French in 1645 and into
English in 1652 and which did not fail to have a profound effect
upon European poets and philosophers from Corneille and Descartes up to Schopenhauer and Nietzsche. Gracián's philosophy
of life was mirrored in *El Oráculo manual y arte de prudencia*
(*The Clear Oracle or the Art of Prudence*, 1647), a collection of
three hundred maxims about life and worldly wisdom which was
translated into French under the title of *L'homme de cour* (*The
Courtier*, 1684) and which influenced the *Maximes* of La Rochefoucauld and *Les Caractères* of La Bruyère. It was appreciated
by Voltaire and Goethe and again by Schopenhauer, who translated it. The baroque stiltedness and obscurity of form came to
the fore especially in *El Criticón* (1651), Gracián's most significant work, a philosophical novel analyzing men and customs
through the eyes of Critilo, the man of reason, and his companion Andrenio, the natural man of impulse and instinct—a contrast
of two types which became significant in the following century of
Voltaire and Rousseau.

C. OTHER LITERATURES

Classical Influences

The Baroque was affected much less by the influence of re-vived or re-evaluated cultures and literatures than was the Ren-aissance. Since the Baroque Period was one of consolidation, even regression, before the forward momentum built up during the Renaissance could rush on, classical and oriental influences are much less apparent. This does not mean that such influences were not at work. Indeed, it suggests that they were more subtle and, therefore, in some ways more interesting to the reader. The stylistic influence of Antiquity served as a much-needed complement to the basic experience of the Baroque, which was religion.

The function which classical literature had in the shaping of the literature of the early seventeenth century perfectly illus-trates the typically Baroque. Just as the word Baroque in its derivation implies the disruption of an inherently perfect form, so the typically baroque literature makes use of the theoretically perfect classical form and distorts it out of classical shape by trying to force into it more than the form can hold. Many a ba-roque drama gives the impression that the author has used a per-fect classical mould which cracked when he poured into it the molten metal of his conception. In the plays of a Corneille or a Lohenstein, for example, one feels that Aristotle, or one of his modern interpreters such as Scaliger or Castelvetro, was called upon to approve every scene. But one also feels that the action and characters of the play are constantly straining against the Aristotelian chains. And so one pole of the painful paradox that shapes most of baroque literature can be seen to consist of the restraining influence of classical form. The individual author has a conception that is too bold, too awe-inspiring, too explosive in its demoniacal emotion to be expressed, but he knows that to put his conception across coherently he must discipline it into some kind of form. The form which was readiest at hand was the form derived from classical Antiquity—or, in the case of lyrical poetry, the Petrarchan sonnet, which, for instance in Gry-phius' *Sonn- und Feiertagssonette,* was likewise broken and vio-lated in every way.

The study of the influence of classical literature upon that of the Baroque will obviously, then, be a different kind of study from that of the influence of classical literature upon the Renaissance. During the Renaissance, classical literature—its spirit, its meaning, and its form—was discovered. During the Baroque, classical literature was used perforce as a guide, the one norm to hold onto in the storm of life. The investigator of classical influences during this period will, then, probably want to determine the way in which classical form tended to discipline baroque expression, and the way the conflict between classical restraints and baroque abandon was resolved—if, indeed, it ever was resolved by a baroque author. And further he will want to examine the profoundly interesting problem created by the attempts on the part of these authors to synthesize the classical and the Judeo-Christian traditions.

The DRAMA of the Baroque Period reflects classical influences in two ways. In the typical drama of England and Spain we find that the classical form has all but disappeared. To be sure, the form which we do find we recognize to have derived from classical models during the Renaissance, but it has been thoroughly adapted to native taste. Ben Jonson (*Sejanus, Catilina*), Virués (*Semiramis*) and Cervantes (*La Numancia,* 1586) were really the only ones in England and Spain to endeavor to conform to certain neo-classical rules—and the interesting verse essay on the *Arte nuevo de hacer comedias* (*The New Manner of Writing Comedias,* 1609) by Lope de Vega indicates just how little he thought of the new-fangled neo-classical rules and how determined he was to keep on writing in the irregular Spanish tradition, as his public wanted him to. The same independent attitude can be seen in authors before Lope, in Juan de la Cueva's *Ejemplar poético* (1606), which imitated Horace's *Letter to the Pisos* rather cavalierly. After Lope, a very free interpretation of old rules and standards can be noticed also in *La nueva idea de la tragedia antigua, o ilustración al libro de la Poética de Aristóteles* by González de Salas (1633). About the only neo-classical model the Spanish and English playwrights were willing to follow were the plays of Seneca. The licence to depict violence, horrors, and bloodshed, which the Renaissance had taken over from Seneca, became quite unbridled in the Baroque, and we feel that it was typical of the drama of the period to include on its stage murders, torture scenes, rapes, lunatics, and ghosts. Spanish naturalism and Senecan horror formed a

murderous combination especially in the plays of Cristobal de
Virués (*Casandra, Atila, Dido,* 1579 ff.)—and the same excesses among the baroque English dramatists finally led to the
closing of the theatres in 1642. Among the English translations
of Seneca, those issued by Thomas Newton (*Seneca His Tenne
Tragedies,* 1581) are particularly noteworthy.

In France we see that the authors had been much better
schooled in neo-classical principles, for they strove heroically
to include within Aristotle's "single revolution of the sun",
enough fantastic experience to require a lifetime of living for
the ordinary man. Typical of the baroque use of classical models
was the attitude expressed during the famous *Querelle du Cid.*
Although Corneille included in his play two duels, a mighty
battle, a break and partial reconciliation between lovers, and
a number of other minor events, he was criticized for letting the
action of *Le Cid* run for so long as thirty-six hours. From
Opitz on Germany also tried to follow the neo-classical pattern,
and in Holland Vondel translated Horace's *Poetic Art* in 1654.
Whether or not such baroque dramatists as Mairet, Scudéry,
Gryphius, Lohenstein, Vondel, Vos or even the Jacobean playwrights were accurately imitating classical drama is irrelevant.
The fact is that they thought they were using classical form,
as defined by the neo-classical critics and as they found it in the
plays of Seneca and Euripides, and it is of just as much interest
to us to study the influence of one literature upon another when
the influence derives from misconceptions as when the earlier
literature is thoroughly and properly understood.

Although Seneca and Euripides were still the only two classical dramatists generally emulated, knowledge of Sophocles
(Garnier's, Rotrou's and Opitz' *Antigone,* Tasso's *Re Torrismondo,* and especially the many Dutch translations by Vondel)
and of Aeschylus was gradually increasing. We find in Milton's
Samson Agonistes (1671) a moving and revealing effort to write
an Aeschylean tragedy and an interesting attempt to blend
classical and Hebraic traditions. In the field of the comedy we
can point not so much to Terence (though La Fontaine adapted
his *Eunuque* in 1654) but to Plautus, whose influence was especially marked (Lope, Hooft, Larivey). We find the *Miles
gloriosus* treated in the *Spaansche Brabander Jerolimo* (1617)
by the Hollander Brederoo (who mixed the play with elements
from *Lazarillo de Tormes*), in *Vincentius Ladislaus* by Heinrich

Julius, Duke of Brunswick, and, above all, in *Horribilicribrifax*
(1663), Gryphius' incisive comedy about the bragging and
polygot soldier of the Thirty Years' War. And in Italian comedies the ridicule was naturally often aimed at the much-hated
Spanish soldier who was a braggart and a dandy at the same
time—as, *e.g.* in the anonymous Sienese play *Gl' Ingannati* of
1531, which was emulated by Charles Estienne in France (*Les
Abusés*, 1540) and expurgated in the Spanish version of Lope
de Rueda (*Los Engañados*, 1567).

The EPIC shows even more effectively than the drama the
earnest wish of baroque authors to reconcile in some kind of
coherent synthesis the seeming conflicts between pagan, classical form, expressive of satisfaction and pleasure in this life,
and Judaic, Christian soul-searching, with its implication that
nothing in life is finally meaningful. Virgil still dominated the
form of the epic, but the classical machinery of gods and god-
desses was transplanted from Homer and Virgil to a Christian
world. We can go back to Camoens with his *Os Lusiadas* to see
the attempt to include pagan as well as Christian gods in the
action of a single story—but after that beautiful example of
Renaissance harmony and tolerance, the tension between the
pagan tradition and the newly awakening Christian intransigence became too great (Spenser's *Faerie Queene*, Tasso's *Gerusalemme liberata*) and the typical baroque epic, in undisguised
hostility, is therefore either all sensual (Marino's *Adone*, 1623)
or all Christian (Du Bartas' *La Semaine*, Fletcher's *Christ's
Victorie and Triumph*, Thomas Heywood's *Hierarchy of Blessed
Angels*, Milton's *Paradise Lost*). As the seventeenth century
progressed in the worldly and skeptical attitudes of some of its
poets, ridicule and scorn were heaped either upon the world of
gods, the mythology of Antiquity directly (Bracciolini's *Scherno
degli Dei*, 1626) or upon the poets who had glorified them (Scarron's *Le Virgile travesti*, 1648; Richer's *Ovide bouffon*, 1649;
Picou's *L' Odyssée en vers burlesques*, 1650; Brébeuf's *Lucain
travesti*, 1656; Colletet's *Juvénal travesti*, 1657). In Italy we
can point to *L'Iliade graciosa* by Loredano (1654), and in England to Charles Cotton, who burlesqued Virgil and Lucian.
Among the relatively few straight translations of classical epics
of this period we might mention Vondel's rendering of the
Aeneid into Dutch verse (1646); but burlesqued versions re-

mained popular to the very end of the neo-classical period (N. Lemercier's *La Mérovéide,* 1818).

The MOCK-HEROIC EPICS also achieved great popularity from this time on. Though the Greek *Batrachomyomachia*—a battle between frogs and mice which parodied beautifully the majestic technique of Homer's battle between the Greeks and the Trojans—had been emulated already by John Heywood's *The Spider and the Fly* (1556) in England and Georg Rollenhagen's *Der Froschmeuseler* (1595) in Germany (both authors using their poems to describe the struggle between Protestants and Catholics), it was now especially Alessandro Tassoni who, in 1622, with his *La secchia rapita* (*The Stolen Waterbucket*), gave real popularity to this genre by building up the trifling feud between Modena and Bologna over a stolen waterbucket into the stately and dignified dimensions of Homeric warfare. Other examples of this mock-heroic technique can be found in *La Gatomaquia* (*The War of Cats,* 1634) by Lope de Vega, the famous *Le Lutrin* (*The Church-Lectern,* 1673) by Boileau, *The Dispensary* by Sir Samuel Garth (1699), and on through *The Rape of the Lock* by Alexander Pope (1712), and *Der Renommist, ein komisches Heldengedicht* (*The Braggart,* 1744) by Friedrich Wilhelm Zachariä, to the *Hasty Pudding* by Joel Barlow (1796), *Knickerbocker's History of New York* by Washington Irving (1809) and Thoreau's battle of the ants in *Walden* (1854) in America. When contrasting, for instance, Scarron with Boileau, or again Butler's *Hudibras* with Pope's *Rape of the Lock,* the student will wish to keep in mind the essential difference between a burlesque and a mock-heroic poem: the former treats an exalted topic in a lowly and vulgar fashion, while the latter builds up a lowly and trivial incident into epic and dignified proportions.

LYRIC POETRY during the Baroque Period reflected notably for the first time the influence of Greek poets. It would seem only natural that the inspired, somewhat exalted quality of Pindar's poetry should find its admirers during this age. It is true that Ronsard had set out to be a French Pindar, but few other poets knew the Pindaric ode until the very late Renaissance or the Baroque Period. It flourished most in England where we find it used by Ben Jonson and Milton even before Abraham Cowley proclaimed himself the inventor of the English Pindaric ode. From these early beginnings on, it becomes an interesting study in itself to examine the adaptations which modern vernacular authors have made in the highly intricate pattern of the strict classical ode. Also the other classical lyric poets, especially Horace, Catullus, and Anacreon continued to influence the modern lyric during this period. Catullus and Anacreon had particular appeal to those poets who fell within the tradition of libertinage, such as Desportes in France, the graceful Cavalier poets of England, or the members of the Second Silesian School in Germany. Horace continued, of course, to exercise a strong influence, especially upon such men as Malherbe and Jonson who were striving to cut back the natural excesses of the evolving baroque lyric.

VERSE SATIRE, known but slightly during the Renaissance, did not really come into its own as a modern form until the Baroque Period, especially after the treatise on the satire which Isaac Casaubon published with his edition of Persius in 1605. The satire had, of course, been used as a mode of metrical expression during the Renaissance, especially by the Italians—Alamanni, Ariosto, and Berni—but it was not really until after 1605 that the formal satire as used by Juvenal and especially Lucian was undertaken. The form was developed in England by Donne (as early as 1595), Hall, Rochester, Jonson and Marston, and in France by Régnier and Boileau, who were especially close to Juvenal and Horace. Such poets as these were naturalizing the form to their native tongues with the result that during the last half of the century the more rationalistic, analytical, and critical sensibilities of the Classical Period had a finely developed form in which they could express themselves perfectly. The Spaniards, as we have seen, excelled especially in the field of prose satire, in which they were heavily indebted to Martial (Gracián), Petronius (Cervantes) and Juvenal (Quevedo).

Baroque PROSE was probably even more fundamentally influenced by classical prose than was the prose of the Renaissance. Growing out of the close study of Cicero during the Renaissance, the vernacular languages saw a highly rhetorical and often elegantly artificial prose style emerging. As vernacular prose became ever more widely and respectably used, its cultivation as an art became ever more exquisite. Cicero remained the first and foremost model for the high style in prose, a style that was intentionally artificial, consciously ornate, contrived, symmetrical, replete with rhetorical figures, and excessively periodic. Probably the best example of a fully developed vernacular style that outdoes Cicero was the euphuistic style of John Lyly and his English followers. The much richer, looser, and more subtle style of the great baroque writers such as Burton, Browne, Gracián, Pascal, Cotton Mather, and Jonathan Edwards reflects a certain complement to the Ciceronian rhetoric in favor of the complex, skillfully devious, often twisted and intentionally unbalanced prose found in Tacitus. The syntax as well as the vocabulary of the German language from the seventeenth century down to our own days likewise indicates the powerful impact of Latin prose upon authors and schoolmasters and, through them, upon the people of an entire nation. Fully as interesting to investigate as this influence upon baroque prose is the dependence of prose writers, religious and secular, upon classical allusions—allusions drawn from classical mythology, history, literature, philosophy, and especially natural history—with Lucretius and Ovid serving as a kind of thesaurus of allusions.

Among the PHILOSOPHERS, the influence of Socrates (significant ever since the days of Thomas Aquinas, Petrarca and Erasmus) on Guez de Balzac (*Le Socrate chrétien,* 1652) and Hofmannswaldau (*Der sterbende Sokrates,* 1681) and the influence of Aristotle on Bacon and Milton should be especially noted; while the importance of Plato and Plotinus, marked in the case of Bruno and Galileo in Italy, was again foremost with Milton and the so-called Cambridge Platonists (Cudworth, Smith, Henry More). Bacon's *New Atlantis,* of course, was derived from a political rather than from a philosophical concept of Plato's. The influence of Plutarch the moralist as well as the historian is particularly evident in Antonio de Guevara's *Clock of Princes,* and Seneca's *Letters* (translated by Quevedo in 1638) and moral essays left a deep imprint on the mentality of an age glorying in Christian stoicism. Seneca himself became a dramatic figure in *La mort de Sénèque* by Tristan l'Hermite (1643) and also in Lohenstein's *Epicharis.* Of significance during this slow growth of libertinism was also the popularization of Epicure by the Italo-French philosopher and critic Gassendi (*De vita et moribus Epicuri libri VII,* 1647) and the English verse translation of Lucretius' *De rerum natura* by Thomas Creech (1682)—and the opposition to such pagan libertinism in works like *The Christian Hero* by Sir Richard Steele (1701).

The NOVEL of the Baroque Period continued in part to develop on the basis of the various Greek models. The pastoral and heroic novels of the early seventeenth century were still developed in essentially the same way as were the *Daphnis and Chloe, Aethiopica,* and so on. The most famous of the heroic novels of the period, Mlle. de Scudéry's *Le Grand Cyrus,* consists of the interminable sequence of fantastic adventures which we find in the Greek novel, and in addition derives its subject matter from Xenophon's *Kyropaedia.* The relationship between Greece and the satiric novel of the Baroque Period is not so close, since the latter depended heavily upon the Spanish picaresque model. But many of its characteristics (the frequent licentiousness, the plot structure which is so loose as to contain no plot, and the inclusion of many often irrelevant short stories within the main story) were certainly similar enough to the characteristics of the Milesian Tales to deserve investigation.

In the field of thematology, the Baroque is fully as rewarding to study for its classical themes as is the Renaissance. While the Renaissance imagination had been drawn to the great themes that made up the bulk of classical mythology, the baroque author as often as not turned to historical figures of Antiquity. A complete list of themes drawn from Antiquity by authors of the Baroque Period would be much too long to be given in anything approaching entirety, but a few examples of plays and novels might suggest the range of interest: the cycle of Troy (Garnier, Shakespeare, Hardy, Opitz, Vondel—and in Portugal Pereira de Castro, who in 1636 wrote an *Ulyssea* on the alleged founding of Lisbon by Ulysses); Sophonisbe (Montchrestien, Marston, Mairet [reworked by Voltaire], Corneille, Zesen, Lohenstein, Lee); Coriolanus (Shakespeare, Hardy); Cleopatra and Mark Antony (La Calprenède, Mairet, Lohenstein, Rojas Zorrilla); Nero (Cyrano de Bergerac's *La mort d'Agrippine,* Lohenstein's *Epicharis* and *Agrippina,* Lee's *Nero*); Androcles and the Lion (Lope's *El esclavo de Roma*); and so on. We might take a single baroque author to illustrate the dominance of classical and historical themes among these: Corneille wrote four plays based on Greek legends, two plays concerning the conflict between paganism and Christianity, and four plays based upon medieval history and legend—but ten plays based on Roman history. The use of classical themes became more and more popular during the Baroque Period until the convention developed, especially in France, which insisted that the drama and epic should use nothing but themes derived from Antiquity. It was only after the Quarrel between the Ancients and the Moderns had been decided in favor of the moderns that "modern" themes (and with them Christian themes, with *le merveilleux chrétien*) were admitted officially into literature.

Oriental, Biblical, and other Religious Influences.

We have described baroque literature as a last attempt of the medieval spirit to assert itself before the heirs to the Renaissance, the rationalists of the late seventeenth and the enlighteners of the eighteenth century, replaced it by a much more secular conception of life. It is, therefore, natural that the Baroque, being a last attempt to restore the impressive and oppressive greatness that had been the Middle Ages, should abound with religious and medieval influences, from St. Augustine (Vondel, Jansen, Pascal) up to Thomas Aquinas (Crashaw) and Thomas à Kempis (Luis de Granada, Corneille). The Spaniards, being the spiritual leaders of this ardent reassertion of religious exaltation, excelled in religious and hagiographic *comedias,* as a few examples will show: Lope wrote *comedias* dealing with *La creación del mundo, El Nacimiento de Cristo, Barlán y Josafá* (a famous christianized version of the legend of Buddha), *Lo fingido verdadero* (the story of Saint Genest) ; Tirso de Molina excelled in his *El condenado por desconfiado* (*Condemned Because of Lack of Faith*) as did Mira de Amescua in his Faustian *El esclavo del demonio* (*The Slave of the Demon*). Of the latter we should mention also *comedias* like *El rico avariento* (the story of Lazarus), *La adúltera virtuosa, Santa María Egipciaca* (which was also treated in *La gitana de Menfis,* by Pérez de Montalbán), and *La mesonera del cielo* (a topic which already Roswitha had treated in her *Abrahamus*). To the many religious *comedias* of Calderón which we have mentioned elsewhere, we might add his *Judas Macabeo, Las cabellos de Absalón, El purgatorio de San Patricio,* and *La cena del rey Baltasar* (which was likewise treated by Moreto, author, also, of *La vida de San Alejo* and of *El más ilustre francés, San Bernardo*). The same religious intensity we have seen in the Spanish mystics (remember their predilection for the *Song of Songs*) and at times even in the Spanish prose-writers, though the latter, like Lohenstein in Germany, were often content to amalgamate their Christian

convictions with a good deal of Senecan stoicism. In the case
of Quevedo we notice the interesting phenomenon of how a work
of the French *renaissance catholique* (which was so richly indebted to the Spanish Catholic reassertion) was translated back
into Spanish, for in 1634 he published a Spanish version of the
Introduction à la vie dévote by St. François de Sales (1609).
Also Crashaw in England was greatly indebted to St. François de
Sales and to the general atmosphere of Gongorism and Marinism.
Some of the most sensual of the baroque poets should be noted
for their religious verse, too—for instance *Les CL psaumes de
David* by Philippe Desportes (1594) and the *Noble Numbers
of Pious Pieces* by Robert Herrick (1647).

We have noted, too, how especially the writers of neo-Latin
and Jesuit tragedies were fond of biblical themes; among the
topics mentioned which continued into the seventeenth century
were the following: the stories of Adam (Andreini's *Adamo*,
Vondel's *Lucifer* and *Adam in Exile*, Milton's *Paradise Lost*);
Noah (Vondel); Joseph (the dramas by Grotius and Vondel, the
novels by Zesen and Grimmelshausen, Calderón's play *Suenos
hay que verdades son*); Jephtha (Vondel's tragedy, Diamante's
drama *Cumplir a Dios la palabra, o la hija de Jefté*); the story
of Saul and his descendants (*Saul le Furieux* and *La Famine ou
les Gabaonites* by Jean de la Taille, *Saul* by du Ryer, *Die Gibeoniter* by Gryphius); David (Peele's *David and Fair Bethsabe*,
Montchrestien's *David ou l'Adultère*, Cowley's *Davideis*, Vondel's
David in Exile); and great biblical heroines like Judith (Opitz),
Esther (du Ryer), Susanna (Heinrich Julius, Jourdan, Vélez de
Guevara), and Ruth (Tirso's *La mejor espigadera*). The story
of the brutality of King Herod or of his relationship with his wife
Mariamne was treated quite frequently—in tragedies by Tirso
de Molina, Tristan l'Hermite, La Calprenède, and Heinsius (the
latter evoking a *Discours sur l'Herodes infanticida de Heinsius*
by Guez de Balzac in 1636); in a novel by Camus; and in two
epics by Gryphius and Marino, respectively (the latter, *La strage
degli innocenti*, translated into German by Brockes in 1715).
Los Pastores de Belén (*The Shepherds of Bethlehem*, 1612) by
Lope de Vega indicates the ease with which the pastoral genre
could be blended with biblical tales about the life of the Holy
Family.

The influence of the Bible in general was most marked in men
like du Bartas and d'Aubigné in France, Grotius and Vondel in

Holland, Böhme and Weise in Germany, Milton in England, and Calderón in Spain. Turning from biblical to general Jewish influences, we notice that they were greatest in Milton, also in this field the most learned of all English poets, and in the great Dutch-Jewish philosopher Spinoza. The power of priesthood, so noticeable in the field of literature, extended so as to include also the field of history, from Bossuet's *Discours sur l'histoire universelle* (*Discourse on Universal History*, 1678) to Cotton Mather's *Ecclesiastical History of New England* (1702).

With regard to contemporary religious problems, the comparatist might wish to investigate the Catholic attitude towards Luther (for instance in Quevedo's *Sueños*) and Protestantism in general (in the *Disputationes adversus haereticos* of 1581 by the Cardinal Bellarmin); the conversion of Protestants like Ben Jonson and Vondel to the cause of Catholicism; the impact of the Inquisition from Rojas, Machiavelli, Marot, *Lazarillo de Tormes* and Luis de León to Tasso, Bruno, Galileo, Campanella and Jansen; or the different aspects of mysticism, old and new, in Langland, Ficino, Thomas à Kempis, Juan de la Cruz, Böhme, Traherne and Fénelon. Then there is the problem of the Jesuit dramatists (*Tragoediae sacrae* by Caussin in 1620, *Ludi theatrales sacri* by Bidermann in 1660), poets (Friedrich von Spee's *Trutznachtigall*, 1649), and moralists (Gracián) and of other authors' indebtedness to them (Gryphius in his *Gibeoniter*) as well as the perennial attacks upon them (from Fischart's *Jesuiterhütlein* in 1580 to Pascal's *Lettres provinciales* in 1657, and from Oldham's four *Satires upon the Jesuits* in 1681 to Isla's *Fray Gerundio* in 1758). The problem of religious allegory—so important since Dante's *Divina Commedia*—leads us to Bunyan's *Pilgrim's Progress* (and to its being parodied by stern antimoderns like Hawthorne). Other investigations might delve into the opposition against the Church and its political ambitions (Sarpi's *Istoria del Concilio di Trento* and his account of the quarrel of Pope Paul V. with Venice); the question of Shakespeare's attitude towards Catholicism; the skillful blending of Petrarchism with the newly quickened religious ardor in Luis de León, Tansillo, Desportes, or Herrick; the first beginnings of the principle of religious tolerance from Nicolaus von Cues, Bodin, Roger Williams, and Zesen's *Die Adriatische Rosamund* (1645) on; the effects of such minor movements as the Rosicrucians (Ben Jonson, Descartes) and Quietism (Mme. Guyon,

Cowper) upon literature; the inception of important religious trends like Jansenism (Pascal) or Puritanism (Ascham, Milton, Increase Mather); the significance of religious oratory from Abraham a Santa Clara in Germany to Jonathan Edwards in America. Also the stories of great conversions of former sinners—noticeable up into the eighteenth century of Defoe's *Captain Singleton*—are basically baroque in attitude. It is entirely befitting that this period should also have witnessed the beginning of the famous Passion Play at Oberammergau (1634).

As to Oriental influences, the Turks in particular among the Mahometans left the greatest impact upon the literature of the Baroque. It had begun with the fall of Constantinople (1453), the loss of Hungary, the sieges of Rhodes (1522), Vienna (1529) and Malta (1565), the crimes of the descendants of Solyman the Magnificent, the battle of Lepanto (1571). Literature, from the late fifteenth century German shrovetide plays up through Luther to Calvin and Montaigne, reflected this Turkish danger, though it was only in the seventeenth century that it became fashionable to mirror the "unspeakable" Turk in novel and drama. It was especially the story of the conversion to Christianity of the famous Iskanderbeg and of his struggle for Albanian independence in the middle of the fifteenth century which interested Spaniards most widely (*Escanderbech*, by Pérez de Montalbán; *El gran Jorge Castrioto y Príncipe Escandenberg*, by Belmonte Bermúdez; *El príncipe esclavo y hazañas de Escandemberg* by Vélez de Guevara)—though it inspired other treatments, too, for instance an Italian epic, *La Scanderbeide*, by Margarita Sarrocchi (1623); a French novel, *Scanderbeg*, by Chevreau (1644); and a Latin epic, *Scanderbegus*, by Bussières (1656). The epic *La Austríada* by Juan Rufo Gutiérrez (1584) dealt largely with the victory of Don Juan d'Austria over the Turks at Lepanto, as did a fine poem by Herrera and a *comedia* by Vélez de Guevara, *El águila del agua y batalla naval de Lepanto* (*The Water Eagle and the Naval Battle of Lepanto*). Cervantes lost the use of an arm in that battle and, when returning to Spain, was captured by Saracen pirates and, as indicated in his *Los tratos de Argel*, was for years kept a prisoner in Algiers (as was the French playwright Regnard exactly a century later). Among the works dealing with the enemy's religion was the drama *El falso profeta Mahoma* by Rojas Zorrilla, in a way a forerunner of Voltaire's famous tragedy. In England, reference must be made to an early scholarly study which opened up a fascinatingly exotic atmosphere, *A General History of the Ottoman Turks* by Richard Knolles (1603), and to Sir William Davenant's *Siege of Rhodes,* a work which practically founded the English opera (1656). In French literature it was Mairet in his tragedy *Le grand et dernier Solyman* (1637) and particularly Mlle. de Scudéry who in her novel *Ibrahim ou l'illustre Bassa* (1641) brought in the exotic and exciting atmosphere of Turkish conquests and perfidiousness. The German Lohenstein, ever anxious to find blood-curdling events and crimes of lust and sex for his Senecan tragedies, dramatized the novel by Madeleine de Scudéry (which Zesen had translated into German in 1645) in his *Ibrahim Pascha* and then added a second tragedy about an entirely different Ibrahim, a pathologically fiendish sultan of Turkey, *Ibrahim Sultan.* Also Settle, in England, dramatized Mlle. de Scudéry's novel, *Ibrahim, the Illustrious Bassa* (1676). Even the great Racine, in his *Bajazet* (1672), was not above treating tales of passions, harems, and crimes—though the restrained manner in which he psychoanalyzed exactly the same milieu as Lohenstein indicates beautifully the fundamental differences, the veritable abyss, between the baroque and the classical technique of treating an offensive subject. In Hungary Zrinyi, in 1651, wrote a *Zrinyiade (Obsidio Szigetiana)* about the futile and heroic attempts by one of his ancestors to stem the tide of the Turkish sweep up the Danubian valley—and the same topic was later treated by Theodor Körner in his well-known tragedy *Zriny* (1814), which was meant to inspire the Germans during the Napoleonic Wars. As to the other Mahometans in Europe, a tragic chapter came to an end in Spain with the expulsion, from 1609 to 1611, of the last descendants of the Moors.

Among the Persian themes reference should be made to Cyrus, who became the hero of the best-known of the baroque heroic novels (*Artamène ou le Grand Cyrus,* by Madeleine de Scudéry, 1648 ff.) and also of a *comedia* by Lope de Vega (*Contra el valor no hay desdicha*) and a tragedy by Quinault (*La mort de Cyrus,* 1656). Vélez de Guevara, like Marlowe in England before and Nicholas Rowe after him, also wrote a *comedia* about *El gran Tamorlán de Persia*—and, shifting the oriental background slightly, he, like Virués and Corneille, wrote an *Atilo azote de Dios (Attila, the Scourge of God).* Persia was likewise de-

picted in Gryphius' martyr-tragedy, *Katharina von Georgien,*
which showed a staunch heroine and ardent Christian who fell
into the hands of the shah of Persia, to whose desires she would
not submit. Gryphius also made use of a Byzantinian topic
when he, in his *Leo Armenius,* the first German neo-classical
tragedy, made use of the theme of political conspiracy and assassination in the East Roman Empire in the early ninth century. Among the few Germans of the seventeenth century to
acquire a first-hand knowledge of the Near East was the poet
Paul Fleming who made a trip from Moscow to the Caspian Sea
and Persia—and among the fertile brains to imagine the most
unbelievable oriental tales of lust, adventure, and wholesale
butcheries was Heinrich Anselm von Ziegler, author of the
monstrous novel about Burma, *Asiatische Banise oder blutiges
doch mutiges Pegu (The Asiatic Princess Banise or Bloody yet
Courageous Pegu,* 1688).

Italy.

The Italian Baroque brings up the name of but one poet of
great international significance, Torquato TASSO (1544-95),
who was to exert an influence abroad during the otherwise well-
nigh complete literary sterility of seventeenth century Italy.
In the pathetic figure of Tasso can well be studied the gradual
progress from the day of the Italian Renaissance to the night of
the Jesuitic Baroque—and, with regard to style, from the free
creativeness of the age of Ariosto to the increasing tyranny of
the neo-classical rules such as they were formulated by Scaliger
and others. It is, therefore, deeply symbolical that Tasso's mind
suffered from this double onslaught and that this fearful man
spent the last years of his life in insanity. One of the most
melodious and lyrical poets of Italian literature, of a mellowness
of versification and an elegiac tenderness of mood unequalled by
others—as indicated both by his *Gerusalemme liberata (Jerusalem Delivered,* 1575) and his pastoral play *Aminta* (1573) —
Tasso, in restraining the sensuous colorfulness in his descriptions of the Orient and the fairy-like environment of miracles,
enchantresses, and bold deeds of Christian valor, wanted to conform with the censorship both of the Church and of the new
literary taste and hence eschewed Ariosto's ribaldry, accepted
the restrictions of epic rules and regulations, and brought order
and a genuine Christian fervor into his glorification of the first

Crusade, whereas Ariosto, more likely than not, would have emphasized nothing but the amorous intercourse between Christians and Mahometans. Fearful lest he had not restrained himself sufficiently, Tasso later rewrote the entire epic under the title of *Gerusalemme conquistata* (1593), a work which, however, can not for a moment compare with the beauty of *Jerusalem Delivered*.

Richard Carew translated the first five cantos of *Jerusalem Delivered* into English in 1594; a complete English version by Edward Fairfax, dedicated to Queen Elizabeth, appeared in 1600. Diederich von dem Werder in 1626 rendered the epic into German, addressing it to German nobility, whereas his later translation of Ariosto (1632) was written for the people who were interested in reading about *Orlando* in the form of a chapbook. Lope de Vega imitated Tasso in Spain (*La Jerusalén conquistada*, 1609) ; du Bartas in France and, above all, Spenser and Milton in England borrowed from him for their own epic poetry. Shortly before Boileau's condemnation of Christian marvels in his *Art poétique* of 1674 there flourished in France an entire school of French epic writers who, in Tasso's fashion, wanted to combine and glorify both Christian ardor and noble deeds of valor: *Alaric ou Rome vaincue* (*Alaric or Defeated Rome*, 1654) by Scudéry, *La Pucelle ou la France délivrée* (*The Maid, or Delivered France*, 1656) by Jean Chapelain, *Clovis ou la France chrétienne* (*Clovis, or Christian France*, 1657) by Desmarets de Saint-Sorlin, *Saint Louis ou le Héros chrétien* (*Saint Louis, or The Christian Hero*, 1658) by Pierre Le Moyne and *Charlemagne* (1664) by Le Laboureur. Striking episodes from *Jerusalem Delivered*, like the sufferings of Olinde and Sophronie, and particularly colorful figures like Tancred, Clorinde, or Armide (Quinault-Lulli in 1685 even made an opera, the most important opera of the century, about the latter), were widely imitated all over Europe. Voltaire made use of Tasso as well as of Ariosto in his *Henriade* and in his flippant *Pucelle d'Orléans*; Wieland in his youth preferred Tasso, with his Christian ardor, to Ariosto, though he later changed his mind. With the dawn of Pre-Romanticism, the poets of the Baroque as well as of the Renaissance became objects of respectful attention. In England Richard Hoole translated both Tasso's *Jerusalem Delivered* (1763) and Ariosto's *Orlando Furioso* (1773 ff.) ; in Germany Wilhelm Heinse, one of the most ardent Italy-enthus-

iasts and a pioneer in German Italomania, translated Tasso into
prose, and in 1800 Johann Gries was even able to reproduce
exactly the beautiful *ottava rima* in his German translation of
the epic. A landmark in Tasso's fame abroad is, of course,
Goethe's beautiful psychological tragedy (1790) into which
Goethe, falsely assuming a love-affair between Tasso and the
Princess Leonore of Ferrara, poured all his own problems about
his life at court of Weimar and his unhappy love for Frau von
Stein. Among the romanticists attention should especially be
called to Byron's *Lament of Tasso* (1817).

Equally important as Tasso is the beginning of the Italian
OPERA and its gradual spreading abroad—a trend which will
take the literary musicologist interested in such matters from
Peri (*Dafne,* 1597—with Rinuccini the author of the libretto),
Monteverdi (*Orfeo,* 1607), and Scarlatti in Italy to Opitz
(*Dafne,* 1627) and Schütz in Germany, Lulli in France, Purcell
in England. A study of these beginnings in their many ramifications might lead, too, to an investigation of English masques
(Ben Jonson) and French ballets (Benserade) and to a description of the growing and emphatic opposition of the classicists to
this most baroque of all semi-literary genres.

Of very great significance for Europe was also the development of the Italian improvised comedy, the COMMEDIA DEL-
L'ARTE (1550 ff.)—for though Italy somehow did not seem to
have the strength nor the discipline to continue the genres of the
classical tragedy and comedy, which required a strict submission to rules and verisimilitude, she certainly had a flair for
developing the swiftly moving dialogues and brilliant improvisations of the *commedia dell' arte,* in which the actors, without
having in mind anything but a vague outline of the plot, improvised their dramatic events skillfully as they went along.
The *commedia dell' arte* encouraged the creation of stock-
characters who would always incarnate the same traits on the
stage: the bragging soldier, the ingenue, the doctor, the funny
person (called *harlekin* or *pulcinella*), the amorous widower,
the scheming mother—and by their very reliance on quick-
witted repartee and their habit of spicing their performances
with hastily picked-up local gossip, these actors really dealt a
death-blow to the amateur-stages of colleges and burghers which
had been so prevalent during the sixteenth century, because for
this kind of brilliant improvisation real professionals were need-

ed, not well-meaning but slow-witted amateurs. Italian troupes of wayfaring actors spread all over Central Europe, from Vienna to Paris and down to Madrid, and by their very great influence on the technique, the quick build-up, and the fluent dialogue of Molière they contributed much to the development of the French classical comedy. The history of Italian playmaking especially in France and of the Italian theatres in Paris (1576 ff.) is a long, important and honorable one. Indicative of the repertory of these Italian troupes is Gherardi's collection *Le théâtre italien* (1694 ff.). Though the Italian comedians were expelled in 1697, they were permitted to return within a few years.

Among the intermediaries we might mention Giordano Bruno and the Cavaliere Marino. Bruno was a visitor to Paris as well as to England; his relationship with the great Elizabethans deserves ever new scrutiny, especially the problem of his possible influence on Shakespeare's *Hamlet*, his friendship with Sidney (to whom he dedicated his *Candelaio* of 1582), and his subsequent influence upon the Holland of Spinoza, the England of Milton and Coleridge, the Germany of Goethe, Schiller, and Kolbenheyer. Marino, a visitor to France from 1615 to 1623, was the author, above all, of the glitteringly voluptuous epic *Adone*, which he dedicated to Louis XIII, and the great hero of the poets and ladies of the Hotel de Rambouillet. We have already discussed the peculiarities of the baroque style; any intensive study of the relationship between Gongorism, Marinism, Metaphysical Poetry, and *préciosité* could do no better than use Marino as the focus of the investigation. His popularity in Paris, where he was a protégé of Marie de' Medici, would certainly suggest some connection between his style and French *préciosité*, and also the relationship between Marino and poets of England (Crashaw), Germany (Hofmannswaldau), and Spain (Góngora and Calderón) is certainly worthy of study. Another intermediary of significance was Pierre Larivey, a born Italian and naturalized Frenchman who, in his comedies (*Le Laquais, La Veuve, Les Jaloux, Les Ecoliers*, 1579 ff.) passed on to the French the great skill and fluent technique of the Italian Renaissance comedy. Turning from Italians to other intermediaries, we must mention the most outstanding foreigner to travel in Italy: John Milton. While in Italy (1638-39) Milton may have visited Galileo, who was incarcerated by the Inquisition. Among the friends who furthered his knowledge of Italy should be named the Diodatis, a Calvinist family of Italian extraction whom he met both in Geneva and in London. Also Crashaw, destitute after his conversion to Catholicism, went to Italy, where he died within a few months (1649).

Foremost among the historical events in Italy mirrored in literature was the abortive attempt of the Spaniards to get hold of Venice in 1618—a conspiracy inspiring various popular *Venice Preserved* versions from Saint Réal (*Histoire de la conjuration des Espagnols contre la République de Venise,* 1674) and Otway (1682) up to Hofmannsthal. Otway's drama was imitated by La Fosse in France in 1698—an event quite noteworthy because it was the first time a Frenchman had presented a play in the manner of the English. Then there was the insurrection of the Neapolitans against the Spanish viceroys, such as depicted in a Dutch tragedy, *Mas Anjello* by Asselijn (1668), a German drama, *Masaniello,* by Christian Weise (1683), and, much later, a prose account by the Duke of Rivas (*Sublevación de Nápoles capitaneada por Masanielo,* 1848). Further investigations in this none too cheerful problem of Hispano-Italian relations during the two (in the case of Southern Italy even three or more) centuries of Spanish domination might yield still more material; it was the kind of dismal background which Alessandro Manzoni described so powerfully in his famous novel *I promessi sposi* (*The Betrothed*). Of Italian origin was also *Cardenio und Celinde,* a tragedy by Gryphius (1648) which is sometimes called the first bourgeois drama in German literature.

England.

Besides Spain, also England and Holland experienced a Golden Age in literature around 1600—but the subsequent hegemony of French Classicism retarded the appreciation and spreading of the knowledge of English literature till after 1700, and linguistic difficulties tended to isolate Dutch literature. The beauties of English literature during the late Elizabethan period and during the first half of the seventeenth century are too well known and too sparkling to require any recapitulation here. The English drama of the period has come to be regarded as among the greatest artistic achievements of modern Europe. The lyric poetry, especially of such poets as Donne, George Herbert, Marvell, and others, failed even in England until the twentieth century to be included among the finest lyric expression of modern times. Since the greatness of English literature of this period was relatively slow in establishing itself—even in its homeland—it does not seem strange that the influence it exerted in other countries was not felt until much later. It was not until the reaction against French-dominated Neo-Classicism had set in during the eighteenth century and the pre-romantic sensibility and taste had begun to develop that England herself began to value her own literary heritage at its true worth, and this native re-evaluation was paradoxically assisted by the re-evaluation being made in other countries, notably in Germany. Because this re-discovery of the English literature of the late sixteenth and early seventeenth centuries contributed vitally to the development of Romanticism, we will defer a discussion of the fame of English authors until that time.

At this point only a few observations will be made about the problems that might face the comparatist in the Baroque Period in England. The first of these is the suitability of the term Baroque to English literature. This term is almost never used by scholars in English literature to describe the age that produced the great plays of Shakespeare; the lesser plays of Middleton, Heywood, Beaumont and Fletcher, Massinger, Webster, Shirley, and Ford; the rich, subtle, complex, and infinitely intricate poetry of Donne, Herbert, Traherne, Vaughan, Carew, Crashaw, Suckling, Marvel; and the greatest *corpus* of Christian religious poetry which any Protestant country has ever produced—Milton's two epics and his *Samson Agonistes*. Historians of English literature seem to prefer to let the name of the ruler of England fall willy-nilly over the literature, so that the periods of this literature are designated by the irrelevant (to literature) coronations and deaths of kings and queens. Thus the period with which we are dealing is variously referred to as Late Elizabethan, Jacobean, Carolingian, Cromwellian, and Restoration. Or the whole body of literature from John Skelton to *Paradise Lost* is subsumed under the title of the Renaissance. The student will want to look at English literature of this period in its relationship to European literature and then ask himself whether there is not such a difference between the poetry of Surrey and of Donne, of Spenser and of Milton; the prose of Ascham and of Browne, of More and of Burton, of Sidney and of Bunyan; the drama of Lyly and of Webster, of Peele and of

Massinger—whether there is not such a difference between the style, intent, and substance of the writing in England in 1570 and in 1640 as to make the distinction between Renaissance and Baroque a useful, indeed an imperative one to be applied in England. For in some ways the literature of England from about 1600 to 1675 is more illustrative of the meaning of the term Baroque than is the literature of any other country. The inner psychological conflicts and paradoxes embodied in the character of Hamlet; the subtle, often obscure, convoluted sentences of Burton; the jagged, complex, allusive, and paradoxical style of Donne; the profound and boldly expressed religious convictions of Milton—surely all of these have really little in common with the grace, the delicacy, the wonderful good humor of Boccaccio, Chaucer, Ariosto, Ronsard and those other men who typify the Renaissance.

If, then, as all of the evidence would suggest, the term Baroque is eminently appropriate to England, the comparatist will be interested in defining the limits of the Baroque Period in England in relation to the Baroque in other countries. He might well take as his clue the division which many Shakespearian scholars make between the serene, lighter Renaissance comedies and the primarily historical tragedies on the one hand and the problem-comedies and "dark" tragedies on the other. This would suggest that Shakespeare in himself marks a change from the Renaissance to Baroque, and that the change can be dated around 1600. Certainly the conflicts in and out of literature between the Cavaliers and the Puritans, between the exuberance for life of the Renaissance and the neo-asceticism of the Counter-Reformation are characteristically baroque; and when these conflicts were resolved politically with the Restoration of Charles II in 1660, we might say that the Baroque Age was coming to its close and the Age of Neo-Classicism was dawning. This leaves the gigantic figure of Milton, all of whose major works appeared after 1660, extending beyond the Baroque Era—but Milton's own life seems so intimately a part of the Commonwealth movement and all that it stood for, that we might well say that his *Paradise Lost* in thought, though not in its classical form, indicates the culmination of the English Baroque.

Foremost among the immediate contributions which England made to European literature during this period were the so-called ENGLISH COMEDIANS, who from the last decades of the sixteenth century on began to travel all over northwestern Europe and whose performances contributed greatly to the spreading of the knowledge of Elizabethan and Jacobean dramas abroad. These dramas, of unequalled vitality, great in their clashes of conflicting passions, a real mirror of life and of the height and the depth of the titanically aspiring English nation, in their colorfulness comparable only—if comparable at all—to the equally irregularly and vigorously pulsating Spanish *comedia*, were at first particularly popular at the courts of the German aristocrats, whither English Comedians had first been invited by the Duke Heinrich Julius of Brunswick. From the middle of the seventeenth century on, when French Comedians, in the wake of the French victory in the Thirty Years' War, began to supersede the wayfaring English troups at the aristocratic courts, these English Comedians sank in their social prestige and clientele and were increasingly compelled to perform their plays in towns, villages, and hamlets, before an ignorant populace that knew even less English than the aristocrats. This accelerated the rapid deterioration of these English dramas in which gross gestures and wild gesticulations had to make up for the subtleties of useless words; and the nefarious habit of granting ever more importance to the jester, the pickelhering (the harlekin of the Italian *commedia dell' arte,* called Hans Wurst in German) who, more likely than not, was the only native German among these troupes and who gradually usurped the leading role for himself, contributed even more to the obscene degradation of these plays. Tragedies like Marlowe's *Faustus* and Shakespeare's *Titus Andronicus* (the crudest and most Senecan of Shakespeare's early plays) were particularly popular in Germany, and translations of *Hamlet* as *Der bestrafte Brudermord* (*The Punished Fratricide*) indicate the prosaically didactic trend of these plays.

Among the intermediaries of this period we must mention— apart from the sojourn in England of Italians like Bruno and Germans like Weckherlin—the residence in France of religious refugees like John Barclay and Crashaw. Barclay was born in France, spent but a few years in England, and went to Italy in the year of the publication of his *Argenis* (1616), where he died five years later. An expatriate for political rather than for religious reasons was Thomas Hobbes, who spent eleven years in France (1641-52), where he became a friend of Descartes.

In the field of thematology, the England of this period has given Europe fewer great topics than the England of the Renaissance: Gryphius condemned the Puritan presumptuousness of rebelling against a God-willed king in his tragedy *Carolus Stuardus* (1649); and Victor Hugo, previous to his tragedy on *Mary Tudor*, turned his attention to *Cromwell* (1827), as did Villemain before him (*Histoire de Cromwell*, 1819). Another topic, though of Italian origin, should be mentioned here, for as an English comedy it is popular to this very day: Ben Jonson's *Volpone* (1605), mirroring the hard-boiled facts of living and cheating in Renaissance Italy, was recently reworked both by Stefan Zweig in Austria and by Jules Romains in France. We have seen a certain Austrian predilection for English (or Spanish) plays also in other connections: Richard Beer-Hofmann in his *Der Graf von Charolais* (1904) adapted Massinger and Field's *The Fatal Dowry* (1619), and in 1905 Hofmannsthal reworked Otway's *Venice Preserved*.

Holland.

The Golden Age of Dutch culture—all the more admirable because it occurred in the midst of a brutal and interminable war of liberation against the Spaniards—produced great poets (Vondel), artists (Rubens, Rembrandt), scholars (Grotius), and, a little later, philosophers (Spinoza) that left their deep imprint on Western civilization. In the field of literature and philosophy, though, we must say that linguistic difficulties tended to isolate the Dutch to such an extent that their works (except, perhaps, in Germany) hardly became known unless, like Spinoza, the only truly international figure, they wrote in Latin rather than in Dutch. In literary criticism we can point to the neo-classicist Daniel Heinsius, a follower of the Italian and French critics, who in turn influenced Germans like Opitz. Cultural relations between the Protestant nations of Holland and Germany were particularly lively; at a time when Germany was devastated by the Thirty Years' War Holland seemed a center of culture which many German poets were anxious to visit (Gryphius, Zesen, and others). The biblical dramas (*Joseph*), patriotic dramas (*Gysbrecht van Aemstel*, 1637), and more or less neo-classical dramas (*Electra*) by Joost van den VONDEL (1587-1679) are particularly interesting, for, like Corneille, Vondel stands on the borderline between Baroque and Classicism.

His influence abroad was frequently important: Gryphius imitated his *Leuwendaalers* in *Die geliebte Dornrose* (1660), his *De Gebroeders* in *Die Gibeoniter*; and Vondel's powerful tragedy on the presumptuousness of *Lucifer* (1654) was one of the sources for Milton's *Paradise Lost*.

With SPINOZA (1632-77) we come to the question, too, of Jewish influences, and to the tragic problem of refugees serving as intermediaries, for like León Hebreo in Italy Spinoza was a descendant of expelled Spanish-Portuguese Jews who had found shelter in Amsterdam. The influence of Spinoza's pantheism was immense, especially in the case of Shaftesbury in England and Lessing and particularly Goethe in Germany; indeed, much that was finest in Goethe's religious warmth and in the whole golden age of German Idealism around 1800 would have been unthinkable without Spinoza's all-pervading presence. Later, he became a popular figure for the Young Germans who strove for religious and racial tolerance, as proven by Auerbach's biography of 1837 and by Gutzkow's *Uriel Acosta* of 1847 (the latter, though dealing only indirectly with Spinoza's world, being one of the few fine tragedies of that period).

In spite of the Anglo-Dutch war under Cromwell, political and cultural relations between Holland and England became ever more active in the course of the seventeenth century, as indicated by the intermarriages between the Stuarts and Oranges and the later succession, in 1688, of a Dutchman to the throne of England. Nor should we forget the fact that besides English Comedians, Dutch Comedians also wandered all over Western Europe during the seventeenth century, from France to Scandinavia, but again particularly in Germany, popularizing the tragedies of Vondel and a new Dutch version of *Titus Andronicus* by Jan Vos, called *Aran en Titus* (1641)—a tragedy which the comparatist may well wish to investigate with regard to its relationship to, and common source with, Shakespeare's play. Franco-Dutch relations, after early beginnings in the days of Grotius (who lived in Paris from 1635 till 1645) and of Descartes (who lived in Amsterdam and died in Sweden) became likewise intense from the middle of the century on—though the Dutch served as receivers rather than as emitters of literary values. Later residents in Holland, apart from religious refugees like the Pilgrim Fathers at the very beginning of the seventeenth century and the Huguenots at the very end of that century, included Shaftesbury, Voltaire and Chesterfield—not to mention monarchs like Peter the Great of Russia.

In the field of thematology, finally, Egmont became an internationally attractive figure, as indicated especially by Goethe's tragedy (1787) and by Beethoven's music. Also the tragic life and death of Barneveld, treated by Vondel and again by Verwey in 1895, found an occasional echo abroad, for instance in the drama by Fletcher and Massinger (1619) in England.

France.

One of the very first names to be mentioned in any discussion of French baroque literature is the name of DU BARTAS, author of *La première semaine ou La création du monde* (*The First Week or the Creation of the World*, 1578), together with d'Aubigné a powerful figure among Huguenot writers, a militantly religious poet and thunderer. Du Bartas' work went through more than thirty editions in less than six years; he was translated into Dutch in 1609 and into Spanish in 1612, and through the English version by Joshua Sylvester (1606) he became an inspiring force for English Puritanism. His German translator was Tobias Hübner (1619), who like his friend von dem Werder, the translator of Ariosto and Tasso, was a member of the *Fruchtbringende Gesellschaft* and, together with Opitz, was the first to introduce the Alexandrine meter into German literature. Du Bartas' impact upon the Puritans is evidenced especially by Milton, who used du Bartas, Andreini's *Adamo*, and Vondel's *Lucifer*—not to mention Dante and many others—as a source for his *Paradise Lost*, and also by Mrs. Anne Bradstreet in Massachusetts (*The Tenth Muse lately sprung up in America*, 1650). Several of Vondel's early works (*Easter*, 1612; *The Ancestors*, 1616; *The Splendor of Solomon*, 1620) are entirely derived from du Bartas.

France's leading contribution to European literature in the first decades of the seventeenth century was what we might call the GALLANT-HEROIC GENRE, which in novel as well as in drama satisfied best the baroque love of bombast and of exotic and erotic details, and which lasted well into the Age of Rationalism. Outstanding among its authors in the field of the novel was Honoré d'Urfé with his epoch-making *Astrée* (1607 ff.—and translated into German in 1619 and into English in 1620) which still indicates the pastoral sources of this genre, enriched, as it were, with elements borrowed from the *Amadis* and built up into grandiose types of amorous and martial adventures and gallant discussions. There were also La Calprenède with his *Cléopâtre*; Georges and Madeleine de Scudéry with their *Ibrahim, Le grand Cyrus, Clélie*, and others. While still baroque in the kaleidoscopic excesses of episodes, these novels foreshadowed the slow growth of Classicism, too, for they laid ever more stress on fine psychological analyses and minute descriptions of emotions and passions—a method of literary expression dear to the later Racine and Mme. de la Fayette.

While the heroic novel became most popular in France, its spread into other countries is deserving of study. In Germany we find a bombastic medley of gallant pompousness, statesmanship, artificialities of style, and exotic atrocities in such novels as Lohenstein's *Arminius* (1689), with its setting in the Teutoburg Forest; Zesen's biblical tale of *Assenat* (1670) and her marriage to Joseph in Egypt; the novels of Anton Ulrich, Duke of Brunswick—*Octavia* (1685), telling of ancient Rome, and *Aramena* (1669), of ancient Syria; and finally Ziegler's *Asiatische Banise* (1688) with its accounts of lust and crime in Burma. Germany went well beyond France in this kind of novel to create a type of story that is almost pathological in its feverishly fantastic excesses of plot and style. The heroic novel in England, equally dependent upon France (Mlle. de Scudéry and La Calprenède were translated from 1652 on), took a somewhat gentler turn, perhaps because the prominent novelists were mostly women. Mrs. Katherine Philips, the "matchless Orinda", led the way for English women, not to emulate the French novelists, but to live like the heroines of the French heroic novel. It was a follower of Mrs. Philips, Roger Boyle, Earl of Orrery, who wrote the most famous English heroic novel, the *Parthenissa* (1669).

In the drama, elements of the gallant-heroic can be found in Alexandre Hardy and especially in the plays of Georges de Scudéry and Pierre du Ryer (whose *Argenis*, for instance, was based on the immensely popular Latin work by John Barclay, a novel which was translated by Opitz in 1626 and which also supplied the plot for a play by Calderón, *Argenis y Poliarco*). But it is especially in the plays of Corneille that we see the gallant-heroic most effectively typified. Corneille is often regarded as the first of the classical dramatists, and we have already pointed out that the Classical Period in France could with reason be dated from the première of *Le Cid*. But Corneille is not truly classical; he never completely mastered the strictures of classical form as did Racine. These strictures mastered him. In his characters, in his plots, in the violent antagonisms, tensions, and conflicts which form his plays, Corneille is typically baroque. Indeed, his super-human characters have been given a rather baroque epithet: *monstres de volonté*. While Corneille may, therefore, be regarded as helping to make the transition between the baroque and the classical style and attitude, his influences in other countries was essentially baroque. We have already discussed Corneille's debt to classical and Spanish drama. His relationship with England and Germany, however, was that of a contributor rather than a receiver. He, along with the Spanish drama, contributed tremendously to the development of the "heroic play" of Restoration England. Dryden's *Conquest of Granada* (1672) perhaps best illustrates all of the characteristics of the heroic play as well as some additional ones that make this drama even more baroque than those of Corneille. This and other heroic plays by Dryden (which Buckingham satirized in his *Rehearsal*), along with plays by Otway and Nathaniel Lee, provide a host of examples of the influence of the French heroic novel and drama, combined with the influences of Spain. In Germany the heroic drama became even more violent and bombastic at the hands of Lohenstein (*Ibrahim Pascha, Cleopatra, Agrippina*) and of Hallmann (*Maria Stuart*).

In any discussion of intermediaries, the promulgation of the Edict of Nantes (1598) and, almost one hundred years later, its unfortunate revocation (1685) should play an immense role, for the flood of Huguenot refugees, their colonies in Holland, Switzerland, Prussia, England, and America, and the indefatigableness of their writers and printing presses abroad contributed to a most lively intellectual intercourse indeed, with Huguenots being instrumental in spreading abroad the cultural and literary values of France and, later, in rechanneling into France ever so many foreign ideas that would not easily have found their way to the French intelligentsia without the help of these Huguenots. A particularly significant work produced by a French Huguenot in Holland was Bayle's *Dictionnaire historique and critique* (1697), which went through many editions and foreign translations.

With regard to French thematology reference can be made to

several historical events and figures that received repeated treatment in the literature of other countries. Jeanne d'Arc at last began to emerge from the Middle Ages and was treated for the first time by Fronton du Duc (*Histoire tragique de la Pucelle de Domrémy*, 1580) and later by Shakespeare (*Henry VI*), Benserade (*La Pucelle d'Orléans*, 1642), Chapelain (*La Pucelle, ou la France délivrée*), and Antonio de Zamora (*La Poncella de Orleans*)—though the two most famous and antipodal treatments of this inspiring figure were of course the flippant epic, *La Pucelle d'Orléans*, by Voltaire and the beautiful tragedy, *Die Jungfrau von Orleans*, by Schiller. Other treatments of her life and death include the tragedy *Joan of Arc* by Southey (1796), the prose-account by Mark Twain (1896), *Saint Joan* by G. B. Shaw (1923) and modern French versions like *Le Mystère de la Charité de Jeanne d'Arc* by Péguy and *Jeanne d'Arc au bûcher* by Claudel. The great figure of Henry IV, indubitably one of the finest kings France ever had, inspired writers from Mamignati in his epic *Enrico, ovvero la Francia conquistata* (1623), and Voltaire in his well-known *Henriade*, up to Heinrich Mann, author of *Die Jugend des Königs Henri Quatre* and *Die Vollendung des Königs Henri Quatre* (*The Youth and the Maturity of King Henry IV*, 1940). The tale of the conspiracy and the execution of the Duke of Biron in 1602 was represented by Chapman (*Conspiracy and Tragedy of Byron*, 1608), Pérez de Montalbán (*El Mariscal de Viron*), and also by Christian Weise in Germany. Other works dealing with seventeenth century French history were Bulwer-Lytton's drama, *Richelieu* (1838) and Dumas' famous novel *Les trois Mousquetaires* (1844).

Germany.

In the midst of all this, Germany—with the exception of her mystics (Böhme) and her other religious poets (Gerhardt) and sectarian leaders (Zinzendorf and others), who exerted a very considerable influence abroad—was really only a recipient of trends and values from abroad. Martin Opitz, the promoter of the French Alexandrine meter, the translator of Sophocles, Seneca, Barclay, Sidney and the first Italian opera in Germany, illustrates best this German indebtedness to foreign values— just as Fischart, the translator of the *Amadis* and of Rabelais, before him, and the Nürnberg poets of the type of Harsdörffer and Claj, who translated Marino, Góngora and Montemayor, after him, were indicative of the same literary impotence. Indeed, even the *Fruchtbringende Gesellschaft,* the patriotic literary association which was intended to put an end to this aping of foreign literatures and vocabularies, was an imitation of the *Accademia della Crusca* in Florence. One important figure in seventeenth century German thematology was Wallenstein, though he did not achieve great fame in literature before Schiller's trilogy of 1799 and its translation into English by Coleridge and its adaptation into French by Benjamin Constant.

III. CLASSICISM AND ENLIGHTENMENT

A. GENERAL OBSERVATIONS

The Classical Period brought to richest fruition the best influences of Antiquity upon modern thought. Most of the factors which contributed to the growth of classical ideals and principles have already been mentioned in connection with the influence of Antiquity upon the Renaissance and Baroque Periods. But this period should be approached from other directions than Antiquity alone. First of all, in the largest sense, the Classical Period can be seen as a perfect synthesis of the two preceding movements that had bitterly contested against one another: of the Renaissance with its often pagan mentality and its sometimes glitteringly shallow style, and of the Baroque with its reassertion of an orthodox Christian mentality and a too often artless style that was heavy with contorted thought—for paganism and Christianity and form and thought were now happily blended. The comparatist, in searching for a definition of the term Classicism, will carefully keep in mind these antecedent periods and study how the authors of the Classical Age used the alembic of ancient models to distill elements of the Renaissance and the Baroque into new and unique creations of their own. He will want to sort out these modern elements which were thus distilled and will, therefore, need to examine the relationship between the literature of Classicism and the history, philosophy, religion, science, and even mathematics of this and the earlier periods.

Certainly it was no accident that political absolutism was triumphant during the period when absolutism in literary form and taste was established. Nor was it an accident that relative stability and even rigidity in the social structure of Europe existed concurrently with stability and even rigidity in literary form and style. These and many other problems of the relationship between literature and non-literary phenomena of this era are especially rewarding to study. For example, the cult of propriety, decorum, and *bienséance* in literature can be examined as a manifestation of the enormously increased emphasis placed

upon manners and genteel conduct by the aristocracy which
during this period was deprived more and more of any kind of
military or governmental duties and which had little to do but
study means of living gracefully. Indeed, this particular problem can be extended and the literature of the period can frequently be studied as the diversion of the aristocracy. Thus the
whole subject of the effect of a relatively small and homogeneous
segment of society upon taste, conventions, and even upon authors themselves becomes a significant one. The manner in
which the new theories of clarity and dignity affected the architecture of France or even the gardens and parks of the age of
Louis XIV likewise affords interesting vistas into the very essence of classical mentality.

Although the relationship between philosophy and literature
during any age is eminently pertinent in literary studies, this
relationship seems especially important during the Classical
Age. For no period in modern European history had a more
fully developed body of literary theory and principles, and however much these theories and principles owed to Antiquity, they
required a contemporary foundation and justification in modern
philosophy. Thus, it becomes virtually necessary, if one is to
understand the period, to examine the relationship between the
philosophical method of Descartes or the theory of knowledge of
Locke and the literature and literary theories of the late seventeenth and early eighteenth centuries. Also experimental science
was beginning to develop and for the first time the physical
sciences began to exert an influence on literature. This influence
became ever more pervasive, especially during the eighteenth century (Buffon), and contributed to the decline of imaginative literature and the rise of expository prose as the dominant mode of
expression. One need only review the influence which the physical sciences had on Bayle, Fontenelle, Swift, Voltaire, and especially on the encyclopedists to realize how very important this
influence was. The resulting philosophical materialism was perhaps most noticeable in Diderot and also in La Mettrie (*L'homme
machine*, 1748).

And finally the influence which changing religious, or quasi-
religious, ideas had upon literature during this era is almost too
obvious to mention. First, during the late seventeenth century,
Catholicism, as a result of its successes during the Counter-Reformation, exerted a new and strengthened influence. Opposing

orthodox Catholicism were such forces as Puritanism in England as well as the Jansenist movement in France. The conflicts involving these forces were bound to affect literature, and the result can be studied in such authors as Dryden in England and Racine in France. Then, in the eighteenth century, the ever-increasing popularity of quasi-religious Deism was reflected so transparently in much of the literature that it seems often to substitute for imagination and genuine insight.

But however interesting and important these and similar problems of the relationship between literature and non-literary phenomena may be, it is still true that the controlling influence upon the Classical Period was the influence of Antiquity. So strong was this force that the history of the impact of Antiquity upon the Renaissance and the Baroque is really only the history of the development of Neo-Classicism into the fully developed Classicism of the late seventeenth century. This history has been sketched in the preceeding chapters and need not be repeated here.

Insofar as countries other than France produced genuinely classical literature, they did so for the most part in imitation of France, rather than of Antiquity. Classicism first triumphed in France, in part because of the strong tradition of Neo-Classicism in that country and in part because of the absolutistic political supremacy which France acquired—and it spread from Paris into the other nations of Europe. The Classical Period can most conveniently be said to begin perhaps not with Corneille's *Cid*, but in 1660, and certainly no later than 1674 when Boileau published his *Art Poétique*, which became both a manifesto and handbook of classical theory and practice. From France, Classicism spread into England and reached its imitative perfection in the early decades of the eighteenth century, with Addison's *Cato* of 1713 and Pope's works best typifying the degree of success which this essentially foreign mode of expression had on English soil. It spread into Spain likewise during the eighteenth century and produced such neo-classical tragedies as Huerta's *Raquel* (1778), or, worse, the rewriting of the irregular *comedias* of the *Siglo de Oro* as they should have been written, emasculated and anemic *refundiciones*, such as those by Don Dionisio Solis (*e.g.* Lope's *El mejor Alcalde el Rey*, Tirso's *Marta la piadosa*, and Calderón's *El Alcalde de Zalamea*). Other works and trends indicating the strength of French influences in Spain

were neo-classical tragedies like *Numancia destruida* by Ignacio
López de Ayala, Forner's condemnation of baroque stylistic irregularities in his *Sátira contra los abusos introducidos en la
poesía castellana* (1782), and an excessively gallicized vocabulary
by Feijóo and others and satirized, in turn, by Isla and Cadalso.
In Germany, Neo-Classicism replaced the expended Baroque
largely because of the work of Schottelius who tried to stand-
ardize the German language, and of Daniel Georg Morhof, whose
Unterricht von der deutschen Sprache und Poesie (*Instruction
on the German Language and Poetry,* 1682) pointed to better
French models than Opitz had been able to know.   Finally, by
drawing on the precepts and examples of both France and Augustan England, Gottsched gave Neo-Classicism in Germany a short-
lived victory between 1730 and 1740.   After a first beginning
of colonial literature during the baroque century of New England
Puritanism America also, in the second half of the eighteenth
century, was influenced by the double wave of Neo-Classicism
and Enlightenment emanating from France, as best exemplified
by the Connecticut Wits, Franklin and Irving.   Neo-Classicism
completed its circle when it returned to the country of its real
birth with the comedies of Goldoni, which in spite of their pre-
romantic sympathy for the lower classes were French-inspired
regular comedies that helped do away with the *commedia del-
l'arte*—and with the tragedies of Alfieri, who in spite of his Gallo-
phobia was completely imbued with French culture and neo-
classical technique.

Another general problem which the student of Classicism
will want to examine is the problem of literary style and form
of classical literature.   He will, for example, need to determine
which genres were especially popular and which unpopular with
classical authors, which seemed peculiarly adapted to classical
expression and which seemed incapable of being used at that
time.   One great casualty should be noted right at the beginning:
the almost complete lack of lyric poetry—for in an age of rationalism and aristocratic etiquette the wild outpourings of the human soul about love or the beauties of nature were evidently
misplaced and quite impossible.   In spite of the pleasant verse
fables of La Fontaine and the promising beginnings of Chénier,
France really had no great lyrical poet from Ronsard at the end
of the sixteenth century to Lamartine at the beginning of the
nineteenth century—and the same dearth of genuine lyricism

before and after 1700 we notice also in the England of Pope, the Germany of Gottsched and the Spain of Iriarte. The Virgilian epic, potentially considered the most exalted of all literary genres, was held in very high esteem, it is true; but the failure of Voltaire's *Henriade* (1723) indicates that the period under discussion did not seem particularly propitious to patriotic epics —and the only masterpiece produced, Goethe's *Hermann und Dorothea* (1797), was Homeric rather than Virgilian, idyllic rather than heroic, bourgeois rather than aristocratic. That left the drama as one of the most popular genres—the classical tragedy from Racine to Lessing and Alfieri, and the comedy which, from Molière to Wycherley and Goldoni, more and more developed into a social satire. This elegant and witty spirit showed itself also in the immense popularity of satires proper, from Dryden, Swift, Parini, Isla, Forner, Zachariä, and Voltaire to the Connecticut Wits, as well as of burlesque (Scarron, Butler) and of mock-heroic poems (Boileau, Pope). Neo-classical rules and regulations waged a victorious war also on the so-called irregular genres that defied their narrow definitions, such as the tragi-comedy, the pastoral drama or the religious play which, after Corneille, were doomed to give way either to the straight tragedy or the straight comedy.

The Quarrel Between the Ancients and the Moderns.

Another result of the influence of Antiquity upon the Classical Period is most interesting: the reaction against that influence which exploded in the Quarrel between the Ancients and the Moderns. This quarrel had been foreshadowed in Italy, but it broke out in full force in France and England and then continued to simmer along in the eighteenth century in Germany and Switzerland. It was clear that modern men, in the name of their dignity and self-respect, would sooner or later begin to protest against the supremacy of rules, against their constantly being told that they and their literature were inferior to the Greeks and Romans who alone were truly great and truly worth imitating—and though these rebellious Moderns were not yet as radical as the later pre-romanticists, we notice nevertheless at this time a first crack in the monolithic concept of neo-classical authoritarianism, the first rumblings of a discontent and a self-assertion which like a seismographic needle indicated the coming of the storm of 1789.

The Italian upholders of Ariosto's free inspiration as opposed to the servile observation of rules attempted by Tasso; the disciples of Bacon in England and Descartes in France who in the name of philosophy and reason proved that the Moderns were more ancient, more experienced, better trained by history and science than the Ancients had ever been; the friends of Desmarets de Saint-Sorlin who proclaimed that the poetic treatment of biblical tales and Christian miracles was far superior to the tales of pagan mythology (*Discours pour prouver que les sujets chrétiens sont seuls propres à la poésie héroïque*, 1673); the English rebels who defended the greatness of their own Shakespeare against the pro-French pro-Ancients; Bodmer in Switzerland who eulogized the true poetic greatness of Milton against the niggardly neo-classical aspersions by Gottsched in Germany —all of these authors indicated that each century had its own tastes, and that the concept of eternally valid rules of beauty will not always be believed. Further, when the Moderns under the leadership of Perrault (*Le siècle de Louis le Grand*, 1687; *Parallèles des Anciens et des Modernes*, 1688) and Fontenelle (*Dialogue des Morts*, 1683; *Digression sur les Anciens et les Modernes*, 1688) began examining their own basic assumptions, they enunciated the uniquely modern doctrine of Progress in justification of their claim that those living today can be and, indeed, are superior to the Ancients. The victory of the Moderns over the Ancients in this quarrel marks the end of an epoch and prepares the ground for the beginning of another.

Enlightenment, Rococo and Storm and Stress

The reasons for and characteristics of the gradual transition from seventeenth century Classicism to eighteenth century Enlightenment will bear particularly close scrutiny—among them the gradual decrease of pagan themes and of pro-royal and pro-religious sentiments and the emerging of a modern, progressive, at times hard-boiled and cynical attitude towards Church and State. One great fact must be borne in mind, though: that the enlighteners, in spite of their modernism with regard to Church and State, were still thoroughly pro-classical in their literary convictions. They might say the most radical things against Pope or King—but they never really challenged the authority of Boileau, though, like Voltaire, they might try, here and there, to enlarge the restrictive concepts of Greek and

Roman imitation by introducing cosmopolitan topics about Asia (*Mahomet, L'orphelin de la Chine*), Africa (*Zulime*) or America (*Alzire*). But essentially the enlighteners poured new wine into old casks; they expressed their militant ideas about the increasing spiritual and political dignity of man essentially in the old literary forms handed down to them by the neo-classical admirers of Antiquity. Their criticism of the *status quo* might often make them unnecessarily nasty (Pope) and atheistic (the encyclopedists)—indeed, their spleen might at times degenerate into appalling misanthropy (Swift) ; on the other hand, they had a firm will to reform their contemporaries before it was too late, and frequently they managed to become downright lovable if they handled the many vexing problems with urbane wit and good humor (Wieland, Irving).

In their earnest intention to work for the improvement of their contemporaries they displayed a reformatory zeal which distinguished their satire most advantageously from the shameless and conniving laughter of the Restoration wits, and they lashed out against worthless young aristocrats (Parini's *Il Giorno*), the debauchery of princes (Lessing's *Emilia Galotti*), the corruption of governments (Sir Philip Francis' *Letters of Junius*), the bombast of baroque oratory (Isla's *Fray Gerundio*), the arrogance of priests (Paine's *Age of Reason*) and of potentates (Alfieri's *Della Tirannide*), or even against the facile optimism of their own mentality (Voltaire's *Candide*). Often they suffered hardships at the hands of governmental censorship, as Voltaire's imprisonments in the Bastille (1717, 1726), his exile in Holland (1713, 1722, 1737) and other countries, and the burning of his books (*Lettres philosophiques*, 1735) indicate. Especially beautiful and inspiring were their efforts, from Roger Williams around 1640 through Shaftesbury down to Lessing's *Nathan der Weise* and *Die Erziehung des Menschengeschlechts* (*The Education of the Human Race*, 1780), to work for racial and religious tolerance (Voltaire's *Traité sur la tolérance*, 1763) and to propagate the ideal of a future great age of man's freedom and dignity (*Projet pour rendre la paix perpétuelle en Europe* by the Abbé de Saint-Pierre, 1713; *The Columbiad* by Joel Barlow; *Zum ewigen Frieden* by Kant, 1795). Also the founding of the *Helvetische Gesellschaft* in Schinznach in 1761 which vainly strove to abolish many injustices in the old Swiss Confederacy, was a distinct product of the Age of Enlightenment. Its reverse side, its rather dull materialism and utilitarianism, can be noticed especially in Benjamin Franklin's *Poor Richard's Almanach* (1732 ff.), with its proverbs about time and money and virtue and their interrelationship.

During the Age of Enlightenment, the before-mentioned linkup of literature became particularly intimate with history and philosophy, for it was one of the main tenets of the enlighteners to blur the exact delimitations between the various arts and types of literary expressions and to mix everything together into popular philosophy and political literature, a belletristic *mêlée* of various disciplines which the Germans so significantly called "angenehme Gelehrsamkeit"—a blissfully indifferent intermixing of techniques which was perhaps best illustrated by the literary-philosophical-scientific-moral essays of Feijóo in Spain (*Teatro critico-universal*, 19 vols, 1726-60) and which was stopped in at least one case, when Lessing in his famous *Laokoon* (1766) insisted again on an exact delimitation of painting and poetry. The exploitation of political history for political and literary purposes became very important among these enlighteners, distant sons of Machiavelli: thus, Bolingbroke's *Letters on the Study of History*, Hume's *History of Great Britain* (1754-61), Gibbon's *Decline and Fall of the Roman Empire* (1776 ff.), Montesquieu's *Considérations sur les causes de la grandeur des Romains et de leur décadence*, (*Considerations on the Causes of the Greatness and Decline of the Romans*, 1734), Voltaire's *Histoire de Charles XII* (of Sweden) or Johannes von Müller's *Geschichte der schweizerischen Eidgenossenschaft* (*History of the Swiss Confederacy*, 1786-95)—or, with history transformed into a gently satirical mock-heroic, *Knickerbocker's History of New York* by Washington Irving (1809). It should be emphasized that in the field of enlightening philosophy England chronologically preceded the thinkers of France; Hobbes' *Leviathan* (1651) and Locke's *Essay on Toleration* (1667) and *Essay on Human Understanding* (1690), though rooted in philosophy, political science and religion, were of immense importance for literature, too, and no study of the sources of Rousseau or the backgrounds of the American and French Revolutions would be complete without them. The same precedence of England holds true of the problem of theodicy such as treated by Milton, formulated by Leibniz (*Essai de Théodicée*, 1710) and echoed in Pope and Lessing; and of the school of Deism which ranged from Bolingbroke to Voltaire, Lessing, and Paine (*The Age of Reason*, 1794 ff.).

Rococo literature has a place in all this inasmuch as its representatives were the very parasites against whom the enlighteners were fighting. A product of the aristocracy, best incarnated perhaps by the portly crowd at the court of Versailles, the ladies in powdered wigs and the gentlemen with padded calves in the company of Mme. de Pompadour, Mme. du Barry or Queen Marie Antoinette, these Rococo poets idealized a way of life that knew of no tragedies, no broken hearts, no political qualms, no social strife, no degrading poverty. Anacreon and Ovid were the models for these pseudo-shepherds of elegance and amorousness to emulate; Casanova and the dainty porcelain figures of Sèvres and Meissen were the products of this atmosphere. The operas by the Italian Metastasio in Vienna, the comedy *Le jeu de l'amour et du hasard* (1730) by Marivaux in France (with its influence upon Goldsmith's *She Stoops to Conquer*) and Pope's Rococo-epic *The Rape of the Lock* (1712) in England represent best the spirit of this essentially neo-classical school, seekers of beauty and happiness, which—attacked by the enlighteners (Parini) and the Storm and Stress dramatists— came to such a rude end when the Reign of Terror began on what is now known as the Place de la Concorde in 1792. Strangely enough it was the Germans (of whom one would not normally expect such a taste) who produced the most exquisite works of the Rococo: the art-center of Dresden, the residence of August the Strong of Saxony; the so-called Anacreontic Poets around 1750 (Hagedorn, Gleim, and others) ; young Goethe who, while a student in Leipzig, wrote a delicate pastoral drama *Die Laune des Verliebten* (*The Wayward Lover*, 1768)—and, above all, Christoph Martin Wieland, the greatest Rococo-poet of them all (*Musarion, Agathon, Oberon*), the greatest refiner of the German language, the outstanding representative of French delicacy and neo-classical refinement in German literature, the indispensable forerunner of the greatness of German literature that was soon to follow. The philosophy of Shaftesbury, the paintings by Watteau, or the minuets by Couperin lend themselves to striking comparisons with the literature of the Rococo.

The scholar will want to look into the relationship between, and the international manifestations of, Classicism, Enlightenment and Rococo, and also of Enlightenment and Storm and

Stress—for these two complementary and yet mutually hostile movements somehow remind him of the relationship between Humanism and the Reformation. Both of them were opposed to the *status quo* and both worked for the betterment and the modernization of Church and State: French-inspired Enlightenment (like Humanism) in the name of reason, of moderation, of skepticism, of willingness to compromise—German-inspired Storm and Stress (like the Reformation) in the name of irrational ardor, radical solutions, popular uprisings. There was very much which Humanism and Enlightenment, Erasmus of Rotterdam, Ariosto, Voltaire and Wieland had in common—just as there was very much that the Reformation and the Storm and Stress, Luther, Calvin, Klopstock and Rousseau had in common, and it is a thousand pities that in both cases the far more radical German wave killed the compromises suggested by the more moderate intellectuals of the type of Erasmus and Voltaire. The Storm and Stress, like the Reformation, was an avalanche of the masses rather than the work of an intellectual aristocracy; it accused the Enlightenment of not having gone far enough in the task of freeing mankind from the yoke of 1700, of having allowed itself to become involved in rationalistic quibbling and philosophical windmill-fighting—and so, by 1750, a new, a second, a German-inspired wave, the pre-romantic Storm and Stress, carried through the political, religious and literary liberation of man which the Enlightenment apparently had been unable to do. Hence the enmity between Enlightenment and Pre-Romanticism: Voltaire and Rousseau both hated the *status quo*, but they hated each other even more—and the same enmity can be seen in Germany between Wieland the enlightener and Klopstock the exalted pre-romanticist.

B. THE CONTRIBUTIONS OF FRANCE

The Golden Age of French culture—more dignified and yet less colorfully romantic than the Age of Elizabeth in England and less overflowingly wealthy, above all, than the Golden Age of the Germany of Goethe, Kant, and Beethoven—none the less achieved an immediate and all-pervading success abroad such as England and Germany never experienced, because the French cultural empire which extended from the court of Catherine the Great in Russia to the sturdy French settlers in Louisiana was based not only on the poets, the religious thinkers, the artists of France, but also—and perhaps even more so—on the French military victories, the generals and diplomats and the thousands of lesser lights following in their footsteps: refugees, journalists, cooks, crooks, dancing masters, barbers and courtesans, who all left a very deep imprint on the thoroughly gallicized culture of Western Europe. What France gave to the Western Europe of that period was far more than a mere literary hegemony—it was an entire new way of life.

With Germany defeated in 1648 and Spain (and hence also Italy) in 1659, there was no power, neither military nor cultural, to oppose the will of the victor; and after the return of the Stuarts from their French exile in 1660, England also became a willing follower, not to say a vassal, in the train of Louis XIV. Only in stubbornly freedom-loving Holland did there arise a man, William of Orange, who in his just wrath and as King of England after 1688 was going to be the architect of a great European coalition against aggressive France. The political and cultural glory of France reached its apex from 1660 to 1690, though one may insist that it lasted on, till the death of Louis XIV in 1715. Yet even then, with the shifting from Classicism proper to Enlightenment, the power of the French cultural empire remained undiminished so long as there was a spark left in Voltaire, its admirable and valiant last champion to defend it—and though French military hegemony may be said to have come to an end with the Spanish War of Succession in 1713, the impetus of its culture was so great that its intellectual power lasted till the death of Voltaire in 1778, just as the Italian Renaissance lasted beyond the Fall of Florence and the Spanish *Siglo de Oro* beyond the death of Philip II. The correctness of the assertion that this French Golden Age really died only with Voltaire is not refuted by the fact that the first Anglo-German and pre-romantic onslaughts against this empire became noticeable from the 1720's on.

The student of French literary greatness will notice that in the transition from the age of Boileau to the age of Voltaire French cultural leadership was not lessened materially, but that it changed its character as it stoutly fought back at the slowly growing Anglo-German opposition that dared to defy the classical edicts emanating from France. Although many of the ideas germinated during the Enlightenment later grew into pre-romantic weapons which were used against French Classicism, the Enlightenment itself was the logical outgrowth of French Classicism. Once Descartes had provided the intellectual method for rationalism and once the Moderns had won in the Quarrel between the Ancients and the Moderns, it was inevitable that some such development as the Enlightenment represents should occur and that friends as well as foes of the French system should avail themselves of the weapons supplied. In approaching this century, the comparatist becomes aware of the fact that with the victory of the Moderns in the Quarrel and with the accompanying diminution of the prestige of the Ancients, Classicism lost one of its strongest props. When the spread of the Cartesian method is added to this loss of the classical literary aesthetic, the student will understand in part why the eighteenth century was an age of prose which produced very little significant imaginative literature. He will also understand why the new century used the rationalistic method developed since Descartes to destroy many of the values for which the Classical Age stood. Looked at in this way, it will not seem paradoxical that the country which had the most to lose—France —was the country which gave birth to some of the most progressive ideas of Enlightenment. For this reason the interplay of ideas, particularly political and economic, which are contained in the expository prose of the period, is particularly informative.

Among the intermediaries, only a few names can be mentioned, for the number of foreign visitors attracted to Paris and to the Versailles of Louis XIV and XV was legion. Their role among the epigones throughout eighteenth century Enlightenment was far greater than during the few decades of the seventeenth century when Classicism had actually reached its finest

fruition.   More important among the unofficial ambassadors
of French culture in England than Huguenot refugees and translators of the type of Abel Boyer was Saint-Evremond, a noble-
man exiled from France who, apart from a trip to Holland,
spent the last decades (1661-1703) of his life in the England of
Charles II and William and Mary.   His prolonged stay was reciprocated by visitors extending from the age of Hobbes and
Cowley to the age of Garrick, Walpole, Goldsmith, and Sterne,
who all knew France intimately well.   The Stuarts before 1660
and after 1688 spent their exile largely in France; Shaftesbury,
besides being familiar with France, had spent much time among
the Spinozists and French Huguenots in Holland and died in
Italy; Bolingbroke was an exile in France because of his pro-
Stuart sympathies; Hume for a while was secretary to the English embassy in Paris.   In connection with Boileau we shall later
have to mention an international group of Jesuit critics who
followed in his footsteps.   Then we must refer, too, to the very
significant role of the French salons as transmitters of French
culture, salons in which the Swiss Rousseau and the American
Benjamin Franklin were initiated into the values incarnated by
France, and which often channelled French influences into specific directions, like the salon of Mme. du Deffand (the friend of
Horace Walpole) with regard to England, the salon of Mme.
d'Houdetot with regard to America, or the salon of Mme. Geoffrin
with regard to Poland.   Nor should the salon of the Swiss Mme.
de Necker in Paris (1764-90) be forgotten, in which her daughter, the future Mme. de Staël, received her enviably cosmopolitan
outlook.   Royal courts did their share in propagating French
culture abroad: thus the Stuarts in England from 1660-88, the
Bourbons in Madrid and in Parma; thus also the intimate link
between Poland and Lothringia, which made Nancy a meeting-
place between French culture and Polish aristocracy.   In Germany mention might be made of Frédéric-Charles Bressand,
courtier and translator of Racine at the court of Brunswick—
and among the Germans and the Swiss residing in Paris the
intermediary role especially of Melchior Grimm (*Correspondance
littéraire, philosophique et critique,* 1753-97) and of Henri
Meister should be emphasized.   Also La Harpe, one of the few
neo-classicists to survive Voltaire, was a Swiss by birth.   Often
French culture reached Germany not through Frenchmen, but
through thoroughly gallicized Italians: thus Algarotti and

Denina who enjoyed great popularity in Berlin, and the Marquis Lucchesini, a member of the Prussian Academy and well-known for his published conversations with Frederick II, entered the Prussian diplomatic service. Among the members of the *Encyclopédie* reference should be made to the German Baron Holbach; nor should we forget Voltaire's trips to England and Prussia, nor, above all, Diderot's trip to Russia, where French Enlightenment was instrumental in initiating modern Russian literature. Under Frederick the Great the intellectual life of Prussia was gallicized to such an extent that the Royal Academy in Berlin in 1783 proposed for discussion the theme of the universality of the French language—a contest which was won by Rivarol through his *Discours sur l'universalité de la langue française* of 1784. Italians residing in Paris extended from Gassendi in the seventeenth century to Conti, Galiani and Goldoni in the eighteenth century, while among the Spaniards mention should be made of Luzán, Meléndez Valdés, Cadalso and Moratín. Feijóo's *Paralelo de las lenguas castellana y francesa* contained in his *Teatro crítico* (1760) is a further indication of the subservience of Europe to the power of France. At the very end of the century and during the Napoleonic era the Belgian Prince de Ligne, a resident mostly of Vienna, may be mentioned as one of the last great intermediaries of classical French culture abroad.

The Tragedy.

The classical principles and forms were brought to perfection first in the drama, and indeed the classical drama is that literary form which was most widely used and most completely developed. We have already discussed how Pierre CORNEILLE (1606-84) in his neo-classical dramas beginning with *Le Cid* helped prepare the way for the restrained, economical, highly polished, and subtly analytical tragedies of Racine. Although we have discussed Corneille as a baroque author, we indicated that he was essentially a transition dramatist—one who retained some of the bombast and rhetoric, some of the baroque taste for the abnormally heroic and superior-willed individual, and some of the inability to economize his material sufficiently to squeeze it all into the classical mold. But Corneille was also classical in the extent to which he was more interested in psychological analysis than in overt action, and in the extent to which his style achieved dignity, decorum and polish. It really makes little difference whether one calls him classical or baroque, but insofar as he was known abroad he was regarded as one of the great modern classicists. In both his subject matter and his style he contributed especially to the English drama of the Restoration Period and to the German drama around 1700, as has already been suggested, and this contribution helped to prepare for the entrenchment of French Classicism later on in these two countries.

Jean RACINE (1639-99) was, of course, the great tragic dramatist of French Classicism. After writing two tragedies in the style of Corneille, Racine produced nine undisputed master-pieces, of which six (*Andromaque, Bérénice, Britannicus, Phèdre et al.*) are classical both in subject matter and form and three are classical only in form, taking their subject matter from the Bible (*Esther, Athalie*) or from Turkish history (*Bajazet*). Racine's greatness, and the quality which his countless imitators in France and abroad were never able to capture, lay in the exquisite subtlety of his probings of human feelings. These probings were revealed in a marvelously restrained, economical, and perfectly controlled development of his plots through his perfectly polished style. Racine's genius was to make his audience feel and perceive volcanic emotions tearing his characters apart even though the surface of their language and actions seems placid and contained. Perhaps it was that Racine's foreign admirers had read Corneille first, perhaps it was that they did not have a language as precisely tooled as French, or perhaps it was that they simply lacked the genius, sensibility and insight of Racine— but whenever the English, Germans, Italians, Spanish, or Russians attempted to write a classical tragedy such as he had written, the result seemed artificial, oratorical, bombastic or sentimental. Nevertheless try they did. No dramatist in modern history had so many immediate imitators as did Racine. The influence of Shakespeare on the dramas of other countries may be more enduring and more far-reaching; but only Racine, with the help of Corneille, had the effect of imposing a tight mold on the drama of virtually all of Europe.

The French classical tragedy spread to the rest of Europe not only as a result of direct imitations of Racine himself, but also as a result of the continuing cultural dominance of France throughout the eighteenth century and of the continuing dominance of Racine over the drama of that French culture. Looked at in this way VOLTAIRE, who prided himself on being the successor to Racine's tragic crown, was in effect an intermediary, for the spread of French classical drama into Spain or Russia, for example, was given impetus even more by the dramas of Voltaire than by those of the man whom he imitated.

The student who is interested in tracing the evolution of the classical drama in the various parts of Europe will need to examine how all three of these French dramatists contributed to the development of the tragedy in the several countries. He will need to investigate, in addition to the use the English made of Corneille (the translations of the *Cid* by Rutter, of *Pompey* by Mrs. Katherine Philips, the adaptation of his *Horace* in William Whitehead's *Roman Father* etc.), the contributions of Racine to the tragedy of Thomas Otway, Dryden, and especially Addison, whose *Cato* (1713) was the one English play which attempted wholeheartedly, but unsuccessfully, to be truly a classical tragedy. Best-known among the Racine translations and adaptations were *Mithridates* by Nathaniel Lee, *Titus and Berenice* by Thomas Otway and then especially the amazingly popular *Distrest Mother* (*Andromaque*) by Ambrose Philips (1712) which, in contrast to Corneille's distant tragedies on Roman history or Spanish honor, afforded a real and throbbing heart-interest. However, the net effect of the classical influence in England will probably be estimated to have been bad. What is good in the English drama of the Restoration and Augustan periods is usually native; the bathos, bombast, and absurd attempts to expand the form are merely the results of the English inability or unwillingness to create the kind of masterpiece of simplicity which a Racine play is. As to the colonies: also the first American tragedy, Thomas Godfrey's *Prince of Parthia* (1767), was entirely conceived in the prevailing French neoclassical fashion.

The results in Germany were even more fantastic than they had been in England. The prevailing Senecan taste in seventeenth century Germany brought about even worse disfigurations of the classical tragedy than they had in England—as seen, for instance, in Claussen's two additions to his translation of the *Cid* (*Der Cimena Trauerjahr* and *Der Tod des Cids*, 1655) and in Christopher Kormart's version of *Polyeucte* (1669). Later, when the baroque excesses gave way to Gottsched's Neo-Classicism, the translations of the Gottschedians from the dearly beloved French (for instance, in the six volumes of the *Deutsche Schaubühne*, 1740-45) became flat, wooden, monotonous (Gottsched's *Iphigenie*, 1732), with not a spark of Corneille's greatness or of Racine's fire left beneath the dry regularity of German Alexandrines. Both the bombast of the late seventeenth century and the pedestrian sobriety of the early eighteenth produced thoroughly unsatisfactory results, and Lessing's later unjustly violent attacks upon the classical French drama in his *Literaturbriefe* (*Letters on Literature*, 1759 ff.) can in part be understood only in the light of what these Gottschedians tried and failed to do. Gottsched should, however, be given credit for having cleared the German stage of the grotesque and even obscene performances which, largely due to the influence of the English Comedians, had been prevalent until the troupe of Mrs. Neuber in Leipzig began to emulate French Classicism (1727 ff.). Gottsched's attempts to give to the stage a repertory of classical drama by copying, among other things, his own *Der sterbende Cato* (*Dying Cato*, 1732) largely from Addison's tragedy, at least had the effect of giving dignity, seriousness, and stilted formality to the German theatre. But in spite of his rather pedantic attempts to create almost singlehanded a German classical dramaturgy, it was not until Schiller published his translation of Racine's *Phèdre* (1805) that the German language ever knew a really genuine and pure version of one of Racine's plays. The purity of Schiller's translation can undoubtedly be attributed to the fact that in this case one great classical poet was translating another great classical poet. In this connection, mention must be made also of Goethe's translations of *Mahomet* and *Tancrède* by Voltaire (1802).

The influence of the French classical tragedy from Corneille to Voltaire was especially interesting also in Spain because most Spanish authors of the eighteenth century were constantly oscillating between imitation and rejection of the French models and fashions which were imposed upon them by the fact that with Philip V (1700-1746) the Bourbons of France had succeeded the Habsburgs of Austria. In spite of increasingly bitter satires against the apers of France (Isla's *Fray Gerundio*, Cadalso's *Cartas marruecas*), there were Spaniards who were anxious to imitate and translate not only the great leaders of French literature, but also their disciples abroad such as Metastasio, Alfieri and Goldoni in Italy. In fact, they even translated back

into Spanish those French authors who had originally been inspired by Spain—such as Corneille, Molière, Le Sage, Houdart
de la Motte, or Beaumarchais. Among the translators we can
name José de Clavijo y Fajardo (Racine's *Andromaque*, Voltaire's *Semiramis*) ; Ramón de la Cruz (Racine's *Bajazet*, Metastasio's *Attilio*, Voltaire's *Ecossaise*, Beaumarchais' *Eugénie*) ;
García de la Huerta (Voltaire's *Zaïre*) ; Tomás de Iriarte (Voltaire's *Orphelin de la Chine*) ; Olavide (Racine's *Phèdre* and
Mithidrate, Voltaire's *Zaïre*). The translation of Corneille's
Cinna by Pizarro Piccolomini in 1713 had given impetus to this
vogue of neo-classical translations; among its later manifestations we can name the Spanish version of Alfieri's *Virginia* by
Dionisio Solis (who also translated his *Oreste*) and Rodríguez
de Ledesma (who also translated his *La congiuria dei Pazzi* and
Voltaire's *Mahomet*). The prohibition of performances of
autos sacramentales by royal decree in 1765 certainly constituted
a great victory for the partisans of French Classicism and Enlightenment. The fact that Bretón de los Herreros (the translator also of Scribe, Delavigne and Dumas) likewise rendered into Spanish Racine's *Andromaque* and *Mithridate* and Voltaire's
Mérope indicates that neo-classical influences lasted well into the
middle of the nineteenth century—as attested also by Hartzenbusch's imitation of Voltaire's *Oedipe* and by the Alfieri-imita-
tions in Quintana, Martínez de la Rosa, the Duke of Rivas and
Gertrudis Gómez de Avellaneda (*Saul*, 1858).

While the Spaniards oscillated between the new French models
and their own native traditions, the Italians, having no such
rich dramatic traditons of their own, oscillated between the
French models and the original Greek and Roman patterns upon
which they were based. Thus, Metastasio and Maffei, who were
predominantly inspired by the Ancients—while Frugoni at the
court of the Bourbons in Parma, Martelli, the introducer, into
Italy, of the French Alexandrine meter, and Alfieri, the greatest
of them all, stood distinctly under the spell of France. Alfieri's
tragedies (*Oreste, Antigone, Virginia, Merope, Bruto, Saul,
Filippo*, and others), of an exaggerated and studied simplicity,
are striking examples of the greatness and barrenness of works
created with the brain and by sheer will-power alone. Among
the translators, Baretti's rendering into Italian of Corneille's
tragedies should be especially noted (1747-48), and also the
collection by Paradisi (*Scelta di tragedie francesi tradotte in*

verso sciolto, 1764) contributed greatly to make the Italians familiar with the tragic masterpieces of France. If classical tragedy may be said to have originated in the Italy of Trissino and to have achieved its finest perfection in the France of Racine, it may also be said to have come to an end in the country of its origin, in the Italy of Alfieri.

The Comedy

MOLIÈRE (1622-73)—in many ways far more modern and original than either Corneille or Racine, because for moral or political reasons he could not imitate his predecessors (Aristophanes, Terence, Ariosto) as the others had imitated theirs— fared very badly in England. London's poetasters did not honor him as one of the world's great geniuses, but would rob him unashamedly, steal from him entire scenes, or mix up the actions of two or three of his plays in order to make their comedies "more lively" and to satisfy the English craving for greater action rather than for depth of thought. Dryden (*Sir Martin Mar-all,* 1667), Etheredge (*The Man of Mode,* 1676), Wycherley (*The Plain Dealer,* 1677), Congreve (*The Double Dealer,* 1694) and Vanbrugh (*The Cuckold in Conceit,* 1707) were the chief culprits in these cases of unadulterated plagiarism. Also the moral tone of these comedies was changed, because Molière's earnestness of social criticism became transformed by the Restoration crowd into such shameless laughter at the crimes of greed and sex that Jeremy Collier in 1699 was indeed justified in writing a condemning *Short View of the Immorality and Profaneness of the English Stage.* This immorality was somewhat mitigated when after the expulsion of the Stuarts new monarchs like William and Mary and Ann to some extent silenced the voices of the wits and rakes. In the beginning the English dramatists rarely honored Molière with a literal translation; even *The Miser* by Shadwell is more noted for its brazen "improvements" than for its accuracy.

The German title of a translation of *Tartuffe, Der vertrackte Jesuit und Intrigenmacher* (*The Confounded Jesuit and Intriguer*) and the imitation of *Les Précieuses ridicules* in Christian Reuter's acid *L'honnête femme oder die ehrliche Frau zu Plissine* (1694) are perhaps indicative of the rather dull and pedestrian level of moralizing to which Molière sank before and during the era of Gottsched, thought it must be added, too, that he exerted a better influence upon the comedies of Gellert and the early works of Lessing. In general, however, it must be said that Gottsched in his long overdue reform of the German theatre was so busy eliminating the atrocities of the Baroque and the vulgarities of the English Comedians, that he paid great attention only to stately and stilted neo-classical tragedies (*Haupt- und Staatsaktionen,* as he called them). Gottsched's enmity against the "Hans Wursts" almost completely killed off any chance of a literary development of German comedies, a trend best demonstrated by the fact that during the Golden Century of German literature tragedies outnumbered comedies by about ten to one—and even then comedies were rarely hilarious (Kleist), but rather political (Lessing) or philosophical (Grillparzer) in intent. It was only after A. W. Schlegel that Molière was at last fully appreciated across the Rhine. Of special interest in this connection is the drama *Das Urbild des Tartuffe* (*The Première-Performance of Tartuffe,* 1847) by Gutzkow, in which the Young German author used the story of how the censorship had tried to stop Molière's play in order to plead for freedom of thought and of speech.

Much quicker was Molière's success in the Denmark of Ludvig Holberg and the Italy of Carlo Goldoni, who have both been called the greatest disciples of the French master. In fact, Goldoni successfully used Molière's fluent Neo-Classicism in order to combat the popularity of the Italian *commedia dell' arte* and to force Italian actors to observe again the restrictions of texts, rules and careful diction. With his typically Venetian comedies which excelled through the wit and the gentle irony that hovered over their Rococo-atmosphere (*La bottega del caffè, Il bugiardo, La locandiera, Le donne curiose,* etc.), Goldoni achieved great fame not only in Italy and France, but also in the rest of Europe. In Germany he was praised by Lessing and Goethe, and in England Elizabeth Griffith adopted his *Le bourru bienfaisant* in her *The Times* (1779). Goldoni is also significant as an important Italo-French intermediary, not only because of his imitation of Molière, but also because he lived in Paris during the last thirty years of his life (1763-93), writing in French (and dying in most impecunious circumstances during the French Revolution). The Spaniards, finally, emulated and translated both Molière and his somewhat more superficial Italian disciple: thus Ramón de la Cruz with his parody of *L'Amour médecin*

(*La enferma del mal de boda*), Leandro Fernández de Moratín
who had met Goldoni while in Paris and who translated *L'école
des maris* and *Le médecin malgré lui*, and José Marchena y Ruiz,
the translator of *Tartuffe* (*El Hipocrito*) and *Le misanthrope*.

Students interested in thematological themes will find Molière
particularly rewarding, and they can compare his treatment of
Amphitryon and *Don Juan*, or of lawyers, doctors, servants or
ingenues with Plautus, Terence, the *Celestina*, Ariosto, Lope or
Tirso de Molina before him or with Lessing, Goldoni, Sheridan
and others after him.

Boileau

The question of the significance of Nicolas de Boileau-Des-
préaux (1636-1711), the high-priest of French Classicism, brings
up, above all, the significance of his *Art poétique* (*Poetic Art*,
1674) which prepared the groundwork for the power of Neo-
Classicism at home and abroad. This very important book was
one of the chief pillars of French cultural hegemony. Among
Boileau's foreign disciples we might mention Dryden, Soame
and Ozell in England who translated him; also Thomas Rymer,
the most narrow-mindedly didactic neo-classicist England ever
produced, author of *Tragedies of the last Age Considered* (1678),
must be mentioned in this connection. Pope in his *Essay on
Criticism* (1711) as well as in most of his other works was infinitely indebted to Boileau—though with reference to this particular work it should be noted, of course, that Pope's accent
was slightly different and that he was writing down precepts essentially for critics, while Boileau had tended to guide poets.
The influence of Boileau's *Lutrin* upon Pope's *Rape of the Lock*
we have mentioned in connection with the mock-heroic epics;
John Dennis subjected both works to a running comparison, very
much to the detriment of his arch-enemy Pope. Also the English satire in the age of Dryden and Pope drew heavily upon
Boileau, though the satirists of ancient Rome (Juvenal) provided
the primary inspiration. We might say that Dr. Johnson was
about the last representative of Boileau's concepts of literature,
and, in view of the fact that he was surrounded by a whole group
of pre-romanticists clamoring for exactly the opposite ideals,
it certainly seems erroneous to designate the middle of the English eighteenth century as the Age of Dr. Johnson. Outstanding among these enemies of Neo-Classicism was Joseph Warton

who, in his *Essay of the Writings and Genius of Pope* (1757),
denied this disciple of Boileau the very name of poet and spoke up
in favor of a pre-romantic regeneration of poetry.

In Germany, Daniel Georg Morhof with his *Unterricht von
der deutschen Sprache und Poesie* (*Instruction in the German
Language and Poetry*, 1682) had not yet felt the full impact of
Boileau's Classicism—that was left for Gottsched and his well-
known *Versuch einer kritischen Dichtkunst* (*Attempt at a Critical Art of Poetry*, 1730). Neo-Classicism had not been too successful in baroque Germany so long as it had been backed up
only by the wave emanating from Scaliger and Opitz; now,
however, it had a much better chance to achieve supremacy because it derived its strength from the second and much finer
wave emanating from the France of Boileau and his contemporaries. Gottsched's dictatorship over German literature was as
absolute and stultifying as Pope's dictatorship over English
literature; his great enemies were, first, Bodmer, who around
1740 defended the religious miraculousness of Milton against
the Gottschedian slurs and naggings deriving from similar attacks by Boileau upon the Christian marvels in Tasso—and,
second, Lessing, who in his famous seventeenth *Letter on Literature* attacked Gottsched and all the French behind Gottsched
in the name of a freer, a Greek conception of Classicism. Yet
so powerful were the French ideals both in Germany and in
Switzerland that when Bodmer's friend Breitinger, also from
Zürich, at the very height of the fight against Gottsched, wrote
a *Kritische Dichtkunst* (*Critical Art of Poetry*, 1740) of his
own, it was far more neo-classical than one might have expected
from that ardently anglophile Swiss. Also Frederick the Great
of Prussia, the idol of the pre-romantic German authors, was
still completely imbued with the spirit of Boileau and Voltaire
when, in his notoriously ignorant and widely criticized essay
De la littérature allemande (*On German Literature*, 1780),
written at the time of Lessing, Wieland, Klopstock and Goethe,
he denied that there had as yet been created such a thing as
"polite" German literature.

We notice the same troubled split of opinions in Spain, except
that the French doctrines, under a French dynasty and under the
impact also of French Enlightenment, lasted well into the age
of Napoleon, even though the smouldering opposition against all
this, and an emphatic wish to return to the *hispanidad* of one's

own native traditions, began even before Ramón de la Cruz.
The French neo-classical pattern became noticeable in Spain
with the establishment of a Spanish Academy in 1714 and the
publication of its authorized dictionary in 1726; and the same
trends continued with the founding of the *Diario de los literatos*
(1737-42—a publication emulating the *Journal des Savants* in
France) and with the francophile *Academia del Buen Gusto* of
the Marquesa de Sarria (1749 ff.). Boileau's ideals were imposed upon the Spaniards in the well-known *Poética o Reglas de
la poesía en general y de sus principales especies* by Ignacio
Luzán Claramunt de Suelves y Gurrea (1737)—though, like
most Spaniards of the eighteenth century, Luzán was thoroughly
familiar not only with Boileau, but also with Italian critics like
Muratori, Gravina, and Crescimbeni. Also Montiano's *Discursos sobre las tragedias españolas* of 1753 are noted for their
pro-classical bias; later, after English literature began to become
known, Montiano also approved of Dryden's and Addison's works.
Particularly well-known was the basic work by the expelled
Spanish Jesuit Juan Andrés, *Del origen, progreso y estado actual
de la literatura,* which was published in Italian in 1782, in Spanish in 1784. Boileau's theories in Spain reached a new climax
in *Las reglas del drama* by the well-known Manuel José Quintana (1791) in which the French models were eulogized and the
many blemishes of Lope and Calderón enumerated. The Frenchman's fine hand can be seen also in the arguments with which
men like Nicolas F. Moratín (*Desengaño al teatro español,* 1763)
and José de Clavijo y Fajardo justified the forbidding of the
performances of the *autos sacramentales*: not only because
they mixed religion with vulgarity, treating of saintly persons and concepts in a spirit of coarse levity, but also because
they violated the neo-classical rules of the established dramatic
genres. In Portugal, finally, Boileau's *Art poétique* was translated by Ericeira as early as 1697.

Just as Boileau's neo-classical ideas in France had been taken
over and expostulated by a whole group of minor Jesuit critics
(Rapin, Le Bossu, Bouhours, etc.), so a more or less unswerving
brand of rationalistic and neo-classical criticism was propagated
elsewhere, especially in the Italy of the notorious Jesuit Saverio
Bettinelli (author, as we have seen, of the one great Italian attack upon Dante) and of the ex-Spaniard Juan Andrés, the librarian of the king of Naples. Others, like the literary histor-

ians Crescimbeni and Tiraboschi (the latter again a Jesuit),
were more independent of France. The entire Roman Arcadia
and its various members (Crescimbeni, Metastasio, Frugoni,
etc.) stood more or less under the influence of France; among the
critical dissertations written by this group were *Della tragedia*
and *Della ragion poetica libri II* by Gian Vincenzo Gravina
(1708). A definite reaction against France began with Muratori, Vico and, as we shall see later, with Baretti, the great enemy
of Voltaire.

Minor French Influences of the Seventeenth Century

In addition to these four giants of French Classicism—Corneille, Racine, Molière, and Boileau—there was a host of lesser
figures whose achievements in other genres helped to give substance and quality to Classicism in other countries. The student
can find more than enough fascinating minor studies in examining the spread to other countries of the work of such people as
La Fontaine, Mme. de la Fayette, La Rochefoucauld, and La
Bruyère. For example, LA FONTAINE—in his *Fables* a disciple of Aesop, in his *Contes* an imitator of Boccaccio and Ariosto—in his turn, through his fables, inspired those of John Gay
in England (1727) and of Christian Fürchtegott Gellert in Germany (1738). In the course of the eighteenth century of Enlightenment and didacticism, fables tended to become ever more
useful and popular; their range extended from those of Dryden
(1700) and Lessing to the *Favole Esopiane* by Pignotti, the
Favole by Bertòla in Italy and the *Fabulas morales* by Saman-
iego and the *Fabulas literarias* by Iriarte in Spain (1782). In
this connection we should mention also the famous dramatic
fables of Carlo Gozzi, the brother of Gaspare, whose plays (*Turandot*, 1762; *L'augellin belverde*; *L'amore delle tre melarance*,
etc.) indicate even more than the comedies of Goldoni the graceful superficiality and lighthearted fancifulness of Italian play-
goers. Among the translations of these plays Schiller's version
of *Turandot* should be especially noted (*Turandot, Prinzessin in
China, ein tragikomisches Märchen*, 1802).

The famous novel by MME. DE LA FAYETTE, *La princesse
de Clèves* (1678) deserves our attention not only because it was
immediately translated into English and transformed into a
Restoration drama by Nathaniel Lee (1681), but also because,
like Barclay's *Argenis*, it is a perfect example of a *roman à clef*,

depicting definite events in French society around 1600 under a
slight literary disguise. In its emphasis on the self-discipline
of a woman who might easily have oscillated between husband
and lover, the novel is an outstanding example of the supremacy
of will encountered in Gracián, Corneille and Descartes. The
comparatist might wish to enjoy it alongside with Goethe's
Elective Affinities—another famous novel teaching classical discipline and the sanctity of matrimony.

The State Novel

We have previously given a brief outline of the state-novel,
from Plato and Xenophon up to Campanella and Bacon. Now
we must take it up again for the recent centuries, because in
view of the enlighteners' immense interest in problems of government and in view, too, of the neo-classical concept that literature should fulfil a didactic purpose, it is not astonishing at all
that state-novels flourished during the eighteenth century as
never before. Not only state novels pure and simple, but also the
many combinations with other types of novels which, as seen
before, lend themselves easily to some semi-pedagogical purpose.

The work to initiate the new popularity of this genre was
Télémaque by Fénelon (1699) about the rich political experience
and wisdom gathered by the future ruler of Ithaca while he was
searching for his long-absent father Ulysses. *Télémaque* was
an international success; among its many foreign translations
we might mention the one by Benjamin Neukirch who, in 1727,
rendered it into German Alexandrine verses. More important
than Marmontel with his *Bélisaire* (1766—imitated in *Eudoxia,
hija de Belisario* by the Spaniard Montengón y Paret, 1793) were
the three state-novels by the Swiss patrician Albrecht von Haller:
the story of *Usong* (1771), a young Mongolian who became shah
of Persia, and the description of enlightened despotism; *Alfred
der Grosse, König der Angelsachsen,* a discussion of the principles
of constitutional monarchy as it surely did not yet exist in ninth
century England; and *Fabius und Cato*, an analysis of the
problems of monarchy versus democracy in which the Swiss
Haller, through the words of Cato, spoke up in defense of his
democratic ideals. Spirited and amusing is also *Der goldene
Spiegel (The Golden Mirror,* 1772), in which Wieland in Germany traced the causes for the rise and the decline of the
fabulous oriental kingdom of Scheschian—a book which netted

him the job of becoming the tutor of the young duke Karl August
of Saxony-Weimar and the honor of being chronologically the
first great author to enter Weimar, the future capital of German
literature.

With *Gulliver's Travels* (1726) by Swift, the state-novel became amalgamated with accounts of extraordinary voyages and
neo-classical satire; with Schnabel's *Insel Felsenburg* (1731), it
began to blend with an enlarged concept of a Robinsonade. There
is no denying that also Voltaire's famous *Zadig* (1748) and
Candide (1759) contain many elements of the state-novel, mixed,
as it were, with the genre of the apprenticeship novel, plus a
good deal of typically Voltairian flippancy. The same is true—
but with flippancy replaced by pessimism and melancholy—
in Dr. Johnson's *Rasselas, the Prince of Abyssinia* (1759).

Rather than dwell on the romanticists—for instance, Melville's blending of the state-novel with another Robinsonade in
Typee (1846) and with the apprenticeship-novel in his fascinating *Mardi*—let us conclude by saying that it was reserved
for the last hundred years to supply us not only with an unusually rich number of ordinary or extraordinary state-novels (Butler's *Erewhon*, Hauptmann's *Die Insel der grossen Mutter*)
but, in conjunction with the Industrial Revolution and the rise of
Caesarism, Fascism and Communism, also with some appallingly
impressing and depressing portrayals of the future: Bellamy's
Looking Backward (1888); Jack London's *The Iron Heel*;
Arnold Ulitz' *Ararat* (1921) and George Orwell's *1984* (1949).

Montesquieu

The first great French enlightener was Montesquieu (1689-
1755), a man who made the whole world the subject of his study
and who not only received suggestions from other countries,
but who gave back, especially to England and America, even
more than he received. *Les Lettres persanes* (*The Persian Letters*, published in Cologne in 1721) call for a definition of a new
genre, a type of state-novel mixed with a travelogue in which two
foreign visitors criticize the political and religious corruption
of a country—a procedure repeated in Walpole's *Letter from
Xo Ho, a Chinese Philosopher in London, to his Friend Lien
Chi, at Peking* (1757), Goldsmith's *Citizen of the World* (1762)
and in Cadalso's *Cartas marruecas* (*Moroccan Letters*, 1793), in

which Chinamen and Moroccans rather than Persians serve
as critics of European nations. A distinct imitation of Montesquieu's work can also be seen in George Lyttleton's *Letters from
a Persian in England to his Friend in Ispahan* (1735). Previous
critics of social conditions had used other devices to escape
punishment by hostile censors: Erasmus in *The Praise of Folly*
had let Dame Folly speak in his stead; the early Swiss enlightener Jakob von Graviseth in his *Heutelia* (1658) had used an ana-
grammatic disguise in attacking the cities and the reactionary
strata of Helvetia; Le Sage in his *Gil Blas* and *Le Diable boîteux*
had excoriated Spain when in truth he meant France. Montesquieu's device of quoting the impressions of travelling "foreigners" now constituted a distinct improvement in technique.

His most important work and the one which helped to change
the political concepts of entire nations was his *Esprit des Lois*
(*The Spirit of Laws*, 1748). Most of the study of the significance
of this work falls into political history, but the student of literature can find that in addition to contributing to the political
ideals of America Montesquieu's treatise made a deep impression
on the writers of many other nations, too. For American readers
he gave such a splendid outline of the old English liberties that
the rebellious colonists used his chapters as a weapon against
the tyrannical perversions of George III. His book contained
some of the finest statements against slavery ever written, and
its emphatic reformulation of the absolute necessity of separat-
ing the three supreme powers of government— the legislative,
the executive, and the judiciary—has found an echo in most
modern constitutions of the free world. Among other enlighteners to take up the inspiring study of English government
mention should be made of Jean Louis de Lolme from Geneva,
author of *La constitution de l'Angleterre*, a work which was
rendered into English in 1775. The comparatist might also investigate how much Montesquieu's theory of the influence of the
climate upon the form of local governments impressed such a
man as Haller in Switzerland, who exemplified this theory in
his three state-novels; or he might investigate how radically
Montesquieu's concept of primitive man, borrowed from Hobbes'
Leviathan and illustrated in the famous Troglodyte-scene of his
Lettres persanes, ran counter to the beautiful theories of the
later Rousseauists. In a way it would be interesting and whimsical, too, to study just how far the French writings of two other

authors after Montesquieu's eulogy of northern climates and peoples, Mme. de Staël and Gobineau (the latter the author of a well-known *Essai sur l'inégalité des races humaines,* 1853) have contributed to the growth of the Germanic superiority complex.

Montesquieu's effect upon the political thought behind the American and the French Revolutions (Jefferson, Mirabeau, Burke), though pertaining mainly to Political Science, is of great interest to every student of human progress. His influence upon the Spain of such statesmen and authors as Jovellanos and philosophers and scientists as Feijóo (both of them enlighteners in the best sense of that word), like the influence of all other French enlighteners, was particularly pathetic in view of the futility of all Spanish hopes for freedom and progress. To Montesquieu's literary and political significance must be added his fame as a historian. His *Considérations sur la grandeur des Romains et de leur décadence (Considerations on the Causes of the Greatness and the Decline of the Romans,* 1734) was again the work of an enlightener, a keenly observing analyser, who, for the benefit of contemporary France, used the awful example of actual history in order to expostulate on the suicidal consequences of royal folly and national demoralisation.

Diderot

The name of Denis Diderot (1713-84) brings up not so much the international repercussions of his various works—though it would be interesting to investigate, for instance, the three great borderline-authors in Europe between Classicism and Pre-Romanticism, Diderot in France, Lessing in Germany, and Goldsmith in England, and to see just how much their work belongs to the camp of Neo-Classicism and how much announces the dawn of Romanticism. Rather, the name of Diderot evokes, above all, the project known as the *Encyclopédie* (1750-72), that most important vehicle of Enlightenment which, printed, sold and bought clandestinely, contained in its hundreds of pages brilliantly dangerous articles which spread the incisive messages of the enlighteners all over Europe, from Portugal to Russia, and as such became the greatest single literary cause for the outbreak of the French Revolution. Diderot, as editor in chief of the *Encyclopédie,* was both a leader and a symbol of the Enlightenment, and some of the diffusion of French ideas can be traced through the personality and the works of Diderot himself.

Herder, Schiller and the German expatriate Melchior Grimm were under his spell; Goethe in 1805 translated his *Le neveu de Rameau* (*The Nephew of Rameau*, 1762) ; rulers like Catherine of Russia consulted him; progressive thinkers like Quintana hoped that Spain might learn and profit from him; romanticists like Coleridge and Manzoni learned to accept or to reject him. The comparatist may wish to investigate particularly the relationship between the encyclopedists (Diderot, d'Alembert, d'Argental, Helvétius, Holbach, Voltaire, and others) and their sensualistic philosophy which derived from Locke or their deistic concept of religion which echoed Bolingbroke and Shaftesbury. Fréron and then especially Rousseau were among the first to rise up against the negativism of the encyclopedists; in Spain they were attacked in *La falsa filosofia* by Fernando de Ceballos, and in the first half of the nineteenth century it was then particularly Chateaubriand and La Mennais who replaced their cold cynicism by a new religious ardor.

Diderot's contributions to the bourgeois drama will be discussed under the heading of Pre-Romanticism; at this point, however, we must still say a word about his pioneering efforts in art-criticism and in blending the provinces of art and literature, such as evidenced in his *Salons* (1759-81—and published in Grimm's *Correspondance littéraire*), for in that he was a forerunner of Heinse (who mixed art and literature in *Ardinghello* and music and literature in *Hildegard von Hohenthal*) and, above all, of Heine's *Salons* in German literature.

Voltaire

Voltaire (1694-1778), one of the greatest Europeans and also one of the finest incarnations of French clarity of thought and cosmopolitanism in the best sense of the word, will always be an intriguing figure for any comparatist, not only because of the values he received from the Romans, the Greeks, or the Italians, but also because of the very great values he and his France gave to the rest of the world. One may object to certain aspects of his character, to the chilling and cold and very often destructive light of his rationalism, to the debunking tenor of so many of his writings (*La Pucelle d'Orléans*), or to his great attacks upon the organized Church (*Mahomet*)—and yet one will still have to hail him as the greatest European since Erasmus, the peer of kings, the man whose word could make or break an author. We

can also hail Voltaire as a great battler for the principle of religious tolerance (for instance in his efforts in 1762 on behalf
of Jean Calas—a tragic figure whose doom was dramatized by
C. F. Weisse and M. J. Chénier), as the last great defender of
the French neo-classical empire (*Le siècle de Louis le Grand*), the
champion of a lost cause who, with wit and elegance, but also
with bitterness and hatred, fought the false gods—Dante, Shakespeare, Milton—whom the foreign barbarians were trying to
substitute for the increasingly discredited incarnations of French
taste, Boileau and Racine.

Directly and indirectly, through his friends and disciples
abroad—Pope in England, Luzán in Spain, Gottsched in Germany, Bettinelli in Italy—Voltaire's influence was tremendous;
his exile in Holland and England, his visit to Frederick the
Great in Prussia (1750-53) and, above all, his last decades in
Switzerland, contributed to the spreading of his fame. As the
Patriarch of Ferney he succeeded in making that estate on Lake
Geneva as much the intellectual center of European Enlightenment as Mme. de Staël, a few decades later, succeeded in making her neighboring estate at Coppet the center of European
Romanticism. It is deeply ironical and tragic that the progressive ideals of the French enlighteners were listened to and heeded
everywhere, in Prussia, in Austria, in Russia, in England, in
America—but not at home, in France. France had to undergo
the horrors of a Revolution before some of Voltaire's ideals
could become reality.

The circle of Voltaire's foreign friends, foes and disciples—
epitomized by his very important *Lettres philosophiques ou lettres anglaises* of 1734 (of which we shall speak in the next
chapter) with regard to England, by the gamut of his relationship with Frederick the Great with regard to Germany, and
by his quarrel with Rousseau and his stay in Ferney with regard
to Switzerland—is so very wide that it includes the names of
most prominent authors or thinkers of Europe: Bolingbroke,
Pope, Chesterfield, Walpole, Fielding, Smollett in England;
Gottsched, Lessing, Wieland, Goethe in Germany; Bodmer, Haller, Rousseau in Switzerland; Bettinelli, Baretti, Rolli, Alfieri,
Monti in Italy; Iriarte, Jovellanos, Quintana in Spain; Franklin, Jefferson, Paine in America; Catherine the Great, Sumarokov in Russia. Especially well-known is the great enmity of
Lessing, who attacked him as the very symbol of neo-classical

petrification and soulless sophistry; of Baretti, who in the name of the greatness of Dante as well as of Shakespeare led the forces both in his native Italy and in England that rose up against the *diktat* of this self-appointed umpire of European taste; of Rousseau who, though more often than not defeated by the elegant blade of Voltaire and his henchmen, the encyclopedists, was gnarlingly resolved to keep at least his own native Geneva free of all the pernicious influences emanating from Voltaire's France. Other men thought differently: Wieland, for instance, often called the German Voltaire or, better, the German Ariosto, held him in great respect, though he was sorry that he could not quite love him—and Goethe, far from approving of the anti-French clamorings of his German contemporaries, even translated his *Mahomet*.

We have quoted Voltaire a dozen times in the past (especially in connection with the classical tragedy) and we shall keep on doing so, for he is and remains one of the great centrifugal as well as centripetal forces of eighteenth century Europe.

C. OTHER LITERATURES

During the peak of the Italian contributions to the Renaissance and the Spanish contributions to the Baroque other nations, too, had had a chance to be quite vocal in expressing ideals of their own: the German Reformation, the Elizabethan drama, the Golden Age of Holland, for instance. It is quite indicative of the thoroughness and the all-pervasiveness of the classical French hegemony over European literature that during the age of Louis XIV hardly a voice could be heard in Western Europe that would not indirectly reflect the viewpoints of France. For French influences were far from being a matter of literary problems only—there was an entire way of life that was evolved in Versailles and that was eagerly emulated everywhere in the so-called polite society of eighteenth-century Europe. Our paragraphs on other modern literatures are, therefore, going to be disappointingly short.

Classical Influences.

The study of European Classicism is essentially a study of the spread of French Classicism aided and abetted by the prestige of the Ancients. Since the models and theories of the Ancients had been affecting the development of modern literature for some two hundred years before Classicism triumphed, it is almost impossible to sift out of the literature of the Classical Period those influences which came directly from Antiquity and those which had become a part of the modern tradition. For this reason the importance of the influence of Antiquity upon the literature of this period is paradoxically not as great as it had been in the Renaissance and Baroque Periods. One might say about the Classical Period that the Ancients had now triumphed completely, and the literature of the period is a monument to that triumph. Although the comparatist will hardly be able to distinguish between the influence of, say, Euripides and Racine upon Addison, he may find it interesting to compare works of Antiquity and of the modern classical authors. He may wish to contrast, for instance, Sophocles and Metastasio, Virgil and Voltaire, Juvenal and Pope.

In epic poetry the great god still remained Virgil, as indicated, for instance, by the translation of Dryden (1697) and the emulation by Voltaire (*La Henriade*, 1723). But besides Virgil

Homer now at long last began to push to the fore, though the full appreciation of the Greek genius came only in the pre-romantic period. But Homer was at least increasingly talked about and quoted as one of the world's greatest; in the Quarrel between the Ancients and the Moderns, for instance, he was cited by the pro-Ancient Boileau, and in the second French phase of that quarrel he even became the real bone of contention, with Mme. Dacier, a conscientious hellenist, in her essay of 1714 (*Des causes de la corruption du goût*) outraged by the elegantly flippant Rococo version de la Motte Houdart had dared to make of her own version of the *Iliad* (1699). Nor was this reprehensible fashion of transforming the *Iliad* into a gallant novel and Achilles into a smooth eighteenth-century gentleman restricted to France alone: Alexander Pope's unfortunate translation of the *Iliad* (1715 ff.) did the same thing for England—though it must be added, too, that Thomas Hobbes, perhaps trained through his translation of Thucydides (1629), did a very much better job in his versions of the *Odyssey* and the *Iliad* (1672 ff.). It is entirely in keeping with the critical and inquisitive mood of this period that the first doubts with regard to the person of Homer and the poetic unity of his two epics were raised during the Age of Enlightenment, in the *Conjectures académiques* by d'Aubignac (1715).

GREEK studies began to make progress—one can see that, too, by the way the *Fables* of Aesop reached a poet, La Fontaine, who best incarnated, reproduced and spread over the rest of Europe the charming and simple didacticism connected with that literary genre, and also by the belated appreciation of Theophrastus in modern Europe. The latter contributed to the Classical Period a form of literature which is in some ways its most typical means of expression and which is its unique contribution to the genres developed in modern literature. Although Casaubon had introduced Theophrastus in 1592 with his great edition of this author's psychological character-sketches, it remained for Joseph Hall (*Characters of Virtues and Vices*, 1608) and John Earle in England and especially for La Bruyère in France (*Les Caractères ou les moeurs de ce siècle, avec un Discours sur Théophraste et une traduction des Caractères de Théophraste*, 1688) to exploit the genre in the modern vernacular. The kind of subtle insight into human character revealed by La Bruyère—both in his translation of Theophrastus and in his own satirical portraits appended thereto—contributed in turn to the psychological analysis found in classical drama and in the evolving psychological novel. This influence persisted well into the eighteenth century in the novel and the drama through such authors as Richardson, Gellert, and Nivelle de la Chaussée.

But it was especially in the field of the tragedy, with Racine, that Greek influences now at last began to prevail; in fact, one might say that this gradual changing over from Roman inspiration to Greek inspiration, from Senecan horror to Sophoclean restraint, is the one great criterion which separates Neo- or Pseudo-Classicism from Classicism proper. Racine, who had enjoyed an excellent hellenistic education among the Jansenists at Port Royal, was the first and only Frenchman to initiate that change with his *Andromaque* of 1667; he was followed—not really by Metastasio, whom the Italians loved to call the Italian Sophocles—but by Goethe and his *Iphigenie* more than a century later, in 1787. Racine's Greek restraint, which insisted that it was sufficient if "une tristesse majestueuse" pervaded the theatre and that the physical representation of horror and gore was utterly inartistic and added nothing to the catharsis, contributed most to the majestic dignity of the French classical tragedy. The simple example of the treatment of the despicable figure of Nero will show the tremendous abyss that separated the baroque mixture of Seneca and Neo-Classicism from the delicacy of Racine's real Classicism: Lohenstein, in his two tragedies *Epicharis* and *Agrippina,* could show Nero only as a monster, in *fortissimo* affectations of murder and incest, while Racine in his *Britannicus,* paying no attention whatsoever to the bestiality of Nero's later life, was interested alone in a fine psychological analysis of the one critical moment when young Nero pondered committing his first murder. Indeed, already Corneille, though less perfectly, had shown the same trend towards self-restraint and delicacy, for in his *Cinna* the Roman emperor, through a superhuman effort, had been able to forgive those who had conspired against him, while in *Epicharis* Lohenstein's Roman emperor, in an exactly identical situation, could only shriek for the blood and the torture of the conspirators. Rarely have such confrontations afforded the comparatist a more convincing chance to delineate the treatment of a classical theme in the hands of a German baroque and a French classical author. No

French successor of Racine could ever equal that fine Greek restraint and artistry, that real Classicism.

Rather than speak of Metastasio's revival of the lyricism of the Greek tragedies—and the *libretti* to his various Rococo operas are very musical and also very shallow indeed (*Didone abbandonata, Catone in Utica, Achille in Sciro, Attilio Regolo, La Clemenza di Tito, Semiramide*, etc.)—we should point to a certain Italian and German reaction against the false neo-classical pathos and tepid amorousness of the later French tragedies, and an attempt to return to the greater simplicity and severity of the Greek models. This can be seen especially in the famous *Merope* by Scipione Maffei (1713) which influenced poets from Pope, Voltaire and Alfieri up to Almeida Garrett in Portugal, Hartzenbusch in Spain and Matthew Arnold in England (1858) ; it can be seen, too, in Lessing's tragedy *Philotas* (1759), a Spartan and a most patriotic play in which there was not one word about women and love. In Spain, finally, Andrés, for all his neo-classical shortcomings, put Greek literature far above Latin literature—and a few years later Estala, in 1793, prefixed his translations of *Oedipus* and of *Plutus* with appreciative *Discursos sobre la tragedia y la comedia griegas.*

Lessing and Winckelmann deserve a special place in this outline of slowly growing Greek influences. In our pre-romantic chapter we shall see how Lessing tried to combine the greatness of Sophocles and of Shakespeare; here we must say a word about his famous *Laokoon* (1766—translated, among others, into English by DeQuincey, 1826), an important fragmentary essay which displays most accurately Lessing's profound knowledge and intuitive understanding of Greek literature and art. The essay— investigating why Laokoon, strangled by the deadly sea-serpents, only groans in Agesander's statue, but yells in Virgil's description in the *Aeneid*—served not only to delineate the different techniques of painter and sculptor on one hand and of the poet on the other (poetry being dynamic, hence capable of showing many climaxes, and sculpture being static, restricted to one moment, the most fertile moment, alone). It also described the Greeks as perfectly normal and modern beings, not callously stoic as Seneca had represented them, nor effeminately amorous as the French and Wieland had shown them to be. Lessing's constant praise of the superior poetic techniques of Homer and Sophocles is particularly worth remembering. Johann Joachim

Winckelmann, Germany's first great archeologist, a student especially of Greek sculpture, conceived of Greek art as representing "edle Einfalt und stille Grösse" (noble simplicity and quiet grandeur) and as such far superior to the turgidity of the Baroque and the frothy frills of the Rococo. Such sentiments, contained in his *Gedanken über die Nachahmung der griechischen Werke* (*Thoughts about the Imitation of Greek Works*, 1754) and *Geschichte der Kunst des Altertums* (*History of the Art of Antiquity*, 1764) did not fail to influence profoundly Lessing's, Goethe's and Schiller's later concept of the Greeks as essentially restrained, sublimated, Apollonian characters. This Classicism of Goethe and Schiller will be discussed in our next chapter, for in spite of its being rooted in Winckelmann and Lessing, it was permeated with a good deal of pre-romantic warmth, too. The importance of Winckelmann was also appreciated by foreigners: *La gloria de las artes* by Meléndez Valdés (1781) was influenced by him, and Walter Pater wrote an essay about him (1867). Among the French authors who preceded and at least in part influenced these German deliberations on the essence of art were Dubos (*Réflexions critiques sur la poésie et la peinture*, 1719) and Batteux (*Les Beaux Arts réduits à un seul principe*, 1746)—the latter translated into German in 1759 by Johann Adolf Schlegel, the father of the well-known critics of the Romantic Period, August Wilhelm and Friedrich Schlegel.

A new influence of Antiquity which appeared for the first time in the field of literary criticism was the influence of Longinus with his *On the Sublime*. Although this great critical treatise had been published in 1554 by Robortello, it did not receive any real attention until 1674, when Boileau translated it and when, in 1694, he added his *Réflexions sur Longin*. From this time down to the present day Longinus has continued to grow in stature until he now occupies a place next to Aristotle as one of the great critics of Antiquity. It is hardly possible to say that Longinus contributed anything materially new to the theories of modern Classicism, for these theories had been fully developed before he became generally known, but the classical critics, from Boileau to Pope and from Dryden to Voltaire, all borrowed from him whenever they wanted further justification for their essentially Aristotelian and Horatian critical theories.

This growing pre-occupation with Greece naturally did not mean that modern interest in ancient ROME subsided—for that interest remained alive from Saint-Evremond (*Réflexions sur les divers génies du peuple romain,* 1663) up through the historical investigations by Montesquieu and Gibbon. Among the translators of Horace's *De Arte poetica* mention might be made of Iriarte in Spain and of George Colman in England. Neoclassical comedy was particularly indebted to the Romans: Molière and Dryden treated the story of *Amphitryon;* Terence-influences and translations are evident in the works of Regnard in France, Colman in England, and Leandro de Moratín in Spain, and Diderot was noted for his *Réflexions sur Térence* of 1762. With regard to the philosophical poetry contained in *De rerum natura, L'Anti-Lucrèce* by the Cardinal de Polignac (1747) achieved a particularly great significance, for this scholastic refutation of Epicureanism went through many translations (Latin 1748, English 1757, and so on), though it did little to undermine the carefree atmosphere of the Rococo (just as the *Anti-Machiavel* by Frederick the Great did little to undermine Machiavellian statecraft). Lyrical poetry—insofar as it managed to subsist during the Classical Period— showed itself only in the verse satire and, later, in the pleasantly shallow effusions of the Rococo poets from Matthew Prior in England to Hagedorn in Germany, and from Jean-Baptiste Rousseau in France to Meléndez Valdés in Spain who all, somehow, echoed the feelings of Anacreon and Ovid and the tenets of Epicureanism. In the field of the verse satire, however, Juvenal, Martial and Persius were very significant models, showing once more the still substantial leadership of Roman over Greek literature during this age. More important than essays, translations and direct imitations (Buckingham's *Essay on Satire;* Dryden's translations of Juvenal and Persius and his *Essay on Satire* of 1692, and Pope's *Prologue to the Satires* and *Imitations of Horace* of 1733) were the many neo-classical satires written in the manner of Juvenal and others, starting with Boileau, leading to independent masterpieces like Dryden's *Absalom and Achitophel* (1681) and *The Hind and the Panther* (1687), Pope's *Dunciad,* Dr. Johnson's *London, a Poem in Imitation of Juvenal* (1738), Parini's *Il Giorno* and ending with Trumbull's *Progress of Dulness* (1772) and *McFingal* (1782) in America and with Lemercier's *Panhypocrisiade* (1819) in France.

A mere glance at the dramatic works of the classical authors will reveal the immense range of thematological topics treated over and over again, from Racine's *Bérénice* to Voltaire's *Mort de César*, from Gottsched's *Sterbender Cato* to Young's *Busiris*, from Metastasio's *Temistocle* to Alfieri's *Bruto*, from García de la Huerta's *Agamenon vengado* to Ignacio López de Ayala's *Numancia destruida*. We need not draw up a new list of these and similar classical topics, though it might be observed that minor authors were particularly frequent adaptors of these themes—thus Crébillon in France (*Atrée et Thyeste*, 1707, *Electre, Xerxes, Semiramis*), Thomson in England (*Sophonisbe*, 1730, *Agamemnon, Coriolanus*), Johann Elias Schlegel (*Die Trojanerinnen*, 1747) and C. F. Weisse (*Atreus*, 1766) in Germany. Particularly the theme of the rape of Lucrezia and of similarly tragic events seems to have enjoyed a great popularity during this period, from Shakespeare, Heywood and du Ryer up to the versions by Nicolas Fernández Moratín and Alfieri and the *Emilia Galotti* by Lessing.

Religious Influences

In order to avoid a good deal of overlapping in this thought-packed and transitional eighteenth century, we shall delay a brief discussion of Oriental influences till we come to the chapter on Pre-Romanticism; but a word about the manifold biblical and religious influences at work seems more than justified here.

Officially, to be sure, religion may have gone underground during this age of Diderot and Voltaire, disappearing with the end of the Baroque and re-emerging, with a loud trumpet-blow, with the publication of the first three cantos of Klopstock's *Messias* in 1748; unofficially, however, there were far more currents and cross-currents at work than merely those controlled by the classicists and the encyclopedists. Biblical topics all but disappeared in the field of the drama—though one can point to a few exceptions from du Ryer's *Esther* to Alfieri's *Saul* a hundred years later: Racine's *Esther* and *Athalie*, Houdart de la Motte's *Les Macchabées* and Voltaire's *Hérode et Mariamne* in France, Bettinelli's *Gionata* (*Jonathan*) in Italy, Wieland's *Der geprüfte Abraham* and Schönaich's *Mariamne* in Germany. Also notable is the very skillful use which Dryden made of biblical material in his *Absalom and Achitophel*. But gradually religion seemed to give way to rationalism and psychology and to inspire nothing but more or less ardent pleas for tolerance (Locke, Voltaire, Frederick the Great) or sarcastic attacks upon Christian miracles

(Hume). Especially the Baron Holbach among the encyclopedists was notorious for his attacks upon the very tenets of Christianity (*Le Christianisme dévoilé*, 1761; *Le Bon Sens, ou Idées naturelles opposées aux idées surnaturelles*, 1772), and Diderot, in *Le neveu de Rameau* and elsewhere, if possible even surpassed him in this tendency. Yet much of the exaltation of the Baroque managed to survive—leading sometimes to acts of stupid fanaticism (as the Revocation of the Edict of Nantes in 1685), but becoming, more often than not, subdued through the classical dogma and the emphasis on majestic dignity of style— as, for instance, in the impressive *Oraisons funèbres* of Bossuet which more than anything else show the perfect blending of Christian ardor and a classical cult of form. Just as baroque poets formerly had had to live side by side with godless late representatives of Renaissance sensualism, so now they had to live side by side with ever so many rationalists, courtiers and libertines after 1660; the Puritans' sullen withdrawal from the court of the Stuarts (Baxter, Prynne, Milton) makes that sufficiently clear.

Yet away from these courts the power of religion lived on. Although Boileau, in his *Art poétique*, might frown upon the use of biblical lore or "le merveilleux chrétien" in vernacular literature, classical authors from Racine's *Andromaque* to Goethe's *Iphigenie* were eagerly providing their pagan heroines with a thoroughly Christian ethos. In the Catholic camp we can point to the Jansenists, to the powerful figure of Pascal (*Pensées sur la religion et sur quelques autres sujets*, 1670) as well as to the submissiveness of poets from Racine to Manzoni to this creed. We can also point to the *Querelle du quiétisme* which started with Mme. Guyon (*Les torrents spirituels*, 1688), whose mysticism was inspired by Santa Teresa, and which involved Fénelon (to whom the New Englander William Ellery Channing, his biographer, felt particularly attracted) and Bossuet as protagonists before it ended with the defeat of the former (1695-98). On the Protestant side, reference can be made especially to the founding of Quakerism by George Fox (1647), whose representatives were to receive such praise in Voltaire's *Lettres philosophiques*. From William Penn through Thomas Paine and John Greenleaf Whittier up to our own days, Quakers have played an important role in the religious and social liberation of man; their place in literature is unanimously honorable and their stand against slavery especially frequently quoted.

But more important than this and similar movements (the *Herrenhuter* or Moravian Brethren, 1722 ff.; Methodism, 1739 ff.) was the development, as the eighteenth century opened, of a natural religion among certain intellectuals which went under the name of Deism and of which men like Toland (*Christianity Not Mysterious*, 1696), Shaftesbury and Bolingbroke were early representatives. Most enlighteners of the eighteenth century were deists of some sort, accepting the basic principles (but not the embellishing or highly metaphorical details) of the Bible. Among the most beautiful utterances of deistic faith—and superior to the somewhat prosaic reasonings in Paine's *Age of Reason* (1795)—are the words of Rousseau and Goethe, as the Savoyan vicar in *Emile* explained to his pupil and as Faust in the drama explained to Gretchen what they thought the real quintessence of religion was. Also Lessing belonged to this group of rationalizing but nonetheless convinced Christians. Though his publication of the more or less atheistic manuscript of his friend Reimarus (*Fragmente eines Ungenannten*, 1774) made him appear far more radical, Lessing gave many persuasive proofs of his unfailing deistic convictions—as, for instance, in his *Parabel* and his other anti-Goeze pamphlets, his *Nathan*, and in his *Erziehung des Menschengeschlechts* (*Education of the Human Race*, 1780).

In this connection mention should also be made of what was at least in its beginnings a quasi-religious organization: the founding of the Free-Masons in England (1717), from whence it spread rapidly into France (1725), America (1730) and Germany (1740). Among the poets to ascribe a potentially important role to such a secret society of idealistic leaders of men, we must mention, above all, Goethe, who in his *Wilhelm Meister* dreamed that they might bring about a true unity among nations.

An event of considerable significance also in literature, in a way another victory of the Enlightenment over the Baroque, was the banishing of the Jesuits in a number of European states: in 1764 they were suppressed in France, in 1767 in Naples; in 1773 they were indeed expelled even from Rome (though in 1814 the order was again restored to full efficacy). In the field of literature the Jesuits produced an amazing number of neo-classical critics, and their international influence can be seen, for instance, in the critical works of the many Jesuits (Andrés, Arteaga, Isla, Lampillas and others) that were expelled from Spain (1767) and that settled particularly in the north-central Italian provinces.

The Modern Literatures

During the hegemony of French Classicism, any expression of national traditions in neighboring countries was suppressed with an arrogance that was as stupendous as it was, in a way, admirable. Folk-literature in Spain, Germany, England was scorned and replaced by refined classical literature; exuberance gave way to restraint, originality to imitation, ardor to rationalism, homespun simplicity to courtly sophistication. Germany from Opitz to Gottsched, England from Waller through Pope to Dr. Johnson, Italy from Tassoni to Bettinelli, Spain throughout the eighteenth century were all under the spell of France; there is hardly any possibility of enumerating any "original" contributions of theirs which could not be traced back to France. Dante in Italy, Hans Sachs in Germany, Spenser in England, Lope in Spain: they all had to yield to the new order, to bow to the criticism and the obliteration decreed by the disciples of Boileau and Voltaire.

Most independent of all, relatively speaking, was ENGLAND —not English literature, which during this Silver Age was pretty well coordinated, but English philosophy. In this connection it must be emphasized again that, chronologically, English enlightening philosophers preceded the French enlighteners by at least a generation or two. English neo-classical and enlightening literature produced no great figureheads like Voltaire in France or Lessing in Germany (Pope, with his *Essay on Man*, could hardly qualify) ; the writers of England, if they were poets, turned to the ideals of Pre-Romanticism rather than to the sterility (from a poetical viewpoint) of Neo-Classicism. If they were philosophers, they fought their great battles in the second half of the seventeenth century, in the wake of the two great English Revolutions, rather than in the more quiescent eighteenth century. Hence the pioneering significance of Hobbes who in his *Leviathan* (1651) justified the uprising of the English people against a monarch who had failed to keep the social contract freely entered into for the purpose of mutual self-protection. In his *Treatise on Human Nature* as well as in his

Letters upon Liberty and Necessity (1654) Hobbes also spoke pessimistically of the nature of a rulerless people left to its dark instincts alone—sketching a picture of primitive society which was completely different from the beautiful dreams of the later Rousseauists. Hence also the importance of John Locke's two *Treatises of Government* of 1689 which were translated into French in 1691, and of his *Reasonableness of Christianity* which went through two French translations in 1696. Turning from political and religious to philosophical matters, Locke's *Essay in the Human Understanding* of 1690 denied the existence of *a priori* ideas (for instance, of Original Sin, a concept which had driven to despair the men and women of the baroque century) and, by wiping the slate clean and by calling sensual perception the sole basis of human experience, it provided the later encyclopedists around Diderot and Holbach with a philosophical basis for libertinism and atheism. To the fame of these philosophers we should add that of English scientists such as Newton—from Voltaire's repeated praise (in the *Lettres philosophiques ou anglaises*, the *Epître sur la philosophie de Newton* and the *Eléments de la philosophie de Newton* of 1738) and Algarotti's dainty *Il Neutonianismo per le donne* (*Newtonism For the Ladies*, 1737) to Goethe's refutation of Newton's theories in his *Farbenlehre* (*The Theory of Color*, 1810).

Compared with these influences (not to speak of Bolingbroke's impact upon Voltaire, nor of Hume's broken friendship with Rousseau, and reserving a discussion of Shaftesbury for our next chapter), individual influences of English literature in the narrower sense of that word pale into insignificance. Dryden's *MacFlecknoe* of 1682 was translated into German by Wernicke in Hamburg and adapted by Bodmer in Switzerland; Butler's *Hudibras* (1663-68) helped to inspire Trumbull's *McFingal* (1781) in Connecticut; together with Pope's *Dunciad*, *Hudibras* was again adapted by Bodmer for his own controversies. Pope's poems influenced Haller in Switzerland (*Vom Ursprung des Uebels*); in America they served as the chief inspiration of the Connecticut Wits (Trumbull's *Progress of Dulness*, 1772). In French Switzerland Silhouette published a translation of his *Essay on Man* (1736); it was followed by an *Examen sur l'Essai de M. Pope sur l'homme* by de Crousaz. Palissot emulated Pope in France in his *La Dunciade* of 1764 and Antonio Conti translated into Italian both his *Rape of the Lock*

(1739) and his *Epistle of Eloisa to Abelard* (1760). Among the Italian imitators of the *Rape of the Lock* mention should be made also of Pignotti, author of *La treccia donata* (*The Given Lock,* 1808). The writings of Pope were quite popular also in Spain: the *Dunciad* was imitated by Alberto Lista (*El imperio de la estupidez,* 1798), and *La derrota de los pedantes* (*The Defeat of the Pedants,* 1789) by Leandro de Moratín may well be compared with the English satire. Pope's *Essay on Man* influenced not only Meléndez Valdés, but also Juan Pablo Forner's *Discursos filosóficos sobre el hombre* (1787). To turn to English prose: Swift's frightful misanthropy in *Gulliver's Travels* (1727) was misunderstood and, as a children's classic, it became famous all over Europe. The English novels of Fielding, discreetly enlightening in their social criticism and healthily realistic if contrasted with the later tearful tales of Richardson or the chaotic technique of Sterne, became one of the strongest influences in the Germany of Wieland (*Agathon*) and Goethe (*Wilhelm Meister*)—though quite a few French novels of the type of Marivaux' *Marianne* (1731) and *Le paysan parvenu* (*The Upstart Peasant,* 1735) and of Prévost's *Manon Lescaut* (1731) had preceded them in indicating the same trend. In the field of the drama, finally, Addison's *Cato* of 1713 formed the basis for Gottsched's stilted tragedy by the same name.

GERMANY likewise produced very little in the literature from Morhof to Gottsched that was of significance. Her two important contributions to European literature were the philosophy of Leibniz and the literary criticism and the earnest religious Enlightenment of Gotthold Ephraim Lessing (1729-81). Yet even Lessing's works were not immediately echoed abroad; one had to wait until the first pre-romanticists appeared before Germany really began to contribute to the concert of European literature. We shall discuss Lessing again in connection with Shakespeare and the bourgeois drama, and also Wieland (whose *Oberon,* having gone through three French translations before 1800, was rendered into English by John Quincy Adams, at that time American minister to Berlin) will be mentioned again in connection with Shaftesbury. The fascinating personality of the Prussian King Frederick the Great inspired various foreign authors, from the mediocre Spanish dramatist Comella y Villamitjana (*Federico II en el campo de Torgau*) to the renowned Carlyle in England (*History of Frederick II of Prussia, Called Frederick the Great,* 1858 ff.).

Enough has been said about ITALIAN literature—Metastasio, Goldoni, Alfieri, Carlo Gozzi—to indicate its essential dependence upon French influences during the period under discussion. The success of wayfaring Italian comedians in Madrid, Paris, Vienna and Eastern Europe performing the plays of Goldoni and Alfieri helped to consolidate the cause of Classicism (though the tradition of the *commedia dell' arte* was still very potent among them, too). Metastasio is of great interest to the comparatist not only because of his blending of literature and music, but also because in 1730 he was called to the Imperial Court in Vienna where he functioned as *poeta cesareo* and an outstanding representative of Italian culture north of the Alps. A word might still be added about Giuseppe Parini, a style-conscious artist of great integrity and moral earnestness who in his famous satire *Il Giorno* (*The Day,* 1763 ff.) lashed out against the complete unworthiness, the luxury and the arrogance of young aristocrats. Like a mock-heroic epic, *Il Giorno* used the dignified Virgilian example in order to ridicule the vainglorious ignorance and immorality of contemporary aristocracy; though distinctly neo-classical in its entire concept, it also has an anti-French flavor which is natural with any patriot watching the growth of French fads and fashions invading his native land.

While neo-classical Spain did not produce any works that were influential from an international point of view, PORTUGAL should be mentioned on two accounts: Manuel de Melo, in 1646, wrote his *Fidalgo Aprendiz* which, in turn, influenced Molière's *Bourgeois Gentilhomme*; and in 1663 the Portuguese nun Mariana Alcoforado addressed her despairing love-letters to a French officer who had forsaken her—letters, preserved only in their French translation, which went through twenty editions before the end of the seventeenth century and which were translated into English from 1678 on. They became even more appreciated from the age of Pre-Romanticism on and in our own days they were rendered into German by Rainer Maria Rilke. It may be assumed that these *Portuguese Letters,* together with Petrarchism, were among the external factors contributing to the celebrated *Sonnets from the Portuguese* by Elizabeth Barrett Browning. The increasing attractiveness of the mild climate of

Portugal is demonstrated by the fact that Fielding spent his last days there (1754).

AMERICA, finally, was most deeply indebted to European Enlightenment, especially to the political and philosophical aspects of French thought. More significant than the harmlessly satirical and neo-classical tendencies of the Connecticut Wits was the fact that Benjamin Franklin and Thomas Jefferson, while in Paris, became imbued with the wealth and the dangerous fermentation of French political doctrines. What in French salons for years had been a mere game of wits, in America suddenly became a bloody reality—and after 1776 constructive ideals and democratic faith all of a sudden had to replace the merely destructive criticism and flippancy of ever so many French enlighteners. The immortal sentences in the American Declaration of Independence are in the fullest sense of the word the final and imperishably formulated result of all the political thinking that had been going on from Bodin in France to Hobbes in England and from Leibniz in Germany to Rousseau in Switzerland. Thomas Paine, in *The Crisis,* and even more in *The Rights of Man* (1792) and *The Age of Reason,* was completely steeped in the spirit of French Enlightenment, as were Madison's Constitution and Hamilton's *The Federalist.* More important among the intermediaries than visitors of the type of Talleyrand and Volney to encourage that French influence was the early Franco-American poet Philip Freneau. And most beautiful, perhaps, in its vision of a free community of all nations was Barlow's enthusiastic epic *The Vision of Columbus* (1787 ff.), which hailed America as the home of the free, the continent where the oppressed can find shelter, and which in its further implications clearly outlined what has since been achieved in the League of Nations and the United Nations.

IV. PRE-ROMANTICISM

A. GENERAL OBSERVATIONS

Although in most histories of literature it may not be customary to reserve a large special chapter for Pre-Romanticism, we do so for two good reasons: first, because the topic of the Romantic Revolt against Classicism is so very large that it can be more easily handled in two different chapters, one dealing with the eighteenth, the other with the early nineteenth century—and second, because such a double billing gives us a chance to give special credit to the two leading nations inspiring this Romanticism, England and Germany. England's role in combating the tenets of French Classicism was so very great that we might declare her to be the leader of Pre-Romanticism, while the Romantic Period proper coincided so much with the Golden Age of German culture, that we can declare Germany to be the chief inspirer of the early nineteenth century.

Against French skepticism bordering on atheism, against the elegant frivolity of the Rococo and the dull preaching of rules and imitation by Pope and Gottsched, there now arose a powerful Anglo-German reaction which clamored for nature instead of civilization, simplicity instead of artificiality, originality instead of imitation, religion instead of irony, passion instead of convention, lyricism instead of didacticism, literature of the heart instead of literature of the brain. The comparatist will watch with fascination the tide of the battle that was going full blast towards the middle of the century, the defeat of the classical outposts around Bettinelli in Italy, Luzán in Spain, Pope in England, Gottsched in Germany; the rallying of the Old Guard under Voltaire's leadership in France, and finally the defeat of those last French defenders of Boileau, too. Critics often say that Pre-Romanticism, the beginning of the battle against the standards of Versailles, started not really in England and in Germany, but in Scotland and Switzerland instead, for in tradition, mentality and literature these two mountainous lands with legendary heroes, rustic backgrounds and artless sincerity were indeed the very opposite of what the France of Louis XIV and Louis XV stood for.

The English movement of national reassertion, spearheaded by revivals of Shakespeare and Milton, produced figures like

Thomson, Young, Richardson, Percy; Switzerland followed with Haller, Bodmer and Rousseau; Germany under the leadership of Klopstock and Herder produced the revolutionary wave of the Storm and Stress; Celtic influences came in with Ossian; Scandinavian mythology experienced a so-called Nordic Renaissance. Italy joined the battle with Vico and Muratori, who honored again the great men of Italy's own past; with Baretti, who stood up against Voltaire's urbane arrogance; with Monti and Foscolo, who joined the Anglo-German camp. Even Spain, though completely under the thumb of France from 1700 to 1814, began to speak up again in defense of its own glorious but unclassical literature. Even before the time of Voltaire's death in 1778 there happened in literature what happened in political and military history at the time of Napoleon's retreat from Moscow thirty-five years later: all Europe rose up against France and all peoples flowed together from all directions in a united effort to shake off the yoke of French literary or political hegemony. From those two dates on the power of France was broken; she became later, at best, a peer among other European nations, but no longer the undisputed leader.

In their common fight against French Neo-Classicism, all nations of Western Europe had in common certain programs and convictions; but in going back to the poets of their own past, so cruelly discarded and scorned ever since the French had become the supreme umpires of literary taste, they produced different values and revered again different traditions which they lovingly put up in lieu of the shattered French idols. Yet whether they turned to Alpine utopias, to Shakespeare, Calderón, Dante, Tacitus' *Germania* or Iceland's *Edda*—these men all shared a certain concept of literature and a respect for national traditions which are called Pre-Romanticism and which opposed a rich variety of patterns to the dictatorial oneness of French-dominated Classicism. Striking differences in the preromantic camp itself can be noticed, too, if for instance we contrast the English churchyard poets with the representatives of the German movement: for whereas many English preromanticists were satisfied to indulge in gentle elegiac meditation, the German pre-romanticists, inhabitants of a country far less wisely ruled than England, became much more rebelliously aggressive in their fight against the French-inspired *Ancien Régime,* and produced a violently protesting literature against the political abuses of their time which was militantly called *Sturm und Drang* (Storm and Stress) and which in a way was the counterpart of the French Revolution—except that the German equivalent of that revolution was fought with pen and ink. Elsewhere, too, we can notice a distinct difference between the international orientation of the Italian pre-romanticists and the almost exclusively native preoccupation of the Spaniards with their own former *Siglo de Oro*.

B. THE CONTRIBUTIONS OF ENGLAND

The most characteristic development of the eighteenth century is the fact that, as the decades progressed, the intellectual leadership of Europe shifted from classical France to preromantic England. Already the enlighteners had had words of high praise for English governmental principles—but, being neo-classicists at heart, they had as yet abhorred the "barbarities" of English literature. With the growth of Pre-Romanticism, however, also the literature of England was increasingly hailed as a source of inspiration and encouragement in the continent's struggle against the yoke of France—and it is at times amusing to see how the same English authors were enthusiastically welcomed and imitated in romantic Germany and bitterly criticized and rejected in classical France. It should perhaps be emphasized, too, that English literature in its tremendous influence on European Pre-Romanticism did not so much give fundamentally new ideas to Italy, Spain, Switzerland or Germany—rather it merely encouraged these nations really to defy France, to be their own selves and to go back to their own national traditions.

England became the Mecca not only of the enlighteners, but also of the pre-romanticists: from France came Destouches, Prévost, Buffon, Montesquieu, Voltaire, Diderot, and Chénier; from Switzerland Muralt, Haller and Rousseau; from Germany Seume, Lichtenberg, the well-known critic of the English theatre, and diplomats like Borcke; from Holland van Effen; from Italy Rolli, Conti, Baretti, Foscolo; from Spain Leandro de Moratín and others. Foremost among the intermediaries and discoverers of England must be mentioned Beat Ludwig von Muralt with his *Lettres sur les Anglais et les Français* (*Letters on the English and the French*, 1697—published in 1725) and, above all, Voltaire with his *Lettres philosophiques ou Lettres anglaises* (1734—preceded in 1733 by a first English draft, *Letters Concerning the English Nation*), which constitute a book of importance in Comparative Literature second only to Mme. de Staël's *De l'Allemagne* eighty years later. Of considerable significance in this connection are also *Les Lettres d'un Français concernant le gouvernement, la politique et les moeurs des Anglais et des Français* (*Letters of a Frenchman concerning the Government, Politics and Customs of the English and the French*, 3 vols,

1745) by J. B. Leblanc. Foremost among the Italian intermediaries was Baretti, a man significant not only in Anglo-
Italian or Franco-Italian relations, but also in Hispano-Italian
literary problems, and who lived in England from 1751 to 1760
and again from 1766 to 1789. Equally noteworthy was Count
Calepio, the friend of Bodmer, who introduced the Swiss critic
into the beauties of Italian and English literature, particularly
of Dante and Milton. Foremost among the French translators
of English literature were Prévost (a visitor in England from
1727 till 1734 and second only to Voltaire in his Anglophily)
and Le Tourneur; among the Swiss, Bodmer and his friends such
as Waser, Tobler, Grynaeus, the translators of Pope, Milton,
Percy; in Germany, Johann Joachim Bode, the most prolific
translator of them all, who rendered Sterne, Fielding, Goldsmith and others into German. Among the great cities serving
as intermediaries of English influences, the student will want
to dwell on Amsterdam (van Effen), Zürich (Bodmer) and
Hamburg (Brockes).

Shakespeare

During the age of Neo-Classicism, William Shakespeare (1564-
1616) had been treated somewhat shabbily even in his own
native England: Dryden spoke for and against him in his
Essay on Dramatic Poesy (1668) and tried to improve upon him
in his *All for Love* (1678), a neo-classical adaptation of *Antony
and Cleopatra,* and in a similar fashion Davenant redid *The
Tempest* and Buckingham *Julius Caesar.* Thomas Rymer, in
his *Tragedies of the Last Age Considered* (1678), said about the
worst things against him any Englishman ever said, and also
Pope's and even Dr. Johnson's critical editions of his works of
1725 and 1765 respectively did not do him as much justice as he
deserved. That appreciation, in England, started only with
Addison's *Spectator* (1711 ff.), Dennis' *Essay on the Genius
and Writings of Shakespeare* (1712), with Lewis Theobald's
edition of his works (1734), Dodd's *Beauties of Shakespeare*
(1752) and with Young's fundamentally important *Conjectures
on Original Composition* (1759).

In Holland, Scandinavia and Germany, Shakespeare became
first known after 1600 through the wayfaring English Comedians; *Titus Andronicus, Hamlet (Der bestrafte Brudermord)* and
King Lear were especially popular. In his comedy *Peter*

Squentz (1663) Gryphius, without actually knowing of Shakespeare, borrowed the story of Pyramus and Thisbe which, no doubt, he had seen performed by English Comedians in the *Midsummer Night's Dream*. Christian Weise, again without knowing Shakespeare, produced a version of *The Taming of the Shrew* under the title of *Die Komödie von der bösen Katherina* (*Comedy of the Wicked Catherine*), while an anonymous version of 1672 even called it *Die Kunst über alle Künste, ein böses Weib gut zu machen* (*The Art Above all Arts, to Make an Evil Woman Good*). It was only in the eighteenth century that Shakespeare became known by name and that he was knowingly translated. Borcke's translation of *Julius Caesar* into Alexandrine metre (1741) was emphatically attacked by Gottsched, but it also inspired J. E. Schlegel to a first German critical essay about the great Englishman: *Vergleichung Shakespeares und Andreas Gryphs* (*A Comparison of Shakespeare and Gryphius*, 1741) in which the latter was praised for his emphasis on action (as Aristotle would have it), while the former, with his emphasis on great characters, passions and their clashes, was recognized as a genius over whom the rules of Aristotle apparently did not hold sway—an opinion which was later shared by Dr. Johnson, too. In 1757 *Romeo and Juliet* was translated into blank-verse and published in Basel, probably by Grynaeus; from 1762-66 followed Wieland's famous translation of twenty-two dramas mostly into prose—though the Rococo-Wieland naturally had a far greater predilection for the fairy-like comedies than for the darkly impassioned tragedies of Shakespeare. Also the tragedies of Christian Felix Weisse (*Eduard III*, 1758; *Richard III*, 1759; and *Romeo und Julie*, 1767) were distinct copies of Shakespeare, in spite of Weisse's occasional assertions to the contrary.

Especially famous is Lessing's eulogy of Shakespeare in his *Literaturbriefe* (1759 ff.) ; in Letter XVII he called his works far greater than anything the French (or, of course, Gottsched) had ever produced, and in his *Emilia Galotti* (1772) he wanted to amalgamate Shakespeare's gigantic characters with the somewhat freer Greek (rather than French) conception of Classicism of Sophocles. Gerstenberg continued this eulogy in his *Briefe über Merkwürdigkeiten der Literatur* (*Letters about Oddities in Literature*, also called *Schleswiger Literaturbriefe*, 1766 ff.) and, above all, in his *Ugolino* (1768), a tragedy allegedly combining

Shakespearian form with Dantesque thought. During the Storm and Stress Shakespeare was emulated by Klinger; Lenz discussed him in his *Anmerkungen übers Theater* (*Notes about the Theatre*, 1774); H. L. Wagner and Bürger translated his *Macbeth* (1779 and 1783, respectively) and Eschenburg must be noted for having produced the first complete translation of Shakespeare's dramas (1775-82). With Herder's celebrated essay on *Shakespeare* (1773) and Goethe's many works on him or inspired by him (*Götz von Berlichingen* 1773, *Rede zum Shakespeare Tag*, *Wilhelm Meisters theatralische Sendung*, up to his essay of 1813, *Shakespeare und kein Ende*), German Shakespearomania reached its peak. It continued with Schiller, whose *Räuber* (*Robbers*, 1781) reflects *King Lear* and who as an interesting experiment, as it were, even translated Shakespeare's baroque *Macbeth* into a classical German version (1801).

That wild enthusiasm for Shakespeare was, if possible, even increased by the German romanticists: by the supreme eulogies by the Schlegel brothers, the excellent A. W. Schlegel-Tieck translation of Shakespeare which made him a German classic (1797 ff.), and the efforts by Kleist and Grillparzer to emulate him. Also noteworthy are other translations by men like J. H. Voss and others, the many adaptations by Schreyvogel for the Burgtheater in Vienna (1840 ff.), and the expanding of Tieck's love for Shakespeare to the other Elizabethans, as evidenced in his two volumes of translations *Alt-Englisches Theater* (*Old English Theatre*, 1811). The Shakespeare idolatry continued into the Age of Realism when dramatists like Hebbel, Ludwig and Hauptmann studied, worshipped and imitated him and when poets like Bodenstedt, Herwegh and Heyse translated him. The *Deutsche Shakespeare Gesellschaft*, founded in 1865, to this day symbolizes the power Shakespeare holds over the Germans.

The name of Shakespeare had hardly ever been mentioned in seventeenth century France; it was only Voltaire who in his *Lettres philosophiques* began to speak of him with a certain condescension and to borrow from his *Julius Caesar* in his *Brutus* (1731) and *La Mort de César* (1736) and from his *Othello* in his *Zaïre* (1732). Later, however, when fame of Shakespeare in France increased by leaps and bounds thanks to men like Marivaux, Prévost and others, Voltaire in *Du théâtre anglais* (1761) and elsewhere became increasingly frantic and abusive in his condemnation of this "drunken savage" who, here and there, had written a few beautiful lines that were "like jewels hidden in a tremendous dung-hill"—and to his very death, on his last trip to Paris and in his last address to the French Academy, he did not cease abominating the English dramatist. Among the early popularizers of Shakespeare were La Place and Mercier; the former published *Le théâtre anglais* (1745 ff.), eight volumes of translations and analyses. Ducis even better than La Place or Mercier illustrates well the uncertainty of the average Frenchman when reading Shakespeare: his admiration for his great dramas, but also his shock upon seeing so many crude irregularities—and hence Ducis tried to gallicize Shakespeare, to render him more acceptable to the discriminating French taste, to transform his mighty clashes of passions into anemic French illustrations of what propriety and regularity on the stage should be (*Hamlet,* 1769; *Roméo et Juliette,* 1772; *Macbeth,* 1783; *Othello,* 1792). Very significant was the great translation of Shakespeare's dramas in twenty volumes which was finished under the direction of Le Tourneur (1776-82) and which was dedicated to Louis XVI and amended and published again by Guizot in 1821. The influence of the German Shakespeare-criticism, especially of the Schlegels, intensified the French admiration for the Englishman until by 1830 it reached a belated climax somewhat comparable to that in Germany. Rather than mention the praise of Chateaubriand, or Vigny's *Roméo et Juliette, Othello* (1829) and *Le Marchand de Venise* (1839), we should point to Victor Hugo, the greatest French admirer of Shakespeare, who emulated him in his own tragedies and extolled him in his famous preface to *Cromwell* (1827). Among French essays devoted to the great Englishman mention should be made especially of Stendhal's *Racine et Shakespeare* (1823) and of Hugo's *William Shakespeare* (1864). Also Hugo's son, François Victor Hugo, is noted for his well-known Shakespeare translation in fifteen volumes (1859 ff.).

Switzerland should be mentioned because Wieland's translation of twenty-two dramas (1762-66) and the first complete German translation of Shakespeare's dramas by J. J. Eschenburg (1775-82) were both published by Gessner in Zürich—and also the touchingly naive eulogies of Shakespeare by Ulrich Bräker, the Poor Man from Toggenburg, should be included here (*Etwas über William Shakespeares Schauspiele,* 1780). In his various tragedies glorifying republican freedom in medieval

Switzerland as well as in ancient Rome (*Wilhelm Tell*, 1775, *Karl von Burgund; Cato, Julius Caesar, Marcus Brutus, Cajus Gracchus*, and others), Bodmer imitated Shakespeare, especially his *Julius Caesar*, in a very inferior fashion; he is certainly far more important as an intermediary and a critic than as a dramatist.

With regard to the Italians, we should emphasize that both Antonio Conti (the first writer in his country to point to Shakespeare) and Vittorio Alfieri, though inspired by Shakespeare to write their own dramas of freedom (Conti's *Cesare*, 1726; *Giunio Bruto*, 1742; *Marco Bruto*, 1751; Alfieri's *Bruto*, 1798), remained essentially neo-classical in their adherence to rules and unities. We have already spoken of Baretti's emphatic defense of the great Italian masters and of Shakespeare against the aspersions of Frenchmen like Voltaire (*Discours sur Shakespeare et sur M. de Voltaire*, 1777) ; among the translators and adaptors in the Romantic Period we should name Giustina Michiel (*Othello, Macbeth, Coriolanus*, 1798), Cosenza (*Othello*, 1813), Benedetti (*Richard III*, 1819), della Valle (*Romeo and Juliet*, 1826) — and among the large-scale translators of the nineteenth century Michele Leoni (1819 ff.) and Giulio Carcano (1843 ff.). Other Italians to undergo his influence were Monti (*Aristodemo*, 1786), Pignotti (author of a poem about *Shakespeare* in 1799), and especially Manzoni in his historical tragedies (*Carmagnola*, 1820; *Adelchi*, 1822), and poets and critics from Foscolo, Leopardi and Gioberti up to Croce in our own days—not to mention the operas by Verdi (*Falstaff, Othello*).

In Spain, mention should be made of Ramón de la Cruz, whose translation of *Hamlet* was unfortunately based not upon Shakespeare, but upon Ducis' version. Far better was the version by Leandro Fernández de Moratín (1795) who had become acquainted with Shakespeare's works during his sojorn in England—though it must be admitted that his critical *Examen de Hamlet* of 1800 still betrayed many neo-classical prejudices. Rather than refer to partial translations of *Hamlet* by Blanco-White, we might mention the version of *Romeo and Juliet* by Dionisio Solis (1820), of *Othello* by Teodoro de la Calle, and of *Macbeth* by García de Villalta (1838). During the Romantic Age the influence not only of Calderón's *La vida es sueño* but also of Shakespeare's *Hamlet* and *Macbeth* can be seen in *El desengaño en un sueño* (1842) by the Duque de Rivas; later a play by Manuel Tamayo y Baus, *Un drama nuevo* (1867) was parti-

cularly noteworthy because it introduced Shakespeare as a leading dramatic character.

In America, finally, the fame of Shakespeare spread not only
in cities favorably inclined towards the theatre (Charleston,
Williamsburg, and, to a lesser extent, New York), but also
among the Puritans of Boston and the Quakers of Philadelphia.
During the eighteenth century he was still largely performed in
fashionable reworkings (Cibber's *Richard III,* Dryden's *Antony
and Cleopatra,* Garrick's *Romeo and Juliet* and *Taming of the
Shrew,* Shadwell's *Tempest* or Nahum Tate's *King Lear*) ; with
the dawn of Romanticism and the gradual spreading of play-
acting into the unruly Middle West, the original Shakespearian
versions, and among these his dramas of violence and virility
(*Richard III, Macbeth, Julius Caesar*), enjoyed an increasing
popularity.

Milton

Hardly less significant than Shakespeare in the growth of
eighteenth century Pre-Romanticism was John Milton (1608-
74)—again a poet who had not been appreciated by his contemporaries, whose *Paradise Lost* (1667) had been perverted into an
opera by Dryden (*The State of Innocence,* 1677) and whose
greatness was fully established only by Addison's *Spectator.*
Bodmer in Switzerland, impatient with the dull rationalism of
the Gottschedians and inspired by the breath-taking imagination and the religious ardor of Milton, finished a German translation of *Paradise Lost* in 1726. It went through five editions in Bodmer's life-time and in 1740-41 it formed the apple
of contention in the famous literary war between Leipzig and
Zürich, between the adherents of Gottsched who repeated Boileau's condemnations of the use of religious miracles by Tasso
and the adherents of Bodmer who restored phantasy and warmth
to their proper place in literature. In 1752, Bodmer's friend Simon Grynaeus translated *Paradise Regained* and later he also
rendered into German Dryden's adaptation from Milton (*Der
Stand der Unschuld und Fall des Menschen,* 1754).

Klopstock in Germany continued the movement begun by Bodmer, and his imitation of *Paradise Lost, Der Messias* of 1748, was
hailed as the most significant date in German literature of the
eighteenth century because it marked the beginning of Pre-Romanticism, the beginning of the end of the French-inspired

hegemony of rationalistic literature—though it must be added, too, that Klopstock's epic was far too rhapsodic and ethereal in its religious ardor to enjoy a long popularity. Among the later German translations of *Paradise Lost* we might mention the one by Zachariä in 1760. The geniuses of Pre-Romanticism derived inspiration from Milton's epic for two utterly different reasons: to the seekers of a golden age of innocence the picture of Adam and Eve in Paradise was particularly appealing, while the proudly defiant titans of the Storm and Stress who rebelled against the established order of 1770 were enflamed by the awe-inspiring courage and daring presumptuousness of Lucifer.

In France, it was again Voltaire who first discussed Milton in his *Essay on Epic Poetry* of 1727 (later published in French under the title of *Essai sur le poème épique,* 1733) and who flippantly parodied both *Jerusalem Delivered* and *Paradise Lost* in his *Pucelle d'Orléans* (1755). Dupré de Saint-Maur translated *Paradise Lost* into French in 1729. After him, Jesuit critics like Magny (*Dissertation critique sur le Paradis perdu,* 1729) and Routh (*Lettres critiques sur le Paradis perdu et reconquis de Milton,* 1731) expressed their dislike of the unorthodox and unclassical character of *Paradise Lost*; because of its more compact and classical form, *Paradise Regained* was far more acceptable to them. *Le Paradis terrestre* by Mme. du Boccage and other imitations by Roucher, Chénier, and others indicated a growing appreciation of the lyrical qualities of Milton, while Louis Racine in his running comparison of Dante and Milton contained in his *Discours sur le poème épique* extolled the latter as much as he disliked the former. The famous Mirabeau in his *Sur la Liberté de la presse, imité de l'anglais de Milton* (1788) on the eve of the French Revolution made use above all of Milton's prose-writings, transforming the Englishman's words about the freedom of press and the absolutism of the Stuarts into a warning against Louis XVI. Towards 1800 Milton's fame in France increased tremendously with Delille's fine verse translation of *Paradise Lost* in 1804, and especially with Mme. de Staël and Chateaubriand. The former eulogized his greatness in *De la Littérature* (1800) and the latter, the restorer of (Catholic) faith after the devastating drought brought into France by the sceptics around the *Encyclopédie,* crowned a life-time of Milton-devotion (such as evidenced in his *Essai sur la littérature anglaise* and his *Le génie du christianisme*) by his translation of *Paradise Lost* of 1836. Also La Mennais was strongly impressed by the great Puritan—not to speak of the epics of leading French romanticists (Vigny's *Eloa,* Hugo's *La fin de Satan,* Lamartine's *La chute d'un ange* and Soumet's *La divine épopée)* which were all indebted to Milton or to Dante or to both.

In Italy, reference should be made to the translation of *Paradise Lost* by Paolo Rolli (1735), an Italian refugee and language teacher in England; in Spain *La inocencia perdida* (*Lost Innocence*) by Félix José Reinoso (1799) may possibly have been influenced by Milton, while Timothy Dwight's epic *The Conquest of Canaan* (1785), depicting, *mutatis mutandis,* God's leadership of another Chosen People in their conquest of New England, likewise had a markedly Miltonic ring. The epic by Reinoso instigated a lengthy quarrel about the use of Christian marvels in vernacular literature—a quarrel which paralleled the Gottsched-Bodmer feud in German literature and in which also Quintana and Blanco-White were involved. Among the Milton-translations during the Romantic Age we should mention an Italian version of *Paradise Lost* by Papi in 1806, a Spanish version by Juan Escoiquiz in 1812, and a first Portuguese version in 1823.

Shaftesbury

One of the most significant contributors to eighteenth century thought was Anthony Ashley Cooper, the third Earl of Shaftesbury (1671-1713) who published, two years before his death in Naples, his *Characteristics of Men, Manners, Opinions, Times*—for he exerted an equally great influence upon the neoclassicists and upon the pre-romanticists, upon Voltaire, Diderot, Wieland and Schiller as well as upon Gessner and Herder. In opposition to the men of the baroque century weighed down by problems of sin and damnation, Shaftesbury, a disciple of Spinoza, proposed the belief in the essential goodness of man and the mercifulness of God; to the skeptical sensualists of the eighteenth century he opposed a fervent affirmation of religious faith and irrational ideas. Apart from these pre-romantic traits he might also be called the philosopher of the Rococo, for his was a smiling philosophy indeed, tender and human without, however, going to sensual extremes. His admiration for the Greeks and for their wholesome way of life marked an important step forward in the gradually evolving picture and supreme influence of Greece upon eighteenth century thought.

The pre-romanticists hailed him because he freed man from the unnaturalness of French etiquette and restraint and imbued him with a feeling of warmth and piety. Gessner in Switzerland in his *Idylle* emulated this aspect of Shaftesbury's religious tenderness as completely as Wieland, his greatest disciple in Germany, emulated Shaftesbury's mixture of Hellenism and Rococo. Hölty and Voss, two leading representatives of the Göttingen group of poets, were among the early translators of his philosophical essays (1776 ff.). Schiller, in his earnest philosophical quest for permanent values, accepted Kant's Prussian concept of the categorical imperative with regard to man's ethical behavior, but not without mellowing Kant's sternness by the much greater gentleness of Shaftesbury and by replacing Kant's imperative sense of duty by the Englishman's no less all-pervading sense of beauty—for it was through aesthetic considerations, in the name of beauty and harmony, that Shaftesbury hoped to achieve the same goal of man's ethical perfection. Three of the greatest works of the Golden Age of German Idealism—Schiller's *Briefe über die ästhetische Erziehung des Menschen* (*Letters Concerning the Aesthetic Education of Man*, 1793), Herder's *Briefe zur Beförderung der Humanität* (*Letters for the Advancement of Humanism*, 1793 ff.) and Goethe's celebrated apprenticeship-novel *Wilhelm Meister* (1795 and 1829) —are lasting monuments reflecting the greatness and the humaneness of Shaftesbury and of the teacher behind Shaftesbury, Spinoza.

In France, Shaftesbury's gentle and tolerant view of morality appealed to the enlighteners fully as much as to the pre-romantics: Montesquieu's *Lettres Persanes* reflected much of the spirit of Shaftesbury, while Diderot, as leader of the encyclopedists, in his *Principes de philosophie morale ou Essai sur le mérite et la vertu* (1745) helped to make the Shaftesburian philosophy permeate the point of view of many of his followers. Rousseau, on the other hand, took over the basic assumption of Shaftesbury—that man is innately good—and used it as a club with which to cudgel society, and hardened the Englishman's neo-Epicureanism into a new kind of Puritanistic morality.

Journals of Morals and Manners

Joseph ADDISON (1672-1719), along with his sometime collaborator Sir Richard Steele, occupies a central position both in English Neo-Classicism and Pre-Romanticism. While his *Cato* (1713) is the outstanding example of the English neo-classical drama, his *Spectator* of 1711 (preceded by Steele's *Tatler* of 1709) created a new literary genre and provided an international medium for the expression of a newly developing sensibility and for the improved understanding of those authors of the past who were to become so popular among the pre-romanticists. In the wake of Addison's innovation, moral periodicals achieved a tremendous importance not only as vehicles of Enlightenment, in which didactic writers could expound all sorts of literary, political, philosophical, moral, or aesthetic problems dear to the age of Voltaire, but also as vessels containing and propagating the new tenets of Pre-Romanticism, of bourgeois thrift and sentimentality. For the first time in two hundred years the great gap between the intelligentsia and the relatively uncultured population (a gap that had been widening ever since the humanists had begun to write in Latin and since the court poets had begun to use their own learned jargon instead of the plain people's language) was being closed, because these journals tried to appeal both to the high and the low among their potential readers. Morality and all problems pertaining thereto were now taken away from the Church; secularized, they became the subject of public and semi-literary discussions. The sentimental, democratic, and often superficial taste reflected in the pre-romantic movement in general results from the fact that its literature is for the first time appealing to a vast middle-class audience rather than to a select group of sophisticated and refined aristocrats. Two other eminent developments should be mentioned in connection with the increasing literary importance of these periodicals: again for the first time in generations they tried to appeal directly to the women, writing for them and their tastes, and perceiving in them a potentially important clientele —and second, they said what they had to say in a language that was fluent and rational. These periodicals thus were forerunners of modern journalism and as such they were definitely opposed to the baroque cumbersomeness of the preceding age.

Among all foreign imitators of these periodicals, we must emphasize especially the importance of Justus van Effen and must underscore again the great significance of Holland as an intermediary between England, France and Germany. Though a Hollander, van Effen's many journals were far more frequently published in French rather than in Dutch: *Le Misanthrope* (1711-12), *Le Journal littéraire* (1713 ff.—giving, in 1717, the first account of Shakespeare written in French), *La Bagatelle,* (1718 ff.), *Le Nouveau Spectateur français* (1723-27), *De Hollandsche Spectator* (1731-35). The same holds true of van Effen as a translator: he made French translations of Addison's *Spectator* (1720), Defoe's *Robinson Crusoe* (1720) and Swift's *Tale of a Tub* (1721). With a large Huguenot colony in her midst, Holland became a pioneer in spreading English influences through the French-speaking world: the first French translation of the *Spectator* appeared in Amsterdam (1714), as did the important seventeen volumes of the *Bibliothèque anglaise ou Histoire littéraire de la Grande-Bretagne* (1717-28), and the twenty-five volumes of another great pioneering collection, *La Bibliothèque britannique* (1733-47) appeared in The Hague. The influence of Holland on Frenchmen like Bayle and Voltaire, Englishmen like Shaftesbury and Fielding and Germans like Gellert should be especially noted.

Other countries were equally quick in accepting these new English trends. In Switzerland, Bodmer started editing his *Discourse der Maler* (*Discourses of the Painters*) in 1721—indicating by the very title that he did not differentiate greatly between painting and poetry until Lessing's *Laokoon* taught him better. In France, Marivaux published *L'indulgent philosophe* (1728) and *Le Spectateur français* in the Addisonian fashion, and in Italy Gaspare Gozzi's *Gazzetta veneta* (1760-61) and *Osservatore* (1761 ff.) were followed by *La frusta letteraria* (*The Literary Whip*, 1763-65) by the indefatigable Baretti. Also noteworthy is *Il Caffé*, a literary and moral journal of a Milanese society by the same name (1764 ff.). Spanish Addison imitations started with *El Pensador,* a journal edited by José de Clavijo y Fajardo (1762-67). In America, Benjamin Franklin—author, among many other things, of *The Busybody Papers* —confessed that in his convincing and forceful prose he was indebted to Addison rather than to his own American predecessors of the type of the Mathers or of Jonathan Edwards, and Washington Irving imitated him in his own *Salmagundi* papers (1807).

But it was in Germany, above all, where the English *Specta-*

tors, Ramblers, Tatlers, and *Observers* were most frequently imitated, producing some 800 different journals in the eighteenth century alone, though most of them were very shortlived indeed. Outstanding among them were *Die vernünftigen Tadlerinnen (The Reasonable Female Critics,* 1725) and *Der Biedermann (The Honest Man,* 1727) by Gottsched which lent themselves well to the defense of the increasingly contested Gottschedian viewpoints in literature; the German translation of *The Spectator,* undertaken by Mrs. Gottsched (1739-43), who seemed to be unaware of the mare's nest of pre-romantic ideas which were contained in these pages; the *Bremer Beiträge (The Bremen Contributions,* 1744-48) which started out on Gottsched's side but then dared to publish the first three cantos of Klopstock's *Messias; Der nordische Aufseher (The Nordic Spectator,* 1758-61), a very important periodical used by Gerstenberg and others to transmit Scandinavian influences into Germany; Herder's *Fliegende Blätter von deutscher Art und Kunst (Flying Leaves of German Manners and Art,* 1773), the mouthpiece of the Storm and Stress movement; Wieland's *Teutscher Merkur* (1773-95); Schiller's *Horen (Hours,* 1795-97) and, finally, the *Athenaeum* (1798-1800) by the Schlegel brothers, the short-lived mouthpiece of the early romanticists.

The contributions of Addison and Steele to this phenomenal European outburst of moral periodicals lay not merely in their creations of the new medium. Their *Spectator* essays on Shakespeare, Milton and the popular ballad helped directly to introduce these new literary influences into the stream of Pre-Romanticism—stimulating, for instance, Lessing's appreciation of Shakespeare, Bodmer's ardent defense of Milton and Herder's growing interest in folk-literature.

The Reawakening of Lyrical Poetry

James THOMSON's *Seasons* (1726-30) stand on the threshold of a new beginning of lyricism, when the cold pallor of Neo-Classicism was at last being replaced by a new warmth and exuberance, a love of nature and intense religious ardor. England's poets were at the head of that movement: Thomson introduced the vogue of descriptive nature poetry, Young added his predilection for night and solitude, Gray advanced the popularity of meditative churchyard poetry, Blake enriched literature through his powerful visionary language, Burns sang again of the little problems of the common man, as did George Crabbe, and Bishop Percy awakened a deeper understanding for the ballads and the folksongs of the past.

Thomson's influence upon *Die Alpen* (1729) by Haller in Switzerland is disputable, but he certainly influenced Barthold Heinrich Brockes in Hamburg who translated him and also imitated him in his *Irdisches Vergnügen in Gott* (*Earthly Delight in God*, 1721-48) ; Ewald von Kleist emulated him in his *Frühling* (*Spring*, 1749), the only finished part of his planned descriptive nature poem *Die Landlust* (*Rustic Delight*) ; and also the poets of the German Storm and Stress, the so-called *Göttinger Hainbund* (The Grotto League of Göttingen) were indebted to him, as was young Goethe. In France, Thomson preceded Rousseau's message of a return to nature; he was translated and emulated by Saint-Lambert (*Les Saisons*, 1769), Roucher (*Les Mois*, 1779) and André Chénier, the greatest poet of the French eighteenth century. Also Delille, the poet of the Empire, showed distinct traces of Thomson's influences, mingling them, as was perhaps unavoidable among those who preferred rustic peace to the turmoil of the world, with the *Beatus ille homo* theme of Horace and Virgil (*Les Jardins, L'Homme des champs ou Les Géorgiques françaises*, 1802). Other manifestations of the same basic beliefs can be found in the Italy of Bertòla (*Poesie campestri e marittime*, 1779) and of Pindemonte (*Poesie campestri*, 1785), as well as in the Spain of Meléndez Valdés (*La felicidad de la vida del campo*, 1779).

Very often descriptive nature poetry tended to blend with churchyard poetry and with a typically pre-romantic love for solitude and meditation such as found in GRAY'S celebrated *Elegy Written in a Country Churchyard* (1750). It was translated into Italian by Cesarotti in 1772; in France it went through no less than four different translations in the first twelve years of the nineteenth century. The very titles of some English poems are indicative of the new trend in literature; thus *The Pleasures of Imagination* by Mark Akenside (1744), *The Pleasures of Melancholy* by Thomas Warton, *The Meditations among the Tombs* by James Hervey, *The Grave* by Robert Blair, and so on. Perhaps the most important work of this type was Edward YOUNG'S *Night Thoughts* (1744). Le Tourneur rendered into French both Hervey's *Meditations* and Young's *Night Thoughts* (1769), and his French version then became the basis for the

Portuguese (1785) and the Spanish (1789) renderings of the *Night Thoughts*—the latter undertaken by Juan Escoiquiz. The *Night Thoughts* were translated into German by J. A. Ebert (1752), and they also inspired what is undoubtedly the greatest work of this type in German literature, *Die Hymnen an die Nacht* (*The Hymns to the Night*, 1797) by Novalis. Of a similarly pensive mood was Goldsmith's *Deserted Village* (1770) which in its atmosphere and different accent is often contrasted with Goethe's poem *Der Wanderer*. Continental poets and thinkers eagerly followed the new English trends: thus *Die frühen Gräber* (*The Early Graves*) by Klopstock, *Einsamkeiten* (*Solitudes*, 1760) by Cronegk, and *Die Vergnügungen der Melancholey* (*The Pleasures of Melancholy*, 1765) by Zachariä in Germany, and *Les Tombeaux* (*The Graves*) by Bridel in Switzerland (1779). In Spanish literature sepulchral moods are evident from *Las noches lúgubres* (*Dark Nights*, 1798) by Cadalso (inspired, as were Novalis' *Hymns*, by the death of a beloved woman) and *La noche y la soledad* by Meléndez Valdés up to Cienfuegos (*La escuela del sepulcro*) and Espronceda (*El estudiante de Salamanca*) —while in Italian literature reference should be made to *I cimiteri* by G. B. Giovio (1804) and *Alla melanconia* and *I cimiteri* by Ippolito Pindemonte (1806). In his *Sepolcri* (1807) Ugo Foscolo blended this type of pre-romantic poetry with proud allusions to Roman antiquities. In his eight volumes of translations, *Idée de la poésie anglaise* of 1749-71, the Abbé Yart (known especially for his translations of Milton's minor poems) tried to make a good deal of this and other English poetry accessible to French readers.

The folksongs and also the border-ballads, which had flourished at the very end of the Middle Ages and which, in their reflection of the genuine emotions of the people expressed in a simple and yet forceful language, had always been scorned by the French-inspired poets from the sixteenth century on, had for the first time been praised again in Addison's *Spectator*—and after him the rapid growth of the appreciation and cultivation of genuine folk-poetry was to become one of the great characteristics of romantic literature. Burns achieved considerable popularity in nineteenth century France, especially with Angellier; in Germany he might perhaps be compared to Matthias Claudius and in America, above all, to John Greenleaf Whittier, whose poetry (*Snow Bound*, 1866) reflects the same tender and homelike quality. It was, however, Bishop PERCY with his *Relics of Ancient English Poetry* (1765) who initiated a real wave of enthusiasm for late medieval lyrical poetry. The forgeries of the unhappy Chatterton (whom Vigny in his beautiful tragedy of 1853 represented as a tragically gifted genius broken by the lack of appreciation in a heartless world) were a consequence of the same enthusiasm which was evidenced also in Beattie's *The Minstrel* and Scott's *Border Minstrelsy* of 1802-1803. In Germany, this love of folksongs and ancient ballads produced many beautiful results: Bürger, commonly called the founder of German ballad-literature, emulated Percy in works of his own; he became particularly famous for his *Lenore* (1773), a ballad skillfully translated into English by Sir Walter Scott (1795) and forming the basis for Irving's *Spectre Bridegroom*.

Far greater than Bürger's or Bodmer's efforts to translate Percy and to collect ballads of their own was Herder, the author of *Die Stimmen der Völker in Liedern* (*The Voices of Peoples in Songs*, 1778), the greatest folklorist of the century, the philosophical leader of the *Sturm und Drang*, a fine intuitive critic and translator, enthusiastic, above all, about real folk-literature (*Urpoesie*) which he opposed to the shallow, artificial and salon-begotten literature of France. Inspired by Herder, also young Goethe set out to collect folksongs and to write folksongs (*Heideröslein*) and ballads of his own (*Der Erlkönig*). This reawakening of medieval culture and literature continued, of course, into and beyond the age of Romanticism: reference might be made to the beautiful medieval ballads of Uhland (*Des Sängers Fluch*), to the greatest folksong collection in the history of German literature, *Des Knaben Wunderhorn* (*The Cornucopia of the Youth*, 1806) by Achim von Arnim and Clemens Brentano —and, in a slightly different vein and genre, to the very significant collections made by the brothers Jakob and Wilhelm Grimm of old German fairytales (*Kinder- und Hausmärchen*, 1812) and of heroic sagas (*Deutsche Sagen und Heldengeschichten*, 1829). The Schlegel brothers should be hailed as the direct continuators of Herder's efforts on behalf of the simple and heartfelt folk-literature which Europe had enjoyed before the Neo-classical Period.

New Bourgeois Ideals in the Novel

Whereas the literature of Neo-Classicism had been essentially aristocratic, the literature and taste of the Pre-romantic Period were increasingly dominated by the up-and-coming bourgeoisie which made its influence felt again for the first time since the end of the Middle Ages. This can be seen particularly in the amazingly rich output of the English novelists, from Defoe to Fielding, Richardson and Smollett, all of them exponents of bourgeois mentality, of a new realism, and, at times, a new pre-romantic sentimentality.

Daniel DEFOE's *Robinson Crusoe* (1719) was more than a mere glorification of manual dexterity and Christian perser-verance; it indicated also the increasing disillusionment with European civilization and the wish to get away from it all, to return to a state of Puritan simplicity and wholesome living. Though Germany had produced a Robinsonade some fifty years before, with the *Continuatio* of Grimmelshausen's *Simplizissimus* (1670), the world was not ready for this message of a return to nature until Defoe's book appeared, which was immediately trans-lated into most European languages. Schnabel's *Insel Felsen-burg* (*Island Rock-Castle*, 1731) was the best among the more than fifty Robinsonades produced before 1770, combining adventure and exoticism with utopian dreams about a new Juda to grow from the twelve sons of the hero who, married to a strange medley of shipwrecked brides, established twelve tribal settlements on the island and who pervaded the atmosphere of the entire book with the bourgeois ideals of thrift, industriousness and piety. *Paul et Virginie* (1787) by Bernardin de Saint-Pierre was the outstanding French imitation of Defoe, a book of tearful sentimentality, contrasting the innocence of the island of Mauritius with the moral corruption of France in the best manner of Rousseau, and ending in utter tragedy. Best known among the later Robinsonades was *Der schweizerische Robinson* (*The Swiss Family Robinson*) by Johann Rudolf Wyss which was written in 1813, when the endlessness of the Napoleonic Wars made Europeans doubly anxious to exchange their strife-torn continent for some blissful island. Such novels, combining the traits of *Robinson Crusoe* with the romantic longing for a golden age of innocence, and with man's ever-present predilection for exotic landscapes and for utopian dreams, can be found throughout the nineteenth and twentieth centuries. Their frequent and close connection with state-novels is evident and natural.

The works of Samuel RICHARDSON (1689-1761), for a while the saint of his contemporaries, were eminently successful, in part because of the veil of tenderness and sentimentality which he spread over his minute and realistic descriptions of middle-class life and the problems of morality. These works were also important because they started the vogue of the epistolary genre, novels in form of letters which allowed the author to discard the calm objectivity customary for novels, and to transform every letter into a prose poem, an emotional outburst of the hard-pressed heroine. Richardson started this vogue with his *Pamela or Virtue Rewarded* (1740), which we might call a picaresque novel in reverse, because the lowly-born heroine rose high in society and became a gentlewoman through chastity and senti-mental steadfastness, rather than through immoral scheming. Rousseau in his *Julie ou la Nouvelle Héloïse* (1762), Goethe in *Die Leiden des jungen Werthers* (*The Sufferings of Werther,* 1774) and Foscolo in his *Ultime Lettere di Jacopo Ortis* (*The Last Letters of Jacopo Ortis,* 1802) all continued the fashion of the painstakingly psychoanalytical epistolary novel; it was a genre unusually well suited for the mood of Romanticism. Also Gellert in Germany should be noted as an admirer of Richardson whose novel he tried to emulate in his well-known *Das Leben der schwedischen Gräfin von G---* (*The Life of the Swedish Countess of G---,* 1748). An even greater success was Richard-son's tearful tale of the seduction and death of *Clarissa Harlowe* (1748) : it was imitated in Lessing's drama *Miss Sara Sampson* (1755) and hailed by Haller in Switzerland and Eschenburg in Germany. Least successful was Richardson's description of the priggish *Sir Charles Grandison* (1753) : Wieland's drama *Clementine von Porretta* was based upon it, but it was parodied, among others, by Musäus in his *Grandison der Zweite* (*Grandison the Second,* 1760). But even so, Richardson's influence upon the emotional emancipation and the excessive sentimentali-ty of his age was tremendous; European Wertherism would have been unthinkable without his contributions. In France we can point to Diderot's *Eloge de Richardson* (1761), and we must underline especially the role of the Abbé Prévost, the translator and popularizer of all three novels of Richardson (1742, 1751, 1755)—though Haller chided him for having falsified the ending of *Clarissa Harlowe*. Prévost's own works, to be sure (for instance his *Manon Lescaut* of 1731, contained in his *Mémoires d'un homme de qualité*) display a rather cold and detached analysis of the workings of human passions—but through him the techniques of Richardson and other English novelists nevertheless exerted a distinct influence upon the novelists of France. In 1786 Le Tourneur provided the first accurate French translation of *Clarissa Harlowe,* complete, with a tragic ending.

As to the other great English novelists: Henry FIELDING's greater and calmer realism in *Joseph Andrews* (1742) and *Tom Jones* (1749) constituted a welcome antidote to the excesses of Richardsonianism—and both Wieland after his stay with Bodmer, and Goethe after the writing of his *Werther,* were glad to revert to the far preferable technique of Fielding, the former in his *Agathon* (1766) and the latter in his *Wilhelm Meister* (1795). The same can be said of Tobias George SMOLLETT whose novels (*Roderick Random,* 1748; *Peregrine Pickle,* 1751; *Humphrey Clinker,* 1770), because of the rich Spanish heritage they received from Cervantes and from the picaresque tales, could be depended upon to be less lachrymose and more healthily realistic than the sentimental Pre-Romanticism of Richardson and his followers. Also Oliver GOLDSMITH contributed his share: though his *Vicar of Wakefield* (1766) was sentimental and as such was dearly beloved by Herder and actually experienced by Goethe in his own Sesenheim idyl (as described in his autobiography), he was a more consummate and objective artist and thus remained a favorite with Goethe (for instance in his *Hermann und Dorothea,* 1797) at a time when he had long ago overcome the absurdities of Wertherism and Richardsonianism. *The Vicar of Wakefield* was translated into German under the title of *Der Landpriester von Wakefield* (1767); in France the novel experienced a vogue especially around 1800 when it went through five translations in six years.

An English novelist of an entirely different flavor and influence was Lawrence STERNE, the author of the whimsical *Tristram Shandy* (1760 ff.) and of the *Sentimental Journey* (1768). Though Sterne was humorous, pleasantly ironical and eminently sane in his outlook on life and love, he nevertheless contributed—especially in his first work—a rambling style, an involved, arabesque, utterly incoherent manner of telling a story which still is the despair of all classically-minded readers and which, of course, appealed greatly to the romanticists and to their own meandering ways of epic presentation. Bode's German translation of *The Sentimental Journey* (*Die empfindsame Reise*, 1774) went through four editions in four years; Foscolo's Italian version (*Il viaggio sentimentale*) appeared in 1813. Wieland should be included among the greatest German admirers of Sterne; and in his gentle humor, his compassion for little people and little problems and his hopelessly involved style and miniature descriptions also Jean Paul, the author of *Schulmeisterlein Wuz* (1793) and of *Quintus Fixlein* (1796) was one of his outstanding disciples. Eichendorff's *Aus dem Leben eines Taugenichts* (*From the Life of a Good-for-Nothing*, 1826) and Wilhelm Raabe's *Chronik der Sperlingsgasse* (*Chronicle of Sparrow's Lane*, 1857) are likewise greatly indebted to the author of *Tristram Shandy*. In America, Longfellow's *Hyperion* (1838) might be said to represent a distant echo of the *Sentimental Journey*, though Paul Fleming's journey was far more sentimental than the gayly amorous adventures of the immortal Yorick.

In an entirely different atmosphere we should also mention the growth of the Gothic novel which began with Horace WALPOLE's *Castle of Otranto* (1765) and which, as *roman noir* or *Schauer-* and *Räuberroman,* became widely popular also in France and Germany, though it was constantly in danger of degenerating into mere trash. After Mrs. Ann Radcliffe's *Mysteries of Udolpho* (1794) and *The Italian, or Confessionals of Black Penitents* (both works immediately translated into French), this type of novel reached a peak especially in Matthew Gregory Lewis' *Ambrosio, or The Monk* (1795). Most of these novels brought the prestige of Italy and Spain, the lands of unspeakable villains and dastardly crimes, to a new and undeserved low. Lewis also wrote a Gothic drama, *The Castle Spectre,* which in 1801 was imitated by Quintana in *El Duque de Viseo.* Gothic elements prevailed in the English novel from Beckford's *Vathek* (1786) up to Mrs. Shelley's *Frankenstein* (1818) ; among the defenders of this genre may be named Sir Walter Scott (*Apology for Tales of Terror,* 1799). In Germany, reference must be made especially to Schiller's *Geisterseher* (*Ghost-Seer,* 1789), to *Rinaldo Rinaldini* (1798) by Christian August Vulpius, Goethe's brother-in-law, and, even more so, to the famous novels by E. T. A. Hoffmann (*Die Elixiere des Teufels,* 1815, *Nachtstücke,*

1817, and others), which, in turn, had a very profound influence on the sombre tales of Dostoevski. Zschokke in Switzerland published his *Abällino der grosse Bandit* both as a novel (1794) and as a drama (1795); it was imitated, among others, by Pixérécourt in France (*L'homme à trois visages*, 1801). Also the tragedies of the Storm and Stress (Gerstenberg's *Ugolino,* Schiller's *Räuber,* and others) and especially the later fate-tragedies (Werner, Grillparzer) loved to exploit the Gothic element of horror. In America, the Gothic novel may be said to have begun with Charles Brockden Brown's *Wieland* (1798) and to have led to the masterpieces of Edgar Allan Poe (*The Pit and the Pendulum, The Cask of Amontillado, Berenice, The Fall of the House of Usher,* and others). In modern times the Gothic novel has become quite influential upon the technique of the surrealists—as evidenced in Gracq's *Le château d'Argol.*

New Trends in the Drama

New bourgeois ideals came to the fore also in the field of the drama, especially in *George Barnwell, or The London Merchant* (1731) by George LILLO—a mediocre play which, in spite of such forerunners as the anonymous Elizabethan *Arden of Feversham* (1586), Gryphius' *Cardenio und Celinde* (1648) and the moralizing comedies of Sir Richard Steele (*e.g. The Tender Husband,* 1703), is often hailed as the first bourgeois drama. For the first time since Boileau it became clear that the neo-classical assignment of tragedy to emperors and princesses alone was wrong, and that the Aristotelian pity and fear could be aroused by domestic and bourgeois tragedies, too, as in the case of the crime and the punishment of George Barnwell, whose misdeeds Lillo found described in an old ballad—or in the case of a second play by him, *The Fatal Curiosity* (1736), in which an impoverished old couple unwittingly murdered a rich stranger who happened to be their own long lost son.

Diderot in France continued this trend with his *Le fils naturel* (*The Illegitimate Son,* 1757) and *Le père de famille* (*The Father of the Family,* 1758) in which the study of milieu formed a significant part; he was also influenced by Edward Moore's similarly conceived drama, *The Gamester* (1753), which he imitated in his own *Le Joueur* (1760). More important than Diderot's rather unsuccessful plays were his critical essays, *Entretiens sur le Fils Naturel* (1757) and *De la poésie dramatique* (1758), in

which he derived from English models an entirely new theory
of the drama. This theory, with its insistence that drama should
treat social and domestic problems, should create characters who
are types of a given society, and should imitate nature realistically, foreshadows the dramatic theories of Realism. Diderot
found an ardent proponent in Sedaine, who may be mentioned
especially for the bourgeois and didactic spirit of his *Le philosophe sans le savoir* (*The Philosopher without Knowing it*, 1765
—a play which was imitated in England in William O'Brien's
The Duel of 1772). Greatly contributing to the newly emerging
bourgeois drama was also the *comédie larmoyante*, or sentimental
comedy, usually accredited to Nivelle de la Chaussée as the
founder (*Le Préjugé à la mode*, 1735—translated into Spanish
by Luzán—and *L'Ecole des mères*, 1741) ; it was a new dramatic
genre which inspired *A Comparison between Laughing and Sentimental Comedy* by Oliver Goldsmith (1773). The trend towards a
new bourgeois realism was continued by Baculard d'Arnaud and
especially by Beaumarchais, whose *Eugénie* (1767) was imitated
in England in *The School for Rakes* by Elizabeth Griffith (1769).
In the field of theory we should point to the anti-classical preface
to Beaumarchais' *Eugénie* and then especially to Sébastien
Mercier's important *Du théâtre, ou Nouvel essai sur l'art dramatique* of 1773 (the latter translated into German by Heinrich
Wagner in 1776). A few years before, in 1769, Mercier also
wrote an adaptation of Lillo's play, *Jenneval, ou le Barnevelt
français*—to be followed by yet another *Barnevelt* by La Harpe
in 1778.

These French bourgeois dramas were introduced into Italy
through a translation by Elisabetta Caminer: *Composizioni
teatrali moderne* (1772)—and in Spain we can point to *El delin-
cuente honrado* by Jovellanos (1774) as a representative of this
new genre. But the impact of Lillo and Diderot was particularly great in the case of Germany. Lessing acknowledged his
great indebtedness to Diderot, asserting that while the Frenchman's own plays were indeed weak, his statements concerning a
new kind of drama had given his own dramatic taste an entirely
new direction. So taken with Diderot's theories was Lessing
that he translated his plays and his *Entretiens* in 1760. He also
started the new bourgeois genre in Germany with his first full-
length play, *Miss Sara Sampson* (1755), which is an amalgamation of the technique of Lillo and the basic plot of the tragic

death of a seduced maiden which he found in Richardson's
Clarissa Harlowe. The *comédie larmoyante* found its German
advocate in Gellert, whose plays like *Die Betschwester* (*The
Hypocrite*, 1745) echo Nivelle de la Chaussée. The Storm and
Stress authors of bourgeois dramas intensified their flaming
protests against social iniquities—for instance Klinger in *Das
leidende Weib* (*The Suffering Woman*, 1775), Lenz in *Die Sol-
daten* (*The Soldiers*, 1776), Wagner in *Die Kindermörderin*
(*The Infanticide*, 1776) and Schiller in *Kabale und Liebe* (*Intrigue and Love*, 1783). Theirs were among the first thesis-dramas
in European literature and they thus foreshadowed the distant
plays of Hebbel, Ibsen and Shaw. The most popular writer of
sentimental bourgeois dramas around 1800, as will be seen in the
next chapter, was August von Kotzebue.

As to Lillo's second play, *The Fatal Curiosity*, it was translated into German and formed the basis for many popular fate-
tragedies in which the irresponsible romanticists amidst an
abundance of Gothic paraphernalia were anxious to blame their
own evil doings on some supernatural power—such as *Der 24.
Februar* by Zacharias Werner (1810), with a plot quite similar
to Lillo's, or the even more absurd *Der 29. Februar* by Adolf
Müllner (1812). Even the great Grillparzer began in the Lillo-
Werner tradition with his *Die Ahnfrau* (*The Ancestress*, 1817),
a colorful play of haunted castles, gypsies, robbers and in-
cestuous passions, and it was only towards the end of Romanticism that August Graf von Platen with his sarcastic parody *Die
verhängnisvolle Gabel* (*The Fatal Fork*, 1826), written in the
manner of Aristophanes, began to put an end to this genre,
though traces of it can be seen as late as in Otto Ludwig's *Der
Erbförster* (*The Hereditary Forester*, 1850).

Young and Other Literary Critics

The new attitudes toward literature, the new tastes which
evolved during the eighteenth century, and the new concept of
the very nature and purpose of literature which became in effect
the foundation of romantic literature were all explored in literary criticism. While the literary criticism contained in the moral
periodicals, the discussions of the newly discovered virtues of
Shakespeare, Milton, and the popular ballads all foreshadow the
pre-romantic critical aesthetic, it was primarily Edward Young's
Conjectures on Original Composition (1759) which first promul-

gated the basic assumptions of this new aesthetic. Young insisted that there are really two kinds of writers: first, the original genius, who copies nature directly and who, therefore, establishes his own rules for the form of his creation; and second, the imitator, who copies the works of the original genius and who, therefore, derives rules of form from the works of others. This theory provided the means for demolishing the neo-classical principles which were still advocated by Dr. Johnson in England and Voltaire in France. Once this license was given to the individual author to allow his own genius to create without any restrictions whatsoever, the way was opened for an entirely new conception of what literature is, a conception that was ultimately formulated by such romantic critics as the Schlegel brothers and Coleridge. Young's essay, which reaffirmed several concepts already outlined in Addison's *Spectator,* might be regarded as the final and decisive salvo in the Quarrel between the Ancients and the Moderns (in spite of some later skirmishes in the French citadel of Neo-Classicism). Young was quickly translated into French and German and found supporters in Nicolai, who defended and supported his new ideas in the *Literaturbriefe;* in Lessing, who criticized Young but whose disagreement with the Englishman, whether Lessing knew it or not, was purely verbal; and especially in Herder, Hamann, and a little later in young Goethe. One might say that Young's theory of literature was one of the foundation stones for the German *Sturm und Drang,* for the young rebels of this movement all shared the conviction that they were original geniuses (*Kraftgenies*) whom no rules and no conventions could possibly bind.

Among other English critics who contributed to the critical principles both of the Storm and Stress and later Romanticism we should mention again Joseph Warton and his famous *Essay on the Writings and the Genius of Pope* (1757 ff.), for by redefining the quintessence of poetry and by refusing Alexander Pope the title of being a poet, he dealt a hard blow at neo-classical verse-making all over Europe. Joseph's younger brother, Thomas Warton, is noteworthy above all because of the loving care with which he, in his *History of English Poetry* (1774 ff.), restored older literature (Chaucer, Spenser, etc.) to the place of which it had been unjustly deprived by the neo-classical school— a tendency fully emulated in their own native literature by Bodmer in Switzerland, Herder in Germany and Gozzi in Italy.

Henry Home's *Elements of Literary Criticism* (1762) for the first time approached the problems of criticism from the point of view of the subjective effect of a piece of literature upon the reader, rather than from the point of view of the characteristics of the piece of literature inherent within its own objective identity. Home not only contributed to Herder, but provided the basic point of view of literary criticism which can be found in most romantic criticism and which reaches its extreme statement in the theories of E. A. Poe and later in the attempts of I. A. Richards to reduce literary criticism to the analysis of the psychological effect of poetry upon the bio-chemical organism of the reader. Any discussion of the growth of critical concepts should also include the names of Alexander Baumgarten in Germany, commonly hailed as the founder of aesthetics (*Aesthetica*, 1750 ff.), Edmund Burke in England (*Philosophical Inquiry into the Origin of Our Ideas on the Sublime and Beautiful*, 1756—an essay greatly praised by Lessing), and the *Investigaciones filosóficas sobre la bellezza ideal* (1789) by yet another expelled Spanish Jesuit, Esteban Arteaga.

In Germany, the Storm and Stress was prepared for in literary criticism and the new ideas were proclaimed to the world in critical manifestoes, ever since Bodmer, in his *Kritische Abhandlung über das Wunderbare in der Poesie* (*Critical Essay about the Miraculous in Poetry*, 1740) and other treatises written in defense of Milton, had restored the importance of phantasy and vivid imagination in a literature hitherto dulled by French rationalism. In his *Briefe die neueste Literatur betreffend* (*Letters Concerning the most Recent Literature*, usually referred to as *Literaturbriefe*, 1759 ff.), which Lessing published with the collaboration of his two friends Nicolai and Mendelssohn, are found some of the most important critical statements of the newly evolving aesthetic which tried to bridge the abyss that separated Shakespeare from Aristotle. We have seen in our previous chapter that Lessing's *Laokoon* (1766), the most important critical essay of the period, does not express so much a pre-romantic point of view as it does anticipate the *Klassik* of Goethe and Schiller and the critical theories of modern Symbolism. In the period extending from Gerstenberg's *Briefe über Merkwürdigkeiten der Literatur* (*Letters Concerning Oddities in Literature*, 1766 ff.) to Schiller's *Ueber naive und sentimentalische Dichtung* (*Concerning Naive and Sentimental Poetry*, 1795) and beyond, no man was more important for the emancipation of the poets' creative genius from the stifling yoke of neo-classical imitativeness than Johann Gottfried Herder. In such critical works of his as *Fragmente über die neuere deutsche Literatur (Fragments about more Recent German Literature,* 1766), *Kritische Wälder (Critical Improvisations,* 1769) as well as in his essays on *Ossian* and on *Shakespeare* (1773), this undisputed critical and philosophical leader of the German Storm and Stress conceived of a poet as a sacred harbinger of great truths, an original genius inspired by God alone, living in closest contact with the soil of his nation and the soul of his people. Herder, more than any other single individual, was responsible for the development of the historical approach in literary criticism.

C. OTHER LITERATURES
Classical Influences

With the decline of the Neo-Classicism of France it was to
be expected that the Roman influences behind France would likewise decline and that the star of GREECE would be rising to a
far greater eminence than Boileau's and Pope's pre-occupation
with Homer or even Racine's admiration for Euripides and Lessing's admiration for Sophocles would indicate. To the pre-
romanticists eulogizing original geniuses who had dared to defy
the Roman-French rules, the Greeks now appeared as original
creators, too, who had shaped their own literary standards and
who thus were far superior to the polished imitativeness of the
Romans. For the first time now the values were reversed as
they should have been reversed ever since the time of Scaliger,
and Homer deservedly took his place above Virgil, Pindar above
Horace, Sophocles above Seneca.

Though the new phase of Hellenistic studies may be said to
have begun in England, with Thomas Blackwell's *Enquiry into
the Life and Writings of Homer* (1735), Robert Wood's *Essay
on the Original Genius and Writings of Homer* (1775) and William Cowper's verse-translation of the *Iliad* and the *Odyssey*
(1791), it was nonetheless the Germany of Lessing, Winckelmann and Goethe which contributed most to this new and profound appreciation of Greek values. Wieland, to be sure, had
spoken of the Greeks with great admiration—yet he had conceived of them as such urbane, sensual and graceful Rococo
characters (*Musarion, Agathon*) that Goethe later rebuked that
interpretation in his satire *Götter, Helden und Wieland* (*Gods,
Heroes and Wieland*, 1774). Lessing was a careful student of
Aristotle whose *Poetics* he interpreted far more elastically than
the French had ever done—and though in his tragedy *Philotas*
(1759) he represented the Greeks as rather Spartan characters,
he mellowed and humanized that impression considerably in his
Laokoon (1766), the work that indicates best his profound
knowledge of Greece and his great love especially for Homer
and Sophocles. Herder's friend and teacher Hamann should
be noted for his aphoristic *Sokratische Denkwürdigkeiten* (*So-
cratic Memorabilia*, 1759) and for Herder himself Greek culture
was one of the primary sources of human thought. Klopstock,
the great reviver of German lyrical poetry after the drought of

the French neo-classical period, and the great experimenter in all types of versification with which he aimed to break the monopoly of the French Alexandrine meter, was especially enamoured of the Pindaric odes, the construction of which he did not quite grasp; Goethe later followed him in imitating Pindar. During his youth Goethe hailed the concept of original Greek geniuses to such an extent that he represented the Greeks as titanic, superhuman and defiant characters, as in his *Prometheus,* or, as in *Götter, Helden und Wieland,* as boisterous and tough Herculeans; later in his life, however, he followed Winckelmann's dictum of "noble simplicity and quiet grandeur." In their love of ancient myths and lyrical dramas the Stolberg brothers translated Aeschylus and Sophocles as well as Homer. Voss, another member of the Göttingen Poets, is famous for having produced the very best translation of the *Odyssee* (1781) and the *Ilias* (1793) in the German language. Distinctly Homeric influences can also be seen in the growing popularity of the idyllic epic, of which Voss' *Luise* of 1783 (a forerunner of Goethe's *Hermann und Dorothea*) is an early example. No discussion of Greek influences in the German eighteenth century would be complete without at least a reference to the important investigation of the origin of the Homeric epics contained in Friedrich August Wolf's *Prolegomena ad Homerum* (1795). This interest in ancient Greece—and, concurrently with it, Europe's interest in the modern Greek struggle of independence against the Turks, commonly called Philhellenism—reached its peak particularly in the Romantic Period.

But a few years before the climax of Romanticism, Europe witnessed a last flaring up of Classicism, of Greek-inspired Classicism rather than French-inspired Classicism though. Foscolo in Italy and Chénier in France—both born in the Near East and of Greek mothers—were pioneers in this re-emergence of Greek classical ideals which were to be blended with modern problems; they were followed by the Italian Monti, the Englishmen Keats and Landor, and, above all, by Goethe and Schiller in Germany. For German Classicism appeared only now, from 1785 till 1805; what had existed before, under Gottsched, had merely been Neo-Classicism. We mention Goethe's and Schiller's Classicism in this chapter on Pre-Romanticism, rather than under the heading of Greek and Roman influences upon Classicism proper, because the impetuosity of their own Storm and

Stress youth had permeated these two men with a passionate
ardor and an exultant warmth which distinguished their classical works after 1785 most noticeably from whatever other
classcial works Voltaire, Pope or Gottsched may have written.
Taking advantage of the far more humanized interpretation of
Greece such as furnished by Lessing, Winckelmann and the pre-
romanticists, Goethe, after his immensely important trip to
Italy (1786-88), now blended Greek myths with modern Christianity (*Iphigenie in Tauris*, 1787) and in his Homer-inspired
epics he combined the stately Greek gait with medieval (*Reineke
Fuchs*, 1793) or with modern German (*Hermann und Dorothea*,
1797) stories. The so-called Helena-act in the second part of his
Faust was but another effort of Goethe's to create a perfect synthesis between Greece and Germany, between pagan Antiquity
and modern Christianity—and ballads like *Die Braut von Korinth*
(*The Bride of Corinth*, 1797) indicate clearly that in the last
analysis he preferred the former to the latter. So also Schiller:
he, too, in his poem *Die Götter Griechenlands* (*The Gods of
Greece*) extolled the Greek way of life; through his translations
of Euripides (*Iphigenie in Aulis*) he trained himself in a con-
cise classical style; in *Die Braut von Messina* (*The Bride of
Messina*, 1803) he emulated Sophocles' *Oedipus*, and in his other
classical dramas he tried to strike a happy balance between
Greek classicism of form and modern romanticism of thought
(*Wilhelm Tell*, 1804). Both Goethe and Schiller thus conceived
of the Greeks as classically restrained artists capable of sub-
limating their sorrows into products of finest art—an interpretation which differed not only from that of Wieland or of young
Goethe, but also from that of the later romanticists.

Far less can be said of ROMAN influences, which were not
considerable during the Pre-romantic Age. In France, we can
point to Delille, who combined his love for Thomson's descriptive
nature poetry with the lyrical poems of Virgil, creating, in his
Géorgiques françaises (1769), an atmosphere that was Rococo
and pre-romantic at the same time. Virgil's poems were also
translated in England, *e.g.* the *Eclogues* and *Georgics* by Joseph
Warton. In Germany, Goethe emulated Ovid and Horace in his
own *Römische Elegien* (*Roman Elegies*, 1795); he applied that
strictest form of classical versification in order to speak guarded-
ly of the freest topic he was ever to discuss: his passionate
love-life with Christiane Vulpius. Elsewhere the word "elegy"

was to obtain the modern connotation of melancholy pensiveness which it did not have in Rome and with Goethe: thus Gray's *Elegy Written in a Country Churchyard*, and the elegiac tenderness of so many pre-romanticists of the type of Blair or Ewald von Kleist. Significant is the notorious translation of Petronius by Heinse (*Die Begebenheiten des Enkolp*): it reveals a trend towards utter amorality which is not entirely unexpected in this first great German admirer of the unbridledness of the Italian Renaissance. A milestone in man's investigation of the Roman past was reached with the publication of Edward Gibbon's *Decline and Fall of the Roman Empire* (1776 ff.); among its foreign translations was the Spanish version by José Mor de Fuentes.

Biblical and Oriental Influences

After the skepticism and rationalism of the Enlightenment, Anglo-German Pre-Romanticism was marked by renewed manifestations of CHRISTIAN fervor and, to some extent at least, by a return to the religious ardor which had been so characteristic of the Baroque Age. The religious indifference which had spread from the England of Locke to the Germany of Reimarus and the France of Diderot had failed to take root especially in England, where the frivolous crowd at the court and in the literature of the last Stuarts was soon replaced by what in the eighteenth century might best be called the atmosphere of the English country parson. Klopstock, with the publication of the first three cantos of his *Der Messias* in 1748, likewise heralded a new era of religious exaltation which recaptured much of the spirit that had animated Gryphius. The influence of Jakob Böhme's mysticism remained potent not only in Germany, but also in England (Milton, Blake), and the spreading of Methodism and Quakerism in England, of Pietism in Germany and of Quietism in France kept religious ardor burning through the very age of Voltaire. The same religious warmth manifested itself also in the literature of Switzerland; it extended from the profoundly religious attitude in Haller to the stern Calvinism that permeated so many of Rousseau's writings, and from Bodmer's treatment of religious topics (*Noah*, 1750) and Gessner's famous idyls (*Der Tod Abels*, 1758) to Lavater's *Hundert christliche Lieder* (*One Hundred Christian Songs*, 1776).

More important even than the rising fame of Milton's great Christian epic throughout the eighteenth century, or the impact of these religious currents upon the genius of Goethe (*Die Höllenfahrt Christi, Ganymed* and *Die Bekenntnisse einer schönen Seele* contained in *Wilhelm Meister*) is the commanding figure of Emanuel Swedenborg, the influential scientist, theologian and mystic of eighteenth century Sweden whose works (*De cultu et amore Dei,* 1745; *Arcana coelestia,* 1749 ff. and others) had the effect of a real revelation upon the rest of Europe and upon America. His influence was particularly great on Blake and Coleridge in England, on Lavater in Switzerland, Goethe in Germany, Emerson in America; a society of Swedenborgians (The New Church Signified by the New Jerusalem in the Revelation) was established in England as early as 1788; another in America in 1817.

This new religious warmth, indicated in Rousseau's *Profession de foi du vicaire savoyard* (*The Profession of Faith of the Savoyan Vicar*) in *Emile* and coming to the fore, in France, especially with Chateaubriand, permeated likewise the finest works of the Golden Age of German Idealism. Already Hamann, the teacher of Herder, called religion the one true basis and inspirer of all great literature; in his *Briefe zur Beförderung der Humanität* (*Letters to Advance the Cause of Humanism,* 1793 ff.), Herder himself envisaged a future ennobled by such lofty principles of religious and racial tolerance as to make these letters one of the finest expressions of German Idealism. The same warm humanitarianism can be found in Lessing and Goethe: the latter, in his *Iphigenie* (1787), created a "barbarian" king, Thoas, who was fully as noble and generous as the christianized Greek heroine of the drama, while the former, the great friend of Moses Mendelssohn, in his *Nathan der Weise* (*Nathan the Wise,* 1779), created the admirable figure of a Jew whose integrity and greatness of character were far superior to the bigotry of certain Christians. Essays such as Lessing's *Die Erziehung des Menschengeschlechts* (*The Education of the Human Race,* 1780) and Herder's *Die älteste Urkunde des Menschengeschlechts* (*The Oldest Document of the Human Race,* 1774) and *Vom Geiste der ebräischen Poesie* (*Of the Spirit of Hebrew Poetry,* 1782) indicate the same broadness of outlook, both with regard to the great cultural contributions of the Jewish people and with regard to the symbolical and literary (rather than narrowly dogmatical) interpretation of the Bible.

During the eighteenth century also the knowledge of, and the influences from, the MAHOMETAN and more distant oriental countries increased considerably. The relatively naive rationalism of many of the enlighteners had made them assume too readily that people living in distant lands must be more reasonable in their way of life than Europeans, and that religions other than Christianity must produce a greater tolerance. Hence the invention of critical travellers from Persia (Montesquieu), China (Goldsmith) or Abyssinia (Dr. Johnson), the meaningful oriental dramas and tales by Voltaire (*Mahomet, Zadig*) and the fundamentally anti-Christian tenor of his investigation of oriental cultures in his *Essai sur les moeurs* (*Essay on Manners,* 1756) ; hence also the admiration of Sultan Saladin as a truly "enlightened" monarch and the favorable picture drawn of him in Lessing's oriental drama *Nathan der Weise*. One of the earliest biographies of Mahomet was written by Boulainvilliers in France (*La vie de Mahomet*, 1730) ; and in his Italian exile the Jesuit Andrés was one of the first to point to the vast indebtedness of Spanish culture to the Arabs (*Cartas sobre la música de los árabes,* 1787). The pre-romanticists, on the other hand, with their aversion to the immorality of sophisticated civilization, looked nostalgically, but not very closely, at the less sophisticated and more natural cultures of the East. Although this interest is perhaps even more apparent in the writings of the enlighteners (Marmontel's *Contes moraux* in France, Haller's *Usong* in Switzerland, Wieland's *Der goldene Spiegel* in Germany) than in those of the pre-romantics, it is so closely allied to the enthusiasm for the older primitive cultures of Europe that it is essentially a pre-romantic tendency (Collin's *Persian Eclogues*, 1742 ; Herder's mostly oriental *Lieder der Liebe*, 1778). Oriental influences—at times with the strong implication of the superiority of a colorful and exotic culture over the drabness and decline of Europe—henceforth ranged all the way from Goethe's worshipful hymn *Mahomet* about the divine mission of a great human being to the fantastic tale of adventure as evidenced, for instance, in *Vathek, an Arabian Tale* (1786) by William Beckford, an Englishman writing in French.

With Antoine Galland's version of the *Arabian Nights* in twelve volumes (1704 ff.) a new veritable storehouse of exciting, fabulous and exotic tales was opened up for European poets and readers. Although many tales of this frame story, known as early as the tenth century, but probably collected in its modern form sometime in the fifteenth century, had been known in the Middle Ages through Spanish intermediaries (in the *Conde Lucanor* by Don Juan Manuel, the *Libro de Buen Amor* by Juan Ruiz, Archpriest of Hita, and others) and, even more, in the form of European analogues in Boccaccio and Chaucer, the French translation of the complete collection was something fascinatingly new for eighteenth century bibliophiles. English translations extended from the *Arabian Nights Entertainment* of 1705 up to and beyond the masterful version by Sir Richard Burton (1885).

Although various seventeenth century authors, from Lope de Vega's *El triunfo de la fe en los reinos del Japón* of 1608 to Settle's romanticized drama *The Conquest of China* (1676) had begun to write about the FAR EAST, it was really only at the very end of that century that European-Asiatic mutual cultural relations were finally established. Leibniz, after studying the first translated Chinese texts available, in his *Novissima Sinica* (*Latest News from China*, 1697) advocated a lively cultural interchange with the Far East; among the earliest travel-accounts available were *Relazione sulla China* by L. Magalotti (1697), *Idée générale du gouvernement et de la morale des Chinois* by Silhouette (1729) and *Histoire et description générale du Japon* by Charlevoix (1736). To these we must add accounts of the Near and the Middle East of the type of the *Voyage en Turquie, en Perse et aux Indes* by Tavernier (1682) and the *Voyage en Perse et aux Indes orientales* by Chardin (1711). Man's intellectual horizon was immensely enlarged also by the new circumnavigations of the world by Dampier (*Voyage Round the World*, 1697), Bougainville (1766-69), and by Cook (1768-71)—and Diderot's *Supplément au voyage de Bougainville* (1772), and Bernardin de Saint-Pierre's *Voyage à l'Isle de France* (1773) and *La chaumière indienne* (*The Indian Cottage*, 1790) indicate clearly that the writers of the eighteenth century were not slow in claiming these new spheres for the field of literature. But the most important book in this field—at any rate the one to underscore the leading role of the Jesuit Fathers in opening up new geographical and cultural frontiers—was the *Description géographique, historique, chronologique, politique et physique de l'Empire de la*

Chine et de la Tartarie chinoise, which Father Jean-Baptiste du Halde published in 1735. Du Halde himself had never been in China, but he based his work upon numberless reports from Jesuit Fathers, foremost among them the learned sinologist Joseph Henri Prémare, author of *Notitia Linguae Sinicae,* one of the earliest Chinese grammars in Europe. It was Prémare, too, who in 1731 translated into French the story of an almost complete liquidation of a dynasty and the belated revenge by the sole surviving member which he called *L'Orphelin de la Maison de Tchao,* which du Halde printed in 1735, and which then entered into European literature under the name of the *Orphan of China* in the grossly distorted versions of William Hatchett (1741) and Arthur Murphy (1756) in England, Metastasio in Vienna (1752) and Voltaire in France (1753). Du Halde's work became quickly known all over Europe; its reproduction of Prémare's French version of the first authentic Chinese drama to become known in Europe was translated into English by the later Bishop Thomas Percy in *Miscellaneous Pieces Relating to the Chinese* (1762) and in Germany it may have influenced Goethe's *Elpenor* (1781). Also Gozzi's version and Schiller's translation of *Turandot, Princess of China,* should again be mentioned in this connection.

The Nordic Renaissance

The destruction of the literary hegemony of France and the weakening of the Graeco-Roman foundation upon which the principles of Classicism were based naturally brought to the fore the traditions of Northern Europe—not only of England and Germany, but also of the early Germanic tribes in Scandinavia and the ancient Celtic settlers of Britain. Tacitus' *Germania,* long ignored during the Middle Ages and at last discovered again by the humanist Conrad Celtis, assumed a new and great importance during the eighteenth century, for in its contrasting of Germanic virility and of Roman (read: French) decadence, it contributed to the increasing animosity against the system of Versailles. Germanic heroes like Arminius or Hermann der Cherusker became popular again: though already Hutten, Scudéry and Lohenstein had written about him, he was now hailed as a symbol of the Germanic opposition to Roman civilization, and epics and tragedies about him from Möser (1749) and Schönaich (1751) to Klopstock (1769),

Kleist (1821) and Grabbe (1838) significantly underscored this line of thought. Also Pindemonte in Italy wrote an *Arminio* (1804) in which he blended Klopstockian and Ossianic influences. Entirely in keeping were the efforts of the pre-romanticists from Bodmer on to familiarize themselves with, and appreciate the beauties of, oldest German and English literature, the *Nibelungenlied* (1757), *Beowulf, Parzival,* Walther von der Vogelweide, and others. Bodmer imitated the *Nibelungenlied* in his epic *Chriemhildens Rache* (*Kriemhild's Revenge,* 1757); he should also be noted for his *Sammlung von Minnesingern aus dem schwäbischen Zeitpunkte* (*Collection of Minnesingers of the Swabian Era,* 1758) and his *Altenglische und altschwäbische Balladen* (1781). Herder followed suit with his essay *Von der Aehnlichkeit der mittleren englischen und deutschen Dichtkunst* (*Of the Similarity of Middle English and German Poetry,* 1776). In a small way this trend had been initiated already in the seventeenth century: in 1639 Opitz published an edition of the *Annolied*; the year 1665 witnessed the first edition of the Gothic Bible of Wulfila, with a Gothic-Latin dictionary; and even Lohenstein's heroic novel on *Arminius,* though bombastic, was none the less sincerely patriotic.

It was, however, the purity of Germanic traditions in SCANDINAVIA, particularly the heroic songs and the valorous mythology of the Icelandic *Edda* that now became so supremely important that we may well speak of a Nordic Renaissance. Scandinavian lore of the Golden Age around 1100 had hardly become known as yet, in spite of the beauty especially of Icelandic literature and in spite of sporadic Nordic influences during the preceding centuries such as evidenced in *Hamlet,* a topic which Shakespeare had found in Belleforest's version of the account given in the *Danorum regum heroumque historiae* (*The Accounts of Danish Kings and Heroes,* 1514) by Saxo Grammaticus. In 1575 Saxo Grammaticus was translated into Danish by A. S. Vedel, a scholar also noted for his *De scribenda historia Danica* (1578). From the seventeenth century on, the *Edda* became increasingly known; in 1636 Ole Wormius published *Runir, seu Danica litteratura antiquissima* (*Runir, or the Oldest Danish Literature*), and ultra-patriotic men like the Swede Rudbeck insisted that the long lost Atlantis must have been in the North Sea region near the coast of Norway.

Paul Henri Mallet, a Swiss citizen from Geneva and long

a resident of Copenhagen, in his fundamentally important *Introduction à l'Histoire du Danmark* of 1755 and in the various literary and religious monuments appended thereto (*Monuments de la mythologie et de la poésie des Celtes, et particulièrement des anciens Scandinaves*, 1756) opened up to amazed Western European readers a world hitherto ignored, a eulogy of the values and standards of our Nordic ancestors not falsified by what Roman or other Mediterranean historians have since then told us about them. Mallet's "discovery" proved to be immensely important in the gradual growth of Pre-Romanticism: Bishop Percy, the author of *Five Pieces of Runic Poetry translated from the Icelandic Language* (1763), translated the *Monuments* in his *Northern Antiquities* (1770), Sir William Temple, Gray, Collins and others took to writing runic odes in the manner of their Anglo-Saxon forefathers, and in 1784 Edward Jerningham wrote on the *Rise and Progress of Scandinavian Poetry*.

Klopstock, who likewise spent nineteen years of his life in Copenhagen (1751-70), forsook his biblical poetry in favor of sturdy Germanic effusions (for instance, his three bardic dramas *Die Hermannsschlacht, Hermann und die Fürsten* and *Hermanns Tod*). Gerstenberg from Schleswig-Holstein, a German by birth but a Dane by citizenship and as such eminently qualified to serve as an intermediary between Germany and the North, helped to make the *Nordischer Aufseher* (*Nordic Spectator*, 1758-61) the mouthpiece of this Renaissance and to cultivate the new fashion through his *Gedicht eines Skalden* (*Poem of a Bard*, 1766) as well as through his drama *Minona oder die Angelsachsen* (1785). Also Schütze from Hamburg-Altona, the translator of Mallet, joined this wave of Germanic enthusiasm in his *Schutzschriften für die alten Deutschen* (*Defensive Writings for the Old Teutons*, 1746-47)—and even formerly anacreontic poets like Gleim and Wieland suddenly became ultrapatriotic and nordic, especially after the outbreak of the Seven Years' War, with Wieland's Valkyries assuming the functions of enchanting houris, and with Gleim displaying his martial spirit in his *Preussische Kriegslieder von einem Grenadier* (*Prussian Warsongs of a Grenadier*, 1758—followed by Gerstenberg's *Kriegslieder eines dänischen Grenadiers*, 1762).

Space forbids us to elaborate on the continuation of this

Nordic Renaissance and to speak also of the wealth of Scandinavian literature after 1750 which, tutored by French Enlightenment and German Romanticism, broke forth in full blossom in the nineteenth century; nor can we speak of the frequent and profitable use which these Scandinavian authors themselves (for instance Tegnér) have made of ancient Germanic lore. It should be emphasized, though, that these ancient Germanic strains have continued to permeate West European and even American literature of the nineteenth and twentieth centuries, as evidenced in England by the various works of the scholar and translator Sir George Dasent (1842 ff.) and especially of the poet William Morris (*Sigurd the Volsung and the Fall of the Nibelungs*, 1876; *The House of the Wolfings*, 1889). We shall see that also Longfellow in America was often indebted to Scandinavian sources and to the Finnish *Kalevala*, and an echo of pagan literature—Roman as well as Nordic—can also be found in the *Poèmes barbares* by Leconte de Lisle in France (1857) and the *Odi barbare* by Carducci in Italy (1877). German literature was especially frequently inspired by old Germanic themes—from Friedrich de la Motte-Fouqué (*Der Held des Nordens*, 1810; *Die Fahrten Thiodolfs des Isländers*, 1815) to Wagner's *Nibelungen*-tetralogy (1853), Hebbel's *Nibelungen*-trilogy (1862) and to more recent dramas like Samuel Lublinski's *Gunther und Brunhild* (1908), Paul Ernst's *Brunhild* (1909) and *Chriemhild* (1910) and novels like Hans Friedrich Blunck's *Urvätersage* (*Sagas of Our Ancestors*, 1927 ff.) and Will Vesper's *Das harte Geschlecht* (*The Hard Race*, 1931).

Ossian and Other Celtic Influences

The hoax perpetrated by James MacPherson in 1760 and the enormous popularity of Ossianic lore during the decades afterwards give us a chance to speak, somewhat belatedly, of much older strains of Celtic influences which had made their impact felt since the peak of the Middle Ages: the ARTHURIAN romances and, closely allied with them, other Celtic tales about Erec, Iwain, Tristan and other chivalrous heroes and lovers of the past. The comparatist, in investigating the origin of these legendary tales about King Arthur and the Knights of the Round Table at the time when Celtic Britons fought the Anglo-Saxon invaders, will use as a basis the *Historia regum Britan-*

niae (*The History of the Kings of Britain*) by the twelfth century Benedictine chronicler Geoffrey of Monmouth which will introduce him into the lore connected with King Arthur, Queen Guinevere, the magician Merlin, Lancelot and others. Rather than dwell on Geoffrey's translators (Gaimar and Wace, who rendered him into Anglo-Norman, and Layamon, who translated him into English), the student of Celtic lore may wish to investigate how individual Arthurian knights became connected with the legend of the Holy Grail and of Joseph of Arimathia which, in the hands of English, French and especially German medieval poets, blended oriental and Hebrew strains with the richly chivalrous background of Celtic legends. Among English continuators of these legends should be mentioned Walter de Map who, around 1200, systematized and spiritualized the stories of Lancelot, of Arthur and of the Grail. In medieval French literature the Celtic impact was supremely important especially in the case of Chrétien de Troyes (1170) and Marie de France; in Germany, mention should be made, above all, of Wolfram von Eschenbach's *Parzival* (1200) and his deeply symbolical quest of the Grail—while other Germans like Hartmann von Aue and Gottfried von Strassburg retold the stories of Erec, of Iwain and of Tristan and Isolde, respectively.

Of great significance is also the connection which exists between this Celtic world of chivalry, adventures and fairy-like miracles and the *Amadis de Gaula* in Spain and Portugal. Through the largely Anglo-French background of the *Amadis* these Celtic influences became an integral part of Southern European literatures, too. In England proper, the stream of Celtic lore began to diminish after Sir Thomas Malory, around 1470, had written his great compilation of Arthurian romances, generally known as the *Morte d'Arthur*—though it might be noted that the first Tudor, Henry VII, in view of his Welsh ancestry, was anxious to perpetuate these traditions, to the point, for instance, of naming his first-born son Arthur and of having a large Round Table built for himself. Yet even though these Celtic contributions proper began to decline, they lived on, in Spain and abroad, in the immense popularity of the *Amadis* and *Palmerin* romances—and, combined with different romanesque backgrounds, in the new interpretations of love, chivalry and adventures such as depicted in Ariosto's *Orlando furioso,* in the endless heroic-gallant novels of the type of d'Urfé and Scudéry and the pastoral novels and plays rampant all over Renaissance and baroque Europe. They persisted also, in a prosaic and pedestrian form, in the *Volksbücher vom sterbenden Rittertum* (*Chapbooks of Dying Knighthood*) which late medieval German poetasters were wont to compile for their bourgeois readers. With his dramatic opera *King Arthur* of 1691, Dryden cultivated Celtic lore even in the midst of the Neo-Classical Period.

With his *Fragments of Ancient Poetry, collected in the Highlands of Scotland and translated from the Gaelic Language* of 1760 (followed by his *Fingal,* 1761, *Temora,* 1763, and *The Works of Ossian, Son of Fingal,* 1765), James MACPHERSON started another and entirely different strain of Celtic influences. Though the songs of Ossian, an old and blind bard, the last of his tribe, singing of heroic deeds of valor and pathetic tales of love of yore, were essentially products of MacPherson's own rich imagination, the Scotsman provided them with so much genuine Celtic material found on his folklorist excursions, and ennobled them with such a rich and sonorous biblical language, that the immense international success of his works became quite comprehensible. Here at last there seemed to be a genuine document of oldest Nordic origin describing our ancestors as men and women of tenderness, and adding a sombre northern landscape of cliffs, forests, oceans and mist of a beauty and a melancholy unimagined before. Through his *Critical Dissertation on the Poems of Ossian* (1763) MacPherson's friend Blair added to the fame and the prestige of his work. The followers of Rousseau eagerly welcomed Ossian as confirming their theories about the goodness of primitive tribes, while the students of the *Edda* with rising doubts noted that something was wrong with this sweetly sentimental and modern text. More important than Turgot and Suard among the French translators of Ossian was Le Tourneur (1777), and Ginguené provided a new translation with a lengthy preface as late as 1810. Among other echoes of Ossian in France we should mention the tragedy *Oscar, fils d'Ossian,* by Arnault (1796) which was translated into Spanish by Gallego; and *Balder, fils d'Ossian, poème scandinave,* by Saint-Geniès (1824). In Italy, the Abbate Cesarotti produced a translation (1763-72) that was hailed as one of the finest in Europe; it served as the basis for the Spanish

verse-translation by Montengón y Paret (1804), another former
Spanish Jesuit residing in Italy. Distinct Ossianic echoes can
also be found in Monti's *Il bardo della Selva nera* (*The Bard of
the Black Forest*, 1806) and in Pindemonte's *Arminio*. In Germany (where Ossian was translated more often than in all
other countries together), we should point to the renderings of
the Bavarian monk Denis (who wrote under the pseudonym of
Sined the Bard, 1768), of Herder and of Stolberg, and the
lengthy passage contained in Goethe's *Werther* spread the fame
of Ossian even further afield. MacPherson's essay *Concerning
the Era of Ossian* was translated into German by Christian
Felix Weisse (1770), but it was Herder who dealt most enthusiastically with this wonderful new genius, discussing him
in his essay *Ueber Ossian und die Lieder alter Völker* (*About
Ossian and the Songs of Old Nations*, 1773), translating many
passages in *Vom Geist der ebräischen Poesie* (*Of the Spirit of
Hebrew Poetry*, 1782), and comparing *Ossian und Homer* in a
lengthy article in 1795. Bodmer in Switzerland hailed the book
for its sombre descriptions of mountains just as the Scandinavians welcomed it because of its fine portrayals of the North Sea.
Schiller admired the biblical tenor of its language and its style
which was so epic, so lyrical and so dramatic all at the same
time; and in America an echo of the prevailing mood of Ossian
can be found in Cooper's *Last of the Mohicans*, for Uncas, too,
roaming through silent forests, was the last of his tribe.

Racial differences were completely discarded by these enthusiasts, because the ancient Germans and Celts were more or
less the same thing for them, and Schütze in Hamburg claimed
Ossian as eagerly for his country as he had claimed the valor-
ousness of the Scandinavian *Edda*, while in Britain the Irish,
the Scotch and the English all saw in Ossian the pure incarnation of their own folk-spirit. All northern European nationalities were united in extolling Ossian as the finest Nordic voice
against the prevailing Roman-French Neo-Classicism until
Baour-Lormian, in his *Poésies galliques* (1801), asserted that
Ossian, of course, belonged to France, because the French, too,
the ancient Gauls, had been Celtic. Towards the turn of the century the power of Ossian can still be seen in the music of Mendelssohn-Bartholdy (*Fingal's Cave*) and in the fact that Napoleon took copies both of Ossian and of Goethe's *Werther*
along on his Egyptian expedition. During the Age of Romanti-

cism, however, the fame of this ingenious forgery definitely began to decline.

At the same time, however, European literature witnessed an enthusiastic revival of the somewhat more authentic traditions of Arthurian and other CELTIC ROMANCES, and this revival persisted and increased throughout the nineteenth and twentieth centuries, as European and later American scholarship brought to light and re-evaluated the great wealth of Celtic literary traditions. It was not so much France (*La Table ronde* by Creuzé de Lesser, 1812) or Spain (*Los encantos de Merlín* by José Zorrilla) but especially England and Germany that contributed most to the renascense and various reworkings of these Celtic tales. More important than the burlesque poem *Arthur and the Round Table* by John Hookham Frere or Bulwer-Lytton's *King Arthur* (1848) was the activity of Matthew Arnold, beginning with his *Tristram and Iseult* (1852) and extending especially to his scholarly works *On the Study of Celtic Literature* (1867) and *Essays in Celtic Literature* (1868). Other English treatments include the poems by William Morris (*Defence of Guenevere*, 1858) and by Lord Tennyson (*Idylls of the King*—among them *Guinevere*, 1859, and *The Holy Grail*, 1869); *Tristram of Lyonesse* (1882) by Swinburne and *The Wanderings of Oisin* by W. B. Yeats (1889). In Germany, Immermann wrote *Merlin* (1832) and *Tristan und Isolde* (1841)—but these works, of course, were far surpassed by the significance of the operas by Richard Wagner (*Lohengrin*, 1847; *Tristan und Isolde*, 1859; *Parsifal*, 1877). In our own century and country we can point to the very human and rather unheroic presentation of Arthurian characters in the poetic works of Edwin Arlington Robinson (*Merlin*, 1917; *Lancelot, Tristram*) which—entirely apart from the Irish Renaissance of the last two generations—demonstrates anew the deep irrational values of the Celtic soul and the importance and wealth of its somewhat belated influence upon Western thought.

Switzerland

In the eighteenth century, German-Swiss and French-Swiss literature assumed an importance far beyond the actual size of the country, because in view of the genuinely democratic government and the idyllic and rustic atmosphere prevailing in some (but by no means in all) Swiss cantons, it was to be expected that her thinkers and ideals would assume leadership in the great European fight against the civilization and the literature of Versailles. The first continental to point to the values emanating from England and to dare to write a running comparison between England and France, very much to the disadvantage of the latter, was the Bernese Beat Ludwig von MURALT with his *Lettres sur les Anglais et les Français* (*Letters on the English and the French*), which in their composition, though not in their publication (1725), preceded Voltaire's *Lettres anglaises* by at least three decades. They constitute a very important book for any comparatist bent upon studying the earliest impact of English culture upon continental mentality.

In 1729, Albrecht von HALLER—not only a political enlightener as his state-novels have indicated—wrote an epochmaking poem *Die Alpen* (*The Alps*) which, though still rationalistic and written in the Alexandrine meter, nevertheless was a real revelation of the hitherto ignored beauties of the Alps and, perhaps even more important, of the virtuousness and simplicity of the Swiss mountaineers. At the same time as Thomson in England, and long before Rousseau, Haller here preached a return to nature, and replaced the lifeless screen of nature hitherto shown in Rococo-pastorals by really seen, minutely observed, and enthusiastically described portrayals of Alpine scenery. In the first fifty years, *Die Alpen* went through thirty translations in five different languages; among the French translators of this and other poems by Haller (*Versuch schweizerischer Gedichte,* 1732) we should mention especially the version by his friend and fellow-countryman Tscharner (1750). Through Haller, the role of Helvetia as an idyllic democracy and as an effective antidote against the corruption of modern civilization received a powerful impetus. In England, Haller was emulated in George Keate's poem *The Alps* (1763), while Marmontel in France kept in step with the new fashion with his pastoral comedy *La bergère des Alpes* (*The Shepherdess of the Alps,* 1765). The same period should be noted for the slow beginnings of a general European interest in mountain climbing. Stanyan prepared the way with his long descriptive *L'Etat et les délices de la Suisse* (*The State and the Delights of Switzerland*), published in four volumes in Amsterdam in 1714, and in 1742-43 the *Proceedings* of the Royal Society in London printed the first account of excursions to the glaciers of the Alps. Tourism started around 1775; H. B. de Saussure, who in 1779 had published his *Voyages dans les Alpes,* was eight years later the first to climb the Montblanc. The entire trend was further encouraged by the *Lettres sur les contrées pastorales de la Suisse* (*Letters on the Pastoral Regions of Switzerland,* 1795) by the Swiss patrician Bonstetten.

Among the Swiss literary cities and figures the Zürich of BODMER and Gessner was more important even than the Bern of Muralt and Haller, for Zürich soon became one of the great centers of Anglophile activity, an undisputed leader in the literature of German-speaking lands. Of Bodmer we have already spoken: his translation of Milton's *Paradise Lost,* his successful struggle against Gottsched, his clever use of the satires of Butler, Dryden and Pope in combating his own enemies, his great contribution in restoring imagination and warmth to literature from whence French Classicism had expelled it, his efforts on behalf of Dante, of medieval ballads and of the long forgotten Middle High German literature. Of equal importance was Solomon GESSNER (1730-88), the Swiss Theocritus, the successful publisher of Wieland's and Eschenburg's Shakespeare-translations, but well-known in literature especially for his famous *Idylle* (1756) which had a real European vogue spreading from Italy and Spain to Poland and Scandinavia. Gessner's works (*e.g. Der Tod Abels*) had much of the sensuousness and of the delicate fragrancy of the Rococo in them except that they were at the same time deeply religious and excessively sentimental, too—thus representing a true picture of that problematical generation before the outbreak of the French Revolution that was so elegiac in its yearning for a long-lost golden age of innocence which Haller thought to have found in the Swiss Alps and the Robinsonades in some exotic climes, and which Gessner now realized had existed only, if ever, in the days before Cain slew Abel. Gessner was translated into French by Michel Huber, Turgot and Meister (1762) and praised by Diderot and Rousseau. His works, especially the *Death of Abel,* became immensely popular in England and his influence upon Wordsworth, Coleridge and Byron (*Cain*) should be especially noted. In Spain, he was emulated by Meléndez Valdés whose works, like his, were on the border-line between Rococo and Pre-Romanticism. Bertòla translated him into Italian (1777) and likewise wrote an *Elogio di Gessner,* and also the *Idyllen* by Johann Heinrich Voss in Germany were partly influenced by him.

Greater even than any of these German-Swiss authors was Jean-Jacques ROUSSEAU (1712-78) from Geneva, who achieved his greatest success in France where he was so revolutionary because he was a Calvinist among Catholics, a republican among royalists, a plebeian among courtiers, a romanticist among neoclassicists, a Swiss among Frenchmen. His message about the corruption of modern society and the need for a return to nature (contained in the *Discours sur les sciences et les arts* of 1750 and his *Discours sur l'origine de l'inégalité* of 1755 and translated into German by Mendelssohn in 1756) found an enthusiastic welcome among all the underprivileged of the *Ancien Régime*, especially among the dramatists of the Storm and Stress who repeated this message *ad nauseam* (for instance Schiller in his *Räuber*) and with Herder, who became the leading Rousseauist of Germany. In Italy, Rousseau was rebuked in Genovesi's *Lettere sulla questione se sien più felici gl' ignoranti o gli scienziati* (*Letters Concerning the Question of Whether Ignorant or Learned People Are Happier*, 1764). Rousseau's *Lettre à d'Alembert sur les spectacles* (*Letter to d'Alembert on the Theatre*, 1758) displayed an ardently pro-Swiss and anti-French attitude; it was a Puritan condemnation of theatrical performances and of actors and actresses comparable to the worst the Church Fathers of the Middle Ages or the fanatical English Puritans of the seventeenth century (such as William Prynne in his *Histriomastix* of 1632) had ever said against comedies and tragedies. In particular, the letter represented a bitter excoriation also of Voltaire and his followers who planned to invade and demoralize the idyllic peace and innocence of Calvinistic Geneva by founding a theatre there.

The Calvinistic tenor of his pedagogical novel *Emile* (1762) and its influence upon later educators of the type of Pestalozzi (who softened its radicalism) and Basedow is particularly noteworthy; in Spain it was imitated by Pedro Montengón y Paret (*Eusebio*, 1788). It certainly constitutes an outstanding document of the fundamentally anti-intellectual attitude of the romanticists who, averse to excessive bookish learning, were inclined to rely more on the work of their hands and the feelings of their heart than on the powers of a rationalizing brain. *Julie, ou la Nouvelle Héloïse* (1762) is far more than just an-

other allusion to the famous tale of the seduction of the medieval
nun Heloisa by her tutor Abelard (as also treated, for instance,
in Pope's *Epistle of Eloisa to Abelard,* 1717) ; it is, on the contrary, one of the most important novels of the entire century,
an outstanding example of the excessive sentimentality of the
pre-romanticists and a fervent defense of the rights of the
flesh against the laws of society—the tale of two lovers amidst
the idyllic and imposing scenery of the Swiss Alps written with
such an intensity that readers like Goethe and Byron, commis-
erating their lot, would pilgrimage to the shores of the Lake of
Geneva where Julie and St. Preux had lived, loved and suffered.
It inspired imitations like William Russell's *Julia, a Poetical Romance* (1774). Rousseau's third work published during that
important year 1762, *Le Contrat Social* (an idealized picture of
what the democracy of Geneva might have been), contained an
important political message which inspired European revolutions from 1789 to 1917 and political and social thinkers from
Mirabeau and Burke to Marx and Lenin—a message which,
because of its emphasis of the rights of the majority over the
minority, has become responsible not only for some fine aspects of democracy, but also for the despotic ruthlessness of
modern People's Republics. Particularly interesting to a comparatist with a flair for political science are also Rousseau's
draft for a constitution for Corsica and a plan for a political
reorganization of Poland (*Projet de constitution pour la Corse*
and *Considérations sur le gouvernement de Pologne*), for they
naturally started out from a basically Swiss pattern.

Rousseau's *Confessions* (1765 ff.) finally are but another
indication of his lyrical, high-strung and at times extremely
pathological character; comparable to the *Confessions* of St.
Augustine, they certainly offer a first example of the unbridled
exhibitionism, the breast-beatings and vain-gloriousness of ever
so many later romanticists. The writing of autobiographies
became quite popular around 1800, and poets representative of
that self-analyzing trend ranged all the way from the calmly
restrained Goethe (*Dichtung und Wahrheit*) to Chateaubriand
(*Mémoires d'outretombe*) and Alfieri (*Vita scritta da esso*).

Scores of detailed studies of Rousseau's influence in France
(Bernardin de Saint-Pierre, George Sand, the Revolutions of
1789, 1830 and 1848, the Commune of 1871), Germany (Herder,
Schiller, Jean Paul, Fichte, Hegel), England (Hume, Burke,

Shelley, Byron), Spain (Feijóo, Jovellanos, Meléndez Valdés, Iriarte, Quintana), Italy (Leopardi, Manzoni), among the Slavs (Mickiewicz, Tolstoy), and in America (Paine, Thoreau) attest to the unusual significance—in the good and the bad sense— of this father, not only of French, but in many ways of general European, Romanticism.

With the appraisal of English mentality by Muralt and with the important literary activities of Bodmer and of other translators (Grynaeus from Basel, the translator of *Romeo and Juliet* and of *Paradise Regained,* Clément from Geneva, the translator of Lillo's *London Merchant,* and many others) Switzerland's noble task of serving as a cultural mediator between nations was by no means over; we shall see later, with Mme. de Staël and Benjamin Constant, that she also contributed, as no other nation did, to the international appreciation of German literature, and, with Mme. de Staël, Sismondi, Burckhardt and Meyer, to the discovery of the greatness of Italian culture, particularly of the Italian Renaissance.

Among foreign travellers to be inspired by Switzerland we might mention Montesquieu and, above all, Voltaire, who found a shelter at Ferney near Geneva (1759 ff.); the English historian Edward Gibbon, who spent many years in Lausanne (1754 ff.); the visits of Klopstock (1750) and Wieland (1754) in Zürich and the former's ode *Der Züricher See* (*The Lake of Zürich,* 1750); the impact of his numerous trips to Switzerland upon young Goethe (in his *Schweizerreise* and in such poems as *Gesang der Geister über den Wassern*). Indeed, among these visitors we might mention also the Danish poet Baggesen, who as a result of his trip through the Alps in 1792 wrote a German epic glorifying the Jungfrau: *Parthenäis oder die Alpenreise, ein idyllisches Epos.* Among the international themes contributed by Switzerland, mention might be made of the story of William Tell, such as described in Tschudi's *Chronicon Helveticum* (1570) and as encountered again in the famous drama by Schiller (1804) and the opera by Rossini (1829). Other treatments of the story of Tell range from the early tragedy by Lemierre in France in 1766 to Bodmer in Switzerland (1775), Sheridan Knowles in England (1825) and Gil y Zarate in Spain (1843). Indeed it is noteworthy that Tell and the general theme of the struggle for freedom in the oldest democracy of the Old World should have found a quick echo also in the oldest democracy of the New World, for William Dunlap's play *The Archers, or The Mountaineers of Switzerland*, was performed in New York as early as 1796—eight years before Schiller.

The Noble Savage

The preceding three discussions of Nordic and Ossianic influences and of Gessner and Rousseau have indicated the growing conviction of these pre-romanticists who were all disillusioned with the corruption of modern civilization, that primitive men in primitive society were good, noble and virtuous and that history and civilization, far from indicating progress, really indicated a retrogression, a constantly growing alienation from the golden age of man's innocence and bliss. Hence the tremendous popularity not only of Rousseau's early essays, of Gessner's idyls, or the tender sentimentality found in Ossian or in Milton's description of Adam and Eve, but also of scenes of modern virtuousness which approximated the vanished ideals of bygone centuries: Defoe's *Robinson*, Haller's *Alpen*, Bernardin de Saint-Pierre's *Paul et Virginie*. Like Charles Moor, the hero in Schiller's *Räuber*, the poets of the Storm and Stress were convinced that peace and virtue could be found only by reverting to the primitive life of a rebel against society, a robber in the Bohemian forests. Herder searched for true poetry (*Urpoesie*), the expression of the real soul of a people, not among the courtiers of France, but among the Indians of America, the Negroes of Africa, the Eskimos of Greenland. The romanticists continued this trend and travelled to distant lands to find simplicity and happiness among primitive men: thus Chateaubriand and Lenau who went to America, Volney who visited the Near East, Melville who found peace in the South Seas. Students of the *Edda* or believers in the martial qualities of ancient Germanic or Celtic tribes soon clashed with the touching descriptions of noble savages contained in Rousseau or MacPherson—but these dissidents did not diminish the ardor of those who were firmly resolved to see their dream of a new golden age come true in some distant climes.

Entirely in keeping with this trend was also the awakening conscience of Europe against slavery, against a brutal system of human exploitation which destroyed the idyllic innocence among primitive peoples. Aphra Behn's *The History of the Royal Slave, or Oroonoko* (1688—and dramatized by Thomas

Southerne in 1696)—the story of the perfidiousness of white men and of the sufferings and the pitiful deaths of Oroonoko and his wife in the West Indies—was one of the first graphic descriptions of the horrors of slavery. Mrs. Behn was followed by enlighteners of the type of Montesquieu in his *Esprit des lois* and by the Quakers in England and America. The famous story of *Inkle and Yarico,* such as told by Steele in his *Spectator,* likewise contributed to the intensification of this trend—the tale of how a materialistic and unscrupulous young Englishman rewarded the loyalty and love of a native maiden who had rescued, sheltered and trusted him by selling her and his as yet unborn baby into slavery as soon as he could return to a white settlement. More important than the popular imitations by Chamfort, Gessner, Bodmer and Gellert is the fact that Yarico in this story represented one of the finest incarnations of the noble savage yet told, while the despicableness of Inkle confirmed the worst fears about the rottenness of Western civilization.

Other Literatures

Up till 1750, GERMANY was definitely a receiver rather than an emitter of important literary trends—and it is mainly from this angle that we have discussed her in the three preceding chapters. The slow growth of Germany's literary significance abroad can be gauged especially well by a number of French works: *La Bibliothèque germanique ou Journal littéraire d'Allemagne, de Suisse et du Nord* from 1720 till 1759 published eighty volumes of increasingly important literary information; Huber's first attempts to familiarize the French with German poetry (*Choix de poésies allemandes* in four volumes) were followed by discussions and translations in Bielefeld's *Progrès des Allemands dans les belles-lettres et les arts* (1768) and by four volumes of translations in Junker and Liébault's *Le Théâtre allemand* (1772). Italians likewise became increasingly preoccupied with German literature; thus Corniani in his *Saggio sulla poesia alemanna* (1774) and the significant discussions by one of the leading Italians residing in Germany: Denina's *Sur le progrès de la littérature du Nord de l'Allemagne* (1783) and *La Prusse littéraire sous Frédéric II* (1790).

The period of Germany's real leadership in European literature started with the publication of Goethe's *Werther* (1774) and will be outlined in our next chapter. That leaves the names of only two important Germans to be mentioned in this discussion of Pre-Romanticism: Klopstock and Herder. Friedrich Gottlieb Klopstock, the German "Milton," the author of *Der Messias* (1748 ff.), of religious dramas of the type of *Der Tod Adams* (*The Death of Adam*, 1757) and of bardic dramas such as his trilogy on *Hermann der Cherusker*, the reviver of German lyrical poetry, enjoyed only a brief popularity at home (among the Göttingen Poets) and abroad—in France (Soumet, Sainte-Beuve), Italy (Pindemonte, Monti), England (Blake) and also in Scandinavia and America, where his religious exaltation was appreciated. His *Messias* was translated into French from 1750 on (by Tscharner), into English in 1763, into Italian in 1783. His *Der Tod Adams* was equally acclaimed; it was translated into five languages, no less than nine times into French alone.

Far more important was Johann Gottfried Herder (1744-1803), perhaps more even than Rousseau the great antipode of Voltaire, the first great folklorist, the worshiper of Shakespeare and Ossian, the leading disciple of Rousseau in Germany, the inspirer of the Storm and Stress, the teacher of Goethe, the forerunner of the Schlegels in his cosmopolitan and intuitive understanding of world literature, and of the Grimms and others in his deep love for ancient Germanic lore. In his *Ideen zur Philosophie der Geschichte der Menschheit* (*Ideas about the Philosophy of the History of Mankind*, 1784 ff.) he was, above all, the formulator of a philosophy of history which is comparable only to Vico's efforts in Italy (*Scienza nuova*, 1725 ff.) and which in its irrational and deep fathomings of mankind's past transcends the similar endeavors by enlighteners of the type of Montesquieu and Voltaire. Herder's advocacy of a return to native folklore as a basis of literature was influential above all in the slowly awakening Slavic countries, from Serbia to Poland and from Bohemia to Russia; in France his translator Quinet and also Michelet became his disciples; in England he was studied by Wordsworth, Coleridge, William Taylor of Norwich and others.

Another German contribution of this period was the tall tales usually connected with the name of Baron von Münchhausen—though models for such tall tales can be traced through the picaresque novels back to Antiquity. The first to publish some adventures of the pleasant liar Münchhausen on his travels to Russia was a German fugitive from justice residing in England, Rudolf Erich Raspe, whose English text of 1785 was translated back into German and considerably enlarged by Gottfried August Bürger in 1786 and again in 1788. Though there are certain German forerunners of this type of braggart's tale (such as *Schelmuffsky* by Christian Reuter, 1696), it is especially the Munchhausiad of Bürger which has entered into world's literature and which, for instance in America, may have helped to inspire the tall tales of Paul Bunyan.

FRENCH literature can be omitted in this chapter, for Rousseau was discussed in the Swiss subdivision and all the other writers of this period have been shown to be receivers rather than emitters: Bernardin de Saint-Pierre, Mercier, Diderot, Roucher, Chénier, Delille and others. One phenomenon should be emphasized in this connection: the violently anti-French character of many European writers in the second half of the eighteenth century—not only of pre-romanticists like Herder, of whom one would naturally expect it, but of authors who, because of the neo-classical and rationalistic character of many of their writings, were more indebted to France than they were willing to admit. Thus, for instance, Muralt in his *Lettres sur les voyages* (*Letters on Travelling*, 1725) and Haller in *Fabius und Cato* in Switzerland, Lessing in his *Literaturbriefe* in Germany, and especially Alfieri in Italy, author, among other things, of *Misogallo* (1798), a series of bitterly vituperating epigrams against France.

Also SPAIN continued for a while to be a receiver rather than an emitter; the indebtedness of Ramón de la Cruz, Cadalso, Feijóo, Clavijo or Meléndez Valdés to France or England indicates that sufficiently. Yet in the course of that same eighteenth century the tide gradually began to turn; Spaniards reverted to Spanish themes, to their own great masters of the past for inspiration, and the opposition against France began to rise to such a pitch that the so-called "afrancesados" were bitterly persecuted until the ascension to the throne of the notorious Ferdinand VII in 1808 suddenly forced Spain's leading thinkers to look upon France again as a friend and a refuge rather than an enemy. Ramón de la Cruz showed the pre-romantic trend in his parodies of neo-classical tragedies and even more in the

wonderful realism of his folk-scenes, especially of Madrid in his
sainetes—short plays which are often called the best source of
information about life in eighteenth century Spain. Among
the essayists and dramatists to eulogize the great figures of the
Siglo de Oro we should name Francisco de Molina with his *Discurso en defensa de Lope de Vega* (1768) and García de la
Huerta with his *La Escena española defendida* (1786). In his
seventeen volumes of *El Teatro español*, Huerta also rehabilitated
and republished Calderón. At times the literary feud between
French Neo-Classicism and Spanish traditions became exacer-
bated by unnecessarily tactless phraseology; Forner's emphatic
Oración apologética por la España y su mérito literario of 1786,
for instance, was a reply to Masson de Morvilliers' notorious
inquiry in *La Nouvelle Encyclopédie* of 1784 into the question
of what we owe to Spain and what she had done for Europe
during the past two, four or ten centuries. In the Berlin Academy also the Abbé Denina hastened to the defense of older
Spanish literature (*Réponse à la question: Que doit-on à l'Espagne?* 1786). At times these Spanish self-assertions and
counter-offensives were aimed not only against the French, but
against the English (*Cuatro cartas de un español a un anglo-
mano* by P. Estala, 1804) and also against Italian neo-classicists who, while under the spell of France, had dared to speak
unfavorably of Spanish literature: thus Javier Lampillas,
another Jesuit expelled from Spain and living in Ferrara, who
defended Spanish literary excellence as far back as Lucan,
Martial and Seneca in his *Ensayo histórico apologético de la
literatura española contra las opiniones preocupadas de algunos
escritores modernos italianos* (*Apologetic Historical Essay on
Spanish Literature against the Biased Opinions of Some Modern
Italian Writers*, 1782-86), written both in Spanish and in Italian and aimed especially at neo-classical fellow-Jesuits like Bettinelli and Tiraboschi. It was entirely in keeping with this
patriotic and pre-romantic reassertion of the Spaniards that
the medieval text of the *Poema del Cid* should have been published for the first time by Tomás Sánchez in 1779. In the field
of thematology, about the only Spanish story of the eighteenth
century which became known and treated abroad was the love-
affair of the Buffon-translator and Addison-imitator José Clavijo
y Fajardo which Goethe, through the intermediary account
given by Beaumarchais, dramatized in his Storm and Stress

tragedy *Clavigo* (1774). In 1870, Goethe's play was translated into Spanish by Gustavo Adolfo Bécquer.

In ITALY, reference should be made to the philosopher of history, Giambattista Vico, one of the most fertile minds of the century, whose *Principii di una Scienza nuova d'intorno alla comune natura delle Nazioni* (*Principles of a New Science Concerning the Common Nature of Nations*, 1725 ff.), possibly influential upon Herder, were propagated by Quinet and translated by Michelet. Outstanding among the Italians that began to rise up against Voltaire's France were also Lodovico Muratori (author of *Rerum Italicarum Scriptores*, 1723; *Antiquitates Italicae medii aevi*, 1738, and *Annali d'Italia*, 1744), the first to return to the study of medieval history and a correspondent of Leibniz; Giuseppe Baretti, a long-time visitor to England (1751 ff.), an adherent of English Pre-Romanticism, an inveterate enemy of Voltaire (*A Dissertation upon Italian Poetry*, 1752; *The Italian Library, Containing an Account of the Most Valuable Authors of Italy*, 1752; *An Account of the Manners and Customs of Italy*, 1768, *Discours sur Shakespeare et sur M. de Voltaire*, 1777); Gaspare Gozzi, the defender of Dante against Bettinelli (*Difesa di Dante*); Calepio, the friend of Bodmer, the champion of native Italian traditions (*Paragone della poesia tragica d'Italia con quella di Francia*, 1732); Paolo Rolli, another "fuoruscito" in England, the translator of *Paradise Lost* (1735); Vincenzo Monti, the emulator of Klopstock and Herder who, like Foscolo, tried to combine Greek and pre-romantic influences (*Prometeo*); Ugo Foscolo, another refugee in England, the imitator of *Werther*, the translator of Sterne, a friend of the romantic poets and a contributor to the *Edinburgh Review*—they all are men to fascinate a comparatist interested in the gradual liberation of Italy from the yoke of Neo-Classicism. Abroad, the *Bibliothèque italienne ou Histoire littéraire de l'Italie* of Geneva which issued eighteen volumes between 1728 and 1734, should be mentioned among the very first publications to awaken an interest in Italian culture.

Among foreign visitors were the critic Luzán, who stayed in Italy from 1715 till 1733 and who was a disciple of Vico, and the noted Charles de Brosses, author of *Les Lettres familières écrites d' Italie en 1739 et 1740*. Rousseau, while in Turin, momentarily renounced his Calvinistic faith, and in 1743-44 he was briefly connected with the French embassy in Venice.

Addison was one of the first English literary figures to pay renewed attention to Italy; in 1703 he wrote *A Letter from Italy*
and in 1705 *Remarks on Several Parts of Italy*. Gray and Walpole travelled in Italy from 1739-41; they were followed, among
others, by Smollet (*Travels Through France and Italy*, 1766).
Foremost among the Germans to be deeply inspired by the landscape and the literature of Italy were Meinhard, Winckelmann,
Jagemann, Heinse and Goethe. Winckelmann spent the last
thirteen years of his life (1755-68) in Italy, among the art
treasures of Rome, where he became converted to Roman Catholicism, and Jagemann, a runaway Augustinian monk and
likewise a great lover of Italian art, later became librarian at
the court of Weimar and an enthusiastic exponent of Italian
culture north of the Alps (*Antologia poetica italiana*, 1776;
Briefe über Italien, 1778). Wilhelm Heinse, author of *Ardinghello* (1787), a novel which strangely combines the physical
prowess of the German Storm and Stress with the amorality
and keen aestheticism of the Italian Renaissance and an utopian
dream of a full life on some blessed island in the Mediterranean,
can certainly be called among the first in chronology as well as
intensity of all those German lovers of Italy (from Waiblinger
and Heyse down to Ricarda Huch and Heinrich Mann) who
seem to prefer her to their own native Germany—while Goethe
(as evidenced in his *Italienische Reise*, 1786-88, his *Römische
Elegien*, 1795 and even his *Venezianische Epigramme*) owed to
Italy a new youth, a new life, and the last decisive step in his
gradual development from the Storm and Stress to Classicism.

V. ROMANTICISM

A. GENERAL OBSERVATIONS

The complex literary and cultural phenomenon of the Romantic Revolt provided a body of writing which is exciting for its freshness, originality, and spirit of proud individualism. Virtually all literary historians agree that the literature of the period designated by the term Romanticism is in a way very homogeneous, but because the works of different authors, of different countries, and of different times within the Romantic Period itself are so infinitely varied and individual, any definition of the term Romanticism becomes forbiddingly difficult. It is this homogeneous variety, this uniquely individualistic expression of a universally prevalent sensibility and *Weltanschauung* that makes the term Romanticism and the period of the Romantic Revolt so complex and so fascinating to study.

There is only one way to approach a definition of Romanticism, and that is by studying the Romantic Period as the product of the past. It is the product of the individualism characteristic both of Renaissance Humanism and of the Protestant Revolt, of the Cartesian faith in the power and right of the individual to seek and discover truth for himself, and of the conviction of the enlighteners that men can change this world to ameliorate human suffering and happiness. From Humanism the romanticists inherited their faith in the dignity of the human being. From the Protestant Revolt they inherited their firm conviction that the individual must seek union with the Divinity by himself (in spite of the fact that many romanticists gave up the lonely struggle and turned to orthodoxy—mostly Roman Catholicism —for help). From Cartesianism they inherited a philosophical justification for their individualism, but they made a crucial substitution in Descartes' "I think: therefore I am"; for them it was "I feel: therefore I am". From the Enlightenment they inherited their idealism and aspirations for a better and more humane world.

But while Romanticism can thus be regarded as a synthesis of the past, upon closer examination we find that it is also a rebellion against the past. And, indeed, the best way to understand the complex meaning of the term "Romanticism" is to define it in contrast with the term "Classicism". While Classicism implied the use of reason to discover truth, Romanticism implied the use of emotion, intuition, and instinct; while the former glorified the advancement and sophistication of civilization, the latter glorified the simplicity and innocence of primitive life close to nature; while the former accepted the institutions of society, government, and religion as a part of an ordered universe, the latter denied that there is a known order in the universe and felt that the institutions of society, government, and religion should be constantly changed to fit the organic needs of man. This polarity between Classicism and Romanticism can be expressed as a series of contrasts, such as reason *vs.* emotion, the typical *vs.* the individual, the universal *vs.* the particular, the clarity and satisfaction with the present of the Mediterranean world *vs.* the obscurity and the melancholy longing for the unknown of the Nordic world, the critical sensibility *vs.* the intuitive sensibility, the finite *vs.* the infinite, the sculptural *vs.* the musical, completeness *vs.* incompleteness, and so on and on. Such polar contrasts as these have validity not so much in comparing individual authors of Classicism and Romanticism (for instance, Racine *vs.* Wordsworth) as they do in comparing the collective character and sensibility of the two great movements of European literature.

Amidst all of the confusion which develops whenever an attempt to define Romanticism is made, there remains the persistent desire to find a single common denominator which will fit all of the varied manifestations of the Romantic Period, from the democratically inspired French Revolution to the tyranny of Metternich, and from the rigid ethics of Kant to the moral rebelliousness of Byron. Various common denominators can be predicated, but the use of any one of them usually requires a twisting of the interpretation of a considerable portion of romantic literature in order to make it a product of the common denominator. Defining Romanticism as the revolt of the individual to assert himself and his rich emotional life, and claim the world as his own is supported by the examples of such men as Goethe in his *Faust* and *Wilhelm Meisters Lehrjahre* (*Wilhelm Meister's Apprenticeship*), F. Schlegel in his *Lucinde,* Byron in his own life and in most of his poetry, Chateaubriand in *René* and *Atala,* Foscolo in *Le ultime lettere di Jacopo Ortis,* Zorrilla in *Don Juan Tenorio;* but this militant individualism is hardly characteristic of Goethe in his *Wahlverwandtschaften* and *Wilhelm Meister's Wanderjahre* (*The Elective Affinities* and *Wilhelm Meister's Travels*—if, indeed, these are typically romantic works), Chateaubriand in his ardent Catholicism, the orthodoxy of the later years of Wordsworth and of the American transcendentalists. It would seem (and the example of Goethe makes that particularly clear) that the individualism of the early Romantic Period shaded into social consciousness during the later period.

Another possible common denominator is the metaphysical one: most of the romanticists shared a belief that the universe is not the ordered, well planned, and smoothly running mechanism which earlier philosophy, classical and Christian, implied that it was; they conceived of the universe as unknown and virtually unknowable, an organism rather than a mechanism, which is constantly changing and the ultimate reality concerning which can only be dimly perceived by intuition. Equating Romanticism with "organicism" helps to explain the romantic theory of art, the romantic desire for social and political reform, and the romantic rejection of tradition, but it does not explain the return to Neo-Platonism which is predicated on the assumption of absolute aesthetic values and absolute perfect forms, nor again does it explain the Catholic revival characteristic of so many romanticists.

Defining Romanticism as the triumph of emotion over reason provides another possible common denominator that will support Shelley, Novalis, Lamartine, Espronceda, and others, but it will not explain Wordsworth's rejection of pure feeling as a means to truth nor the essential rationality of many of Goethe's dramas. The search for a common denominator for Kant and Hegel, Blake and Byron, Emerson and Poe, Goethe and Novalis, de Maistre and Musset, the French Revolution and the Congress of Vienna, the cosmopolitanism of the Schlegel brothers and the nationalism of Kleist, and all of the other seeming contradictions characteristic of the period is a worthwhile pursuit, and if it fails to find a universally applicable common denominator at least it will contribute to an understanding of the period.

The problem of defining the general concept Romanticism carries with it the corollary problem of determining the dates of the Romantic Period. As has been seen, literature characteristic in many ways of Romanticism exploded into being in Germany during the Storm and Stress as early as 1750 and 1760.

Interest in folk poetry, the Middle Ages, the dark and obscure in human life was apparent in England from Percy, Gray and Blake on. Rousseau, in many ways the Father of Romanticism, published his major works during the same period. But so long as the restraining forces of Johnson in England, Voltaire in France, and Lessing in Germany were effective, it seems more appropriate to speak of Pre-Romanticism rather than Romanticism. Politically, Romanticism is best represented by the French Revolution, so that the year 1789 might possibly be used to mark the beginning of the Romantic Period, but this year is still ten years earlier than the first real flood of romantic literature. The years 1797-98 are significant for the publication in Germany of Wackenroder's *Herzensergiessungen eines kunstliebenden Klosterbruders* (*Outpourings of an Art-loving Monastic*), of the art ballads of Goethe and Schiller and for the establishment of the principal German critical magazine of Romanticism, *Das Athenäum*; for the publication in England of the *Lyrical Ballads* by Wordsworth and Coleridge, and for the coming to the fore, in Italy, of Monti and of Foscolo. But the Romantic Period did not officially begin in France, Italy, Spain and America until later, in spite of the appearance of such demonstrably romantic works as Mme. de Staël's *De la Littérature considérée dans ses rapports avec les institutions sociales* (*On Literature considered in its Relationship to Social Institutions*) in 1800 and Chateaubriand's *Atala* in 1801. Regardless of how one might date the Romantic Period in any individual country, the best initial date for European Romanticism would seem to be the round figure of 1800, a year which is somewhat late for Germany and England, but somewhat early for the other countries.

Before trying to define a terminal date for Romanticism, the student may wish to investigate the correlation among the various European countries of the periods of Romanticism: the first and second generations in England; the *Frühromantik* of the Berlin-Jena school and the *Spätromantik* of the Heidelberg school in Germany (not to speak of other aspects such as Patriotic Romanticism or Swabian Romanticism); the group in Milan (Pellico, Breme, Berchet, and others) in Italy; the "Pre-Romanticism" of the early Restoration period in France, and so on. Though the importance of salons persists, courts and princes cease to be centers of attraction, and poets prefer to assemble in productive albeit ephemeral local schools and groups. There can be little doubt that in each country there are significant differences between the literature written by those who were reaching maturity when the French Revolution occurred, and the literature written by those who matured later without ever having enjoyed the pure, hopeful and undiluted idealism that had existed before 1789 and who consequently did not suffer quite so personally and immediately the terrible disillusionment that followed. We must distinguish, too, between the ones who retreated into their imaginations and thus escaped the political realities of the period of Napoleon and of Metternich and the ones who expressed their romantic sensibility by means of intensely patriotic and nationalistic writing and activity. And finally there is the problem, suggested earlier, of examining the religious development from pantheism during the early Romantic Period to orthodoxy later on.

Fixing the terminal date for Romanticism poses the same questions as selecting the initial date. It could be argued with force that the Romantic Period has not yet ended, that the Symbolist Movement is a continuation of the Romantic Movement, that the socialist trend in politics is a continuation of the romantic political revolt, and that the contemporary destruction of traditional forms in art and music is a continuation of the romantic artistic rebellion against the past. But there is a sufficiently significant difference between the literature of, say, 1810 and 1880 to justify our seeking a new terminology to distinguish the later period from the earlier. Perhaps the most satisfactory means of seeking a terminal date for Romanticism would be to determine when the later type of literature became predominant. In England, much of Romanticism lost its meaning and freedom with the death of Shelley (1822) and of Byron (1824), when a great age gave way to the Victorian morality that was to follow. In Germany, it might be argued that the end of the Golden Age of German literature (indicated by the death of Goethe in 1832) signified also the end of Romanticism; it was the age, too, when epigones like Platen and Grillparzer preferred the Classicism of Italy and Greece to the formlessness that had been Romanticism. France, Italy and Spain, having begun Romanticism later, were also later to terminate it. In France it broke forth with Hugo's *Cromwell* in 1827, survived the great decisive battle raging around *Hernani*, but may really be said to have come to an end with the failure of *Les Burgraves*

(1843), if not before, and with the coming of poets like Théophile Gautier. In Italy, the enthusiasm whipped up by the ardor of Romanticism and the tenets of the French Revolution, led in spite of momentary setbacks and disillusionments, straight into the tempestuous era of the *Risorgimento,* a period of national resurrection which had been prepared by neo-classical (Parini, Alfieri), romantic (Manzoni, Leopardi) as well as realistic (Carducci) patriots. In Spain Romanticism, which in truth meant a return to the old idols of the *Siglo de Oro* symbolized by Cervantes, Lope and Calderón, and which in the field of the drama reached a climax in 1835, with *Don Alvaro o la fuerza del sino* (*Don Alvaro or The Power of Fate*) by the Duque de Rivas, likewise gave way only slowly and reluctantly to the new school of Realism emerging after 1850. It is not difficult at all to point to various anti-romantic statements by poets who at least in some phases of their creative art have been identified with Romanticism—among them Leopardi (*Discurso di un Italiano intorno alla poesia romantica,* 1818), Heine (*Die romantische Schule,* 1836) and Lamartine (*Cours familier de littérature,* 1856 ff.).

It is easier to define the more specific characteristics of romantic literature than it is to define the movement as a whole, although all these characteristics are the logical consequences of the fundamental attitudes of the age. The reaction against the past and the belief in the organic nature of the world led inevitably to the development of new modes and forms of expression. In poetry traditional, classical forms were rejected in favor of freer, less disciplined lyric forms, which are often close to folk poetry. The art ballad, the personal lyric, and the song (*Lied*) became the favorite means of poetic expression because these forms allowed for the projection of the subjective feelings of the poet and became in effect a creation of what was inside the poet rather than an imitation of what was outside him—which had been the classical concept of the purpose and nature of poetry. In prose the novel, short story, and especially the fairy-tale, among the loosest, least rigid of all literary forms, became the favorite mode of expression because they too allowed the greatest freedom to the author to create the world of his own imagination. It is significant that the genre which dominated the period of Classicism should be the genre least successfully used by the romanticists: the drama—for romantic drama is quite often closet drama, consisting of plays like Goethe's *Faust,* Shelley's *Prometheus Unbound,* Byron's *Manfred* or Longfellow's *Christ*-trilogy which are philosophical, lyrical or epic in intent rather than dramatic (unless, of course, they be colorful Shakespearean spectacles as in Kleist, Hugo or among the Spaniards). The final genre which dominated Romanticism was that of literary criticism (A. W. and F. Schlegel), and in this area the best critics were no longer concerned (as critics since Horace had been) with determining to what extent a piece of literature conformed or did not conform to preestablished rules, but rather they were concerned with redefining anew the very nature and purpose of literature.

Just as in their cultivation of new literary forms the romanticists rebelled against their immediate past, so in their selection of materials and themes they also rejected the eighteenth century heritage. While among the classicists the psychological concern was with the conflict between reason and passion, with emphasis upon the control of passion by reason, among the romanticists the interest was in the exploration and dramatization of the passions as providing the only valid mode for meaningful experience. The classicists chose most of their material from Antiquity, treating the mythological and historical characters as if they were sophisticated, modern representatives of a highly developed civilization. The romanticists chose their themes from their own lives, from the common people who lived close to nature, from the Middle Ages as well as from Antiquity —but in borrowing themes derived from Antiquity, the romanticists were interested in exploring the mysterious, the occult, and the uniquely and rebelliously individual. Instead of treating the stories of Sophoclean and of Euripidean drama, the romanticists preferred to modernize such legends as Prometheus (Goethe, Monti and Shelley) and Hyperion (Hölderlin, Keats and Longfellow). The mysticism, mystery, and exotic atmosphere which the romanticists read into the Middle Ages appealed to the age even more than anything in Antiquity, so that a great many works made use of medieval subjects, themes or settings (by Schiller, Tieck, Keats, Coleridge, Scott, Longfellow, Hugo, Manzoni, Hartzenbusch, Rivas and others). Even many works which presumably have contemporary settings are enshrouded in a medieval atmosphere, as for instance Novalis' *Heinrich von Ofterdingen* (1799).

Various problems grow out of the romantic taste both in literary forms and in materials and themes. Among the interesting studies which could be made in literary forms would be examinations of the development of the "art ballad", imitative of the folk ballad, in the hands of Bürger, Goethe, Schiller, Uhland, Scott, Coleridge, Keats, Hugo and others—or, similarly, the development of the artistic fairy-tale out of the popular fairy-tale (as in Goethe, Tieck, Brentano, de la Motte-Fouqué, Chamisso, Hoffmann or Hauff). Any investigation of the revival of the personal lyric would have to restrict itself to certain themes in lyric poetry, such as the great popularity of the "dejection" poem among such poets as Coleridge, Shelley, Novalis, Lenau, Heine, Lamartine, Musset, Vigny, Leopardi and Espronceda.

Closely allied to this study would be the larger problem of that remarkable phenomenon usually referred to as *Weltschmerz* or *mal du siècle*—that fashionable maladjustment of the individual which induces in him utter melancholy and overwhelming sadness in the face of the materialism, misunderstanding and blindness of the world to the sensitive feelings and intuitive understandings of the artistic individual. The first manifestation of *Weltschmerz* came as early as 1774 in Goethe's *Werther*, which by virtue of its amazing international popularity helped to establish the fashion. This lonely isolation of the sensitive individual from the world at large became steadily worse during the Napoleonic wars and especially afterwards, with the growing industrialization of Western Europe and the intensification of social iniquities and class struggle, in which a poet felt ever more thrust aside and impotent to realize his idealistic hopes. Actual poets to serve as symbols of unhappiness were Camoens (in the poem by Garret, 1818) and Chatterton (in the tragedy by Vigny, 1835). In Eastern Europe the same mood of complete despair prevailed because of the tyranny of the Holy Alliance and the hopelessness of national aspirations. While the *Weltschmerz* can be studied as it is reflected in the works of Goethe (*Torquato Tasso*), Novalis (*Hymnen an die Nacht*), Lenau, Heine, Byron (*Childe Harold*), Shelley, Longfellow (*Hyperion*), Chateaubriand (*Atala, René*), Musset (*Confessions d'un enfant du siècle*), Senancour (*Obermann*), Foscolo (*Le ultime lettere di Jacopo Ortis*), Leopardi, Espronceda, Słowacki, Krasinski up to Thomson's *City of the Dreadful Night* and Thomas Hardy's novels, it can also be studied as it seems to be directly embodied in the apparently maladjusted and often tragic lives of so many of the romanticists. Poe, Coleridge, DeQuincey, and Hoffmann turned to alcohol or opium as a means of escaping their maladjustment; Hölderlin, Lenau, Don Juan Arolas and Gérard de Nerval became insane; Pellico in Italy, Larra in Spain and Mickiewiez and Słowacki in Poland were imprisoned or exiled because of their patriotic endeavors; Foscolo, Byron, Shelley, Heine, Platen and Stendhal became voluntary expatriates because they could not live with their native societies; Chateaubriand and Lenau came to America in their search of peace and happiness; Byron, Shelley, Keats, Wackenroder, Novalis and Espronceda all died in their twenties or early thirties before they had had a chance to fulfill the great promise of their youth; Chatterton, Kleist, Larra and Gérard de Nerval committed suicide; Pushkin and Lermontov were killed in duels; Körner, Petöfi, and in a way Byron, died fighting for freedom. Even among those authors who seemed able to adjust themselves to the world, there is strong evidence of their feeling of isolation from that world, and opposition to its materialism: Wordsworth and Eichendorff turned to nature and their own imagination; Grillparzer and Mörike passed their lives in frustration; Vigny found bitter comfort in a profound philosophical pessimism; Hugo, that "mirror" of the nineteenth century, became increasingly inimical to the trends in France until he finally spent the period of the second Empire in militant exile. Only Goethe, and to a lesser extent Schiller, seemed able to become genuinely a part of the world of their day. During the French Revolution and the Age of Napoleon, to be sure, Goethe appeared to be an Olympian who looked down upon the world rather than a member of that world who looked around himself; after 1815, however, as the second parts of his *Faust* and *Wilhelm Meister* indicate, he delved into the very core of the social, economic and political problems of the world around him. This typically romantic feeling of the futility of the individual's attempts to reconcile the world with his ideals produced in philosophy the extreme pessimism of Schopenhauer, whose ideas were formulated during the romantic upheaval (1819), but became generally known and popular only a few decades later.

The relationship between literature and philosophy is very close during the Romantic Period, so that it becomes at times impossible to separate the one from the other. For example, Coleridge's criticism, along with that of the Schlegel brothers, who influenced Coleridge, introduced the fashion in England of making literary criticism a kind of philosophy. Coleridge's own interest in philosophy and in particular the associational psychology of Hartley color much of his poetry and all of his criticism. Shelley became a disciple of the political philosopher Godwin and embodied many of the latter's ideas in his more ambitious poems. In Germany, the influence of Spinoza's pantheism upon Goethe, Kant's ethics upon Schiller, and, among the romantic philosophers, the influence of Schelling's mysticism upon Novalis, Fichte's nationalism upon Kleist, Hegel's historism upon Hebbel, and Schopenhauer's pessimism upon Wagner reveals how closely allied the literature and philosophy of the period were. Indeed, as German Romanticism was understood abroad, especially in England and America, philosophy and literature became indistinguishable. Turning from philosophy proper to social and political thought, reference should also be made to the works of that type by Sismondi and Constant and to the early socialist planning of Saint-Simon and Fourier and their repercussions abroad, especially in New England.

Since the romanticists felt that poetry is closely akin to music, the relationship between romantic literature and music provides other significant problems. With the cultural significance of Germany coming ever more to the fore, it was natural that her distinguishing traits, the essentially romantic qualities of her literature and her distinct predilection for music and philosophy, should begin to permeate the culture of the rest of Europe, too. Thus there were various attempts, for instance in Bürger, Novalis, Coleridge and Musset, to make of poetry a kind of verbal music. Then there is that rich body of romantic lyric poetry which has since been set to music. Probably no period in world literature has provided more texts for art songs than the period of German Romanticism, with such composers as Schubert, Schumann, Brahms, and Wolf finding in its poems direct inspiration for their music. And finally the study of poetry and music can explore the similar trends in the two arts —the rejection or fundamental modifications of eighteenth century forms that are apparent in each, and the experimentations designed to discover new modes of expression for each art. The indissoluble intimacy between literature and music can also be seen in Heinse's novel *Hildegard von Hohenthal* (1795 ff.) and in the person of Ernst Theodor Amadeus Hoffmann, novelist, lawyer, concert director, composer of the opera *Undine* (1816— taken from the German tale by de la Motte-Fouqué of 1811) and author of keen musical criticism, especially on Mozart. The same predilection can be observed in Stendhal's plagiarized *Lives* of Haydn, Mozart and Metastasio (1817) and of Rossini (1824).

Finally, during the same Romantic Age literature became also intimately intertwined with a study of and an enthusiasm for Fine Arts: thus Stendhal's preoccupation with Italian painting, Tieck's and Wackenroder's ardent love of medieval art as found, for instance, in Nürnberg (*Franz Sternbalds Wanderungen; Herzensergiessungen eines kunstliebenden Klosterbruders*) and apprenticeship-novels dealing with artists of the type of Mörike's *Maler Nolten* (*Painter Nolten*, 1832).

The Political Problems of Romanticism.

The great impact of political history upon romantic literature between 1789 and 1848 is best characterized by three terms: French Revolution, Napoleon and Holy Alliance. Since Romanticism paradoxically marks the beginning both of the artist's isolation from society and his direct involvement in the political, social and economic problems of society, the study of the relationship between literature and political events is particularly fruitful. Few romantic authors were untouched by the tremendous democratic idealism which accompanied the outbreak of the French Revolution or by the increasing disillusionment which, in the days of Robespierre and even of Napoleon, accompanied its deterioration into tyranny. Despite the disillusionment following the Terror and the subsequent establishment of the Empire, these ideals were never really lost after 1815, but rather became the foundation of a new kind of patriotic fervor and militant advocacy of the freedom of man. One could profitably study the reactions of the various romantic authors to the Revolution and its aftermath, from the enthusiasm and subsequent disillusionment of Burns, Wordsworth, Coleridge, Klopstock, Schiller, Wieland, Foscolo and Monti to the implied rejection of the Revolution and the more or less overt welcoming of Napoleon by Goethe, Heine, Manzoni, Hugo and others. Then the Napoleonic conquest supplied the cause for revived nationalism which was especially keenly felt in

Italy and which led to especially bitter struggles against the French invaders in Spain and in Germany.

Among the scores of poems, dramas, novels, speeches and studies dealing with the first rumblings and the actual outbreak of the French Revolution are Goethe's *Der Grosskophta*, Alfieri's *A Parigi sbastigliato*, Pindemonte's *Francia*, Blake's *The French Revolution*, Burke's *Reflections on the Revolution in France*, Goethe's *Die natürliche Tochter, Der Bürgergeneral* and *Die Aufgeregten* up to Carlyle's *History of the French Revolution* (1837) and beyond (Dickens' *The Tale of Two Cities*, Hugo's *Quatre-vingt-treize*, Anatole France's *Les Dieux ont soif*, the Baroness Orczy's *The Scarlet Pimpernel*). Individual leaders of that Revolution became frequent objects for dramas and poems; thus Danton and Robespierre as treated by Southey and Coleridge (1794), Büchner (1835) and others. The invasions of other countries produced violent echoes, ranging from the marvelous *Chant de guerre pour l'armée du Rhin* (*La Marseillaise*) by Rouget de Lisle (1792) in France to Holland (Helmers' *Funereal Song of the Grave of Holland*, 1795), Italy (Monti's *La Bassvilliana*), Switzerland (Lavater's *Schweizerlieder* of 1798, W. L. Bowles' *The Sorrows of Switzerland*), Spain (Martínez de la Rosa's *Zaragoza*, Gallego's *El dos de mayo*), Germany (Goethe's *Kampagne in Frankreich*, Fichte's *Reden an die deutsche Nation*, Reuter's *Ut de Franzosentid*, Luise von François' *Die letzte Reckenburgerin*, Sudermann's *Der Katzensteg*, Paul Ernst's *York*) and Russia (Tolstoy's *War and Peace*). But it was, of course, the figure of Napoleon which evoked the greatest number of works, such as Foscolo's *A Bonaparte liberatore*, Nodier's *La Napoléone*, Byron's *Ode to Napoleon*, Gaudy's *Kaiserlieder*, Quinet's *Napoléon*, Scott's *Life of Napoleon Bonaparte*, Rivas' two odes on *Napoleon destronado* and *España triunfante*. Grabbe's and Mussolini's dramatizations of the Hundred Days, Lermontov's *The Last Domicile* and Manzoni's *Il cinque maggio* (translated into German by Goethe), up to Rostand's *L'Aiglon* (1900). The impact of the whole period on Goethe, Fichte, Byron, Carlyle, Monti and Mme. de Staël should be particularly noted.

It is through a study of the relationship between these political events and literature that one can best examine the functions of the many intermediaries in contributing to the development of a truly pan-European romantic literature, for the constant

movement of intellectuals from one country to another provided
a constant interchange of literary ideas. Chateaubriand and Delille were not only cultural emissaries abroad, but, even more
important, they brought back to France from England, America,
and Germany many of the tenets of Romanticism. The great
number of French expatriates included not only men who served
as important intermediaries between France and other nations,
but included such men as Adelbert von Chamisso and Friedrich de
la Motte-Fouqué, who became German citizens and poets writing
in the German language. The greatest example of the influence
of the Napoleonic Wars on the interchange of literary ideas is
provided by Mme. de Staël, whose vigorous opposition to Napoleon forced her into frequent exile and who during her travels became a disciple of German Romanticism. Her *De l'Allemagne*
(*About Germany*, 1813) was the most important single book
for the spread of German ideas and German literature, while
her estate at Coppet in Switzerland became the principal nerve
center (1802-11) where the great literary leaders of Europe
met (the Schlegel brothers, Chamisso, Shelley, Byron, Monti,
Sismondi, Oehlenschläger) and through which literary impulses
from every part of Europe were transmitted to every other part
of Europe. Hardly less important than the stream of French
emigrants in the emitting and receiving of literary influences
were the many Italian political emigrants (Foscolo, Mazzini)
who, while abroad, revived the awareness of the importance of
Italian culture and literature and who, upon their occasional
return to Italy, brought back the leading ideas of English or
German Romanticism.

After the Napoleonic Wars there followed the even greater
disappointment and oppression of the Age of Metternich—
which led to new political struggles fought partly by the romanticists, partly by what might be called the "Young Europeans".
The relationship between Romanticism and Young Europe deserves a word of clarification. The oppression of subjected
states, national minorities or democratic aspirations which is
usually associated with the Holy Alliance under the leadership
of the Austrian Foreign Minister Prince Metternich and which
lasted from Waterloo in 1815 till the dismissal of Metternich in
1848, confronted the romantic authors of Europe with a burning issue which they were far from unanimous in solving. England had done her great battling on behalf of freedom in the

days of Byron and Shelley; after their deaths this relatively
best governed of all great European nations, apart from some
platonic expressions of compassion for the suppressed in other
lands (the Brownings), showed little direct interest in the tragic new and, more often than not, abortive revolutions abroad.
German romanticists were even worse: they had fought valiantly against Napoleon, from the battle of Jena to the battle of
Waterloo, under men like Kleist, Arndt, Körner—but with the
coming of Metternich, the late romanticists gave up in despair
and disillusionment, seeking escape in the beauties of nature
(Eichendorff), in weird fantasies (E. T. A. Hoffmann), preaching utter passivity (Grillparzer's *Der Traum ein Leben, Ein
Bruderzwist im Hause Habsburg*) if not downright subservience
to despots (Grillparzer's *Ein treuer Diener seines Herrn*). One
reason for this lack of civic courage—apart from its being a national trait—lay undoubtedly in the fact that ever so many German romanticists were Catholics and hence essentially conservative and, perhaps even more important, that very many among
them were aristocratic by birth (Kleist, Chamisso, de la Motte-
Fouqué, Arnim, Novalis, Eichendorff, Lenau, Platen) and
hence not likely to spearhead a revolution against Metternich.
The reaction against the Holy Alliance in Germany and Austria
therefore occurred not with the romanticists but with the so-
called Young Germans (1835 ff.) who in their militantly defiant
and belligerent attitude against political oppression were most
contemptuous of the spinelessness of the romanticists—and
from the Young Germans the term spread all over Europe to include among the Young Europeans all those who fought political reactionaries in France and Spain and foreign oppressors in
Greece, Poland, Italy, and Hungary. The Young Germans were
forerunners of Realism, political pamphleteers and journalists fighting for immediate political and social issues rather
than dreaming nostalgically about the glory of the Middle Ages;
among their leaders we can name Laube (*Das junge Europa,*
1833), Herwegh (*Gedichte eines Lebendigen,* 1841), Heine,
Gutzkow, Börne, Wagner, and Freiligrath. To them might be
added, in Switzerland, the name of Gottfried Keller. For the
others, the frustrated or the passive ones who were content to
lead peaceful and quiet lives apart from the great turmoils of
their times, the unheroic term "Biedermeier" was coined, and
among them we can name Mörike in Swabia, Grillparzer in Aus-

tria, Stifter in Bohemia, perhaps Jane Austen and the Brontës in England; it is a mood represented in art by Ludwig Richter and Karl Spitzweg.

In other countries, however, the romanticists did not fail their compatriots in their struggle for personal freedom and national emancipation; indeed, with its strong emphasis on national traditions and racial traits (which it had inherited from Herder), Romanticism soon spearheaded the various national longings for political and literary self-expression. In France during the upheaval of the Revolutions of 1830 and 1848 it would be hard to say where Romanticism ended and political Realism began, for the over-towering figure of Victor Hugo, the inveterate enemy of the despotism of Napoleon III (*Napoléon le Petit*, 1852; *La vision de Dante*) held together the two periods before and after 1850. These Young Europeans were so busy fighting against their own reactionary governments that they had no time fighting each other on a national basis, though we should mention the fact that a warlike tension between Germany and France around 1840 produced Hoffmann von Fallersleben's *Deutschland über alles* (*Germany above Everything*), Schneckenburger's *Die Wacht am Rhein* (*The Watch on the Rhine*) and Becker's *Sie sollen ihn nicht haben, den freien deutschen Rhein* (*They shall not have it, the free German Rhine*)—the latter sarcastically answered by Musset's *Nous l'avons eu, votre Rhin allemand!* In Italy, too, the *Risorgimento*, the desperate attempt to achieve national unity and independence, which lasted through Carducci, Mazzini, Cavour and Garibaldi (all of them Young Europeans, like Chateaubriand, Lamartine, Hugo or Béranger in France) was borne equally by those whom we might still call romanticists and by those who were realists. Among the journals of restless Italian exiles in Paris, *La Giovine Italia* (*Young Italy*, 1831-34) and *L'Esule* (*The Exiled*, 1832-34) should be mentioned—the former edited by Mazzini; and among outstanding patriotic works, *Del primato morale e civile degli Italiani* (*Of the Moral and Civil Primacy of the Italians*) published by Gioberti in Brussels in 1843 and Mazzini's three volumes entitled *Scritti di un Italiano vivente* (*Writings of a Living Italian*, 1847). In Spain, the fight was made more complicated because to the Spaniards France was not only the liberator, the homeland of Enlightenment and the great Revolution, but also the oppressor, the France of Napo-

leon's invading armies. After 1814, however, when the French
had been expelled and when it was a question of fighting against
the native Spanish despotism of Ferdinand VII, the Spanish romanticists, whether at home or in exile in France or England
(the Duke of Rivas, Espronceda, Martínez de la Rosa, Larra,
and others) participated to the hilt in the political upheavals
that beset Spain for several decades and that produced so pathe-
tically few results with regard to true liberalization. Among
the journals to keep alive the spirit of resilience among the
Spanish émigrés in London were *El Español*, edited by Blanco-
White (1810-14) and *Ocios de españoles emigrados en Inglaterra* (*Leisurely Thoughts of Spanish Emigrants in England*,
1824-26).

In America, the great and burning issue was not freedom
in general, but union versus secession, slavery versus anti-sla-
very, the North versus the South—and here, too, the literary
leaders from Thoreau's and Channing's pamphlets to Whittier's
and Longfellow's poems and from Lowell's *Biglow Papers*
(1848) to Harriet Beecher Stowe's *Uncle Tom's Cabin* (1852)
more than fully did their share, confirming the noble tradition
that Romanticism should not be only a movement of idle dreams
and fantasies, but a strong and militant element in the task of
building up a new and better world. And in the pathetic and
suppressed countries of Eastern Europe, too, it was Romanticism which, by its emphasis on native lore and old folk-tradi-
tions, kept alive the flame of national consciousness and of militant opposition against the foreign oppressor: thus in Greece,
which finally won its freedom from the Turkish yoke; thus in
the Hungary of the martyred Petöfi and the Poland of the exiled
Mickiewicz—countries which had to endure more failures and
longer delays even than Italy before the foreign oppressor, at
least for a generation or two, could at last be expelled from the
native soil. Especially tragic were the two Polish uprisings of
1831 and 1863, which were ruthlessly suppressed by the Russians
and which sent abroad new waves of Polish refugees.

Out of all these political endeavors and subsequent sufferings
in which Romanticism played such a vital role, there grew a rich
body of literature ranging from the abysmal pessimism of Słowacki in Poland to Pellico's autobiographical account of his incarceration from 1820-38 (*Le mie prigioni*, 1832, and immediately translated into most European languages) and from *El*

sueño del proscripto by the Duke of Rivas (1824) and Heine's flight to Paris to Petöfi's death on the battlefield. European compassion for the plight of Italy aroused the wrath of Byron as well as of Elizabeth Barrett Browning (*The Casa Guidi Windows*, 1851) against the Austrian oppressors, and the plight of Poland called forth, for example, Count Platen's *Polenlieder* (*Polish Songs*); but this European compassion was greatest for the Greek struggle for independence from the yoke of the Turks (1821-30). The ensuing Philhellenism (which with its emphasis on a burning modern problem was quite different from the everlasting European admiration for ancient Greece) was noticeable among many warm-hearted idealists of the period, extending from the England of Byron and Shelley to the France of Chateaubriand and Fauriel (*Chants populaires de la Grèce moderne*, 1824), from the Germany of Hölderlin (*Hyperion*), Müller (*Lieder der Griechen*, 1821; *Lord Byrons letzte Liebe*) and Mosen (*Der Kongress von Verona*) to the Spain of Vayo (*Grecia, o la doncella de Missolonghi*, 1830), and from the Italy of Monti to the America of William Cullen Bryant. The fight against national oppression soon turned against any discrimination because of race or sex, too: thus Auerbach's *Spinoza* (1837) and Gutzkow's *Uriel Acosta* (1847) on behalf of Jews, and other novels by Gutzkow (*Wally die Zweiflerin*, 1835) and George Sand in favor of the emancipation of woman. Already Mme. de Staël, in her *Delphine*, had spoken in defense of a greater role of women in society, and with Jane Austen, Charlotte and Emily Brontë and George Eliot in England, Annette von Droste-Hülshoff in Germany and, above all, the militant George Sand in France and Margaret Fuller and Harriet Beecher Stowe in America, they certainly began to conquer for themselves a notable place in literature.

Among refugees from the oppression of the rulers of the Holy Alliance and serving as important literary intermediaries, mention should be made, above all, of the strong colonies of Spanish, German and Polish émigrés abroad. France, in 1789 as well as in the days of the July and the February Revolutions of 1830 and 1848, respectively, became a great center of liberal thought, the home of freedom rather than of oppression, with Paris sheltering a great number of Spaniards (from Meléndez Valdés and Leandro F. de Moratín up to Espronceda, Larra and Zorrilla), Germans (Börne, 1830-37; Heine, 1831-56) and

Slavs (Słowacki, Krasinski). Switzerland followed as a close second, serving as a shelter not only for endangered leaders of the Italian *Risorgimento* (Mazzini), but also for Germans like Wagner and Herwegh, Poles like Mickiewicz and Słowacki, and Spaniards like Villalta—while again others found a home in England (Foscolo, 1815-27; G. Rossetti, Freiligrath, Trueba y Cossio).

B. THE CONTRIBUTIONS OF GERMANY

Of the five great literatures of Western Europe, German literature was the last to dominate one of the great European movements. It is true that during the Middle Ages Germany had produced some of the finest works in European letters and during the Reformation, of course, she had left her deep imprint on the mentality of the modern world. But at most other times (partly because of the chaotic weakness of the Holy Roman Empire and partly because of the catastrophic devastation of the Thirty Years' War) Germany had received rather than given, and had absorbed what her richer neighbors had produced. It is, however, a testimonial of the forcefulness of German Romanticism that it came to dominate both Europe and America in spite of the fact that Germany in 1800 enjoyed neither political nor economic power. Italy's Renaissance had been supported by the economic strength of the Italian city states; Spain's period of European literary greatness came in the wake of her exploitation of the Western hemisphere; France's greatness was a reflection of her political, military and economic hegemony in Europe; and England's influence on European literature came at the same time that the British Empire was acquiring political and commercial domination of the world. But Germany's cultural greatness came in spite of her abject and helpless political, military and economic position in Europe.

Although German Romanticism dates from about 1790 to 1830, the Golden Age of German culture may be said to have extended from 1748 until 1848, from the publication of the first three cantos of Klopstock's *Messias* to the successful March Revolution which expelled Metternich. More accurately, this Golden Age might be said to coincide with Goethe's life, from 1749 until 1832. Its influence abroad, after translations of such German-Swiss authors as Haller and Gessner had prepared the way, began with the publication of Goethe's *Werther* in 1774. From this time on German domination of European thought and literature continued up to the days of Carlyle in England and the transcendentalists in America who were the mirrors of German Romanticism abroad. German culture achieved its richest fruition during the first decade of the nineteenth century, with men like Goethe in literature, Kant in philosophy, and Beethoven in music—each a giant in his own field and each numbering among the handful of giants in the whole history of world literature, philosophy and music. Through her two great cultural centers Germany paid back with interest whatever she had received in the past from her neighbors: Weimar, the home of Wieland, Goethe, and Herder; and Jena, the city which sheltered an amazing galaxy of illustrious men: Schiller, the two Schlegels, the two Humboldts, the philosophers Fichte, Schelling and Hegel, the poets Tieck and Brentano, and, somewhat later, the composer Liszt. Weimar and Jena, together with that outpost of German Romanticism abroad, the estate of Mme. de Staël at Coppet on the Lake of Geneva, now became the great centers of European culture and of international pilgrimages—so much so that their names were often emulated as when, for example, some American critics called Cambridge and Concord the Weimar and Jena of American literature.

The nature of Pre-Romanticism and Romanticism was such that it was natural for England and then Germany to become leaders of these two movements. The German mentality had little of the purely aesthetic interest which had been so strong in the Italian Renaissance, little of the political maturity and social mindedness that had produced the French Revolution, little of the sophistication, courtly refinement, and respect for formalism that permeated the Age of Classicism. German poets, with the great exception of Goethe, were individualistic rather than courtly conformers, romantic rather than classic, philosophical rather than aesthetic, lyrical rather than satiric. With her very great predilection for music (from the baroque grandeur and sublimity of Bach and Händel through Haydn and Mozart to the romantic masterpieces of Beethoven, Schubert, Weber, Mendelssohn-Bartholdy, Schumann and somewhat later Wagner, and to Brahms, Bruckner, and Mahler) it was natural that the chief emphasis both of Germany in particular and of European Romanticism in general should be on lyrical poetry giving vent to man's innermost feelings and aspirations, rather than upon satiric, expository, or even epic and dramatic poetry. With her predilection for philosophy, for metaphysical speculations, for mysticism, and for other forms of essentially Protestant searchings for the way to God, it was natural that Germany in particular and European Romanticism in general should oppose the Cartesian rationalism of France and should lean towards that which was irrational and mystical in man's life. Just as Luther in the sixteenth century had asserted the individual's right to seek God without help from Rome, so now German leaders led the way in expounding an even more individualistic kind of religious quest, as is indicated by such names as Schleiermacher, Schelling, Strauss and Feuerbach and, abroad, Channing, Renan, La Mennais, and Kierkegaard.

Just as lyricism and mysticism, characteristic of Romanticism, were more a part of the German character than of that of any other country, so still another characteristic of Romanticism was peculiarly Germanic: the return to the valorous and picturesque traditions of the Middle Ages, to the beauties of medieval literature and the heart-felt simplicity of folksongs. This desire to search back into the past was doubly strong in a nation like Germany which had been hopelessly defeated in the Napoleonic Wars and which in its humiliation therefore hungered for the memory of former splendor, as for example under Barbarossa. We have seen that Herder, the first great folklorist of modern Europe, was the pioneer of all this and that through his disciples, the Schlegel and Grimm brothers, he became one of the great inspirers of this trend which became evident not only in Germany and Scandinavia, but also in Spain and, above all, in other hopelessly subjected countries of Eastern Europe, such as Lithuania, Poland, and Hungary. They likewise strove to reassert their national identities by going back to older national glories and racial traditions, as exemplified, for instance, in Mickiewicz's *Konrad Wallenrod* (1828).

Germany contributed not only to the essential temper and sensibility of Romanticism or to the fund of romantic ideas, or, through her authors, to the literature of other nations. She also contributed what might legitimately be called an entirely new genre: that of the apprenticeship novel or *Bildungsroman*. This genre is typically German in its emphasis upon the subjective quest of the hero for a philosophy of life and upon the psychological crises and personal experiences of the hero alone. In its lyrical subjectivity the *Bildungsroman* violates the supposedly objective and epic character of the average novel and does not delineate a broad canvas of human society with the hero serving merely as an observer of that society as we find, for example, in the Spanish picaresque novel or in the works of Balzac or Zola. This personal emphasis in a long soul-searching

narrative can be traced far back into the German past to Wolfram von Eschenbach's *Parzival*; it can be seen to distinguish
Grimmelshausen's *Simplizissimus* (1669) from the seventeenth
century picaresque novels of Spain and France, and Wieland's
sensitive *Agathon* (1766) from the eighteenth century sentimental novels of England and France.   Later, Goethe's *Wilhelm
Meister* (1795 and 1829) became the finest product of this type
of novel; among the romanticists who tried to emulate him were
Tieck with his *Franz Sternbalds Wanderungen* (1798), Novalis
with his *Heinrich von Ofterdingen* (1799), and Mörike with his
Maler Nolten (1832).   The apprenticeship novel, developed primarily in Germany, has been the medium of expression for some
of the most important prose since the Romantic Period, in Germany and elsewhere.   In modern Germany there have been, for
example, Wassermann's *Christian Wahnschaffe* (*The World's
Illusion*, 1919) and Thomas Mann's *Joseph und seine Brüder*
(1933-44), in which Mann makes of Joseph an apprentice who
must find for himself a way of meaningful life.   Among the
foreign examples of this essentially German type of novel one
can point immediately to Carlyle's *Sartor Resartus* (1833 ff.)
and even perhaps to Dickens' *David Copperfield* (1850), to Melville's *Mardi* (1849), Gottfried Keller's *Grüner Heinrich* (1854
ff.), Romain Rolland's *Jean Christophe*, and above all to Thomas
Wolfe's *Look Homeward, Angel* (1929).

Among the intermediaries who came in contact with this
Golden Age of German Literature and made its masterpieces
known abroad, a special shrine must be given to Mme. de Staël,
who visited Germany in 1803-04 and again in 1807-08; and among
her French-Swiss fellow-countrymen, mention should be made of
Louis Bridel and Benjamin Constant, both from Lausanne, the
latter the author of an essay *Réflexions sur le théâtre allemand*
(1809).   In France, after the flood of wars and refugees had
abated, it was men like Gérard de Nerval, Quinet, Hugo,
Michelet, Nodier and Renan who were most exposed to German
influences.   Among these, Nerval was particularly active: in
1840 he published a collection of translations, *Choix de ballades
et de poésies de Goethe, Schiller, Bürger, Klopstock, Uhland*, to
be followed in 1852 by *Loreley, souvenirs d'Allemagne*.   During
the early days of the Napoleonic conquests *Le Spectateur du
Nord*, published in Hamburg from 1797-1802, tried to serve
as an intermediary between the two countries; afterwards, it

was especially the *Revue des Deux Mondes* (to which, among others, also Saint-René Taillandier contributed) which distinguished itself by publishing frequent discussions of German literature. In this connection, mention should be made also of *La Revue germanique,* published in Paris by Dollfus and Nefftzer (1858 ff.).

English travellers and intermediaries—beside Wordsworth, Coleridge and Scott—included Henry Crabb Robinson the diarist, who knew Goethe, Schiller, Herder, Wieland and other leaders of German thought. Foremost among the English Germanophiles was also William Taylor, noted for his *Historic Survey of German Poetry with Translations* (1828-30) and for his translations of Bürger's *Lenore* (1796), Lessing's *Nathan der Weise* and Goethe's *Iphigenie* (1794). Among Carlyle's indefatigable Germanophile labors, mention should be made of his translations from Goethe, his four volumes of *Specimens of German Romance* (1827), his essay on *German Poetry,* his lectures on German Literature, his two trips to Germany in 1852 and 1858, and the publication of his *Frederick the Great* (1865). Among the journals, *The Edinburgh Review,* founded by Francis Jeffrey, Sydney Smith and others in 1802, was outstanding in the space and the thoroughness of treatment it gave to the field of German literature.

American travellers included Washington Irving, who was introduced to German literature through Sir Walter Scott and whose *Sketchbook* (1819) and *Tales of a Traveller* (1824) betray manifold German influences (for example, that of Musäus upon his *Legend of Sleepy Hollow,* perhaps also the influences of the Kyffhäuser legend upon his *Rip van Winkle*). George Ticknor, the translator of *Werther* (1814), the predecessor of Longfellow and Lowell at Harvard, was a close student of German as well as of Spanish literature and, while in Germany, was personally acquainted with various literary figures, among them King John of Saxony, the noted translator of Dante. In the width of her sympathies a peer of Emerson, Longfellow and Lowell, Margaret Fuller was one of the leading intermediaries between European Romanticism and New England Transcendentalism; her essays and translations, largely published in *The Dial,* paid particular attention to German literature and, while in Italy with her husband, the Marquis Ossoli, she was in the midst of the abortive revolution of 1848. Minor American intermediaries were George Henry Calvert, James Freeman Clarke, Frederick Henry Hedge, and among the Germans emigrating to America, Charles Follen.

Among the Italians we have already mentioned the indebtedness of Monti and Foscolo to German literature; to them we can add men like Bertòla, not only the translator of Gessner, but also the author of *Idea della poesia alemanna* (1779) and of *Idea della bella letteratura alemanna* (1784) and a traveller in Switzerland and Germany (*Lettere*, 1795); and Giovanni Berchet, the translator of Gray, a lover of old English, Spanish and German romances who in his essay *Sul cacciatore feroce e sulla Eleonora di Goffredo Augusto Bürger* (*On the Wild Huntsman and the Leonore of G. A. Bürger*, 1816) advised a breaking away from neo-classical concepts in literature. In Spain, finally, it is significant that two leading romanticists, the dramatist Juan Eugenio Hartzenbusch and the scholarly critic Juan Nicolas Böhl de Faber were of German parentage; the latter, a disciple of the Schlegels, encouraged a return to older Spanish literary ideals and passed on many ideas of German Romanticism also to his daughter Cecilia Böhl de Faber, the noted novelist who wrote under the name of Fernán Caballero. In Scandinavia, reference should be made to the long discussion between Steffens and Oehlenschläger in 1802 in which the former passed on to the latter, and through him to the literature of the North in general, the quintessence and the powerful impact of German Romanticism—while the Dutchman Bilderdijk became imbued with German literature during his long exile from French-occupied Holland.

Goethe

Although Johann Wolfgang von Goethe (1749-1832) helped to inspire German Romanticism and abroad became the virtual symbol of romantic Germany, his career actually encompasses most of the major developments in literature over a hundred year period. He began writing in the Rococo style (*Die Laune des Verliebten*, 1768) and a few years later, after having met Herder, became the leader of the *Sturm und Drang* with his Shakespeare emulation in *Götz von Berlichingen* (1773). His *Leiden des jungen Werthers* (*The Sorrows of Young Werther*, 1774) catapulted him into international fame and made him, willingly or not, a symbol of everything that the world wanted to see of dark passions, melancholy, and sad love of nature in the German temperament. Goethe's German and international fame continued to grow constantly, although most of his works from 1787 to 1805 (*Iphigenie auf Tauris, Torquato Tasso, Reineke Fuchs, Hermann und Dorothea,* and others) are classical in style and intention rather than romantic. It was the publication of *Wilhelm Meisters Lehrjahre* (*Wilhelm Meister's Apprenticeship,* 1795) that helped to initiate Romanticism in Germany, for in this first part of Goethe's great apprenticeship novel men like Friedrich Schlegel, Tieck, and Wackenroder found what they formulated into the principles of Romanticism. Wackenroder and Tieck in particular saw in Wilhelm Meister's attempts to find meaning in life through some form of art the essential character of the romantic temper. When one adds, as Wackenroder did, that art and religion are essentially the same, one finds the essence of the quest which came to be symbolized as the search for the Blue Flower (the symbol actually used in Novalis' *Heinrich von Ofterdingen*)—the search for absolute and pure beauty which is a revelation of the divinity and which, if ever successful (which it never was), would lead the individual to truth and to the complete life. The appearance in 1808 of the first part of *Faust* strengthened Goethe's international reputation so that, even though he was scorning the moral spinelessness and the pro-Catholic tendencies of ever so many romanticists whom he had helped to spawn, he became the virtual symbol of European Romanticism. The major products of his old age, the second parts of *Wilhelm Meister* and of *Faust* also foreshadowed what was to come generally only late in the century: Realism and Symbolism. In his ethical emphasis upon socially useful activity as the way to a meaningful life Goethe anticipated the social consciousness of the realists and later naturalists, and in his style and method of embodying his ideas in his stories he anticipated the symbolists.

Thus, however much Europe may have looked to Goethe as the cultural leader of the age and however much the romanticists in every country may have found of their own sensibilities in his works, Goethe at one time or another was actually everything—a classicist and romanticist, as well as a momentary disciple of the Rococo, a leader of the Storm and Stress, and a typically late nineteenth century realist using the style of the symbolists. As one might expect, it was those works which

come closest to Romanticism that were most widely read and
most widely influential on other authors: *Werther, Faust I,* and
Wilhelm Meister I, along with his earlier lyric poetry which includes some of the greatest ballads, (*Der Erlkönig, Der König
von Thule* and, later, *Die Braut von Korinth, Der Gott und die
Bajadere*), hymns (*Prometheus, Mahomets Gesang*) and personal
lyrics (from *Willkommen und Abschied* and *Mailied* in 1770 to
the *Marienbader Elegie* in 1823). Furthermore, as might be
expected, it was in those countries which had the closest affinity
to the German temperament that Goethe became the most influential: England and America.

Innumerable translations of *Werther* started in France in
1776, in England in 1779, in Italy in 1781, in Spain in 1803; he
became not only a "best seller", but a serious social problem.
There was such an alarming number of suicides which could
be indirectly traced to *Werther* that the book had to be banned
in Leipzig and Copenhagen. A wave of popularity for Wertherian romances swept Europe and spent itself only after the
entire *Weltschmerz* atmosphere had subsided. In Germany
Werther was imitated (Miller's *Siegwart, eine Klostergeschichte*)
as well as parodied (Nicolai's *Die Freuden des jungen
Werthers*); even Goethe himself, in his *Der Triumpf der
Empfindsamkeit* (*The Triumph of Sentimentality,* 1779) made
fun of the excessive Richardsonianism and Wertherism of his
age, and an anonymous English work in 1786 was called *The Letters of Charlotte during her Connection with Werther*. Just before the turn of the century Scotland became an intermediary to
introduce Goethe into England, with commendatory articles in
the *Edinburgh Review* and translations by Scott of the *Erlkönig*
and *Götz von Berlichingen* (1799). Wordsworth and Coleridge,
following the example of William Taylor of Norwich, went to
Germany together as young men (1798-99), and both came to
know some of Goethe's works. Lord Byron's tremendous admiration for Goethe was reciprocated so that after Byron had
called upon the aging Goethe, the latter hailed Byron as the
prototype of the modern man, the artist who would unite the
romantic and the classical, modern Europe and ancient Greece,
comparable indeed to Euphorion, the son of Faust and Helen of
Troy. Byron, of course, modeled his *Manfred* upon *Faust,* and
echoes of various of Goethe's poems occur throughout Byron's
poetry. Among the earliest translations of *Hermann und*

Dorothea (of which there now are ten) was the one by Holcroft (1801), and *Faust* was rendered into English by Hayward (1833). But the admiration for Goethe in England reached the point of worship in the figure of Thomas Carlyle, who translated many of Goethe's works, including the complete *Wilhelm Meister* (1824 ff.) and who, in his *Sartor Resartus,* wrote an English apprenticeship novel attempting to incorporate the essence of German romantic philosophy to which Goethe had helped introduce him. Following Carlyle, Goethe became almost as much of an institution in nineteenth century England as Shakespeare had become in Germany. Matthew Arnold, for example, ranked Goethe among the greatest figures in world literature and owed considerably to Goethe for his own humanistic and cosmopolitan criticism; and G. H. Lewes wrote a *Life of Goethe* (1855) which is still extremely readable today. The *Publications* of the English Goethe Society (1886 ff.) are an indication of Great Britain's continued interest in the greatest poet of Germany.

In America, Goethe was even more influential than in England. The Romantic Period in the United States marked the first real movement in American literature to break away from the traditions of England and, without a strong native tradition of their own, American authors turned at least in part to Germany. Irving came to know Goethe through Sir Walter Scott; his *Buckthorne* is *en miniature* an American *Wilhelm Meister,* while his *Devil and Tom Walker* is an Americanized *Faust.* Emerson studied Goethe and devoted an important essay to the great sage of Weimar, as did also James Russell Lowell. Margaret Fuller, who had become enthusiastic about Germany through reading Mme. de Staël, became a kind of American Mme. de Staël by virtue of her enthusiasm for German literature and philosophy; among her translations mention should be made of her version of *Torquato Tasso.* Melville's *Moby Dick* (1852) combined the typical quest theme of the German apprenticeship novel with a strong suggestion of Faustian overtones; his *Mardi* about Taji's never-ending search for Yillah is an outstanding American example of blue flower-seeking German apprenticeship-novel indeed. The later historian George Bancroft corresponded with Goethe while studying in Germany. Bayard Taylor's translation of *Faust* (1870) became a standard book for Americans and is still widely read and reprinted. But it was Longfellow, the greatest intermediary of them all, who did most for Goethe: he translated many of his lyric poems, emulated the form and tone of *Hermann und Dorothea* in his own *Evangeline* (1847) and combined in his *Golden Legend* (1851) Hartmann von Aue's epic of *Poor Henry* and Goethe's *Faust*. The direct and indirect influence of Goethe can be traced down to the present day in such works as the apprenticeship novels of Thomas Wolfe, the Faust theme in Stephen Vincent Benét's *The Devil and Daniel Webster* (1937) and Hart Crane's *For the Marriage of Faustus and Helen*.

Although Goethe was never quite the force in other countries that he was in England and America, he had a surprising following in those countries which by temperament would seem least attracted to German Romanticism. In France, his popularity during the 1830's was so great that the expatriate Heine complained that France was becoming more like Germany than Germany was. From the translation of *Faust* by Gérard de Nerval (1828), the operatic versions of *Faust* by Berlioz and by Gounod, the Wertherian *Obermann* by Senancour and the Goethe-like mysterious forces that work behind the scenes of many of Balzac's novels, through Quinet, Gautier and Flaubert to the modern Maurice Barrès, Romain Rolland, André Gide, and Paul Valéry, Goethe's popularity has remained constant. Other early French translators of *Faust* are Albert Stapfer (1823) and Blaze de Bury (1840); in 1821 the former also translated *Les oeuvres dramatiques de Goethe*. Early imitations of *Werther* in France include *La dernière aventure du jeune d'Olban* (*The Last Adventure of Young d'Olban*, 1777) by Raymond de Carbonnières and *Le peintre de Salzbourg, journal des émotions d'un coeur souffrant* (*The Painter of Salzburg, Journal of the Emotions of a Suffering Heart*, 1803) by Nodier. An especially notable example of a Wertherian romance written in French is the *Adolphe* (1806) of Benjamin Constant, providing an account of his unhappy love-affair with that other great Swiss admirer of Goethe, Mme. de Staël. In Italy, *Werther* was quickly imitated in Sografi's tragedy *Verter* (1794) and in Foscolo's *Le ultime lettere di Jacopo Ortis* (*The Last Letters of Jacopo Ortis*, 1802), in which the Italian described the amorous as well as the political broodings over Italy's continued servitude to foreign conquerors as contributing factors for Jacopo's suicide. Manzoni's *Il Conte di Carmagnola* echoes both *Egmont* and Schiller's *Wallenstein*, while later in the century also Carducci and d'Annunzio reflect Goethe's fame. *Faust I* was rendered into Italian by Scalvini in 1835, *Faust II* by Gazzino in 1862. A notable Spanish translation was made by T. Llorente in 1882; yet even before that date Spain was drawn to the German drama, which influenced such works as *El diablo mundo* by Espronceda (1841) and *El drama universal* by Campoamor (1869). In Poland, reference can be made to a particularly strong influence of *Hermann und Dorothea* upon the idyllic and nostalgic picture of rustic peace and affluence in the free Poland of yore in Mickiewicz's *Pan Thaddeus* (1834). On his way to his exile in Western Europe, Mickiewicz was yet another visitor of the patriarch of Weimar.

While his influence on Western literature has been great, it may be that Goethe's most important contribution was the example he provided of the modern "universal man", a sensitive and perceptive author who feels all of the isolation from, and the misunderstanding by, society, as well as the lonely dedication to art that other romanticists have felt ever since, but who through sheer will-power forced himself to adjust himself and to avoid the tragic fate of Werther and Tasso. Because of his amazing variety of interests and accomplishments, he became more than merely a man of society; rather, he became the distillation of the best that a given society contains. To many authors from Arnold to Mann, Goethe has remained a fascinating proof that the artist in the modern world is not condemned to the ivory tower and that the world in all of its multifarious complexity belongs to the artist as much as it does to the scientist, the politician, or the business man.

Schiller

Friedrich Schiller (1759-1805), like Goethe, can be regarded as a romanticist only in some of his works, for, although his career did not embrace as many tendencies as Goethe's, he did evolve from the Storm and Stress to a Greek-inspired kind of Classicism. But in spite of his later admiration for Greece and even for Racine, Schiller remained all of his life most heavily indebted to Shakespeare and Rousseau, so that even his "classical" dramas (with the exception of his very Sophoclean *Die Braut von Messina*, 1803) represent a fascinating blending of Greek and Shakespearian ideals, a kind of union of both Classicism and Romanticism which made Schiller's plays quite acceptable to the romanticists who propagated his fame. In his ballads Schiller often chose Greek topics and form (for instance in the ballads of 1797, such as *Die Kraniche des Ibykus*), but he also wrote more typically romantic ballads on medieval topics (such as *Der Graf von Habsburg*) and was surpassed in this genre only by Uhland. Schiller's philosophy was likewise a blend of classical control and romantic individualism; his *Ueber die aesthetische Erziehung des Menschen* (*Concerning the Aesthetic Education of Man*, 1793) teaches a kind of aesthetic self-discipline which the romanticists would not appreciate—but his persistent defense of individual freedom and of man's inalienable rights to dignity and self-respect aligned him much more intimately with the Romantic Movement than did Goethe's at times Olympian aloofness from the problems of his contemporaries. Indeed, Schiller was hailed in Germany somewhat as Shelley would have liked to be hailed in England, as the poetic harbinger of individual freedom.

One could debate endlessly whether or not Schiller was truly a romantic (he certainly was in *Die Jungfrau von Orleans*, 1801), and whether or not any given work of Schiller's is more classic than it is romantic. Whether such a debate would be worthwhile or not, it would not be germane to the problem of defining Schiller's place in European literature, for his renown was based largely upon those qualities which other nations identified with Romanticism. From his Storm and Stress tragedy, *Die Räuber* (*The Robbers*, 1781), through his transitional work *Don Carlos* (1787), to his later dramas, the *Wallenstein* trilogy (1799) and *Wilhelm Tell* (1804), Schiller found admirers among the romanticists of other countries, while his more self-consciously classical works, such as *Die Braut von Messina* (*The Bride of Messina*, 1803) were much less widely known. But Schiller was not only the greatest dramatist that Germany has produced; he was also one of her greatest poets, particularly in his art ballads, many of which contributed to his fame among the poets and readers of other nations. And finally, Schiller's profound interest in philosophy gave such critical essays as his *Ueber die naive und sentimentalische Dichtung* (*Concerning Naive and Sentimental Poetry*, 1795) a depth and significance that made up for his weakness in close critical analysis. As a historian and a dramatist who took most of his subjects from the history of other lands (for example, *Die Verschwörung des Fiesko zu*

Genua from Italy, *Don Carlos* from Spain, *Die Geschichte des Abfalls der Niederlande* from Holland, *Wallenstein* from Bohemia, *Maria Stuart* from England, *Die Jungfrau von Orleans* from France, *Wilhelm Tell* from Switzerland, *Demetrius* from Russia —not to mention his Greek-inspired *Die Braut von Messina* and his translations of *Macbeth* from Shakespeare and of *Phädra* from Racine) Schiller, even before his premature death, was repaying his foreign debts by contributing both to the literature and to the struggle for freedom in other lands.

In Switzerland—a country which, because of his beautiful *Wilhelm Tell*, has always kept a loving memory of Schiller—he was imitated by Benjamin Constant, who tried to do an impossible and typically French job by squeezing the mighty *Wallenstein* trilogy of eleven acts into one streamlined tragedy of five acts, in which the star-crossed lovers Thekla and Maximilian were given special importance (*Walstein, avec Petit discours préliminaire*, 1809). In France, *Die Räuber* was particularly important from the time of the Reign of Terror down into the period of French Romanticism. In its adapted form, entitled *Robert, chef des brigands* by La Martellière (who, six years later, in 1799, also translated the other early plays of Schiller) it preached a frenzied gospel of freedom and of a Rousseauistic return of nature, all of which pleased the contemporaries of Robespierre as much as the Gothic paraphernalia in the play were pleasing to the contemporaries of Hugo. As French romantic drama developed, Schiller became a model second in importance only to Shakespeare, with the influence of his dramatic practices and of various of his plays appearing in the work of Victor Hugo and Dumas fils. His *Maria Stuart* evoked three adaptations and imitations in 1820 alone; one year later Camille Jordan published the translated *Poésies de Schiller* and Barante *Les oeuvres dramatiques de Schiller*. On the Iberian Peninsula Garrett translated his *Ballads* into Portuguese (1834) and Hartzenbusch rendered into Spanish his *Lied von der Glocke* (*The Song of the Bell*), while Manuel Tamayo y Baus published an imitation of *Juana de Arco* (1847) and an adaptation of *Kabale und Liebe* (*Intrigue and Love*) under the title of *Angela* (1851).

In England and America, Schiller's exalted idealism and Kantian impeccability made him at times more welcome than the oft-suspected Goethe. Coleridge's translation of Schiller's *Wallenstein* (1800) is symptomatic of the impact which the

German romantic had upon the young English romantic, while Wordsworth's *Ode to Duty* seems almost an English transliteration of a typical Schiller poem. A certain English predilection for the bathos of bourgeois dramas (a genre which had originated with Lillo) can be seen in the adaptation of *Kabale und Liebe* by "Monk" Lewis (1797). The English admiration for Schiller reached its climax, of course, with Carlyle, author of a fine *Life of Schiller* (1823). In America, Schiller's plays enjoyed considerable popularity, however little they may be known today, to such an extent even that the legend of William Tell has become as much a part of American folklore as have many native legends. John Lothrop Motley, a student at Göttingen and a class-mate of Bismarck, was indebted to Schiller both for his *Rise of the Dutch Republic* (1855) and for his *View of the Thirty Years' War*. Schiller's noble panegyrics to freedom and integrity also found popularity and imitators in America, notably in Longfellow's *The Building of the Ship*, a glorification of the birth of American statehood, which is patterned closely on Schiller's *Das Lied von der Glocke* (*Song of the Bell*).

August Wilhelm and Friedrich Schlegel

Among the great number of brilliant authors of German Romanticism who are somewhat overshadowed by the towering figures of Goethe and Schiller, the Schlegel brothers (1767-1845 and 1772-1829) stand out as particularly important for their contributions to the formulation of the principles of Romanticism and as intermediaries between Germany and the rest of Europe, and between Europe and the Orient. Through their long stays at Jena, Berlin, Vienna, and Bonn, and especially at that meeting-ground of international Romanticism, the estate of Mme. de Staël at Coppet in Switzerland, they became the leading theoreticians of Romanticism. August Wilhelm's *Berliner Vorlesungen über schöne Literatur und Kunst* (*Berlin Lectures on Literature and Art*, 1801 ff.) and his *Wiener Vorlesungen über dramatische Kunst und Literatur* (*Vienna Lectures on Dramatic Art and Literature*, 1809-11) and Friedrich's *Geschichte der alten und neuen Literatur* (*History of Ancient and Modern Literature*, 1812 ff.) formulated and helped to propagate the basic ideas and attitudes of Romanticism. The *Vienna Lectures* were translated into French in 1813 (by Mme. Necker de Saussure) and into Italian in 1817; in 1814, Böhl de

Faber published lengthy excerpts in Spanish (*Reflexiones de Schlegel sobre el teatro*). John Gibson Lockhart, the son-in-law and biographer of Scott, should be singled out among the English translators of Friedrich Schlegel. Probably nowhere in the whole body of romantic literature can one find a more sensitive and more valid exposition of the distinction between Romanticism and earlier literature than in the criticism of the Schlegel brothers, especially of Friedrich who, though less disciplined, was more of a genius than his older brother. While leading their German contemporaries in the battle against the remnants of the neo-classical hegemony of France, they became the critical leaders of the whole of Europe. One of their, and therefore European Romanticism's, most important assumptions was that literature is the organic product of the individual nation or race—an assumption which they had inherited, of course, from Herder. In undertaking to prove the superiority of the works of German romanticists, who produced organically as parts of the German nation, over the formalized and lately anemic creations of the Age of Classicism, the Schlegels turned also to the literature of many other nations to show how each nation had created its uniquely great modes of expression. Thus, they were important in introducing to Europe such storehouses of literary treasures as those of medieval Catholic Europe (Italy, Spain, Portugal) and of the Orient. August Wilhelm's important re-appreciation of Dante, his epochal translation (with Tieck) of Shakespeare and of the best of Calderón's dramas are important not only for their influence on German literature, but for the contribution these efforts made to the cosmopolitan nature of Romanticism. These efforts were re-enforced by his *Blumensträusse italienischer, spanischer und portugiesischer Poesie* (*Bouquets of Italian, Spanish and Portuguese Poetry*, 1804) and his *Observations sur la langue et la littérature provençales* (1818). Friedrich Schlegel's rediscovery of Camoens indicates the same pro-Mediterranean and pro-Catholic leanings.

The influence of the Schlegel brothers abroad was enormous. Their ideas were spread throughout the Western world in Mme. de Staël's *De l'Allemagne* (*About Germany*, 1813)—in fact, some contemporaries rather ungallantly suggested that August Wilhelm (who intermittently stayed with her from 1804 to 1816) wrote the major portion of *De l'Allemagne*. Victor Hugo's militant program for French Romanticism in his *Préface* to *Cromwell* (1827) was borrowed from them. Coleridge's *Lectures on Shakespeare* (1808) seem at times to edge up to plagiarism rather than honest borrowing from the Schlegel brothers. Because of the Schlegels' championing of national literature, the Scandinavians and the Slavs, as well as the Spaniards and the Italians, turned with redoubled enthusiasm to a reappraisal of their own literature. In Spain, Schlegelian ideas were propagated not only by the Hispano-German Juan Nicolas Böhl de Faber; we find echoes also in Larra's essays on the dramas by Martínez de la Rosa and in the significant and programmatic prologue which Alcalá Galiano wrote to the Scott-inspired legendary romance *El Moro expósito* by the Duque de Rivas (1834).

The Schlegels were not only the very center of European Romanticism from which emanated the literary ideals and principles of the age; also the beginnings of the study of international, indeed of comparative, literature can be ascribed to them. In Germany, their efforts were paralleled by the still somewhat pedestrian and rationalistic Bouterwek (*Geschichte der Poesie und Beredsamkeit seit dem Ende des 13. Jahrhunderts,* 1801-19) ; in Switzerland, they were emulated by Sismondi (*De la littérature du Midi de l'Europe,* 1813). In Holland, W. de Clercq wrote what might be considered the first essay on Comparative Literature : *Treatise on the Influence of Foreign Literatures upon Ours* (1826). Other works to indicate the wider scope of literary interests were Mazzini's *Sopra alcune tendenze della letteratura europea* (*On Some Tendencies of European Literature,* 1829), *De l'unité des littératures modernes* (*On the Unity of Modern Literatures,* 1838) by Edgar Quinet (who three years later became Professor of Southern European Literatures at the Collège de France), *An Introduction to the Literature of Europe in the Fifteenth, Sixteenth and Seventeenth Centuries* by Henry Hallam (1839), and *Histoire de la littérature française au Moyen Age, comparée aux littératures étrangères* (*History of French Literature of the Middle Ages, compared to Foreign Literatures,* 1841) by Ampère. In the field of poetic translations, mention should be made, too, of such broad works as *Poésies européennes* by Léon Halévy (1827) in France and Longfellow's *Poets and Poetry of Europe* (1845) in America.

German Philosophers

While the influence of philosophy on literature is not the primary concern of the comparatist, no study of nineteenth century literature in Europe and America would be complete without at least a brief allusion to the tremendous influence exerted upon it by the German philosophers from Kant to Schopenhauer. At times it is impossible, for example, to disentangle in, say, Carlyle and Emerson, the influence of Kant from that of Schiller. In France, Kant (*Kritik der reinen Vernunft*, 1781) was influential from Charles de Villers to Brunetière; and in America, Emerson studied and appreciated him while the transcendentalists borrowed their very name from one of the leading concepts of Kant's philosophy. In the same way Schelling (*Ideen zu einer Philosophie der Natur*, 1797; *Von der Weltseele*, 1798) inspired much of the pantheism that permeated European Romanticism, from Novalis in Germany to the mysticism of Polish and Russian romanticists. An even greater influence was exerted by Hegel (*Phänomenologie des Geistes*, 1807; *Vorlesungen über die Philosophie der Geschichte*, 1837), who directly, and indirectly through Karl Marx, contributed not only to German literature (for example, Hebbel's dramas), but to the literature of France, from Cousin to Taine and from Hugo to Renan and Maurras; to that of Italy from de Sanctis to Croce; to that of Denmark through Kierkegaard, and through Kierkegaard to a great portion of twentieth century literature; to that of England through Darwin; and, above all, to the literature of America from Emerson and Whitman to the St. Louis Hegelians. Fichte inspired German nationalists like Kleist and Italian fighters for a *risorgimento* and national independence like Gioberti; his influence was great also upon Englishmen like Carlyle who, for this and many other reasons, in recent years was often accused of being a forerunner of National Socialism.

Schleiermacher, the theologian, was important especially for his influence upon the New England Unitarians of the type of William Ellery Channing. Schopenhauer's *Welt als Wille und Vorstellung* (*The World as Will and Idea*), written in 1819, contributed considerably to the late romantic and symbolist developments: Vigny, Balzac, Renan, Laforgue, and Bergson are a few of those who felt Schopenhauer's influence in France; Browning, Hardy, and Lawrence felt it in England; de Sanctis, in Italy; Eminescu, in Rumania; and Thoreau, in America. The basic *Weltschmerz* of ever so many romanticists and the stark pessimism of Schopenhauer contributed greatly to the despairing mood of the mid-century which finally led to rebellion in politics, to Marxism in economics and Naturalism in literature and which was only partly overcome by the philosophy of Nietzsche.

Minor German Influences

Of the great swarm of amazingly original and fecund lesser writers of German Romanticism, only brief mention can be made of a few of the more important whose significance spread beyond the boundaries of Germany. JEAN PAUL Friedrich Richter, an imitator of Sterne, because of his kindly humor often called the German Dickens, was in his loving emphasis on little people and little problems and in his rambling, intricate, and whimsical style in distinct opposition to Goethe's aloof Classicism (*Schulmeisterlein Wuz*, 1793; *Quintus Fixlein*, 1796; *Siebenkäs*, 1796; *Titan*, 1800). In France, Jean Paul's influence was noticeable in Vigny, Hugo, and Gautier; in 1829 La Grange published *Les pensées de Jean Paul, extraits de tous ses ouvrages* and in 1834 Philarète Chasles translated his *Titan*. In England he influenced Carlyle (who published an essay on Richter in the *Edinburgh Review*), DeQuincey, Coleridge, Crabb Robinson and Meredith. In America, Longfellow should be noted for his sensitive discussions of his work, especially in his *Hyperion*.

The strange and tragic early German romantic poet Friedrich HÖLDERLIN is of special interest, not only for his more immediate influence on men like Longfellow, but especially for the revived interest which the twentieth century symbolists of France, England, and America have shown in him. NOVALIS, another of the romantic poets whose promise was snuffed out prematurely, wrote what came to be regarded by many as the archetypical romantic novel, *Heinrich von Ofterdingen*. Heinrich's search for "the blue flower" became for all of Europe the symbol of the romantic quest for a meaningful life. The influence of Novalis did not burn itself out during the Romantic Period, for, in addition to influencing such men as Carlyle, Longfellow, and Senancour, he foreshadowed the symbolists and found admirers among the late nineteenth and early twentieth century symbolist poets and novelists, such as André Gide.

Another German romanticist to influence the Symbolist Movement—and to be mentioned again later, in connection with Poe and Baudelaire—was E.T.A. HOFFMANN, author of weird tales (*Fantasiestücke, Nachtstücke*, 1814-17), which were translated by Loeve-Veimars (*Contes fantastiques d'Hoffmann*, 20 vols., 1829) in France, where they inspired the German-Jewish composer Jacques Offenbach (1880). Loeve-Veimars might be mentioned, too, for his translations of *Les Poésies de Goethe* (1825).

One of the German romanticists most famous in his own day is almost completely forgotten in our age: August von KOTZEBUE. In his bourgeois dramas this German imitator of Lillo appealed strongly to the middle class desire for sentimentality and didactic morality. He took his plots from contemporary German conditions (*Menschenhass und Reue*, 1789; *Die deutschen Kleinstädter*, 1803), though he also had a strong flair for exotic topics (*Die Indianer in England*, 1790; *Die Spanier in Peru*, 1796). *Menschenhass und Reue* (*Human Hatred and Repentance*) was promptly translated into seven languages, four times into French alone; the Spanish version was by Dionisio Solís (*Misantropia y arrepentimiento*, 1800). In England, Kotzebue was hailed as the German Shakespeare and was admired and imitated by Sheridan and Mrs. Inchbald. There exist lengthy special studies devoted to the amazing popularity of Kotzebue in Spain, France, Serbia, Russia, Bohemia and Rumania; also in America he was one of the first Germans to become known on the stages of New York, Philadelphia, Baltimore, or Chicago. Especially William Dunlap was instrumental in adapting Kotzebue to the American theatre; within three years (1798-1800) he introduced no less than six of his plays to the New York stage (*The Stranger, Lovers' Vows, False Shame, The Virgin of the Sun, Pizarro in Peru*, and *Fraternal Discord*).

Of the German lyrical poets of the time—Eichendorff, Lenau, Müller and others—none achieved greater international fame than Heinrich HEINE (1798-1856), an unhappily split personality, a Jew who became Christian, a German who emigrated to France, a bourgeois who preached the coming revolution, a wonderfully gifted poet whose works are often marred by a jarring irony. Heine became very important in France, his adopted country, and also in England and America, where, because of such works of his as *Das Buch der Lieder* (*The Book of*

Songs, 1827) and his more mature *Romanzero* (1851) he was considered a romanticist, though the bulk of his works (*e.g. Deutschland, Atta Troll, Die romantische Schule*) represents him as an anti-romantic Young German. Heine heaped bitter scorn not only upon a Germany docilely submitting to Metternich and Prussia, but, as his *Reisebilder* (*Travelogues,* 1826 ff.) indicate, also upon the John Bull character of the average Englishman. Translations of his poems appeared in France as early as 1834 and, complete, in 1852; among his translators should be mentioned the Italian Zendrini (1866), the American Emma Lazarus (1881) and the Spaniard Teodoro Llorente (the translator also of Goethe, Byron and Hugo). Among his foreign imitators we can name especially James Thomson, Oscar Wilde and Housman in England, George Sand and Baudelaire in France, Carducci and Fogazzaro in Italy, Lermontov in Russia; at times his influence and the influence of his revered model, Byron, would coincide.

Although their influence has been a very different kind, no study of the contributions of German Romanticism to Western literature could be complete without mention of the GRIMM brothers. As the founders of linguistic science (Jakob's *Deutsche Grammatik,* 1819, *Geschichte der deutschen Sprache,* 1848), they presented to every modern nation an entirely new era for scholarly study, and with their collection of old German heroic lore (Wilhelm's *Deutsche Sagen* and *Deutsche Heldengeschichten,* 1829) and, above all, with the fairy-tales collected and published by both of them (*Kinder- und Hausmärchen,* 1812 ff.), they made their names perhaps more widely known than those of any other German romanticists. Among their successors was, above all, the Danish Hans Christian Andersen, whose *Fairy Tales* appeared in 1835.

Finally, there was the towering figure of Richard WAGNER, a romanticist in his glorification of the picturesqueness and the cultural and political prestige of Germany during the Middle Ages, and a Young German in his militant efforts to work for the establishment of an equally impressive Second Reich, a genius significant in the poetry of his *libretti,* but greater still in the music of his operas, who dreamed of an amalgamation of all arts in *Das Kunstwerk der Zukunft* (*The Work of Art of the Future,* 1850). In France, Baudelaire wrote an essay about him as early as 1860, and since 1885 the *Revue wagnérienne* has propagated the fame of a man whose impact upon French poetry has been marked and whose influence, like that of Nietzsche, has at times become quite controversial. The power of Wagner was somewhat less all-permeating in the case of England: his frequent use of Anglo-Celtic themes tended to make him popular, while his anti-bourgeois attitude and the occasionally strong erotic undercurrent of his operas were apt to alienate Victorian England. Among his strongest supporters should be named Swinburne (who emulated the *Tannhäuser*-motif in his *Laus Veneris*), George Moore and George Bernard Shaw (*The Perfect Wagnerite*, 1898), while others like William Morris were no less emphatic in rejecting him.

C. OTHER LITERATURES.

Classical Influences

Although the romanticists rebelled against French Classicism, they by no means rejected the Classicism of Antiquity. Like their immediate predecessors, the pre-romanticists, they valued the masterpieces of Greek originality far above the polished accomplishments of the Roman authors. But they did not believe in absolute standards of beauty, set up for all nations and all ages to follow—and just as they refused to acknowledge the dictatorial leadership of French taste and literature in modern times, they rejected the idea of blindly copying the models of Antiquity. For them—for instance in F. Schlegel's *Geschichte der Poesie der Griechen und Römer* (*History of the Poetry of the Greeks and the Romans,* 1798)—it was not a question of merely imitating the Ancients, but of emulating them in their greatness and of producing something typical of modern times and modern tastes that might compare favorably with what the Greeks had once achieved. Besides, there were other races, ages and literatures—the wisdom of the Orient, or the Catholic fervor of the Middle Ages, for instance—that deserved to be studied and emulated. Greece and Rome, therefore, lost the monopoly of leadership and inspiration they had had among the classicists; their poets remained revered masters to be saluted, but only among many other masters such as Dante, Cervantes, Shakespeare or Ossian, who were equally honored.

Since the concept of the nature of literature of the romanticists was a very different thing from that of the earlier classicists, an entirely new interpretation of Greek myths and literature resulted. While the classicists had seen in Greek, or more especially Roman, art the restraint and objectivity which they admired, the romanticists saw in the literature and myths of Greece individualistic and emotional strivings which, to be sure, were restrained, but which were passionately pulsating nevertheless. While Racine and Goethe had admired and emulated in the Greeks their strong-willed sublimation and the superhumanly marmoreal form with which they held the orgiastic outburst of their emotions in check, romanticists like Hölderlin hailed in the Greeks just this intensity of passions which was seething underneath the masterpieces of Aeschylus and Pindar, and by so doing Hölderlin uncovered aspects of the Greek character which all classicists had hitherto overlooked. In his fundamentally important essay *Die Geburt der Tragödie aus dem Geiste der Musik* (*The Birth of Tragedy out of the Spirit of Music,* 1872) Friedrich Nietzsche later coined significant terms to denote this polarity of the Greek character: their classical restraint and sublimation he called Apollonian, while he named the orgiastic outbursts and romantic conflicts underneath after the oriental god of passion and inebriation, Dionysos.

The result of this new appraisal of Greece was a shifting of idols among the authors of Antiquity. Aeschylus replaced Euripides and Seneca as the most admired of the old dramatists; Sappho replaced Catullus, and Pindar replaced Ovid as the most admired poets. New mythological heroes whose lives were forever symbolical and meaningful replaced the rather mortal and less inspiring former favorites of the type of Achilles, Ulysses or Admetus. Prometheus in particular fired the imagination of the romanticists, because he dared to defy God himself in championing the dignity of man. The lonely Hyperion was the subject of Keats' most ambitious poem and became a modern Greek mortal in the apprenticeship novel of Hölderlin (1797)—not to speak of the heartbreaks of Paul Fleming who, in Longfellow's novel of 1839, was likewise given the name of Hyperion.

We have already spoken of the Greek-inspired works by Goethe and Schiller—not only the dramas (*Iphigenie, Die Braut von Messina*) and epics (*Hermann und Dorothea, Achilleis*), but also the ballads and philosophical poems (*Prometheus* and *Die Braut von Korinth* by the former, and *Die Kraniche des Ibykus, Die Bürgschaft, Der Taucher, Der Ring des Polykrates, Die Götter Griechenlands, Das Eleusische Fest* by the latter) and such adaptations as Goethe's *Die Vögel nach dem Aristophanes* (*The Birds,* 1787) in which Greek mentality and atmosphere prevailed. We now must mention, too, the Greek-inspired works of later German authors, such as *Der Tod des Empedokles* (*The Death of Empedocles*) by Hölderlin, written, perhaps, as a warning against Goethe's self-deification—and Kleist's tragedy *Penthesilea* which, if we compare it with Goethe's *Iphigenie,* illustrates in a nutshell what the classicists meant by the sublime Appollonian and the romanticists by the fiercely unbridled and passionately Dionysian aspects of the Greek character.

In this connection, A. W. Schlegel may also be mentioned for an early essay in Comparative Literature: *Comparaison entre la Phèdre de Racine et celle d'Euripide* (1807) which, as could be expected, was not in favor of the French version. Among all Greek influences, the inspiring impact of Neo-Platonism upon all European romanticists should be especially noted—as indicated, in Germany, for instance, by the big six volume translation of Plato by Schleiermacher (1804-09). After the wave of Romanticism had spent itself and literature began to veer towards Realism, there came to the fore certain epigones or late-born-ones like Grillparzer and Platen who, rather than follow the Young Germans into the dismal field of political pamphleteering, returned to ancient Greece and classical form for inspiration to "stand where Goethe and Schiller stood". Thus Grillparzer in his *Sappho* (1818) and *Das goldene Vlies* (1821), the latter a trilogy dealing with the Argonauts and Jason and Medea—and, above all, in his wonderfully classical and mellow tragedy *Des Meeres und der Liebe Wellen* (*The Waves of the Sea and of Love,* 1831), the story of Hero and Leander. Thus also the lyrical poems of August Graf von Platen: his great admiration for Pindar gave his perfectly chiselled lyrics (*Gedichte,* 1829) a Greek-like clarity and sharpness, in contrast to the hazy and more sentimental poetry of the romanticists. In the manner of Aristophanes he wrote his comedy *Die verhängnisvolle Gabel* (*The Fateful Fork,* 1826) which ridiculed and put an end to the popularity of the romantic fate-tragedies. The same predilection for Antiquity can be seen in Mörike's lyrical anthology of translations (*Klassische Anthologie,* 1840).

In England, Shelley and Coleridge were both great admirers of Aeschylus, and whether he succeeded or not, it was Shelley's intention that his *Prometheus Unbound* (1820) more nearly approximate the lyrical drama of Aeschylus than of the later more technically perfect plays of Sophocles and Euripides. Shelley's *Oedipus Tyrannus* (1820) as well as his lyrical drama *Hellas* (1822) are further indications of his constant preoccupation with Greece; in him, as well as in Wordsworth, Coleridge and others, the influence also of Neo-Platonism was, if anything, even more marked than elsewhere in European Romanticism. Also Wordsworth, the most typically English of the romantics, found in the story of *Laodameia* a means of expressing his newly discovered need for an ethical force stronger than that which he expressed in his early poems. In Keats one should emphasize above all the classical conciseness and chastity of form (*The Grecian Urn*) which makes him a somewhat unusual romanticist, while the case of Byron indicates that the admiration for ancient Greece did not exclude a great compassion for the political struggle for independence of the modern Greeks, for he gave his life trying to contribute to the modern rebirth of the glory that had been the Age of Pericles. English translations ranged from John Hookham Frere's renderings of Aristophanes, and of the *Iliad* and of Aeschylus by John Stuart Blackie (who, in 1834, had also translated Goethe's *Faust*) to *Prometheus Bound* by Elizabeth Barrett (1835)—while new treatments of Greek themes were evidenced in *Prometheus*, a fragmentary drama by Hartley Coleridge, as well as by Tennyson's *Ulysses* (1842). George Finlay, formerly Byron's companion in Greece, added to these endeavors through his *History of Greece* (1843 ff.).

Apart from the Philhellenism of Chateaubriand, Lamartine and others, France between André Chénier and Théophile Gautier and the Parnassians produced little that was under the impact of Antiquity, though the style of the Empire was hellenizing indeed. Poems like Lamartine's *La mort de Socrate* (*The Death of Socrates*, 1823) and Quinet's *Prométhée* (1838) as well as reworkings ranging from Ducis' *Oedipe* (1797) and Lemercier's *Agamemnon* to *L'Orestie, tragédie imitée de l'antique* by Dumas père (1848) indicate the scope of France's indebtedness to ancient Greece, while Michelet added to the Roman studies with his *Histoire romaine* (1831). In Spain, where Neo-Classicism did not really end nor Romanticism really begin till around 1830, the treatment of topics of Antiquity continued in a twilight in which Roman and Greek literature were accorded about the same attention. Manuel de Cabanyes, who died in 1833 at the age of only twenty-five, might be compared to Chénier and Foscolo in his pronounced preference for Antiquity in the midst of budding Romanticism. Translations and imitations of Greek works ranged from Montengón y Paret (*Agamennon, Egisto y Clitemnestra, Edipo* and *Antígona y Emón*, 1820) to the *Edipo* by Martínez de la Rosa (1829), while emulators of Roman literature showed a marked preference for Virgil and Horace—as indicated by the translations by Félix Maria Hidalgo (*Las Bucólicas*, 1829; *Las Eglogas*), Pérez del

Camino (*Las Geórgicas*) and Eugenio de Ochoa (*Eneida*), and, with regard to Horace, by the translation of his complete works by Javier de Burgos (1820) and of the *Poetic Art* by Juan Gualberto González (1844).

It was, however, Italy which most strongly preserved the traditions of classical Antiquity in the midst of the Romantic Age, very often in the person of the same Janus-faced poet. Alfieri forced his rebellious dramas, which clamored for national and personal freedom, into an icily simplified classical form. Foscolo was a romanticist in his imitations of Goethe's *Werther* and of the English Churchyard Poets, but at the same time severely classical, too, in his form, especially in his tragedies (*Tieste*, 1797, and *Ajace*, 1811), and the same can be said of Ippolito Pindemonte, who was a disciple of the Churchyard Poets and a translator of the *Odyssey* at the same time (1818). Also Monti was romantic in his contacts with German literature and, above all, with Mme. de Staël, yet at the same time a glorifier of classical art in his *Prosopopea di Pericle* (1799), a follower of Alfieri in his tragedies (*Caio Gracco*, 1802), the translator of the *Iliad* (1810), a poet who hailed Napoleon as a new Prometheus (*Prometeo*, 1797) and who opposed Romanticism even after it had achieved victory (*Sermone sopra la mitologia*, 1825). Leopardi, the disciple of Greece and Rome (*Ultimo canto di Saffo*, 1822), expressed his abysmal pessimism and despair and his scorn about contemporary Italian conditions (*Paralipomeni alla Batracomiomachia*, 1842) in a style that was coldly classical in its self-imposed restraint and that was far from the self-indulgent tearfulness of many other *Weltschmerz*-poets. The same dualism can be noted in Giambattista Niccolini, a noted romantic dramatist (*Antonio Foscarini, Arnaldo da Brescia, Filippo Strozzi*), yet at the same time an adaptor of Greek dramas (*Edipo*, 1826).

Oriental Influences.

The interest in Mahometan culture and other Asiatic traditions, religions and literatures which had begun as an interest in the exotic on the part of the eighteenth century, developed into a genuine desire to understand and absorb entirely different cultures on the part of the romanticists. Especially the German romanticists, after having breached the Chinese Wall of French Classicism, were not content to point to the beauties of other European literatures alone—Dante, Shakespeare, Calderón; with the catholic taste and unbounded enthusiasm of the Schlegels to guide them, they were supremely important for their investigations also of the cultures of Arabia, Persia and India. One of the most important contributions to an understanding of Oriental literature was made by Friedrich Schlegel with his *Ueber die Sprache und Weisheit der Inder* (*On the Language and Wisdom of the East Indians,* 1808), the product of his long study of Sanskrit in Paris. From 1818 on August Wilhelm Schlegel became the first professor of Sanskrit at the University of Bonn and in 1823 he published the first critical edition and Latin translation of the *Bhagavad-Gita,* and in 1829 of the *Ramayana* with a Latin translation. In these efforts, to be sure, the Schlegels had been preceded by certain English and French translators of ancient Indian literature, for instance by the translations from the *Mahabharata* by C. Wilkins (1785) and of some fragments of the *Vedas* by Anquetil-Duperron (1804).

Through these men and other philologists the language and culture particularly of India became a powerful force in philosophy as well as in literature. The romantic tendency toward mysticism drew various of the romanticists to a study of Hindu philosophy, and the influence of this study, sometimes combined with the ever-present importance of Neo-Platonism, can be found in Emerson and other New England transcendentalists. Hammer-Purgstall's translation of the medieval Persian poet Hafiz in 1812 inspired Goethe in his *Westöstlicher Divan* (*The West-Eastern Divan,* 1819), perhaps the outstanding example of the attraction of the Orient, presenting as a lyrical dialogue between two Oriental lovers, Hatem and Suleika, Goethe's own love for Marianne von Willemer. Quite as important as the poetry contained in the *West-Eastern Divan* are Goethe's notes, which represent as complete and painstakingly scholarly a survey of Oriental studies as was available in Europe at that time. A second translation of Hafiz was made by Daumer, who should also be noted for *Mohammed,* a series of poems in honor of the prophet (1846). The interest in Mahometan culture, potent ever since the days of Herder's *Cid,* Goethe's own *Mahomet* and his performance of such Iberian-Arabic *comedias* as Calderón's *El príncipe constante,* was strong also in August Graf von Platen—not only in his colorful epic *Die Abassiden* (1834), but already in his *Ghaselen* (1821) in which he introduced this unusual metrical form of the Orient into German lyrical poetry. The fascination of the *Arabian Nights* likewise continued to remain potent, as seen, for instance, in the orientalizing fairy-tales by Wilhelm Hauff (*Die Karawane* of 1826, and others). Among later poets and scholars influenced by the Orient, mention should be made of Friedrich Rückert, a most facile translator, for his *Die Weisheit des Brahmanen* (*The Wisdom of the Brahmin*, 1836), and of Friedrich Bodenstedt for his *Tausend und ein Tag im Orient* (*Thousand and One Days in the Orient*, containing the famous *Lieder des Mirza Schaffy*, 1849). Ferdinand Freiligrath should also be named in this connection, although his exotic poems dealt with Africa and America as well as with the Orient (*e.g. Der Löwenritt, Der Mohrenfürst*).

In England, the poets' love for the Orient lasted from Beckford's *Vathek* (1781) till well beyond Edward Fitzgerald's immensely popular adaptation of the *Rubaiyat* of Omar Khayyam (1859) and Kipling's tales from Anglo-India. Southey as well as Byron (just as Pushkin in Russian literature) contributed a colorful and voluptuous interpretation of the Orient to the prevalent romantic exoticism; of the former we can name oriental epics like *Thalaba*, 1801, and *The Curse of Kehama*, based upon an old Hindu legend, 1810, while the latter is famous for his Turkish tales of violence like *The Corsair*, 1814, *Lara*, 1814, and *The Giaour*, 1813 (translated into Polish by Mickiewicz in 1835). Also Thomas Moore's *Lalla Rookh* (1817) with its gorgeous descriptions of Eastern scenes and Shelley's *Revolt of Islam* (1817) should be mentioned in this connection. In France, the first chairs in Sanskrit and Chinese were established in Paris in 1815. The fascination especially of the Near East for French travellers began with Volney (*Voyage en Syrie et en Egypte*, 1787) and Chateaubriand (*Itinéraire de Paris à Jerusalem*, 1811) ; it continued with Gautier, Renan and Flaubert. Of Lamartine, who stayed in the Orient in 1832-33, we should record the three volumes of his *Souvenirs, impressions, pensées et paysages pendant un voyage en Orient* (1835), while Gérard de Nerval contributed to the same trend with his *Voyage en Orient* (1846) and *Scènes de la vie orientale* (1848). The strong impact of the poetry of the Islam is noticeable, too, in Hugo's *Les Orientales*.

But most marked were these Mahometan influences of course in the case of Spain. The reawakening, among the Spanish

romanticists, of the greatness of the poets of the *Siglo de Oro* and
of the topics treated by them, among them Spanish medieval history and the constant warfare between the Christian and the
Arab, naturally contributed to the new emphasis on the influence
of Mahometan culture and themes. The trend showed itself
as early as 1777 with *Hormesinda,* a tragedy by Nicolas F. de
Moratín; but with the coming of Romanticism proper, Spanish
literature began to abound with poems, dramas and novels which
resuscitated the colorfulness of Arabic Spain or the glory of
the *reconquista* which was carried on by the Spanish rulers
of the Middle Ages. In a way Southey's famous English poem
on *Roderick, the Last of the Goths* (1814) served as a forerunner
of a number of Spanish treatments of the coming of the Arabs
in 711, among them the narrative poem *Ommiada* by the Conde
de Noroña (1816), *Rodrigo, ultimo rey de los Godos,* a tragedy
still neo-classical in its pattern by Gil y Zarate (1835), and
Zorrilla's *El puñal del Godo* (*The Dagger of the Goth,* 1842).
In 1833 Noroña also published *Poesias asiaticas,* Arabic, Persian
and Turkish poems which he had translated from the English.
Moorish influences reached their peak between *El moro expósito*
(*The Moorish Bastard,* 1834) by the Duke of Rivas and the
beautiful *Granada, poema oriental* by Zorrilla (1852) ; the latter is also noted for his *Leyenda de Al-Hamar* (1847), while
the former wrote about the tragic expulsion of the Moors in
1609 in his drama *La morisca de Alajuar.* During his exile in
Paris also Martínez de la Rosa wrote a tragedy about the last
struggles of the Moors against Philip II: *Aben-Humeya ou la
révolte des Maures* (1830), thus familiarizing also the French
with this rich and exotic material—though Chateaubriand had
prepared the ground with his famous *Le dernier des Abencer-
rages.* In this connection it is quite appropriate to emphasize
that the study of the Arabic world and of the Arabic impact
upon Spanish culture has always fascinated the best minds
among Spanish scholars because Spaniards, more than anybody
else, are best qualified to take care of that important field of
Comparative Literature and to investigate a civilization to which
the West is so deeply indebted. Among these scholars and works
we can name Spaniards from Don Pascual de Gayangos (*Las
dinastias musulmanas en España*) up to Don Julian Ribera Tar-
ragó (*Bibliofilos y bibliotecas en la España musulmana,* 1896,
La épica entre los musulmanes españoles, 1915, *Música andaluza*

medieval en las canciones de trovadores, troveros y minnesinger,
1923 ff.), Don Miguel Asín Palacios (*El Averroismo teológico
de Santo Tomás de Aquino*, 1904, *La escatología musulmana en
la Divina Comedia*, 1919, *El Islam cristianizado*, 1931) and
Angel González Palencia (*Historia de la España musulmana*,
1925, and *Historia de la literatura arábigo-española*, 1928).
Arabic influences upon Italy were less powerful and their investigation therefore less frequent; among the few scholarly
works in this field we might mention *La storia dei Musulmani di
Sicilia* by Michele Amari (1854). Among outsiders to delve
into this field, we should name the famous German hispanist
Adolf Friedrich, Graf von Schack, whose *Poesie und Kunst der
Araber in Spanien und Sizilien* (1865) was translated into Spanish by Juan Valera (*Poesía y arte de los árabes en España y
Sicilia*).

Religious and Hebrew Influences

While Classicism, though ardently Christian (Racine), had
followed Boileau's advice of dealing with ancient mythology
rather than with biblical themes, and while the eighteenth century of Enlightenment had lost much of the Christian fervor to
the point of treating religion with indifference, if not with
scorn, the Romantic Movement signified an emphatic return
to Christian ardor and in particular to the tenets of the Catholic
Church. In fact, this is one of the few striking differences between German Pre-Romanticism and Romanticism proper:
namely, that the spiritual leaders of the Storm and Stress were
Protestants (Klopstock and Herder, for instance, were Lutheran
theologians, to begin with), while German romanticists were
predominantly Catholic, with an astounding number of converts
from Protestantism among them (Friedrich Leopold Graf zu
Stolberg, Friedrich Schlegel, Zacharias Werner). To be sure,
the treatments of biblical and of hagiographic topics (Tieck's
Leben und Tod der heiligen Genoveva, 1799; Byron's *Cain*,
1817; *Saül* by Lamartine, Soumet, and Gertrudis Gómez de
Avellaneda, *Moïse* by Chateaubriand and by Vigny) as such
might seem to have decreased if compared with the far more
frequent treatments of previous centuries; nevertheless, the
whole atmosphere was so permeated with a religious ardor and
a mysticism closely akin to Neo-Platonism, that Romanticism
can certainly be called one of the great revivals of Christianity.

A mere glance at such works as *Die Christenheit oder Europa* by Novalis (1799), *Le génie du christianisme* (1802) and *Les Martyrs ou le triomphe de la religion chrétienne* (1809) by Chateaubriand, or the *Essai sur l'indifférence* by La Mennais (1817) convinces us of the religious intensity of this period. It existed not only among the Catholics—the reaction against the *Encyclopédie* in France, the powerful revival of Jansenism in Manzoni (*Inni sacri*, 1815) in Italy, the religious poems of Gertrudis Gómez de Avellaneda and of Juan Arolas in Spain or the ardently Catholic mysticism of Coventry Patmore in England (*Poems*, 1844); also the Protestants underwent deeply the impact of religion. That is especially evident in Schleiermacher's *Ueber die Religion; Reden an die Gebildeten unter ihren Verächtern (On Religion; Speeches to its Cultured Despisers*, 1799); in Grundtvig, the great Protestant leader in Sweden; and in the New England transcendentalists who, greatly influenced by Schleiermacher, Kant and other Germans, combined their Romanticism with Protestantism (Emerson's *Over-Soul*), though in the Unitarian Movement they at the same time endeavored to break away from the dogma-bound orthodoxy of seventeenth century Puritanism. In the storms and the passions of life it was rare that a poet ended up in flippant irony (Byron, Heine) or in an almost completely atheistic despair (Shelley's *On the Necessity of Atheism*, 1811; Leopardi's *Pensieri* 1817 ff.); more likely than not, even after the wildest of dissipations, he would avail himself of the comforting reassurances of the Church and thereby, if possible, make his peace with God, too. In the midst of these wholesale surrenders to a medieval mentality of contrition and subservience, Goethe alone had the strength and the pride to stand out as an emphatic individualist and Protestant well capable of coping with the problems of this world and affirmatively responsible for the ledger of his life, treating coolly those whom he suspected of crypto-Catholicism (Kleist, Schelling) and celebrating the Wartburg festivity of 1817, the three hundredth anniversary of Luther's important decision, with more than necessary ardor.

How thoroughly religion permeated Romanticism can best be seen by the example of France: the ardent Catholic Chateaubriand was the first to overcome the aridity left behind by the encyclopedists and to restore religion to its important place in man's life, and his translation of *Paradise Lost* (1836) indicates that he established a spiritual kinship with Milton that was above dogmatic differentiations, and in his *Du Pape* (*About the Pope*, 1819) Joseph de Maistre pushed this Catholic ardor to the point of intransigence. The romantic poets of France excelled in writing religious epics of the type of Vigny's *Eloa* (1823), Lamartine's *La chute d'un ange* (*The Fall of an Angel*, 1838), Soumet's *La divine épopée* (*The Divine Epic*, 1830). The same Catholic ardor can be seen in men like Brizeux, Ozanam and, above all, in La Mennais. Scholarly investigations of the essence of Christianity of the type of Renan's *Origines du Christianisme*, containing, above all, his *Vie de Jésus* (*Life of Jesus*, 1863) may be said to be a direct outgrowth of this romantic ardor, though some of these scholars (in contrast, for instance, to the orthodox Rosmini in Italy) may at times tend to become daringly liberal and individualistic in their conclusions. Thus, La Mennais' *Paroles d'un croyant* (*Words of a Believer*, 1834) in France, David Friedrich Strauss' *Das Leben Jesu* (*The Life of Jesus*, 1835) and Ludwig Feuerbach's *Das Wesen des Christentums* (*The Essence of Christianity*, 1841) in Germany and, above all, Sören Aabye Kierkegaard (*Either —Or*, 1843, *Stadia on Life's Way*, 1845) in Denmark. In England, a strong religious undercurrent was the rule rather than the exception; nevertheless, we can point to a distinct intensification of religious literature from Blake and Cowper through Coleridge especially to Carlyle and Cardinal Newman. Renan's *Life of Jesus* went through more than two hundred French editions and was translated into twelve languages; La Mennais' *Words of a Believer*—immediately condemned in Rome—was rendered into Spanish by Larra and into Portuguese by Castilho (1836) ; and in England we should name George Eliot as the translator both of Strauss' *Life of Jesus* (1846) and of Feuerbach's *Essence of Christianity* (1854). Littré rendered Strauss into French in 1839. Also Kierkegaard's ideas continue to exert a powerful influence, though his beliefs are perverted by his most recent disciples, the existentialists.

With regard to Hebrew influences, we might point not so much to works by gentiles of the type of Byron's *Hebrew Melodies* (1815), but to the increasing importance of Jewish writers and political leaders—for in this age of liberalism and social progress it was but natural that Jews should help inspire the efforts of Young Europe (Heine, Börne), and, indeed, even take over the stewardship of great governments (Disraeli). Women likewise profited by this wave of emancipation and helped inspire the best that was in early nineteenth century literature—not only gentiles like Mme. de Staël, George Sand, Jane Austen, the Brontës, Margaret Fuller, George Eliot, Elizabeth Barrett Browning, but also Jewesses like Dorothea Schlegel, the daughter of the philosopher Moses Mendelssohn, and Rahel Varnhagen von Ense and Henriette Herz, the latter two famous for their spirited salons in Berlin.

Rather than include the progress of Hebrew studies (*e.g.* Renan's *Histoire du peuple d'Israël*, 1887 ff.), or to point to pro-Jewish (*Ivanhoe* by Scott, *Uriel Acosta* by Gutzkow, and *Die Judenbuche* by Annette von Droste-Hülshoff) and possibly anti-Jewish (Fagin in Dickens' *Oliver Twist*) treatments in literature, mention should be made, above all, of a fascinating Hebrew theme which became most popular among the restless seekers of peace and the *Weltschmerz* poets of European Romanticism: namely the story of Ahasverus, the Wandering Jew. In its first published form it was called *Kurze Beschreibung und Erzählung von einem Juden Ahasverus* (*Short Description and Narrative of a Jew Ahasverus*, 1602) and it went through more than fifty new editions and versions in less than a century. It inspired poets like Goethe, Lenau, Quinet, Mosen, Sue, Hamerling and others; of these, the version by Eugène Sue (*Le juif errant*, 1845) was perhaps best known and often imitated (*El patriarca del valle* by Patricio de la Escosura, 1847 and others). Also Scandinavians seem to have had a marked interest in this tale, as indicated by the cycle of poems called *Ahasverus* by the Dane Ingemann (1833) and by *Prometheus and Ahasverus* by the Swede Rydberg around 1890. The weird and tragic medieval tale of Ahasver damned to eternal restlessness for having abused Christ on His way to Golgatha could well compare with other homeless wanderers of the Romantic Age such as Faust, Don Juan or the Flying Dutchman.

Medieval Influences

The revival of interest in the Middle Ages is so universal and so significant a part of European Romanticism (especially in Germany, England and Spain) that the Middle Ages deserve special mention for their supremely important contribution to the literature of this period. Some of the reasons which helped to break down the Voltairian bias against the barbarity and ignorance of the "gothic" Middle Ages have been suggested in the chapter on Pre-Romanticism, in connection with Herder, Percy, Bodmer, Muratori and other pioneers, but only during the Romantic Period itself do they become major forces.

The first and most important influence of the Middle Ages was exerted through the unadorned simplicity and sincerity of folk literature, poetry as well as prose tale, which, after the breakdown of neo-classical stiltedness, was traced back to medieval origins. For the first time systematic collections of folk songs and ballads and of folk tales were undertaken on a broad international scale. Sir Walter Scott's *Minstrelsy of the Scottish Border* (1802) reflects his intense interest and his understanding study of folk poetry depicting essentially medieval life; it led him, in his own poetry and prose, to use the Middle Ages as the setting for many of his works (*The Lay of the Last Minstrel, The Lord of the Isles, Ivanhoe, Quentin Durward, The Talisman, The Fair Maid of Perth, Anne of Geierstein, Count Robert of Paris*). In the same way the works of Goethe (*Reineke Fuchs,* 1793), Novalis (*Heinrich von Ofterdingen,* 1799), Tieck (*Franz Sternbalds Wanderungen,* 1798), Arnim and Brentano (*Des Knaben Wunderhorn,* 1805), Görres (*Die deutschen Volksbücher,* 1807), and especially of the Grimm brothers (*Kinder- und Hausmärchen,* 1812) led the romanticists to an investigation and then an imitation of medieval style, form and atmosphere. Very often this preoccupation with national medieval lore spread across the borders and achieved fame and popularity in foreign countries, as, for instance, Robert Browning's version of the German tale of the *Pied-Piper of Hamelin,* or the great collection and translation of European folksongs published by Sir John Bowring (Russian, 1821; Spanish, 1824; Polish and Serbian, 1827; Hungarian, 1830, and so on). The result of this European revival of medieval folk literature was to provide new and exotic, though often not medieval, moods and styles. For example, the artistic fairy-tale and fairy-drama of Germany, such as deveolped by Tieck (*Haymonskinder, Magelone, Der blonde Eckbert, Der gestiefelte Kater*), Goethe (*Das Märchen*), Brentano (*Die Geschichte vom braven Kasperl und dem schönen Annerl*), de la Motte-Fouqué (*Undine*—very popular in the modern French adaptation by Giraudoux), and Hoffmann (*Nussknacker und Mausekönig*) reveal their medieval inspiration by their tone, intent, and subject matter. Even those *Novellen* of Goethe and Hoffmann which presumably have a modern setting are often bathed in medieval atmosphere.

The Romantic Age was a period of great revivals not only of medieval themes (the *Nibelungen,* the Cid, Joan of Arc, and so on) but also of individual authors. Herder and Bodmer had initiated this trend in the eighteenth century; the linguistic studies by the Grimm brothers, by the philologist Karl Lachmann (*Die Nibelungen,* 1826) and by modernizing translators like Karl Simrock (*Nibelungen,* 1827; *Edda,* 1851) rapidly increased the knowledge of older literatures and of authors like Hartmann von Aue, Wolfram von Eschenbach and Gottfried von Strassburg. Ludwig Uhland showed his profound knowledge of and love for the Middle Ages not only in his famous ballads (*Des Sängers Fluch, Taillefer*) and his dramas (*Ludwig der Bayer*), but also in his professorial lectures and studies (*Walther von der Vogelweide,* 1822). In Italy (Foscolo, Mazzini), as well as in Germany (A. W. Schlegel, Philalethes, Witte), Dante began again to occupy the supreme place due to him, and in England the love of the Middle Ages led not only to a reappreciation of Chaucer (beginning with Thomas Tyrwhitt, in 1775) but also of ever so many medieval aspects of Spenser's *Faerie Queene.* The rich style and metre of Spenser became popular again with John Upton and Thomas Gray and from then on helped to inspire the poetry of English Romanticism; indeed, with G. B. Martelli's translation of 1831 Spenser (not usually popular abroad) became known also in Italy. Among the historians Henry Hallam wrote a *History of Europe during the Middle Ages* (1818), while the Frenchman A. Thierry investigated Anglo-French relations in his *Histoire de la conquête de l'Angleterre par les Normands* (1825).

The constant preoccupation with the Middle Ages became evident also in Spain, France and Italy; it showed itself in the love of spectacular historical tragedies, a revival of national and patriotic romances and also in a reawakening interest in the accomplished artistry of the troubadours and of the vanished Golden Age of Provençal literature. In Spain, we can point to Böhl de Faber's *Floresta de rimas antiguas castellanas* (*Bouquet of Old Castilian Poetry,* published in Hamburg in 1821) and to the *Romancero* by Agustín Durán (1828), a fine collection of medieval lore, with a scholarly discussion of its sources and significance.   Other Spanish efforts in this direction were *Los cantos del Trovador* (1841) by Zorrilla, which, among others, glorified the frequently treated and patriotic theme of Pelayo, king of Asturias, the eighth-century founder of the Spanish monarchy.   Also the so-called *Romances históricos* by the Duque de Rivas should be mentioned in this connection, though they mostly treat post-medieval events in Spanish history; likewise his *Leyendas romanticas*, which were partly in the manner of Scott, partly in the manner of Zorrilla.   With Zorrilla's famous *Granada* (1852) and *La leyenda del Cid* (1882), these medieval tales were naturally frequently tinged with Oriental influences. In France, Villemain wrote his *Histoire de la littérature au moyen âge* in 1828; with regard to the resuscitation of Provençal culture and literature, we should name Raynouard with his *Choix de poésies originales des troubadours* (six volumes of texts and translations published in 1816-21) and again his *Des troubadours et des cours d'amour* (*About Troubadours and the Courts of Love*, 1817), to be continued by Fauriel's *Histoire de la poésie provençale* (1846).   In the field of the novel, the *genre troubadour* had begun with Loaisel de Tréogate as early as 1765. These investigations of medieval chivalry flourished in England from the significant *Letters on Chivalry and Romance* by Richard Hurd (1762) well beyond Browning's profound poem on *Sordello* (1840); in Germany they produced collections like Wilhelm Müller's *Blumenlese aus den Minnesingern* (*Bouquet from the Minnesingers,* 1816).

The wealth of historical novels will be discussed later, in connection with Sir Walter Scott; but here might still be mentioned a few authors and titles of historical dramas with a distinctly medieval background—ranging from Southey's *Wat Tyler* in England to Victor Hugo's *Les Burgraves* in France and Longfellow's *Golden Legend* in America, but again most conspicuous in Germany, Spain and Italy.   Among them might be noted *Das Käthchen von Heilbronn* by Kleist, *Herzog Ernst von Schwaben* by Uhland, *Ezzelino da Romano* by Eichendorff, *König Ottokars Glück und Ende* (*King Ottokar, his Rise and Fall*) by Grillparzer in Germany and Austria; *Macías* by Larra, *El Trovador* by García Gutiérrez (from which Verdi borrowed the theme for his opera), *Los amantes de Teruel* by Hartzenbusch, and Gothic tragedies like *La ley de raza* (*The Law of the Clan*) by Hartzenbusch and *Ataulfo* by Rivas in Spain; and, most numerous in their patriotic ardor, the historical tragedies which helped to inspire the Italian *Risorgimento*: Manzoni's *Carmagnola*, Guerrazzi's *I Bianchi e i Neri* (*The White and the Black*) and Niccolini's *Lodovico Sforza* and *Arnaldo da Brescia* (the latter forbidden and burnt, and therefore printed in France). Hand in hand with this went a loving restoration of pre-classical national dramatic art: thus the collection *El teatro español anterior á Lope de Vega* by Böhl de Faber in Spain, or Tieck's love not only for Shakespeare, but also for the other great Elizabethan dramatists (*Altenglisches Theater*).

England.

It would seem natural that the home of Pre-Romanticism and therefore the seedbed of Romanticism should rival Germany for its contribution to European Romanticism. The Romantic Period in England, a country whose literature had been essentially romantic ever since Chaucer and Spenser, produced a great flowering of lyric poetry and of sensitive prose, but strangely contributed much less to nineteenth century Europe than it borrowed. However, through two men, Scott and Byron, England gave the international community a new literary form and a new, if somewhat ephemeral, literary personality.

Sir Walter SCOTT (1771-1832), the virtual creator of the historical novel, showed his love for historical topics in everything he did, from his collections of English and Scottish ballads to his own art ballads (some of which reflect his interest in the same form in Germany), and to his famous historical novels. In his poetry Scott was much more of a receiver than an emitter, but in his novels which glorified the greatness and the picturesque qualities of the Middle Ages (*Ivanhoe*, 1819) as well as of the Tudor (*Marmion*, 1808; *Kenilworth*, 1831) and Stuart periods (*Waverley*, 1805) he presented to Europe an entirely new literary form, though we should, of course, hasten to add that many historical novels had been written in Europe before him (from Marmontel's *Les Incas ou la destruction de l'Empire de Pérou*, 1777, to Kleist's *Michael Kohlhaas*, 1807) and that he only boosted this genre to a supremely important place. One need search no farther than the most recent best-seller list to determine the importance of the historical novel which Scott was the first to perfect. Almost immediately after his novels began to appear, Scott was imitated at home (Bulwer-Lytton's *The Last Days of Pompeii, Rienzi* and Thackeray's *Henry Esmond*) and abroad. Balzac began his career, when he finally started writing under his own name, by imitating Sir Walter Scott (*Les Chouans,* 1829), while Mérimée's *1572, Chronique du règne de Charles IX* (1829), Vigny's *Cinq Mars ou Une conspiration sous Louis XIII* (1836), Hugo's *Notre Dame de Paris* (1831) and *Quatre-vingt-treize* (1874) and the perennially popular historical romances of Alexandre Dumas père (*Les trois Mousquetaires,* 1844, and *Le Comte de Monte Cristo,* 1845) indicate that the historical novel became the dominant prose form also of French Romanticism and the generations beyond (Flaubert's *Salammbô,* 1862, Anatole France's *Thaïs,* 1894 and *Les dieux ont soif,* 1912). In America, from Cooper's *The Spy* (1822) and *Last of the Mohicans* (1826), through the psychological, but still historical, *Scarlet Letter* (1850) and *House of Seven Gables* (1852) of Hawthorne and the humorous variant in *A Connecticut Yankee at the Court of King Arthur* by Mark Twain down to the present-day surfeit of best-selling historical romances, the historical novel has remained perhaps the single most popular literary genre. A study of Scott's impact upon American culture (so amazingly great especially in the way he was worshipped and emulated in the aristocratic *ante bellum* South) and of his influence in American literature would closely parallel a study of American best-selling novels, from Helen Hunt Jackson's *Ramona* to Allen's *Anthony Adverse* and Margaret Mitchell's *Gone with the Wind.* Indeed, it is not unreasonable to suggest that Scott's romantic and panoramic accounts of historical spectacles are among the ancestors of the super-colossal movie spectacles which Hollywood has made its specialty. A certain predilection for historical novels about early Christians is noticeable both among English (*Fabiola,* by Cardinal Wiseman, 1854) and American writers (*Ben Hur,* by Lewis Wallace, 1880).

Germany was no less fascinated with the new kind of novel which Scott created than were England, France or America. Virtual contemporaries of Scott such as Hauff, with his *Lichtenstein* (1826), set in the turbulent days of the Reformation, and Willibald Alexis, with his novels about early Brandenburg history (such as *Die Hosen des Herrn von Bredow,* 1846) helped to introduce the historical novel to Germany. Later German historical novelists include Gustav Freytag, with his *Bilder aus der deutschen Vergangenheit (Tableaux from the German Past,* 1859) and *Die Ahnen (The Ancestors,* 1872) ; Scheffel, with his *Ekkehard* (1857), set in the region of Lake Constance in the tenth century; and Felix Dahn, with his glorification of the ancient Goths in his *Der Kampf um Rom (The Struggle for Rome,* 1876). The historical novel is still very much alive in Germany, as is demonstrated by Fontane (*Vor dem Sturm,* 1878), Sudermann (*Der Katzensteg,* 1889) and by the international popularity of Lion Feuchtwanger whose subjects have ranged from medieval Germany (*Die hässliche Herzogin,* 1923) to Roman Jewish history (*Josephus*) and of Thomas Mann, with his biblical novels about Joseph and his recent *Der Erwählte (Holy Sinner,* 1951). Switzerland's Conrad Ferdinand Meyer, along with France's Flaubert, came as close to making a genuine art form out of the historical novel as anyone outside of Russia. Meyer's historical subjects are drawn not only from Switzerland (*Jürg Jenatsch,* 1874), but also from England (*Der Heilige,* 1880), Germany (*Gustav Adolphs Page*), Italy (*Die Hochzeit des Mönchs,* 1884) and France (*Das Amulett,* 1873). One of Switzerland's greatest authors of the nineteenth century, Gottfried Keller, also included historical tales in his *Zürcher Novellen* of 1878 (*Hadlaub,* the story of the last minnesinger; *Ursula,* dealing with the Swiss Reformation, and others).

In Italy, one of the first of the imitations of Scott has come to be regarded as the greatest of all Italian novels: Manzoni's *I Promessi Sposi, storia milanese del secolo XVII (The Betrothed,* 1827), the story of two unhappy lovers living near Milan during the period of Spanish domination. Manzoni's work evoked at once a great Italian controversy for or against the historical novel; its immense popularity abroad is attested by the fact that in the first fifteen years of its publication it went through five French translations. Other Italian historical novels—so powerful in their patriotic implications during the fermenting period of the *Risorgimento*— were *Marco Visconti* (1834) by Tommaso Grossi (author, among other things, also of a historical epic and Tasso-continuation, *I Lombardi alla prima crociata,* 1826) ; *Ettore Fieramosca* (1833) and *Niccolo de' Lapi* (1841) by Massimo Taparelli d'Azeglio (both novels dealing with Italian history early in the sixteenth century)—and, above all, the historical novels by Francesco Domenico Guerrazzi (*La battaglia di Benevento*, 1827, *L'assedio di Firenze, Beatrice Cenci*). In Spain, the historical novel extended from *Los Bandos de Castilla* by López Soler (1830) to well beyond *El señor de Bembibre*, an especially famous novel about the Templars by Enrique Gil y Carrasco (1844). Other Spaniards to be influenced by Scott, in their novels as well as in their dramas and poems, were Espronceda (*Sancho Saldana*, 1834) and Martínez de la Rosa (*Dona Isabel de Solís, reina de Granada*, 1837) ; and especially Telesforo de Trueba y Cossío, since 1823 an émigré in England and a popularizer of Spanish culture abroad (*La España romantica*, 1827, first published in English) was under the spell of Scott's historical novels (*Gómez Arias, o los moriscos de las Alpujarras*, 1831), while Nicasio Gallego should be mentioned as the translator of Manzoni. Later, as was to be expectted, the historical tales often blended with regional novels as, for instance, in the *Episodios nacionales* by Pérez Galdós (1873 ff.). The novels of van Lennep (*Our Ancestors*, 1833 ff.) and of Conscience (*The Lion of Flanders*, 1838) in Holland and Belgium, respectively, and of Sienkiewicz in Poland (*Quo Vadis?* 1896; *The Teutonic Knights*, 1897) indicate the universal spread of this new literary genre. And, of course, the greatest of all the historical novels, and in the opinion of some the greatest novel, Tolstoy's *War and Peace* (1868) must be mentioned, too, in connection with Scott's contributions to nineteenth century Europe.

Although the study of the historical novel, and therefore of Scott's influence on the literature of the last hundred and twenty-five years, would provide material for several books in itself, Scott, as has been intimated before, can also be studied for his contributions to poetry and the drama. His popular utilization of romanticized historical topics helped to give impetus to the same kind of utilization of historical materials in such poems as Longfellow's *Hiawatha* (1855), and *The Courtship of Miles Standish* (1858), Scheffel's *Trompeter von Säckingen* (1854) and Meyer's *Huttens letzte Tage* (*Hutten's Last Days*, 1871). In the same way the enthusiasm for historical materials is reflected in the dramas from Hugo (*Les Burgraves*) and Dumas père (*Henri III et sa cour*) up to Rostand (*Cyrano de Bergerac*, 1897, and translated into German by Ludwig Fulda in 1898) in France; Grillparzer (*Ottokar, Libussa*) in Austria; Manzoni (*Adelchi*) and Benedetti (*La congiura di Milano*) in Italy;

Hartzenbusch (*La madre de Pelayo*) in Spain; Hebbel (*Agnes Bernauer*) and Wildenbruch (*Die Karolinger*) in Germany; and Alexis Tolstoy (*The Death of Ivan the Terrible*) in Russia. Finally, among Scott's translators we must mention Giuseppe Niccolini in Italy (also the translator of Byron) and Defaucaufret (also the translator of *La España romantica* by Trueba y Cossío, 1832) in France (38 vols., 1829-42).

The influence of Scott on European literature was the greatest single contribution which romantic England has made, but for at least the first half of the nineteenth century George Gordon, Lord BYRON (1788-1824), seemed to equal Scott, and in some ways exceeded him, in European popularity. Byron's amazing, almost hysterical, popularity on the continent can be regarded as nothing less than a cultural phenomenon of major importance. His fame rested not just on his poetry (*Childe Harold*, 1812 ff., *Don Juan*, 1818 ff.), as influential as that was, but even more upon his personality and his tremendous ability to dramatize himself. In his poetry and personality Byron succeeded in embodying just those traits which were most popular and most admired during the Romantic Period: overpowering *Weltschmerz* that rebels against the tedium of middle class life; perpetual restlessness of spirit which seeks constantly for new experiences; haughty defiance of vested power, whether in the form of English society which exiled him or in the form of political oppressors of subjected countries (all the rabid anti-Metternich poets were Byronians); and above all unashamed, proud individualism, which suggested that the ego could raise itself above society and even above God Himself in its search for self-realization.

The study of the influence of the Byronic personality would alone be a complex one. But on the more measurable level of the influence of Byron's poetry there is no paucity of problems. His *Childe Harold* became another symbol of the restless seeker of meaning in life, largely autobiographical in his wanderings through Spain, Italy, Switzerland, Germany and Greece, comparable to, if less lasting than, Faust, the Flying Dutchman, the Wandering Jew, and the never-satiated Don Juan. In France Byron's influence was especially marked in Lamartine (such as indicated by his poems addressed to Byron and his unhappy attempt to write a *Dernier chant de Childe Harold*), Musset, Vigny, George Sand, Hugo, and Stendhal. A French translation of *Les oeuvres complètes de Byron* by Amédée Pichot began to appear as early as 1814. In Germany, Byron was early hailed as the hope of the future by no less a man than Goethe, who gave a symbolic portrait of the young Englishman in the character of Euphorion, son of Faust and Helen in *Faust II*. He was imitated by Waiblinger, Lenau and Annette von Droste-Hülshoff; but his most eager German disciple was Heinrich Heine. Among the various German translations of Byron the one by Otto Gildemeister (1861, the translator also of Shakespeare and of Dante) deserves special praise. Through his friendship with Mme. de Staël, his residence in Italy, his love affair with the Italian Countess Guiccioli, his imitations of Dante, Pulci and Tasso and his enthusiasm for Italy, Byron did not fail to influence such Italian poets as Pellico, Leopardi and Prati. A first Italian translation appeared between 1818 and 1825; among those who opposed the excessive Byronianism of younger poets was Carducci. Echoes of Byron's poetry and personality were particularly frequent also in Spain; among his disciples should be named especially Espronceda (*El estudiante de Salamanca* and *El diablo mundo*). *Baltasar,* a biblical tragedy by Gertrudis Gómez de Avellaneda (1858) was influenced by *Sardanapal*, while in the field of lyrical poetry we should name the *Poesias* by Juan Arolas (1843) and *La ultima lamentación de Lord Byron* by Nuñez de Arce (1879). In Russia, both Lermontov (*The Demon*, 1839) and Pushkin (in his Don Juanesque *Eugene Onyegin*, 1832) turned more to Byron than to any other author of Western Europe, represented themselves as typically Byronic heroes, and incorporated his personality and sensibility into their poetry. His influence even spread into Scandinavia in the work of Atterbom, Tegnér, and Grimur Thomsen.

Neither Scott nor Byron are today regarded as truly outstanding representatives of English Romanticism. But even though one might agree that Wordsworth, Coleridge, Keats and Shelley were greater literary artists than either Scott or Byron, the impact of these poets was nothing like as important as that of the influence of their more popular inferiors. Even so, one can find interesting problems involving the contributions of Wordsworth, Coleridge, Keats, and Shelley, especially to the poetry and the poetic concepts of Bryant and Poe in America and to the evolution of French symbolist poetry (since one of the leaders of French Symbolism was Mallarmé, whose vocation was teaching English literature). Shelley in particular was admired in France, even before the Symbolist Movement, by such poets as Lamartine, Hugo, Vigny and Baudelaire; in Germany, his idealistic championing of human freedom, like that of Schiller, did not fail to appeal the rebellious Young German poets around 1848 (Herwegh).

The country and the people of England helped to inspire many foreign poets during and after the turbulent years of Napoleon and Metternich. German visitors ranged from Tieck and Arnim to Freiligrath; there were also Mme. de Staël from Switzerland; Foscolo, Mazzini and the elder Rossetti from Italy; Blanco-White, Espronceda, Trueba y Cossío from Spain; Garrett from Portugal; Echeverría from the Argentine. Even Englishmen abroad did not fail to exert a powerful influence; thus, for instance, John Hookham Frere who, while in Malta, acquainted the Duque de Rivas with Shakespeare, Scott and Byron. France was particularly indebted to English history and English literature, as indicated by the dramas of Hugo (*Mary Tudor, Cromwell*), Vigny (*Chatterton*) and Dumas (*Catherine Howard*); by scholarly works extending from Chateaubriand (*Essai sur la littérature anglaise*) to Hippolyte Taine (*Histoire de la littérature anglaise*, 1863); by travel-accounts (Nodier's *Promenade de Dieppe aux montagnes d'Ecosse*, 1821; Pichot's *Voyage historique et littéraire en Angleterre et en Ecosse*, 1825), and anthologies (*Ballades, légendes et chants populaires de l'Angleterre et de l'Ecosse* by Loeve-Veimars, 1825) as well as by learned magazines of the type of the *Revue des Deux Mondes* in which men like Philarète Chasles and later Emile Montégut began to expatiate on English (and American) cultural matters.

Switzerland

Switzerland continued her splendid role, begun in the preromantic era of the anglophile Bodmer, of serving as the foremost literary intermediary between nations. German Switzerland, it is true, in keeping with the somewhat sober mentality of the Swiss people, after the promising beginnings of the eighteenth century, produced practically no great author during the Romantic Period proper—the only two exceptions being Johann Heinrich Zschokke, a native German settled in Switzerland, whose various works (*e.g. Aballino der grosse Bandit*, 1795 and

Stunden der Andacht, 1809) achieved international fame, and Johann Heinrich Pestalozzi, Switzerland's greatest educator, whose books (such as *Lienhard und Gertrud,* 1781 ff.), so much saner than Rousseau's *Emile,* had an immense influence abroad, as seen, for instance, in the description of the so-called Pedagogical Province in Goethe's *Wilhelm Meisters Wanderjahre.* But it was, above all, French Switzerland which now assumed leadership in European Romanticism. We have already spoken of MME. DE STAEL (whose early *Essai sur les fictions* of 1795 was translated into German by Goethe) and of her *cercle* at Coppet, the meeting place of the French and German, of English, Scandinavian and Italian romanticists—and we have likewise emphasized the significance of Mme. de Staël's *De l'Allemagne,* often called the Bible of the romantics, and of minor efforts by Benjamin Constant and others on behalf of German literature. But there is still much to be said about other Swiss efforts on behalf of Italian literature.

It can indeed be argued that Romanticism is not exclusively Anglo-German in its origins and that the colorful lore of old Italy and Spain contributed just as much to the picturesque richness and the medieval pageantry which the romanticists loved to portray. Mme. de Staël used not only Germany, but also Italy in order to batter down the wall of French neo-classical conceit and sterility—and in these endeavors she was valiantly supported by Sismondi and others. Through her frequent trips to Italy (where with her essay *Del modo di tradurre e della utilità delle traduzioni* of 1816 she helped inspire the first phase of Italian Romanticism in Milan, which preceded French Romanticism by more than ten years) and through her ardent friendship with Monti her enthusiasm for things Italian was intensified, and in her novel *Corinne* of 1807 (her reply to the description of her love affair with Benjamin Constant which the latter had presented in his *Adolphe* of 1806) Mme. de Staël did as much for the propagation and the enthusiastic appraisal of Italian culture and literature as she had done for Germany in her *De l'Allemagne. Corinne* was translated into German by Friedrich Schlegel, another great admirer of Italian culture. Because of the width of his scope SISMONDI was perhaps even more important than Mme. de Staël, for he was not only a lover of late medieval and early Renaissance Italy (as his *Histoire des républiques italiennes du moyen âge,* 1807, and his *Histoire de la*

Renaissance de la liberté en Italie, 1832, indicate)—but, in his epochal *De la littérature du Midi de l'Europe* (*The Literature of the South of Europe,* 1813) he also branched out into Spanish and Provençal literature, resuscitating for the romanticists the wealth and the picturesqueness of Mediterranean cultures which their hearts had been searching. Rather than follow Sismondi into the Iberian peninsula (which would have been somewhat unusual for the Swiss), later writers preferred to emulate him and Mme. de Staël in their study and glorification of Italy: thus Johann Kaspar Orelli in his *Beiträge zur Geschichte der italiänischen Poesie* (*Contributions to the History of Italian Poetry,* 1810) and in his *Cronichette d'Italia* (*Chronicles of Italy,* 1822)—and thus also, above all, the famous Jakob Burckhardt in his *Die Kultur der Renaissance in Italien* (*The Culture of the Renaissance in Italy,* 1860) and the novelist Conrad Ferdinand Meyer in his various historical novels dealing with the Italian Renaissance (among them *Die Hochzeit des Mönchs,* 1884, *Die Versuchung des Pescara,* and *Angela Borgia*).

The romantic love of nature and mountains naturally signified also a sudden increase in tourism. We have already spoken of the influence of Swiss landscape upon Goethe (an influence noticeable also in his later works, for instance in the story of St. Joseph the Second in *Wilhelm Meister* and in the Alpine scene in *Faust II*) or upon the Dane Baggesen; to these can be added Byron's treatment of a chapter of Swiss history in *The Prisoner of Chillon* (1816), and the Alpine atmosphere in which his *Manfred* found his death and in which Longfellow's *Hyperion* sought peace and forgetfulness. Among Frenchmen writing or teaching in Switzerland were Balzac and Sainte-Beuve, but nothing symbolizes quite as well the value of Switzerland as a shelter from political storms in which refugees ranging from Louis Napoleon to Wagner and from Mazzini to Mickiewicz spent years of waiting and hoping, than the fact that in 1869 the castle of Rapperswyl near Zürich became a national shrine for Poland in which its sacred treasures were preserved against the day when that unhappy country at last became free again from the oppression by Russia and other neighbors.

Italy

It might perhaps be argued that the literature of France during the Romantic Period was more important than the literature of Italy and should therefore deserve precedence in our discussion. But the Milanese romanticists preceded the *cénacle* in Paris by half a generation and it should be noted, too, (regardless of what Italy and Spain may or may not have produced in literature) that the physical geography, the landscape, as well as the ancient legends, crimes and passions of both peninsulas now became so powerfully important and well-known abroad, that not only Germany and England, with their early poets and critics, but also Italy and Spain with their colorful romanticism in the flesh, can be hailed as important factors which greatly stimulated the originally northern movement. And in the case of Italy (far more than in the case of Spain) it should be added, too, that this land now became the ideal place of sojourn for an amazingly large group of northern romanticists, where they lived, loved and poetized before they (if ever) returned to the various lands of their birth—returning there, as likely as not, by way of Mme. de Staël's estate at Coppet.

French travellers in Italy included Chateaubriand and Lamartine with their repeated stays and Stendhal, Musset and George Sand; especially the works of Stendhal (*Le Rouge et le Noir* and *La Chartreuse de Parme* no less than *Les Promenades dans Rome* and *Les chroniques italiennes*) are full of Italian reminiscences. As for the English romanticists, Italy became a land where they felt far happier than at home. Coleridge went there in 1806; Byron spent his last years in Italy; Shelley and Keats died there; the works of Landor and of the two Brownings can not be separated from the everlasting imprint glorious Italy left upon them; Hazlitt published his *Journey through France and Italy* in 1826 and Beckford his *Letters from Italy, with Sketches from Spain and Portugal* in 1835. Even stronger, if possible, was the attraction of Italy for German poets and artists; it is certainly one of the permanent traits of the Teuton to wish to leave the dreary North, to cross the Alps, and to become human and alive again in Italy. The curing effect Italy had upon Goethe at a critical time of his life (1786-88) is justly famous and symbolical; even before him, Heinse had begun to glorify Italy as no other German had done before him. Besides them there are others, ranging from Tieck, Zacharias Werner, Wilhelm Müller, Eichendorff, Wilhelm Waiblinger to Heine, Platen (who left Metternich's Germany in despair and disgust and who died in Sicily), August Kopisch (the discoverer of the Blue Grotto on Capri) and Heyse. Nor should the great fascination of Italy for Americans be forgotten: it began with Irving, Ticknor and Longfellow; Hawthorne was American consul at Livorno—and the same love of Italy lasted on in the century, as evidenced, for instance, in William Dean Howells, American consul in Venice and an admirer especially of Goldoni. Among Spanish poets in Italy, mention should be made of Martínez de la Rosa, who was twice ambassador in Rome.

It is of course true that the Italian literature of the Romantic Age was no longer as deeply inspiring as the literature of the Italian Renaissance—in fact, we have met most Italian authors of this period as receivers rather than as emitters; but it is nonetheless true, too, that as a geographical and cultural factor Italy remained a power of first-class importance in the history of European Romanticism. To be sure, to some authors Italy remained a country of villainous crimes and dastardliness (as, for instance, to the tellers of Gothic tales); others again thought they could sneer at her, as Lamartine did in his tactless imitation of Byron, *Le dernier chant du pèlerinage d'Harold* (1825) in which he called the oppressed and restlessly fermenting peninsula "la terra dei morti"—a slur which netted him, the attaché to the French embassy in Florence, a duel with an infuriated Italian patriot (1826). For the most part, however, these foreign visitors sympathized deeply with the sufferings of Italy and were inspired by the landscape, the history, the men and women of Italy past and present. Thus Goethe who embraced Italy in his diary of his *Italian Journey*, dramatized the life of Torquato Tasso (rendered into Italian in 1820) and translated the life of Benvenuto Cellini; and Platen, who brought the purity of the sonnet to a new peak unsurpassed since the days of Petrarca (*Sonette aus Venedig*, 1825). Thus also Byron, together with Lamartine the admirer of the Countess Guiccioli, the author of *Marino Faliero* (1820) and *The Two Foscari* (1821); Shelley, whose *Epipsychidion* (1821) was inspired by one Teresa Emilia Viviani; Samuel Rogers in his poem *Italy* (1822); Landor in his *Pentameron* (1837) and *Giovanna of Naples*; Hunt in *The Story of Rimini*; Browning in *The Ring and the Book* (1869) and Mrs. Browning in her *Casa Guidi Windows* (1851). In French Romanticism Italian themes were particularly innumerable: Antoni Deschamps' *Les Italiennes*; Barbier's *Il Pianto*; Musset's *Lorenzaccio* and *Andrea del Sarto*;

Hugo's *Lucrèce Borgia, Angelo, tyran de Padoue* and *La Vision de Dante*; Mérimée's *Mateo Falcone*; Delavigne's *Les vêpres siciliennes* and *Marino Faliero*. Elsewhere Italian themes and atmosphere ranged from Mosen's and Wagner's *Rienzi* in Germany to Hawthorne's *Marble Faun* in America; and of the great Swiss interest in Italy we have already spoken.

Nor should the work of the scholar and the critic be forgotten: ranging from the untiring efforts of the two Schlegels on behalf of Italian literature to Sismondi in Switzerland, to Ginguené's *Histoire littéraire de l'Italie* (1811), Deschamps' *Etudes sur l'Italie*, Fauriel's *Dante et les origines de la langue et de la littérature italienne*, Quinet's *Allemagne et Italie* (1839) and *Les Révolutions d'Italie* (1852) in France, to William Roscoe's lives of *Lorenzo de Medici* (1795) and of *Leo the Tenth* (1805) and Hallam's *Oration on the Influence of Italian Works of Imagination in England*, and to Ticknor's and Longfellow's professorial lectures in America. Particularly fascinating among Anglo-Italian intermediaries were two men: Thomas Mathias, an Italianate Englishman who edited the works of Crescimbeni and Tiraboschi in England (London, 1803) and who, in his *Poesie di scrittori illustri inglesi, recate in verso italiano* (Naples, 1830) translated English lyrical masterpieces into Italian; and Gabriele Rossetti, from 1824 till 1854 a political refugee in England and professor of Italian at King's College in London, who, together with his three children (Dante Gabriel Rossetti, William Michael Rossetti and Maria Francesca Rossetti) became an important spokesman for Italian culture in general and an interpreter (or, in the case of the elder Rossetti, a misinterpreter) of Dante in particular.

Among Italian authors mentioned—Foscolo, Monti, Pindemonte, Guerrazzi—we should underscore again the importance of MANZONI and his indebtedness to Scott, both in his historical novel and his historical dramas. His tragedy on medieval Venice, *Carmagnola*, with a preface against dramatic unities and dedicated to Fauriel, was translated into French by the latter in 1823; and his *Il Cinque Maggio* (*The Fifth of May*, 1821), about the death of Napoleon, went through twenty-seven translations into foreign languages, among them one by Goethe. From an international point of view LEOPARDI was probably the most important Italian romanticist. One of the finest poets of *Weltschmerz*, Leopardi's fame and influence have remained

steady for the last century. He was known in France as early
as 1822 and his power attracted to his poetry no less an author
than Baudelaire. From Musset and Vigny up to the symbolist
Laforgue, Leopardi enjoyed steady popularity. In Germany he
was admired by Heine and especially by Platen, while in England
James Thomson and in America Walt Whitman were drawn to
him. Leopardi's contribution to twentieth century symbolist
poetry has only recently become the object of considerable study;
indeed, his importance in that respect may be second only to
other romanticists such as Hölderlin and Novalis in Germany.
In the field of literary criticism Italian opinions ranged from the
anti-Classicism of Ludovico di Breme (*Intorno all' ingiustizia
di alcuni giudizi letterari*, 1816) to the anti-Romanticism of
Carducci (*Di alcune condizioni della nostra letteratura*, 1867).

Spain

What has been said about Italy can, to a somewhat lesser extent, be said about Spain, too: though her literature with a few
exceptions did not achieve any international fame during the
Romantic Period, the country, the atmosphere, the history, the
colorfulness of Spain nevertheless exerted a powerfully fascinating attraction for the romanticists of other nations. It is
true, of course, that France exerted a great influence upon Spain,
for, having digested the romantic theories supplied by other
countries, she passed them on to Spain, whose Romanticism
started even later than French Romanticism—and this very
significant impact of French literature upon Spain between 1830
and 1850 should never be underestimated. Nevertheless, it is
also true that Spain, at the same time and in the same intensity,
gave back very much, too, because whatever patriotic Spaniards
tried to revive after the sterility of Neo-Classicism—the kaleidoscopic colorfulness of the *Siglo de Oro* and the exciting abundance of life and adventure during the Middle Ages and the
great wars between the Cross and the Crescent—corresponded
so very much to the very essence, the very soul of Romanticism,
that Spaniards merely could skim the cream off their own rich
past in order to present to other Europeans those very episodes
of dazzling chivalry, Catholic fervor and exotic costumes and
architecture they had been looking for. It must be added,
though, that Spaniards like Martínez de la Rosa, the Duke of
Rivas and Bretón de los Herreros indicate that certain classical

ideals survived in the very midst of the Romantic Period, for the former two wrote not only romantic but also quite a few classical dramas (*Moraima, Aliatar,* both written in the manner of Alfieri), while the latter kept on translating Racine, Voltaire, de la Motte-Houdart (and Scribe) at a time when Romanticism seemed definitely established.

Among French authors to be influenced by Spain mention should be made, above all, of Victor Hugo, who learned to know the country as a child while following his father, a French general during the Napoleonic Wars, and who shows Spanish influences in such works as *Ruy Blas* and *Hernani, ou l'honneur castillan* (1830)—the latter rendered into Spanish by Eugenio de Ochoa. Hugo also translated into French some of the poetry of García Gutiérrez. Prosper Mérimée should be noted especially for his *Carmen* (1845), one of the most significant tales to come out of Spain, and rendered doubly famous through Bizet's well-known opera. Mérimée also wrote a *Histoire de Don Pèdre I, roi de Castille,* in which he displayed his love for Spanish medieval history, and an apocryphal collection of plays in the manner of Calderón, *Le théâtre de Clara Gazul, comédienne espagnole* (1825). Other French authors to reflect some of the wealth of Spanish culture were Abel Hugo, the translator of *Romances historiques* (1822); Musset, with his poems entitled *Contes d'Espagne et d'Italie* (1830); Théophile Gautier, known for his *Tra los montes; Voyages en Espagne* (1843) as well as for his fine poems contained in *España* (1845); and Dumas père, whose *Don Juan Maraña* was influenced by Zorrilla. Spaniards in France ranged from José Marchena y Ruiz, who participated in the French Revolution and later returned to Spain with the French army, to Larra and beyond; we have seen that Martínez de la Rosa wrote some of his works in French, and also Riva's *Don Alvaro o la fuerza del sino* (1831), perhaps the most striking romantic drama of Spain, was written in Paris and translated into French by a Spaniard, Alcalá Galiano, a close friend of Rivas. Also Juan Maria Maury y Benítez spent many years in France where he published a collection *L'Espagne poétique, choix de poésies castillanes mises en vers* (1826). Another member of the Spanish colony in France was Eugenio de Ochoa who re-enforced earlier attempts to acquaint France with Spanish works (which went as far back as the translations contained in *Le théâtre espagnol* by Linguet in 1770) by publishing, in Paris, a *Colección de los mejores autores españoles antiguos y modernos* (1838). Ochoa should also be noted for his *Tesoro de romanceros españoles* and, six years later, for his *Catálogo de los manuscritos españoles de las Bibliotecas de Paris* (1844).

German translations began with Herder, Tieck and the Schlegels; the latters' efforts to hail Spanish Romanticism were corroborated by Agustín Durán who in his *Discurso sobre el influjo de la crítica moderna en la decadencia del antiguo teatro español* of 1828 was one of the first to apply the term "romantic" also to Lope and to Calderón and to defend them against neo-classical aspersions. It is not astonishing that also Eichendorff, the author of an essay on German literature viewed from a strictly Catholic angle, should turn to Spain for inspiration and translate from Calderón, while among later German hispano-philes Fastenrath and Adolf von Schack should be especially noted—the latter well-known for his *Geschichte der dramatischen Literatur in Spanien* (*History of Dramatic Literature in Spain*, 1845) which contained many translations. Grillparzer's interest in Spanish literature and his frequent borrowings have been discussed in connection with Calderón and the Jewess of Toledo.

More important, in England, than Byron's trip through Spain and his *Don Juan* are the thorough studies and travels by Robert Southey, author, among other things, of *Letters written in Spain and Portugal* (1797), a *History of the Peninsular War* (1823 ff.), and especially of the *Chronicle of the Cid* (1808) and of the famous poem *Roderick, the Last of the Goths* (1814). Also William Beckford's *Letters from Italy with Sketches of Spain and Portugal* (1835) deserve to be mentioned again in this connection. Other English hispanophiles from Shelley to Fitzgerald have been alluded to in connection with Calderón; to them we can add John Gibson Lockhart, who acquainted his readers with old Spanish lore in his translations of *Ancient Spanish Ballads* (1823). George Borrow, an extensive traveller and accomplished linguist and especially an enthusiastic stu-dent of gypsies, told of his many adventures in Spain as a travel-ling agent of the Bible Society in his still popular *The Bible in Spain* (1843). Among diplomats with literary inclinations men-tion should be made of John Hookham Frere who was both envoy to Portugal and later ambassador to Spain (1802-04). Also the biographer of Lope de Vega, Lord Holland, was significant both as a translator and as a diplomat; Quintana addressed to him *Diez cartas* (*Ten Letters*, 1824) in which he explained post-Napoleonic governmental problems in Spain. Foremost among the intermediaries, finally, was José Maria Blanco y Crespo, who was born in Sevilla of an Irish father and who went to England after the French invasion; his *Letters from Spain* (1822), written under the name of Blanco-White, constitute a first-class source of information about Spanish life and culture.

Italy followed the general trend of exploring old Spanish legends in such works as *Vecchie romanze spagnuole*, a series of translations by Berchet (1837) and *Romanze storiche e moresche e poesie scelte spagnuole* (*Historical and Moorish Romances and Select Spanish Poems*, 1850) by Pietro Monti—but it was, in a way, America which became most strikingly fascinated by Spanish culture. The trend may be said to have begun with the famous traveller Washington Irving who in his later years wrote a great number of works which were imbued with the enthusiasm and the colorfulness Spain had aroused in him: a *History of the Life and Voyages of Columbus* (1828), *A Chronicle of the Conquest of Granada* (1829), *Voyages of the Companions of Columbus* (1831) and, above all, his wonderful *Alhambra* (1832) and his *Legends of the Conquest of Spain* (1835). Also Irving's *Mahomet and his Successors* (1849) may be said to have originated in his constant preoccupation with Spanish-Arabic relations. Among American historians, William Hickling Prescott continued this love either for Spain proper (*History of Ferdinand and Isabella*, 1837, and his unfinished *History of Philip II*) or for her hispanization and christianization of America (*History of the Conquest of Mexico*, 1843, *The Conquest of Peru*, 1847). Other American travellers again turned rather to the literature of this romantic country: thus George Ticknor, author of an excellent *History of Spanish Literature* (1849). Spanish elements can likewise be found in some of Poe's tales of horror (*The Pit and the Pendulum*). Also Longfellow, yet another traveller in Spain, often betrayed influences from that country (such as the drama *The Spanish Student*), though Germany and Italy seemed to attract him more. Longfellow held the first chair of Spanish at Harvard and should be especially noted for his beautiful translations of the *Coplas* of the medieval poet Manrique and of Lope's sonnets *El pastor divino* (*The Good Shepherd*). Finally it should be added, too, that James Russell Lowell was ambassador to Spain (1877) before he held a similar appointment in England.

Entirely in keeping with this interest in picturesque Spain was also the romanticists' love for various islands in the Mediterranean belonging to different nationalities. Heinse with his *Ardinghello* (1787) may perhaps be said to have begun this quest of some blessed island in the Mediterranean for idyllic or amorous living; George Sand, famous for her journey through Italy in the company of Alfred de Musset (1833-34), emulated this idea through her well-known sojourn on Mallorca in the company of the Polish composer Chopin (1838). We have already spoken of Goethe's trip to Sicily and of Platen's death there; likewise we should mention Coleridge's and later Rivas' visits to Malta and Hookham Frere's retirement and death on the same island (1818-46). Especially significant was also the island of Corsica, the birthplace of Napoleon, the object of one of Rousseau's utopian investigations (*Projet de constitution pour la Corse*) and interestingly described in Boswell's *Account of Corsica* (1768); as a background for primitive passions and smouldering vendettas it was introduced into European literature especially through Mérimée's *Colomba* (1840). In his poem *Mateo Falcone* also the German romanticist Chamisso dealt with Corsican history and heroism and so did also the Italian novelist Guerrazzi with his *Pasquale Paoli* of 1860. Finally, there were the Dalmatian islands and the Illyrian coastline, which inspired French travellers (Nodier) and poets like Mérimée (*La Guzla ou Choix de poésies illyriques*, 1827).

France

Even though Romanticism was not an indigenous product in classical France, it would be hard ever to overestimate the significance of that country as the very hub of European intellectual life, the very center of liberalism where, during the dark days from 1815 to 1870—and to a greater extent even than in Switzerland or in England—the political refugees of all nations found a shelter where they could work for the political rebirth of their country (as the unhappy Mickiewicz did, who died trying to organize a Polish Legion to participate in the Crimean War). Especially numerous was the Spanish colony in Paris; although, with the fluctuating fortunes of Spanish internal history, not all of them managed to return to Spain or, once there, to stay on in Spain, these refugees at any rate brought into Spain a real flood of European Romanticism as filtered by France—just as their fathers had brought back to Spain the quintessence of French Enlightenment. Nor should the role of France as a comforter of Italian refugees be forgotten, nor the fact that the Italian *Risorgimento* finally achieved its goal of expelling the Austrians only with the help of France (1859). English visitors in France ranged from Wordsworth (1791-92) to well beyond Thackeray (*The Paris Sketch-Book*, 1840) ; among the echoes of such visits, *France* (4 vols. in 1817) by Lady Morgan caused an especially spirited controversy. German accounts of French life found expression in works like *Briefe aus Paris* (*Letters from Paris*, 1832) by the sensitive Ludwig Börne and *Französische Zustände* (*French Conditions*, 1833) by Heinrich Heine.

The influence of CHATEAUBRIAND persisted throughout this period. Although the *mal du siècle* expressed in his *René ou les effets des passions* (1802) and *Atala* was part of the tradition begun with Goethe's *Werther*, Chateaubriand suggested that the source of this world-weariness lay in some forbidden passion: René's exile from France came because his sister had loved him too passionately, and Atala's destruction came when her passion led her to violate a sacred vow of her mother. This suggestion that the overwhelming melancholy which was so fashionable during the age had a specific cause and that this cause lay in the denial of overwhelming emotion has been echoed frequently in later novels. The parallel between Byron's own life and the fictional life of René is one that Byron, of course, was the first to discover. Chateaubriand's influence remained great throughout the century, not only upon the neo-Catholic authors of France, but also on foreigners like Leopardi, Mickiewicz and Pushkin. His poems and also his tragedy *Moïse* were translated into Spanish by Juan Arolas.

From an international point of view VICTOR HUGO (1802-85) was the greatest of all the French poets of this period—an author, as we have seen, deeply indebted to the values of Germany, England and Spain. He represented not only the high point of French Romanticism, but in his fierce denunciations of Napoleon III he also incarnated the very spirit of Young Europe in its perennial fight against tyranny; indeed, in such novels of his as *Les Misérables* (1845 ff.) he also became a distinct representative of Realism, if not of Naturalism. Hugo's influence at home, upon foreign refugees in France and upon valiant patriots fighting for the advancement of the cause of true humanity abroad was very great indeed; among his immediate disciples or admirers we can name Tennyson, Swinburne, Heine, Freiligrath, Arolas, Carducci and d'Annunzio.

Other French poets likewise passed on to foreign countries not only the fruits of their own rich poetic gifts, but also the values of a Romanticism mainly conceived in Germany and England. Thus, for instance, Lamartine who was less bold than Hugo, and more reassuringly idealistic; his poems were translated into German by Herwegh (1840); he was extremely popular in Russia and found something of a follower even in the realist Turgenev. Musset, a kind of gentler, less egotistical Byron, is especially interesting for his manifold indebtedness to Italy and for the relationship between his poetry and that of Tennyson. Vigny, likewise popular in Slavic countries (especially his *Eloa*), repaid England for some of her contributions by influencing Moore, Campbell and Housman. In connection with Vigny's famous post-Waterloo pessimism mention should be made not only of his *Servitude et grandeur militaire* (1835) in which the soldier is shown as a slave, with his conscience in vain straining against the inhumanity of military discipline— but also of his *Stello* in which he demonstrated that all forms of governments are deeply inimical to poetry and poets. His tragedy *Chatterton,* which expatiated on the same theme of a poet's inability to find happiness in the modern world, was translated into Italian and provided with a preface by Mazzini in 1835. As for Mérimée, his importance as an intermediary should be underscored not only with regard to Spain; he was perhaps even more important because of his early interest in Russian literature and his translations of Gogol and Pushkin.

While the very great international significance of the French novel, from Balzac on, will be pointed out in the next chapter, mention must be made here of the novels of GEORGE SAND, because with her strong emphasis upon the emancipation of womanhood, the rights of the flesh and the sacredness of emotional life (*Valentine, Indiana*) she exerted a strong influence not only upon the romanticists of the type of Gertrudis Gómez de Avellaneda, but also upon the militant Young European au-

thors of the type of Gutzkow (*Wally, die Zweiflerin,* 1835). In
the field of social theory and budding socialism, finally, mention
should be made again of certain novels by George Sand (*Con-
suelo*), and especially of such French thinkers as Saint-Simon
and Fourier, for we find echoes of their theories in the utopian
planning contained in Goethe's *Wilhelm Meister* and, above all,
in the noble experiments by the New England transcendentalists,
for instance of Brook Farm near Boston, concerning which Hawthorne gave such a vivid description in his *Blithedale Romance*
(1852). Their efforts were paralleled by the idealist Robert
Owen, author of *New Views of Society* (1816), who after his
emigration to America inspired planned communities of the type
of New Harmony in Indiana.

America

Second only to the French Revolution in its lasting and
encouraging impact upon the ideals of romanticists and Young
Europeans alike was the American Revolution and the successful and inspiring experiment in democracy carried on on a large
scale in the United States. First among the Europeans to react
to the political impact of the American Revolution was Edmund Burke with his speech on *Conciliation with America*
(1775), and in Germany Schiller lashed out against the sale of
the Hessians in his tragedy *Kabale und Liebe* (*Intrigue and
Love*, 1783). In Italy, Alfieri wrote five odes *All'America libera*
(*To Free America*, 1781) and dedicated his *Brutus* to George
Washington, that other great enemy of tyranny, while Carlo
Botta sought to encourage a people striving for similar liberation from foreign oppression by writing a *Storia della guerra
dell' indipendenza degli Stati Uniti d'America*. French travellers followed in the footsteps of Lafayette to explore the new
country and its *mores*—some of them, like Chateaubriand in his
Les Natchez, raving romantically about the vast virgin continent
and dreaming of the inborn goodness of primitive men beyond
the frontiers of civilization—others, like Crèvecoeur in his *Letters from an American Farmer* (1782) and the famous Tocque-
ville in his *De la démocratie en Amérique* (1835 ff.), observing
and reporting shrewdly and realistically. Chateaubriand's own
Voyage en Amérique (1791, but published only in 1826) has
remained quite a controversial book. His *René* as well as *Atala
ou Les amours de deux sauvages dans le désert* was originally

intended to be included in *Les Natchez*; however, they were rearranged and incorporated in *Le génie du christianisme*. At times, European pilgrimages to America ended in utter disillusionment and tragedy, as when the idealist Lenau became mixed up with Yankee traders in Ohio—which induced him to choose the lesser evil and to return to a Metternich-dominated Europe, where he ended in insanity.

With the beginning of American literature, the cultural relations between Europe and America, which had been initiated by Increase Mather's stay in England and by Franklin's and Jefferson's manifold activities in France, became intensified. We can point to important literary friendships—like Irving's friendship with Scott or Emerson's friendship with Carlyle (and with both Englishmen incidentally doing a fine job of initiating their American friends into the wealth of German literature). At times these relations might become strained—as, for instance, when Irving in his essay *English Writers on America* rejected the haughty condescension with which some British authors treated the fledgeling American literature; gradually, however, the exchange of authors (exemplified best in Dickens' second visit to America and Mark Twain's and Bret Harte's visits to Europe, where they were being lionized) became increasingly popular and fruitful. Goethe in his significant *Wilhelm Meisters Wanderjahre* visualized a growing political, economic and cultural collaboration between the two continents—which made the patriarch of Weimar an amazingly accurate prophet for the events of our own days. The two American journals to devote the greatest space to European literature were *The North American Review* (1815 ff.) and *The Dial*, the latter published by the transcendentalists (1840 ff.).

Though the American authors of the first two thirds of the nineteenth century—as proven by the names of Irving, Longfellow or Margaret Fuller—were far more receivers of influences from, rather than emitters of influences to, Europe, two significant American authors should be mentioned who even before Walt Whitman began to acquire a powerful popularity abroad: Edgar Allan Poe (himself, as we have seen, indebted to the German E.T.A. Hoffmann and also to Dickens) and James Fenimore COOPER (1780-1851). Of Poe's impact upon European, notably French, Symbolism, we shall speak in our next chapter —but Cooper should be mentioned right here, for in spite of the

mediocrity of many of his novels, he was the first to introduce
on a large scale into world literature the theme of the American
Indian. To be sure, already Freneau (*The Dying Indian, The
Indian Burying Ground*) and William Cullen Bryant (*An Indian
Story, An Indian Girl's Lament, The Hunter of the Prairies*)
had spoken of the doomed Indians in tones which indicated the
influence of Ossian; but with his *Leatherstocking Tales* (*The
Deerslayer, The Pathfinder, The Last of the Mohicans*, 1826,
The Pioneers and *The Prairie*), Cooper now created a long-
winded cycle of frontier tales, of exotic landscapes and valiant
warriors that made him quickly famous all over Europe. In
spite of this fame, Cooper did not like what he saw during his
trip through Europe; in his *Gleanings in Europe* (1837) and
Notions of the Americans he delivered a sermon to Metternich-
dominated Europe about the essence of true freedom—though
in another work of his, *The American Democrat*, he indicated
that his concept of freedom was Tory-inspired, to say the least,
and not in keeping with the ideals of Jefferson and Jackson.
Cooper became famous not only because of his *Leatherstocking
Tales* which were well liked because of such striking characters
as Natty Bumppo, Chingachgook and Uncas, but also because
in his *The Spy* (1822, an imitation of Sir Walter Scott's historical novels) he gave the world a first tale about the battles
and intrigues of the American Revolution, and because, in *The
Pilot* (1823) and *The Red Rover* (1831), he carried to a new
height the saga of seafarers, the minute descriptions of sailing
ships, the excitement of storms and naval warfare which Smollett before him and Melville, Joseph Conrad and Eugene O'Neill
after him were to describe with equal enthusiasm and colorfulness. French translations of Cooper began to appear in 1827;
Eugène Sue dedicated to him his own sea-novel *Atar-Gull* (1831).
In 1828 Guerrazzi translated into Italian *The Spy* and *The Pilot*.
In America, Longfellow continued to make use of Indian lore in
his famous *Hiawatha* (1855); it was translated into German by
Freiligrath in 1857. Among the many foreign imitators of
Cooper we want to mention only three: the Austrian Karl Postl
who led an adventurous life in America and who finally died in
Switzerland and who, under the name of Charles Sealsfield,
became one of the leading German-American intermediaries
describing his adventures in such books as *Nathan, der Squatter-
Regulator* (1835) and *Das Kajütenbuch* (*The Cabin Log*, 1842);

Friedrich Gerstäcker, author, among other books of travels and adventures, of *Die Regulatoren in Arkansas* (1845), *Die Fluss-piraten des Mississippi* (1848), and *Gold* (about California); and Robert Louis Stevenson, who published *The Silverado Squatters* (1883) and similar tales.

VI. REALISM - SYMBOLISM

A. GENERAL OBSERVATIONS

The complexities of modern literature necessitate a change in the arrangement of this chapter. In the chaos and the speed of modern living it is no longer possible to cover an entire century or indeed even half a century by one single -ism alone, as it was possible to do in the preceding chapters; instead, the one hundred years since 1850 have produced in rapid succession the following "schools" of literature of which we will mention only the chief ones: Realism, Naturalism, Symbolism, Impressionism, Expressionism, New Classicism, Neo-Romanticism, New Matter-of-Factness (*neue Sachlichkeit*) and so on. Nor is it possible to designate just one nation as the absolute spiritual leader of this period, as could be done before. With Tolstoy, Dostoevski and Ibsen, Russia and Scandinavia became great leaders in the field of the novel and the drama, and after the Civil War America began at last to pay back what she had formerly received from Europe and to assume a strong position of literary importance. Among the older nations of Europe especially France retained an initiative in literary creativeness that demands respect and that caused imitations all over the world—while German literature, though more often than not a mere recipient of values received from abroad, preserved a fascinating importance as the great intermediary (or, perhaps, the great battlefield) of Europe where the forces from the West and from the East clash and where the face of tomorrow will be decided upon. No wonder, therefore, that this chapter—like our own lives of today—will have to break the patterns of yesteryear and to chart its own new course.

For the comparatist who is interested in literary history as well as in the interrelationship of details of style, theme and sensibility among the authors of various countries, one method of organizing the mass of Western literature since 1850 can be to study the literature as falling into one of two large classifications: one class would include that literature which embodies essentially a continuation of the romantic concept of the nature and function of literature, and the other class would include that literature which embodies a reaction against the romantic concept of the nature and function of literature. These two classes cannot, of course, be established as mutually exclusive categories: there will inevitably be overlapping; there will inevitably be epigone classicists who want to pretend that Romanticism never happened; and there will inevitably be, as there were in earlier periods, authors whose genius produces work that defies classification. But at least this method will supply the student with a kind of rough map by means of which he can explore the last century's literature. As his explorations reveal new data, he can alter his map, or even throw it away and draw a new one for himself.

All who attempt to organize the literary history of the last one hundred years in this fashion must decide upon terms which can be applied to these two large and not too clearly defined classes of literature. An examination will reveal that by and large the writing that embodies the romantic conception of the nature and function of literature will be more subjective, will find its ultimate justification primarily on the basis of emotional criteria, and will be less dependent upon traditional forms than the writing of the other class. Writing which embodies a reaction against Romanticism will be more objective, will at least make a more obvious appeal to reason, and will tend to depend more heavily upon its formal presentation. One set of terms, then, which could be used would be "Subjective" and "Objective". But these terms are too generic for historical purposes, carrying with them colorations from earlier literary periods. Perhaps the safest means of choosing descriptive labels for the two classes would be to appropriate currently used critical terms which are broad enough in their generally accepted meaning to be suitable for our purposes and which are extreme enough in their semantic opposition to suggest the differences between our two classifications. Of all the scores of critical terms which have been current during recent decades (such as Expressionism *versus* Impressionism), the two most suitable, however unsatisfactory they themselves may be, are the terms "Symbolism" and "Realism".

In applying these two terms to the literature of the last one hundred years, we should understand that they cannot be applied to temporal sections of this period. Symbolism and Realism have developed and flourished concurrently, and very often the same year has marked the publication of significant works representative of each classification (for instance, 1857: Baude-

laire's *Les Fleurs du Mal* and Flaubert's *Madame Bovary*; or
1922: Eliot's *Waste Land* and Lewis' *Babbitt*). We might say
that Realism can be regarded as the general trend in literature
which reacted against Romanticism, beginning sometime before
1850; and Symbolism can be regarded as the general trend
which to this day continues a few of the essential features of
Romanticism.

Since we are admittedly appropriating our terms somewhat
arbitrarily and are admittedly applying them somewhat loose-
ly, the problem of defining them becomes both important and
difficult. The really essential distinction between the literature
of the two types implied by these disjunctive terms lies in the
fundamental concept of the nature of a piece of literature which
is embodied in the form, style, and intent of the completed work.
As we have seen, the authors of the Romantic Period modified
the classical conception of the nature of literature so that art
became no longer so much an imitation of nature as a new
creation of nature. The distinction between the traditional
classical concept of what literature is and the romantic concept
was perhaps best expressed by A. W. Schlegel who inverted
Aristotle's famous dictum that nature should shape art into the
demand that art should shape nature. On the basis of this new
understanding of the nature of literature, romantic authors as
a group were more concerned with *ex*pressing something from
within themselves than they were with recording the *im*pression
of what lay outside of themselves (Expressionism-Impression-
ism). This same basic approach to the business of writing
was perpetuated by hundreds of post-romantic writers who
often professed extreme antipathy for Romanticism and who
were in effect revolting against many features of Romanticism,
but who, in this respect at least, were one with the romantics.
It is this group of post-romantic writers whom we would include under the general term of Symbolism; indeed, understood
in this way, the term does not seem so very arbitrary if one
recalls that it was again A. W. Schlegel who said that to write
poetry was nothing else but an eternal symbolizing. This application of the term does not mean that such authors as Baudelaire, Proust, Rilke, Kafka, Eliot and others whom we call
symbolists are mere epigone romanticists. It does, however,
mean that these authors, whether consciously or not, are the
natural heirs of Romanticism in that they do not hold with

Aristotle and his two thousand years of followers that the purpose of art is to imitate Nature, but rather they perpetuate the innovation of Romanticism that the purpose of the artist is to create the world for his audience, and that this creation comes largely from within the artist himself and his response to the world and not from a skillful copying of the world outside.

It might well be objected at this point that sucessful authors of all ages have never "copied" the world as it is, but have "created" it by means of artistically organized symbols. But always in the past these symbols were universally accepted and were universally understood by the literate public as representative of various aspects of the world as it is. Certainly no one would have contended that Racine's Phèdre spoke the way a woman in the real world would speak—but the conventions of classical drama which Racine utilized were accepted as being subtly imitative of the real world. And thus by virtue of his use of the conventions Racine was in a very real sense imitating Nature. But after the Romantic Revolt had dispensed with the neo-classical conventions and consciously as an aesthetic policy had encouraged and supported literature which was intensely personal, subjective, emotional and even proudly irrational, there were no longer any universally understood symbols and conventions by means of which the imitation of Nature could be expressed in words. The post-romantic authors whom we would label symbolists undertook to create the world by means of symbols (perhaps not in a very different way than had Racine), but were forced to use highly personal symbols and to create their own forms and conventions as the intent and material of their creation dictated. The nature of their writing is, then, significantly different from the nature of earlier writing in the sense that it is a personal and subjective creation of the world.

With this understanding of the meaning of Symbolism as we are using the term historically, an understanding of the meaning of Realism should not be hard to come by. Realism embraces that group of writers (ranging from the impressionists on the edge of Symbolism to the naturalists, the extremists of Realism) who revolted against the romantic creation of the world and who endeavored, in one way or another, to embody in their writing a realistic imitation of the world as it is. However much of the author may be projected into the works of Dickens, Flaubert, Keller, Fontane, Ibsen, Zola, Chekhov, Lewis, and Steinbeck, the principal method of writing in the works of each of these authors is to represent the world pretty much as it seems to be, and the relatively greater popular success of these authors over the symbolist authors would indicate that the reading public feels that it can recognize the world which these authors represent—while the world represented by the symbolists remains mysterious, unreal and puzzling to all but those who trouble to define for themselves the values of the symbols used to embody the subjective vision of the poet.

Obviously there are many works which embody both the symbolist and realistic impulse. Many of the novels of recent decades have utilized techniques and conventions of narration, description, and dialogue perfected by the naturalists, but have also projected into them intensely personal visions by means of symbols whose values develop organically out of the treatment of the material (Dostoevski, Joyce, Döblin). Likewise the drama since Ibsen and Hauptmann, who both began as realists and moved into conscious Symbolism, has tended to cut across the lines of the distinctions between Realism and Symbolism (as evidenced, for instance, in Ibsen's *Peer Gynt,* in Hauptmann's *Hanneles Himmelfahrt* and also in the dramas of Strindberg, Wedekind and O'Neill). In our historical treatment of literary developments under the headings of Realism and Symbolism we are going to be concerned not so much with classifying authors or works as realistic or symbolistic, but rather with sorting out the significant facts concerning the development of these two kinds of writing. Therefore, when we mention an author as significant in the development and spread of some peculiarly realistic tendency, it will not be for the purpose of pigeon-holing him under Realism, but rather for the purpose of examining how literary methods, techniques, tastes, and sensibilities grow and spread from one country to another.

The next elementary problem that confronts us in approaching this period is the problem of dating the end of the Romantic Period and the beginning of the period of Realism and Symbolism. We might suggest 1832 as our terminal year for Romanticism, since the year of the deaths of Goethe and Scott seems so apt for both Germany and England. But by this year Romanticism was only approaching its peak in Italy, France, Spain, and America, and since it is particularly from France and America that the new impulses of Realism and Symbolism emanated, 1832 seems much too early. Because the precise division between Romanticism and Symbolism is extremely difficult to make, we can probably best seek a dividing date by determining when Realism prevailed over Romanticism. Although Realism was germinating in the Young German movement from 1832 to 1850, in the prose fiction of Gogol in the thirties, in the *Ecole du Bon Sens* and the early Victorians in the mid-forties and in other isolated instances, it did not successfully overthrow Romanticism until the 1850's when Flaubert, Keller, Turgenev, Gautier, Augier, Hebbel, Storm and others first began publishing notable literature which was representative of Realism. And since Realism and especially Naturalism were particularly sensitive to political, social, economic, and even scientific influences, and since the most pervasive political, social and economic impact of the period came from the 1848 Revolution, the year 1850 seems to be the most convenient and the one against which the fewest objections might be raised.

A few other preliminary problems remain before we examine Realism and Symbolism separately and in detail. For instance, there is the problem of the extra-literary influences on the development of literature during the whole century which we are examining. The ever-growing political and social awareness of nineteenth century Europe tended to force the realists (and especially the naturalists who intensified the principles of Realism) to imitate the world around them as they saw it through politically distorting glasses, to make them represent this world as something which ought to be changed because of the debilitating effect it had upon the individual or because by effecting changes Utopia could be achieved in a few generations. On the other hand, this same influence tended to force the symbolists away from the world, to compel them to write for one another and to develop small cults of followers who were proud of the fact that the mass of the public could not understand what they understood. The tremendous successes of the physical sciences and of applied science in industry encouraged the naturalists to take over the objective methods of pure science and the pragmatic purposes of applied science. But this same influence encouraged the symbolists to become ever more non-objective and unscientific in their efforts to reveal that component of man which they felt is not susceptible of scientific study, and to become ever less didactic in their efforts to justify literature as a mode of expression which need not have any pragmatic value other than its value as an experience. The logical extremes of these two tendencies can be found in the avowedly didactic Naturalism of Marxist literature and the esoteric "Art for Art's sake" poetry of some of the symbolists.

Since very often the same extra-literary influence had opposite effects on the literature of Symbolism and of Realism, little more can be said here by way of outlining the problems in this field. The student might find that it would illuminate his understanding of the basic dichotomy that exists in recent literature if he undertook to trace the response to certain political events or ideas in works representative of Realism and of Symbolism. While the ideas of Marx and Engels would seem to have had much more effect upon Realism (the dramas of Shaw and Hauptmann, the novels of Jack London and Dreiser), the results of the spread of these ideas can be found in much symbolist literature (the dramas of Kaiser and Toller). On the other hand, while Freud seems to have become virtually all nine muses for the symbolists, few realists writing today have escaped his influence. Indeed, no period in literary history—perhaps because so much evidence is available, but more probably because authors have never been more fully aware of their dependence upon their society and its culture—offers a greater number of problems for the student interested in the relationship between literature and the events and ideas in the world out of which that literature has grown. From the '48 Revolution to the Cold War, every major political event has seemed to have world-wide repercussions and has, therefore, had direct or indirect influence on literature. And from the publication of Darwin's *The Origin of Species* (1859) to the explosion of the atomic bomb, scientific discoveries have likewise exerted powerful influences on literature. This influence can be examined in its impact upon the basic ideas of such authors as Tennyson and Arnold, or it can be studied for its contributions to the subject matter of literature, from the so-called "science-fiction" of Verne, Wells, and Kellermann to the *R.U.R.* of Karel Capek. In the twentieth century particularly, economic developments and ideas have had fully as much influence upon literature as have political. One might even undertake to work out the relationship between literary trends and economic conditions:

a case in point might be the rapid swing from the highly esoteric symbolist literature of the relatively properous Twenties
to the highly naturalistic and often didactic literature that supplanted it during the depression years. Finally, the student
interested in the relationship between literature and non-literary
phenomena will want to concern himself with the effect of the
changing religious climate of the last one hundred years upon
literature. Some of the most notable symbolist and realist literature alike (Werfel, Kafka, Wassermann, Eliot) seems ultimately predicated on the spiritual vacuum that has been left by the
attacks which the physical and social sciences have made upon
traditional religious beliefs.

Just as the number of problems concerning the relationship
between literature and non-literary events seems countless, so
the number of problems involving literature and the other arts
becomes infinite upon examination. First of all there is the
phenomenon observable in all of the arts of the reaction against
traditional forms. While the symbolists undertook to create
entirely new poetic forms and an entirely new poetic language,
and while the naturalists (rather than the more moderate
realists) rebelled against all of the older conventions of decorum
and *bienséance* of language and style, so composers have often
rebelled against traditional harmonic patterns and painters
have endeavored to develop completely new modes of expression.
The doctrine of organic form implicit in much of Naturalism as
well as Symbolism and replacing the neo-classical acceptance
of fixed conventional patterns is essentially the same as the
doctrine of functional form advocated by the so-called modern-
ists in architecture and design. The relationship between the
other arts and literature can be studied more specifically—from
the Parnassian poetic aesthetic which was based on the aesthetic of the plastic arts to the many modern attempts to incorporate the fugal and canonical patterns of music in poetry.
Likewise, the Realism in the painting of such a man as Thomas
Hart Benton might be studied as reflective of the same tendencies which one finds in the highly programmatic music of the
tone poems of Richard Strauss and the Realism of much contemporary drama and fiction. Indeed, in pursuing such problems as these, the comparatist might undertake to study the
many attempts to interrelate all of the art forms which have
recurrently been made during the last hundred years, from the

operatic attempts of Richard Wagner to the movies of Jean Cocteau. Obviously, if one goes very far in this direction, he soon leaves the field of literary study—but these possible channels of investigation have been mentioned simply to suggest the many possibilities for variety in comparative studies which the modern period offers.

B. THE BACKGROUND OF MODERN LITERATURE

As one would expect of an era which inherited the disillusionment of a Romantic Revolution which had rejected the standards of the past, this period reveals new, varied, and highly self-conscious attempts to discover new forms, new styles, and new modes of expression in the literature of other continents and of the long neglected periods of the past of Western culture. It is only to express a truism to state that each age must reinterpret the past for itself, but no age since the Renaissance has been more persistent in its efforts to rediscover the past than has the post-romantic period. This new exploration into the past of Europe and of other civilizations was given special impetus by the reaction against the romantic interpretation of these cultures and by the development of exact scholarship which for the first time undertook to get at the factual truth about cultures separated from us in time or space. But the primary impetus behind this exploration came from the necessity which most authors felt for finding new forms and new modes of expression.

Classical Influences

The neo-classicists tended to regard the literature of Antiquity through their own eyes and to emphasize the Apollonian serenity, plasticity, and clarity which they wanted to find in it. The romantics tended to emphasize the Dionysian frenzy, mystery, and dark complexity which they wanted to find. Post-romantic authors like Nietzsche, restrained somewhat by the discoveries of exact scholarship, recognized that ancient literature embodies both the Apollonian and the Dionysian. The number of problems growing out of the search for new forms and styles is too great for us to do more than suggest a few of them. Almost any significant poet of the last one hundred years can be studied in his relationship to some lyric poet of Antiquity, from Gautier in France to Stefan George in Germany, and from Swinburne in England to Tate in America. For Matthew Arnold and Walter Pater, a revival of Antiquity seemed the finest means to serve the purpose of enriching contemporary Victorian literature. Of special importance was also the revival of interest in the so-called decadent period of Rome by the French symbolists, who themselves were often referred to as decadents. This interest was continued by the Anglo-American poets of the Imagist Movement and by their successors.

The new use of classical subject matter and the new interpretations of classical themes and legends which both realist and symbolist writers have made is even more interesting. In adapting the historical novel developed by the romantics to their own methods, the realist novelists endeavored both to create the world of Antiquity as scholarship seemed to reveal it to have been and to use this world of Antiquity to project their own ideas. Although there may still be some considerable romanticizing of the classical world in such novels as Flaubert's *Salammbô* (1862), Sienkiewicz' *Quo Vadis?* (1896), and the very popular so-called Egyptian novels by Georg Ebers (*Die ägyptische Königstochter*, 1864; *Die Nilbraut*, 1886; *Kleopatra*, 1894), these novels utilized a wealth of historically accurate detail that set them apart from the romantic historical novel. Most interesting of all for the student of classical influences upon realist and symbolist literature is the study of modern adaptations of classical themes and legends. A sampling of authors who thus re-examine the legends and themes of Antiquity and who modify these legends and themes to express what they have to say to the contemporary world would include at least the following: Mallarmé (*L'Après-midi d'un faune*, 1876, *Hérodias*), Valéry (*La jeune Parque*), Sartre (*Les Mouches*), Anouilh (*Antigone*) and Cocteau (*Orpheus*); Swinburne (*Atalanta in Calydon*, 1865), Arnold (*Empedocles on Etna*), Jeffers (*Medea*) and Shaw (*Caesar and Cleopatra*); Hebbel (*Gyges und sein Ring*, 1854), Hofmannsthal (*Alkestis*), Werfel (*Die Troerinnen*), Ernst (*Kassandra*) and Hasenclever (*Antigone*); Galdós (*Electra*); and O'Neill (*Mourning Becomes Electra*). Two poets in particular have shown a great predilection for themes from Antiquity: Leconte de Lisle in France with his *Niobé*, *Hélène, Vénus de Milo* and other *Poèmes antiques* (1845 ff.) and Robert Bridges in England with *Prometheus the Firegiver* (1883), *Achilles in Scyros, The Return of Ulysses, Nero* (1894) and similar poems and dramas. Often classical themes were used to counteract the influence of the naturalistic dramatic technique as, for instance, in Gide's *Oedipe* and Giraudoux' *Electre*. In a different genre, special attention should also be given to the attempts by Spitteler in Switzerland (*Prometheus und Epimetheus*, 1881; *Der olympische Frühling*, 1900) to revive the Greek epic and the subject-matter of Homer and Hesiod pertaining to it.

Two legends have been especially popular among both naturalist and symbolist authors: the Oedipus legend, in which Dr. Freud saw the recognition by folk wisdom of a basic psychological and sexual phenomenon and which, therefore, became the most important of classical legends for that great host of authors who seized upon Freudian psychology to satisfy their need both for symbols and projection of their concept of the basic importance of the sex drive (Hofmannsthal, Mann and scores of others); and the Odysseus legend, which (as, for instance, in Tennyson) became symbolic of modern man's endless wanderings in search of a spiritually meaningful home. Perhaps the most significant treatments of the Odysseus legend can be found in Ezra Pound's *Cantos,* in which the figure of Ulysses supplies the start of a rather nebulous principle of organization for the whole poem, and especially in Joyce's *Ulysses,* the construction and symbolic values of which are based even in small details upon the Homeric narrative.

Among the great scholars, whose labors have contributed much to making the great classical authors and their works accessible to modern poets and readers are Fustel de Coulanges in France (*La cité antique,* 1864), Jakob Burckhardt in Switzerland (*Die Zeit Konstantins des Grossen,* 1853; *Griechische Kulturgeschichte,* 1898-1900) Marcelino Menéndez y Pelayo (*Horacio en España,* 1885) in Spain and E. K. Rand (*The Founders of the Middle Ages,* 1928) in America. Perhaps even more important have been translators: Leconte de Lisle rendered into French the *Iliade* and the *Odyssée* (1866) and adapted *Les Erinnyes* from Aeschylus (1873); Bryant in America became noted for his versions of the *Iliad* (1870) and the *Odyssey* (1872)—and in England reference should be made, above all, to Fitzgerald, who translated *Agamemnon* from Aeschylus and who adapted the *Oedipus* tragedies of Sophocles in his *The Downfall and Death of King Oidipus;* to Browning's new version of *Agamemnon,* and to the felicitous renderings into English of Virgil's *Aeneid* (1868) and of Horace's *Epistles* and *Satires* by John Conington. Among the more recent translations especially of the Greek dramatists have been those by scholars like Gilbert Murray in England and Ulrich von Wilamowitz-Möllendorff in Germany. During the last fifteen years a large number of younger scholars and poets have begun what appears to be an entirely new wave of classical translations.

Religious and Medieval Influences

The tragic events and global crises of the last two generations have brought forth a new awakening of religious thought and a new flourishing of religious literature. In the second half of the nineteenth century, to be sure, Christianity seemed to reel under the hammerblows of Schopenhauer's pessimism, of Nietzsche's scornful titanism and of the aesthetic amorality of the *fin du siècle* poets. Neither the self-satisfied bourgeois nor the rebellious proletarians saw any reason to fill the increasingly empty shell of Christianity with new strength and a new meaning, and happily tolerant and believing authors like Keller in Switzerland (*Die sieben Legenden,* 1872) were the exception rather than the rule. It took the holocaust of two World Wars to bring humanity back to an awareness of God or at least of the necessity for man to define some moral order in the universe.

Treatments of biblical topics during the Age of Realism ranged from Hebbel (*Judith,* 1841, *Herodes und Mariamne,* 1849) and Otto Ludwig (*Die Makkabäer,* 1854) in Germany to *Baltasar* by Gertrudis Gómez de Avellaneda in Spain (1858) and to *Kain* by Leconte de Lisle in France (1871). Towards the *fin du siècle* it seems as if poets were especially attracted to the glitteringly voluptuous and sadistic Salome, as Wilde in England (*Salome,* 1893), Eugenio de Castro in Portugal (*Salome e outros poemas,* 1896) and Sudermann in Germany (*Johannes der Täufer,* 1898—and the author also of *Sodoms Ende*) indicate. Pathbreaking in a far more genuine reassertion of a new religious ardor and of mystical exaltation were of course the great novelists of Russia, especially Tolstoy with his *Resurrection* and his *Anna Karenina* (1874)—and from them the Germans, ever located at the crossroads of Europe, took over the theme of a *Wandlung,* of man's spiritual regeneration and sublimation. Gerhart Hauptmann in his novel *Der Narr in Christo Emanuel Quint* (*The Fool in Christ, Emanuel Quint,* 1910) could still speak of a new Christ come back to earth who is scorned and vilified by modern base materialists and in *Der Ketzer von Soana* (*The Heretic of Soana,* 1918) he prized man's love for woman higher than life-killing asceticism—but from Rilke's *Geschichten vom lieben Gott* (*Tales about the Dear Lord,*

1904) and from 1914 on, novelists and dramatists all over the Western World spoke with increasing reverence of religious matters, from Thomas Mann's tetralogy on *Joseph und seine Brüder* to Fulton Oursler's *Greatest Story Ever Told* and from Lloyd Douglas' *The Robe* to Pår Lagerkvist's *Barrabas*. Especially powerful and inspiring are three modern Jewish novelists who in their tales, biblical or modern, convey the earnest message of man's great need for a spiritual regeneration: Jakob Wassermann (*Caspar Hauser,* 1908, *Christian Wahnschaffe,* 1919); Franz Werfel (*Barbara oder die Frömmigkeit,* 1929, *Der veruntreute Himmel,* 1939, *Das Lied von Bernadette,* 1942, *Der Stern der Ungeborenen,* 1946) and Sholem Asch (*The Nazarene, The Apostle, Mary, Moses*). Also in France we can point to a very great number of authors, from Bourget, Coppée, Claudel and Barrès to Maurras, Mauriac and Huysmans and in Switzerland and Belgium from Rod and de Reynold to Maeterlinck who by their militant return to the tenets of Roman Christianity have brought about what we might call a new *renaissance catholique.* An emphatically Catholic outlook can be perceived also in England from Coventry Patmore to Hilaire Belloc; in Italy from Rosmini to Papini, and even in the Scandinavian novels of the newly-converted Sigrid Undset. The same religious ardor exists also in the field of the drama: Werfel's *Paulus unter den Juden* (*Paul among the Jews,* 1926), Hofmannsthal's adaptation of Calderón's *Gran teatro del mundo,* the Passion Play in Oberammergau. But it is especially in the field of the novel that the impact of Russian mysticism and of a truly Buddhistic self-abnegation is most deeply felt (though there are novels, too, as Kafka's *Der Prozess* and *Das Schloss* would indicate, in which all mystical longings seem to be thwarted through a cruelly inaccessible God).

The influence of medieval culture and literature upon modern literature is the same in kind as the influence of Classical Antiquity. This impact can be studied in three principal spheres. First, there is the renewal of interest in the poetry of the Middle Ages for the purpose of finding new forms and stylistic methods. The accentual meters of Anglo-Saxon and Middle High German folk literature have been studied and adapted by numerous English, American, and German poets. The intense interest on the part of scholars and poets (Ezra Pound and others) in the lyric poetry of the Provençal troubadours and the Italian *dolce stil nuovo* has contributed in virtually every country to the grace, subtlety and charm of modern lyric poetry. There is also the very special problem of the influence of Dante on modern authors, for perhaps no single non-English author of the distant past has had such a profound influence on the style and sensibility of modern English and American poetry as a whole. The second sphere of medieval influence is that of the appeal which medieval scholastic thought and the seemingly ordered life it would provide have had for so many of the Catholic and converted-Catholic writers of recent decades (*e.g.* Thomas Merton's *The Seven Storey Mountain*). This appeal can be regarded as one aspect of the spiritual problem which is at the center of so very much of serious modern writing.

Finally, medieval legends have been adapted by modern authors in much the same way and for much the same purpose as have the classical legends and themes. Although Tennyson's *Idyls of the King* (1859 ff.) and Wagner's music dramas based on medieval German and Celtic legends are still essentially romantic in their adaptation of materials, the long popularity of Tennyson's poem and the enormous popularity of Wagner's operas are symptomatic of the interest in the Middle Ages. Another instance of this predilection can be seen in the way in which the so-called English Pre-Raphaelites like D. G. Rossetti exalted the greatness of the Middle Ages against the perversity of an allegedly overrated Renaissance. At times old Germanic legends served also as background in an effort to revive the Spartan austerity of oldest Classicism—as, for instance, in Lublinski's *Gunther und Brunhild* (1908) and in Ernst's *Brunhild* (1909) and *Chriemhild* (1910). Medieval Christian legends have been no less popular than the pagan legends. From the satirical *Thais* (1894) of Anatole France to the story of Gregorius in Mann's *Der Erwählte* (*The Holy Sinner*, 1951) the lives of Christian legendary figures have provided the raw material for many a modern story. And of course the Middle Ages have continued to provide the setting for hundreds of historical novels, some good, but most of them adventure stories dressed up with scholarly accuracy (such as Costain's *The Black Rose*, and others).

Oriental Influences

One heritage of Romanticism which Realism and Symbolism did not reject was the heritage of cosmopolitanism. This heritage has been strengthened and given practical support by the tremendous improvements in the means of communication which have been made during the last one hundred years, and especially during the last forty years. The twentieth century author feels himself a very intimate part of the whole world, and particularly since 1941 he has realized that this world very definitely includes all of Asia and Africa as well as Europe.

The interest in India which was cultivated by such romantics as the Schlegel brothers and Emerson was continued through the nineteenth century and exerted direct influence on modern poetry from Whitman, Gautier and Leconte de Lisle through the French symbolists; and their Anglo-American imitators began to study the Vedic hymns in their search for a new poetic idiom. Of even greater influence has been the impact of Indian mystical philosophy as expressed in the *Upanishads* and the *Gita* of the *Mahabharata* upon countless authors who have felt that the modern Western industrialized and commercialized world is spiritually arid. This impact became continually stronger as the finest embodiment of the Indian way of life, Mohandas Gandhi, became more and more to be recognized and respected in the Western world (by Romain Rolland and many others) as both a great political and spiritual leader. Indeed, Gandhi has served not only to attract Western authors to the literature and philosophy of India (Huxley, Isherwood, Koestler, Sheean), but has in a way helped the Western World to re-evaluate its own heritage, for Gandhi himself was well read in Christian literature and as a young man became extremely interested in Tolstoy. One of the principal intermediaries between India and modern Western literature was Rabindranath Tagore whose lectures, translations, and original poetry and prose written in English and French helped not only to acquaint late French symbolist and Anglo-American imagist poets with the poetry and wisdom of India, but who also encouraged a greater knowledge of the poetry of China and Japan. Completely different, yet likewise of great importance, are also the works of Rudyard Kipling (*Soldiers Three*, 1891; *The Jungle Books*; 1894-95; *Kim*, 1901), for though he was a typical representative of British imperialism, he was at the same time a very important intermediary too, whose novels and poems about exotic India and the martial Punjab attracted admiring attention all over the world. Among earlier Anglo-Indians should be noted Thackeray, who was born in Calcutta, and Mountstuart Elphinstone, governor of Bombay and author of a *History of India* (1841) and of *The Rise of the British Power in the East* (1887).

With regard to the Far East and the Pacific, the poetry of China and Japan was virtually unknown until the late nineteenth and early twentieth century. But once it became known it contributed immensely to the development of modern poetry. Notably the imagists, in their desire to find a new idiom, discovered in the delicate lyrics of the Orient the precise style and quality which they were seeking. Lafcadio Hearn, of Irish-Greek parentage, may be called the real cultural discoverer of Japan (*Stray Leaves from Strange Literature*, 1884; *Glimpses of Unfamiliar Japan*, 1894). Even before Hearn, the Orient and the South Seas were being explored by such Anglo-American authors as R. H. Dana (*Two Years Before the Mast*, 1840), Herman Melville (*Typee*, 1846, *Mardi*, 1849) and Robert Louis Stevenson (*The Treasure Island*, 1883). After Hearn, the East inspired the exotic sea-stories by Joseph Conrad (*The Nigger of the Narcissus*, 1897; *Typhoon*, 1903) and the famous China stories of Pearl Buck (*The Good Earth*). Somerset Maugham in his exquisitely told novels and short stories reveals himself to be a connoisseur of the British colonial atmosphere extending from the Pacific through Borneo, the Malay States and India to the Mediterranean, while Katherine Mansfield's tales mirror many aspects of her native New Zealand. In Germany, the appeal of the Orient may be said to have begun with Gerstäcker, author of *Tahiti* and *Die beiden Sträflinge* (the latter dealing with Australia) ; later reference should be made especially to Max Dauthendey (*Lingam*, 1910), who died in internment in Java during the first World War; Alfred Döblin, who teaches Asiatic passivity in the face of sufferings in his Chinese novel *Die drei Sprünge des Wang-lun* (*The Three Leaps of Wang-lun*, 1915) ; and Alfred Henschke, who under the pseudonym of Klabund wrote an oriental fairy-drama (*Der Kreidekreis*, 1925) and who otherwise excelled in Oriental translations and adaptations (*Dumpfe Trommel und berauschtes Gong*, 1915, *Li-Tai-Pe*, 1916). In French literature, finally, the influence of Indonesia upon Rimbaud and Claudel should be emphasized.

The intense interest in the Near East which had begun with Goethe and the Schlegel brothers continued into the late nineteenth century. This interest had also been stimulated by such early nineteenth century Slavic authors as Pushkin and Mickiewicz. Pushkin was of considerable importance as an intermediary between the Western world and the Near East, not only because of the negroid blood in his veins, but also because he was the first to introduce into literature the Crimea and the Caucasus and the reflex of the colorful tribal life in the lands beyond (*The Prisoner of the Caucasus*, 1821). Of equal importance were the *Sonnets of the Crimea* of the Pole Mickiewicz who in 1825 had been exiled into the region of the Black Sea. Paradoxically, the Near East was more completely romanticized during the period of Realism than during the period of Romanticism. Fitzgerald's masterful translation of the Epicurean *Rubaiyat* of Omar Khayyam (1859) of Persia has continued to enjoy steadily increasing popularity, and Fitzgerald's poems might be studied in comparison with a more recent German translation, Klabund's *Das Sinngedicht des persischen Zeltmachers* (*The Wisdom of the Persian Tent-Maker*, 1917). Another example of what might be regarded as a slightly romanticized view of ancient Persia can be found in Nietzsche's *Also sprach Zarathustra* (*Thus Spake Zarathustra*, 1883).

In regard to Africa, France rather than England quite naturally took over the task of serving as the great intermediary. Several modern French authors were born in French northern Africa (Paul and Victor Margueritte, Jean Richepin, Albert Camus), and the cultural impact of France extends from there to the entire eastern Mediterranean coastline too. Foremost among modern French exotic authors is Pierre Loti—for though his novels extend from the coast of Iceland (*Les Pêcheurs d'Islande*, 1886) to Turkey (*Aziyadé*, 1879) and to Japan (*Madame Chrysanthème*, 1887), they dwell with particular intensity on French colonial possessions and on the problems and tragedies encountered in colonial life (*Le roman d'un spahi*, 1881; *Au Maroc*, 1890). Comparatists with an interest in political, social and military problems may find many promising aspects in the literature pertaining to colonialism and imperialism—especially if they should contrast the saber-rattling of Kipling in India with the humanitarian work the Franco-German Alsatian Albert Schweitzer is doing in equatorial

Africa. Other authors besides Loti to deal with Africa were Fromentin (*Un été dans le Sahara*, 1857), L. Bertrand in what is commonly called the best Algerian novel, *Le sang des races* (*The Blood of Races*, 1899); Christopher Wren, who in his *Beau Geste* wrote one of the most gallant books about the French Foreign Legion—and in his well-known *Atlantide*, the story of an old and strangely exotic and erotic legend of the Sahara, also Pierre Benoît conjured up the same picture of the desolateness of desert life. In the twentieth century especially Gide has written extensively about Africa (*Les nourritures terrestres*, 1897, *Voyage au Congo*, 1927, and *Le retour du Tchad*, 1928) and Albert Camus used Oran as the setting for his powerful existentialist allegory (*La peste*, 1947). Two of Hemingway's finest tales, *The Short, Happy Life of Francis Macomber* and *The Snows of Kilimanjaro*, take place in central Africa. Among German authors, Hans Grimm eulogized the greatness and bemoaned the loss of the former German colonies in East and in Southwest Africa (*Südafrikanische Novellen*, 1913, *Lüderitzland*, 1934); he became especially famous through his ambitious plea for a return of these colonies contained in his novel *Volk ohne Raum* (*A Nation without Space*, 1926). With regard to the islands off the coast of Africa it should be recalled that Leconte de Lisle was born on Réunion and that Baudelaire journeyed there in 1841.

Russia

Political as well as literary contacts of Russia with the West really began with Peter the Great and were intensified under the German-born empress Catherine the Great (1762 ff.). In most of her ways Russia lived in such a semi-barbarian seclusion that the Middle Ages may well be said to have lasted till about 1700—and about the only topic of earlier Russian history to become known after a first dramatic treatment abroad in one of Lope de Vega's *comedias* was the story of the false pretenders early in the seventeenth century who under the name of Demetrius claimed to be the sons of Ivan the Terrible. The story was treated in Pushkin's *Boris Godunov*, the ruthless opportunist who ascended to the throne but was defeated by the first Demetrius in 1604; it was also retold in a vast trilogy of historical novels by Alexis Tolstoy (*The Death of Ivan the Terrible, The Czar Fiodor Ivanovich, The Czar Boris*, 1866 ff.);

among the German reworkings of this tale of intrigue, false claims, Polish invasions and political murders were the *Demetrius* tragedies by Schiller and, with altered background, Hebbel (both of them fragments and the last works of their respective authors).

From 1700 on, however, foreign influences began to be felt in Russian literature. Czar Peter himself was widely travelled in the Baltic countries, Germany, Holland, England and France. First, German influences came in with Opitz, Gryphius and Gottsched; a German theatre was established in Moscow in 1674, an Italian opera in St. Petersburg in 1736. But it is perhaps symptomatic of the universally powerful appeal of French Classicism, backed up as it was by the political, military, and cultural dominance of Europe, that for the first time Russian literature really began to revolve into the orbit of Europe by emulating French Classicism. Trediakovsky translated Boileau's *Art poétique* and Fénelon's *Télémaque*; his work, along with that of Prince Kantemir, Lomonosov, Sumarokov, and Catherine II herself, for the first time put Russian literature on the secular European highway which led it to the great achievements of the nineteenth century. However foreign or imperfect it may have been, Pseudo-Classicism was, nevertheless, the first "modern" Russian literary movement, and its brief period of flourishing gave to Russia the medium for sophisticated, secular literary expression at a time when Classicism was about to expire elsewhere. Prince Kantemir imitated the social and political *Satires* of Boileau; Sumarokov wrote the first Russian regular tragedy, *Khorev*, in imitation of Racine. After the production of this work in 1749, Sumarokov played a leading role not only in establishing the French derived classical tragedy as the basis of Russian drama, but became the director of Russia's first permanent theatre (1756) and established in this theatre the French style of acting. As a result of the work of Sumarokov, who regarded himself as the Russian Racine and Voltaire with perhaps a trace of Boileau all rolled into one, and of Lomonosov, the Russian Malherbe, the classical drama very quickly became widely popular, even among the illiterate classes.

Among other authors to indicate the growing contact of Russia with the Classicism and the Romanticism of France, Germany and England should be named the following: Montesquieu's *Esprit des Lois* contributed to the *Instruction to the Committee of Deputies* issued in 1767 by Catherine the Great; the *Fables* of La Fontaine were emulated by Krylov; Karamzin translated Thomson's *Seasons* and, in his *Poor Lisa,* was influenced by Richardson; Ozerov should be noted for his adaptations from Ossian; Zhukovski dramatized Bernardin de Saint-Pierre's *Paul et Virginie,* imitated Gray's *Elegy Written in a Country Churchyard* in his *Thoughts on a Tomb,* and also translated plays from Kotzebue and Schiller; indeed, his ultra-patriotic *The Bard in the Russian Camp* shows traces of the so-called Nordic Renaissance.   More important than other Western influences among minor authors of the early nineteenth century (French and Spanish echoes in Bulgarin's *The Russian Gil Blas* and Scott's influence on Zagoskin and others) is the fact that also the first really great Russian authors like Pushkin, Lermontov and Gogol were distinctly inspired by the West.   The impact of Herder and of later German romanticists was tremendously important not only because of their new emphasis on folklore and medieval sagas (as echoed, for instance, in Gogol's *Taras Bulba* of 1835, a vast prose poem glorifying the barbaric valor of fifteenth century Cossacks), but also because the new racial mysticism initiated by Herder helped to awaken the dormant national consciousness of the oppressed Slavic peoples.   The brooding and grandiloquent *Weltschmerz* of Byron, more often than not coupled with unbridled dissipation—and in many ways so germane to certain aspects of the Russian character—is reflected in Lermontov and even more in Pushkin (*The Prisoner of the Caucasus,* and *The Brother Robbers*), authors who, like Childe Harold and Don Juan, were repelled by the hypocrisy of contemporary society.   More convincing, in the field of the drama, than the influence of Molière upon Gogol's early and excellent comedy *The Inspector-General* (1836) is the clearly visible impact of Shakespeare's *Macbeth* and *Richard III* upon Pushkin's spectacular historical tragedy *Boris Godunov.* The second halves of Rousseau's *Nouvelle Héloïse* and of Pushkin's *Eugene Onyegin* (1832) bear a striking resemblance—but the impact of the Genevan is greatest, of course, on the life and views of Tolstoy.   Mme. de Staël travelled in Russia; certain romanticists like Schiller and Lamartine found a particularly swift audience east of the Vistula.   Among French novelists to inspire Russia (before France, in turn, became deeply indebted to the powerful works of Russian Realism) were Balzac and George Sand; the latter's impressive humanitarianism helped to shape the genius of Dostoevski and of minor writers like Goncharov and Grigorovich.

Russian life and culture, in turn, began to become known in Western Europe from the middle of the eighteenth century on. Voltaire dealt extensively with Russia in his *Histoire de Charles XII* (1731) and his *Histoire de l'Empire de Russie sous Pierre le Grand* (1763); Diderot, the most important French intermediary in this connection, made a memorable trip to the court of Catherine II; Herder in Germany included Russian folksongs in his famous *Stimmen der Völker in Liedern* (*Voices of Peoples in Songs*, 1778). Bachenschwanz dedicated his first German translation of Dante's *Divina Commedia* to Catherine the Great; among other Germans in Russian service, mention should be made of the Storm and Stress dramatist Klinger who ended up as a Russian general, and especially of Kotzebue (whose plays enjoyed a very great popularity in Russia, too), who was assassinated in 1819 while serving as a political informer for Russia in Jena. Though the romantic poets represented the earliest instance of Russian literature to become known abroad (Pushkin, for example, was translated into German by Bodenstedt in 1843 ff. and into French by Mérimée in 1849 ff.), it was, above all, Russian Realism which became a great international success, beginning with Gogol who, because of his *Dead Souls* (1842), is often hailed as the founder of the Russian novel. To these purely literary influences should also be added the impact of violently revolutionary and political works of the type of Herzen's novel *Whose Fault?* (1846).

In the following chapters we shall see that these Russian influences became important especially from Turgenev, Dostoevski and Tolstoy on. In analyzing these influences we must bear in mind that the poets of no other country of Europe ever labored under such frightful handicaps of censorship, despotic persecution and cruelty and that not even the Inquisition of the Baroque or the deadening political oppression in Italy, Spain or Portugal produced as many martyrs among poets as Russia did. In view of the constant oppression of the spirit of research and progress in Russia and of the abysmal ignorance of the vast masses it should be borne in mind, too, that the poet, if and when he spoke, became a voice, too, for all other branches of human activity that were numb and silent—and that his novels at times were apt to deal more with religious, moral, social, legal and economic questions than with purely literary and personal matters. This religious quality, this mystical fervor in much of Russian literature, with its stated or implied contempt for purely materialistic progress, could not fail to have a very great and lasting influence on a Western world shaken by doubts and ever-recurring crises, and it is no exaggeration to say that the new gospel of man's complete inner regeneration (either in the spiritual, truly Christian or then again in the political, communistic sense of the word) which emanated from the East has been one of the most powerful influences of the last hundred years. In nineteenth century Russia men's minds were divided over the problem of whether to cling to native traditions that were increasingly despotic rather than idyllically patriarchal (Dostoevski) or to embrace the values of freedom, human dignity and material progress that came in from the West (Turgenev)—and the Western world, too, has long hesitated about accepting or rejecting what already in the exalted hands of Tolstoy and Dostoevski was a two-edged sword indeed.

Scandinavia

Scandinavia became an important emitter of significant literary influences through Ibsen and, to a lesser extent, through Björnson and Strindberg. Yet, great as they are, the contributions of Ibsen to the world's theatre do not seem typically Scandinavian to the extent that they could not have been made by a gifted writer of some other nationality. We therefore need not search for some outstanding characteristics of Scandinavian literature (as we did in the case of Russia) and can proceed forthwith to sketch the main contacts of Scandinavia with European literature before the age of Ibsen.

In the chapter on Pre-Romanticism we have spoken of the influence of the *Elder Edda* upon the so-called Nordic Renaissance in eighteenth century Europe, and we should underscore also the importance of Snorri Sturluson, author of the *Prose Edda* and of *Heimskringla*, the latter the historical saga of Norwegian kings down to 1187. Also the *Historia danica* by Saxo Grammaticus (ca 1200) was mentioned: it was first published in Paris in 1514 and, through Belleforest, it supplied

Shakespeare with the plot of *Hamlet*. The first Danish translation of the *Historia danica* was made in 1575.

Lutheranism was introduced into Scandinavia through men like Olaus Petri, a Swede; complete translations of the Bible appeared in Sweden in 1541, in Denmark in 1543, in Iceland in 1584. In the seventeenth century should be noted the influence of neo-classical doctrine through Opitz, the cultural contact with France through Descartes' staying at the court of Sweden, the introduction of Alexandrines, the *ottava rima* and other metrical forms. Nordic nationalism between the victories of Gustavus Adolphus during the Thirty Years' War and the downfall of Charles XII at Pultava (1709) led to exaggerated books like Rudbeck's *Atlantica* (1675 ff.) which claimed the North rather than the Mediterranean or Near Eastern countries to be the cradle of civilization and which therefore helped to encourage the Nordic Renaissance among the pre-romanticists. French influences became noticeable in Denmark especially with Ludvig Holberg. In his famous comedies he was a follower of Molière and his *Nils Klim's Underground Journey*, a satirical description of the European countries he had visited (first published in Latin in 1741), reveals Holberg to be a typical child of eighteenth century Neo-Classicism and Enlightenment. In Sweden French influences appeared with King Gustavus III, a patron of arts and letters; with the founding of a Swedish Academy of Letters in 1786 on the French pattern; with the poet Creutz, who became Swedish ambassador to the court of Louis XVI; and, incidentally, with the marriage of a later Swedish ambassador, the Baron de Staël, to Germaine Necker from Geneva, the future Mme. de Staël.

Pre-Romanticism meant the growing influence of England and of Klopstock and Rousseau (for instance in Thomas Thorild); it brought to the fore theosophist seers like Emanuel Swedenborg who died in England and whose efforts to combine science and religion, as we have seen, made him extremely influential among religious seekers, from the Europe of Blake, Goethe, and Elizabeth Barrett Browning to the America of Emerson and Whitman. Among poets and critics we can name Olof Dalin, the follower of Addison; G. F. Gyllenborg, the imitator of Thomson; G. Regnér, in his *Thoughts on the Swedish Theatre* an enemy of French rules; Johannes Ewald, from whom Longfellow translated *King Christian Stood by the Lofty Mast*.

Romanticism brought in the influence, above all, of Germany, and a vogue of polemics between the pro-Scandinavian and the pro-German romanticists and again between the romanticists and the classicists, to which we need not allude. In Denmark Henrik Steffens converted Adam Oehlenschläger to the cause of Romanticism; among the Germans whose influences were most potent were Tieck, Novalis, Schelling and the Schlegels. Oehlenschläger's *Gods of the North* (1807 ff.), a great cycle of epic poems, was entirely in keeping with the romanticists' love for ancient mythology. Likewise mention should be made, above all, of Grundtvig, not only a powerful reviver of Danish Protestantism, comparable to Schleiermacher, but also the translator of the *Historia danica* by Saxo Grammaticus, of *Heimskringla* by Snorri Sturluson and of the Old English *Beowulf*; his critical study on *Northern Mythology* appeared in 1808. With regard to English influences we might point to Blicher's translation of Ossian (1807) and to Ingemann's imitations of Scott's historical novels. The important fairy-tales by Hans Christian Andersen have already been mentioned in connection with the Grimms' fairy-tales—and Rask's beginnings in the comprehensive study of Old Norse philology and literature indicate yet another significant aspect of Danish Romanticism.

Swedish romanticists became familiar with new German trends through Höijer, the popularizer of Kant and Fichte. The adherents of German theories and metaphysics were called Phosphorists, after their journal, *Phosphoros*—while the defenders of native Swedish Romanticism and traditionalism formed the so-called Gothic Society. The clash between Greek and Nordic gods was particularly well satirized in *The Mythologies, or the Dispute of the Gods* by Stjernstolpe (1820), in which the excessive Gothomania of the latter group was ridiculed. Atterbom, author of a famous dramatized fairy-tale *The Isle of Bliss* (1824 ff.), was one of the leaders of the Phosphorists, while Tegnér, well-known for his *Frithiofs Saga* (which was imitated by Longfellow), was one of the mainstays of the Gothic or national group, together with Ling, author of *Symbolism of the Eddas* (1819). Because of their connection with America we might also mention Nicander, the friend of Longfellow and the author of *The Rune Sword* (1821), and Wallin, archbishop and hymn-writer and author of a eulogizing song *George Washington*. Longfellow, incidentally, visited Scandinavia in 1835. Almquist's preaching of a Rousseauistic return to nature, Gumälius' imitations of Scott's historical novels and Geijer's and Afzelius' important publication of *Swedish Folksongs* (1814 ff.) likewise fit into the general picture of European Romanticism. In Norway, finally, reference might be made to the emphatic and anti-Danish patriotism of the Klopstock-imitator Wergeland and to the Norwegian *Fairy Tales* published by Asbjörnsen and Moe (1841 ff.).

Likewise in keeping with Romanticism was the publication, in 1835, in Finland, of the *Kalevala* (*Land of Heroes*), a collection of mythological and heroic legends, published by Lönnrot, the "Finnish Homer", and a distinct influence on Longfellow's *Hiawatha*. It was written in Finno-Ugrian—while other Finnish authors, descendants of Swedish settlers on the Gulf of Bothnia (Creutz, Runeberg, Fredrika Bremer) wrote in Swedish. In his *Songs of Ensign Stal* (1848 ff.) Runeberg, one of the greatest writers in the Swedish language, wrote on the tragic war of 1809 in which Sweden lost Finland to Russia.

The coming of Realism in Denmark was heralded by the anti-romantic critic Heiberg and the coming of Naturalism by the famous literary historian Brandes. We have already spoken of the profoundly religious Danish thinker Kierkegaard; in his bitter opposition to organized Christianity he was another typical member of a generation that chose to face man's great issues critically. In Sweden the trend towards emancipation of women, a goal dear to all Young Europeans, can be seen in the novels of Almquist and of Fredrika Bremer—the latter signicant also because of her trip to and report about America and because of her popularity both in England and the United States. This trend towards Realism and Naturalism was continued with Ibsen, Björnson and Strindberg, though it should always be borne in mind that these authors and others (such as Selma Lagerlöf and Sigrid Undset) were at the same time always capable of neo-romantic and expressionistic tendencies which indicate that in many ways they belong to the camp of Symbolism, too.

America

After absorbing the cultural values that Europe had to offer, American literature began to pay back and to contribute to the literature of the world from Cooper and Poe and then especially from Walt Whitman on. Though American letters have by no means become a dominating force today, they have at least achieved a place of equality with the leading literatures of

Europe. In many cases, to be sure, as in the political and social preoccupations of its muckrakers, American literature has continued to indulge in the same crass and naturalistic exaggeration which European literature had known between 1890 and 1914, and it often seems as if many American authors, because of the undisputed political and economic leadership of the United States, enjoyed a popularity in this world (comparable to the often dubious popularity of Hollywood) which they do not quite deserve.

We have seen how the new American continent entered into the stream of European literature through Ercilla's *Araucana* and how Alarcón had been the first Spanish author to be born in distant Mexico. With regard to the United States we have emphasized the indebtedness of the old colonies to English Puritanism; later, the eighteenth century of Franklin, Jefferson and Paine was indebted to French Enlightenment; and finally the American romanticists from Irving to Longfellow received much of their inspiration from Germany and, to a minor extent, from Spain, Italy and Scandinavia.

A very interesting problem for the comparatist to investigate is the changing attitude of American authors towards Europe. We have alluded to the great spiritual indebtedness to Europe of authors like Irving, Emerson, Longfellow and Margaret Fuller; they cherished Europe not only because of its literary wealth, but also because they preferred the more cultured way of life of the Old World to the robust and wildly pulsating activity and the necessarily crass utilitarianism along the Western frontier. Even Cooper, who looked down upon Metternich-dominated Europe, was an aristocrat and a Tory at heart who was even more shocked by the coming to power in America of uncouth frontiersmen like Andrew Jackson. From Whitman's titanic songs of freedom on, however, the attitude towards the Old World changed completely, for the New World was represented as the home of the free, the land of the future, the hope for the millions of oppressed and handicapped inhabitants of Europe who hungered for a small place of their own in the sun. Whitman was the first, too, to reject European models and standards and to sing of America, of its own greatness and its own dreams. The trend was continued with Mark Twain who refused to be awe-stricken on his pilgrimage to Europe (*Innocents Abroad,* 1869; *Tramp Abroad,* 1880) and who seemed to single out England more than any other nation in order to deride its social injustice, its reactionary caste-system, its medieval cruelties (*The Prince and the Pauper* 1882; *A Connecticut Yankee at the Court of King Arthur*, 1889). In *The Plutocrat*, by Booth Tarkington (1927), the hero, Earl Tinker, feels uncomfortable and contemptuous amidst the smoothness and shallowness of European aristocrats and fourflushers; on a trip through the Mediterranean he is not impressed by the ancient culture of Greece, but, significantly, he worships and fully understands the greatness of Rome, for Romans, like Americans, were essentially men of deeds and not of words, empire-builders who built grandiosely and lastingly—highways, theatres, acqueducts, cities—and who were unrelenting in pushing on the frontiers of the kind of civilization they knew. The same pride in America and her concrete achievements and the same contempt not so much for European as for American expatriates who were ashamed of Pittsburgh or Milwaukee and who preferred Paris or Baden-Baden instead, we notice in *Dodsworth* (1929) by Sinclair Lewis—and though Dodsworth loses his wife to Europe because she prefers the spineless artificiality of social life on the Riviera, Dodsworth himself, a successful builder of cars, an integral part of the great and enterprising concern which is called America, is glad to shake Europe's dust off his feet and to return to his constructive new tasks. Many more examples could no doubt be adduced to indicate that profound change in the evaluation of Europe which set in between the Civil War and the First World War.

It remains for us to point to some significant and typically American trends and contributions before, under the heading of Realism and Symbolism, we elaborate on several authors who were able to translate into words at least some of these indigenous contributions and aspirations. It is to be regretted that some of the finest aspects of our American ideals do not lend themselves to easy expression, for they are very much a matter of the heart only—and neither our politicians nor our novelists seem to be able to put them across to the rest of the world in their most convincing form.

The ideal of true democratic freedom and of the equality of all races in the American melting pot could not fail to make a powerfully important impression on European literature and mentality. On a much smaller scale Switzerland had preceded

America both with her democratic ideas and with her wisely tolerant attitude towards the German, French and Italian elements in her midst. But in America, spreading across a vast continent which was ready to be inhabited and exploited, these ideals were now tried out on a scale so great that the distraught of all Europe were attracted by this noble experiment—the Irish escaping from a famine, the Germans shunning the despotism of Metternich, the races of Southern and Eastern Europe seeking greater economic and political security, the restless and adventurous spirits of all nations in their quest of wider horizons and greater potentialities. The theme of emigration became important in English and Swedish, as well as in German, Italian and Spanish literature—just as, in America, there began an important literature of immigrants, of men and women who, having escaped the poverty and oppression of the Old World, fought desperately, against tremendous odds, to avoid new exploitation and to build up a better life in the New World, as for instance in *My Antonia* (1918) by Willa Cather, the story of a Bohemian girl in the Midwest, and di Donato's *Christ in Concrete* (1939) or d'Agostino's *Olives in the Apple Tree* (1940) about the problems and heartaches of Italian immigrants. Apart from the Indians, individual American themes were as yet of little importance to European writers—*e.g.* the Revolutionary War, the Civil War, the Frontier (which left such a deep imprint upon American mentality and literature) ; indeed, not even the Cowboy achieved such a monumental importance in literature as the Gaucho in South America, who, over and over again, was increasingly treated as a rebel against civilization, a Robin Hood striking back at society (Sarmiento's *Facundo*, 1845; Hernández' *Martín Fierro*, 1879). But, over and above all this, the vision of democracy, of freedom from want and from fear, of what we, in spite of all heartbreaking setbacks and materialistic distortions, call the American Dream, remained a powerful factor in the hearts of men all over the world whose lands were convulsed by war, persecution and hunger. It is not blasphemous at all to say that, in spite of human shortcomings on either side of the ocean, a new star of Bethlehem arose in what America potentially has to offer to mankind—a new light and ideal which has not failed to inspire some of the best thinkers and writers of the last few generations.

For us in the field of Comparative Literature, the peaceful

intermixture of races on the American scene offers not only re-
assuring political promises—it also allows us to perceive the
skeins of all races and the strains of all national mentalities
in the works produced by American authors. To mention only
a few among our contemporaries: besides the Anglo-Saxon
background in a Robert Frost or a Willa Cather, we can point
to the German background of Theodore Dreiser, the Portuguese
ancestry of John Dos Passos, the Italian aspects in Frances
Winwar and Bernard DeVoto; the Armenian contribution in
William Saroyan; the Jewish element in Sholem Asch—all of
them distinct proofs that the intellectual wealth of the Old
World, enriched by new ideals of our own, is mirrored in the
literature of the New World. And this mixture of races and
outlooks is a boon for scholarship, too, for because of our manifold racial backgrounds we Americans seem particularly well
suited to investigate Comparative Literature and to weigh cor-
rectly the delicate problems of the *debits* and *credits* of individual national literatures.

One more important contribution of America must be given
here the emphasis it deserves: through us the voice of negroid
Africa, haltingly and imperfectly as yet, has for the first time
received a chance to make itself heard. Because of his tragic
plight, the Negro has not yet been given the place he so richly
deserves in the history of humanity—and they who today write
about Africa are almost exclusively white settlers or travellers
in that continent. It is only among the sons of the former Negro
slaves in America that the voice of Central Africa was heard
for the first time, in literature as well as in music—not through
the works of privileged and respected mulattos abroad (such as
Dumas in France), but through men and women who, due to our
unfortunate American bias, still completely feel as Negroes.
White Americans began to speak of them and their plight with
ever more compassion and ever less condescension, from Harriet
Beecher Stowe's *Uncle Tom's Cabin* (1852) through the beautiful dramas and stories of Paul Green (*Lonesome Road, In Abraham's Bosom*) to Lillian Smith's *Strange Fruit*, O'Neill's *All
God's Chillun Got Wings*, Anderson's *Winged Victory* and Hod-
ding Carter's *The Winds of Fear*. Later, the Negroes themselves
began to speak up, with humility at first (as in Booker T.
Washington's autobiography *Up From Slavery*), but then with
increasing emphasis, pride, anger and hope, as Americans rather

than as Africans—and Langston Hughes' impressive poem *I, too, am America,* may well serve as a motto for all that has been written by Negroes like Frederick Douglass, James Weldon Johnson, George S. Schuyler, Walter White, Countee Cullen, Claude McKay and others. The beauty and the intensity of feelings of Negro spirituals are especially deeply felt all over the civilized world. But over and above all speculation about the wealth which we might still receive from that vast, promising and untapped reservoir, the soul of the black man, we should pay heed to storm signals like Richard Wright's *Native Son* (1940) —an impressive novel by a thought-provoking Negro—in order to become aware of the greatness and the urgency of the task ahead of us to make the American Dream a real and living concept. We should welcome, rather than begrudge, the fact that the comparatist, unlike many of his colleagues, very often simply cannot afford to remain a passive and scholarly onlooker; his whole profession in the last analysis constitutes also a political creed and he must therefore be willing to leave his books and to start building bridges himself if he really wants to live up to his ideals.

Wars, Revolutions and Expulsions

An unfortunate denominator common to all Western nations at this critical stage of their political and economical history is man's increasing inhumanity towards man in the form of total wars and total revolutions. Some comparatists might wish to investigate the similarity of experience and of suffering brought about by War—from the false nationalism of Tennyson's *Charge of the Light Brigade* (1854) in the Crimean War to the brutal naturalism of Plivier's *Stalingrad* in the Second World War, through Stephen Crane's *Red Badge of Courage* about the American Civil War and Zola's *La débâcle* and Liliencron's *Kriegsnovellen* about the Franco-Prussian War to the immense variety of novels and plays about World War I (*Le Feu* by Barbusse, *Journey's End* by Robert C. Sherriff, *What Price Glory,* by Maxwell Anderson and Laurence Stallings, *Bury the Dead* by Irwin Shaw, *Im Westen nichts Neues* by Remarque, *Die Töchter der Hekuba* by Clara Viebig, *Der Streit um den Sergeanten Grischa* by Arnold Zweig, and others) and World War II (*A Bell for Adano* and *Hiroshima* by John Hersey, *From Here to Eternity* by James Jones, *The Naked and the Dead* by Norman

Mailer, *Mrs. Miniver* by Jan Struther, and others). Certain modern writers might almost be said to have specialized in this subject of War and Death—as Hemingway, who in his *Farewell to Arms* wrote about World War I in Italy and in *For Whom the Bell Tolls* and *The Fifth Column* about the Civil War in Spain. Closely connected with this is the *Heimkehrer*-motif, treating the return of a husband from war (*Karl und Anna* by Leonhard Frank, *Der deutsche Hinkemann* by Ernst Toller) or from some other disaster (*Enoch Arden* by Tennyson). In an age aglow with political passions, our authors find it hard to remain the calm Olympian Goethe was during the Napoleonic Wars; instead, they have become battlers and propagandists, lawyers attacking the social iniquities, physicians examining the ills of our time, prophets announcing the dawn of a new age or the death of a rotten society, soldiers fighting in the first ranks for whatever they believe to be right.

The repercussions of the Russian, the Italian, the German and the Spanish Revolutions have made themselves felt in every phase of modern life; the clash of modern Democracy first with Fascism and now with Communism has intensified man's struggle for survival. Hence the political tenor of ever so much of contemporary literature: the ridicule of militarism (Zuckmayer's *Hauptmann von Köpenick*), the hatred of would-be dictators (Dos Passos' *Number One*), the expiation for political cowardliness (Anderson's *Key Largo*), the rejection of totalitarianism (Lillian Hellman's *Watch on the Rhine*, Brecht's *Furcht und Elend des Dritten Reiches*), the glorification of revolution (Toller's *Feuer aus den Kesseln*, Goering's *Seeschlacht*, Wolf's *Die Matrosen von Cattaro*), the horrors of concentration camps (Wiechert's *Der Totenwald*, Remarque's *Der Funke Leben*), the exaltation of national resistance against totalitarian invaders (Steinbeck's *The Moon is Down*, Sherwood's *There Shall Be No Night*), the hatred of soul-killing machines (Toller's *Die Maschinenstürmer*, Döblin's *Wadzeks Kampf mit der Dampfturbine*). In this feverish atmosphere political convictions range from Pacifism (Bertha von Suttner in Germany, Romain Rolland in France) to Fascism (d'Annunzio in Italy, Hamsun in Norway, Ezra Pound in America) and to Communism (Aragon in France, Toller in Germany)—not to mention the scores of writers, especially in America, whose political thinking at one time or another likewise tilted far to the left.

At the same time, however, the very flood of political radicalism sweeping over us made many of the best grope back into history to help us reaffirm the soundness of our own old traditions (Anderson's *Valley Forge*, Kingsley's *Patriots*, Sherwood's *Abe Lincoln in Illinois*). Many writers died for their political convictions (García Lorca in Spain, Hasenclever in Germany) ; the greatest number, however, managed to escape (though Toller and Stefan Zweig committed suicide in exile)—while again others forsook the ideals of the West (Arnold Zweig, Bert Brecht, Anna Seghers) by returning to a totalitarian system.

Great and pathetic is the literature produced by the innumerable expulsions and emigrations of entire strata of populations—for our age has by far surpassed the cruelty of Spain to the Jews, of France to the Huguenots, of the Holy Alliance to the suffering masses of Italy or Poland. The flood began with the Russian émigrés escaping from the Revolution of 1917; they were joined by Italian refugees in the 1920's and Spanish refugees in the 1930's—with Paris again serving as the most desirable shelter, the perfect embodiment of the spirit of the West. But these waves were soon surpassed by the flood of German refugees—socialists, pacifists, Jews, authors who were mostly expressionists in their literary affiliation—who touched the hearts and enriched the cultures of neighboring lands. Switzerland, the land which once had sheltered Mazzini, Wagner, Nietzsche, Rilke, Lenin, Mussolini, Hesse, Einstein, Paderewski and Rolland, received men like George, Mann and Ludwig; but it was especially America which absorbed most of these intellectuals (Werfel, Toller, Brecht, Remarque, Döblin, Mann). The literature produced by such calamities often dwells on the misery and the pathetic helplessness of refugees (Remarque's *Liebe deinen Nächsten* and *Der Triumphbogen*, and Feuchtwanger's *Der Teufel in Frankreich*) ; it treats of present sufferings in the guise of past persecutions (as Werfel's *Vierzig Tage des Musa Dagh* speaks of the Turkish persecutions of Armenians) and at times even distorts past history in an attempt to find parallel struggles between the forces of light and darkness (as Stefan Zweig's biography of Erasmus and the latter's struggle against the bigotry of a hitlerized Luther)— or then again it proudly points to past achievements especially of the Jews and to their worth and dignity in the face of all vilifications (Wassermann's *Mein Weg als Deutscher und Jude* and Arnold Zweig's *Bilanz der deutschen Judenheit*). The delicate problem of Jew and Gentile, incidentally, was often treated even before World War I, as indicated by Israel Zangwill in England (*Children of the Ghetto*, 1892), Zola's famous *J'accuse!* in connection with the Dreyfus-affair in France (1898) and by Georg Hermann (*Jettchen Gebert*, 1906) and Carl Hauptmann (*Ismael Friedmann*, 1912) in Germany. This problem has, of course, remained alive and is periodically treated in literature, as in Laura V. Hobson's *Gentleman's Agreement* in our own day and country.

Compared to these enormous upheavals and expulsions, the occasional exchanges of poets between France, England and America, though important in themselves, do not assume a tragic significance: under the name of Joseph Conrad the Pole J. K. Korzeniowicz became one of England's best-known novelists; American authors of great repute like Henry James and T. S. Eliot migrated to England and became British citizens; less important young Americans like Julian Green, Stuart Merrill and Francis Vielé-Griffin preferred the background and the language of France—while Ezra Pound, for political reasons, chose Fascist Italy. Among scores of continental writers seeking a new home in America W. H. Auden was the only English poet of note.

For the sake of completeness it remains for us to point to some of the very frequent foreign journeys by late nineteenth century poets, too. Russian, Scandinavian and American authors joined their West European colleagues in their at times lengthy sojourns in France and Italy, in England, Germany or Switzerland. Thus the important literary friendships of Turgenev in Paris, the gambling losses of Dostoevski in Baden-Baden, the three trips of Tolstoy to Western Europe between 1857 and 1861; thus the extended sojourns of Ibsen especially in Italy and Germany (1864-91), of Björnson in Germany, France and Italy and of Strindberg in Switzerland and France; thus the visits of Americans like Mark Twain, Artemus Ward and Bret Harte in England and on the continent, and of Europeans like Dickens (1841 and 1867-68), Trollope, Björnson (1880-81), Hamsun and Hauptmann in America. In France, we have noted that Dumas père, Leconte de Lisle and also Victor Margueritte had been born overseas; to them we can add Jean Moréas, who was a Greek, and Guillaume Apollinaire, who was a Pole by birth, and José-Maria de Heredia, who came from Cuba. To the literature of Spain Cuba also gave Gertrudis Gómez de Avellaneda, while the noted Nicaraguan poet Rubén Darío, greatly indebted to France, also included Spain in his European journey. Other authors to reflect the atmosphere of Spain extended from Barrès (*Du sang, de la volupté et de la mort*, 1893) up to Hemingway. Italy remained a great favorite from the Brownings, Ruskin (*Stones of Venice*, 1853), George Eliot, Swinburne, Pater, and the many works by Francis M. Crawford in England to Burckhardt and Meyer in Switzerland and Ricarda Huch, Isolde Kurz (*Florentiner Novellen*, 1890) and Heinrich Mann in Germany, while Germany was explored by Frenchmen from Michelet and Taine up to Giraudoux and England by Verlaine, Rimbaud and Taine up to André Maurois.

All Voices Shall be Heard

One last characteristic of the literature of the past hundred years is the coming to the fore of nationalities which hitherto had not been given much chance to make their voices heard. We are referring not only to Bulgarian, Rumanian or Estonian literature which, in the wake of an often tragically short-lived national independence, managed to give expression to national ideals of their own; we are referring even more to distinct linguistic sub-divisions within national literatures that insist on a cultural autonomy of their own: Low German, Provençal, Catalan literature. Low German came to the fore again with the poems of Klaus Groth (*Quickborn*, 1853) and the novels of Fritz Reuter (*Kein Hüsung*, 1858). Mistral (*Mireio*, 1859) was the most noted representative of the new Provençal literature; it was discussed, among others, by Saint-René Taillandier in a series of articles in the *Revue des Deux Mondes* (*La Renaissance provençale*, 1859-75) and the enthusiasts of this movement (including even an Irishman, William Bonaparte-Wyse) were anxious to extend closer regenerative literary relations not only to the Catalans but even to their fellow-Latins in Rumania. Catalan literature—silent since the days of Auzias March and the marriage of Ferdinand and Isabella—experienced a rebirth with Rubio y Ors and Verdaguer; the naturalistic novel *La Papallona* (1883) by N. Oller, when translated into French, was even honored with a preface by Zola.

Of greatest importance was also the Celtic revival in Ireland. It was prepared early in the nineteenth century by novelists like Maria Edgeworth, whose Irish novels (*Castle Rackrent,* 1800, *Leonora,* 1806) inspired Scott to transfer the same technique to the locale of Scotland, and by poets like Thomas Moore, the biographer of Byron and the author of *Irish Melodies* (1807) and other works which influenced, among others, Vigny in France. It should be thoroughly worthwhile, too, to investigate the Celtic strains in the works of Chateaubriand or Renan in France or to study the Irish undercurrent in so-called "English" authors from Goldsmith up to Wilde and Shaw. One of the chief promoters of the Gaelic revival was Samuel Ferguson (*Lays of the Western Gael,* 1865), and the whole movement reached its apex towards the end of the nineteenth century with W. B. Yeats, John M. Synge, A. E. (Russell), George Moore and with the founding of the Irish Literary Theatre (1899). The comparatist, apart from marvelling at the richness of this Celtic revival especially in the field of poetry and of the drama, might wish to study also the impact of the ever-present Irish problem upon English mentality, from Queen Elizabeth and Spenser and the brutalities of Cromwell up to our own days of Eamon de Valera.

Within the field of German literature, the poets of Austria, from Grillparzer through Rosegger to Schnitzler and Hofmannsthal, are well worth investigating for their particular traits and for their relationship to Germany as a whole; and perhaps even more fascinating and rich are the Bohemian Austrians (better called Sudeten-Germans) with their wealth of ideas and of beauty, from Stifter up to the three great names, Rilke, Werfel and Kafka—the latter two German-Jewish authors from Prague. In the vast field of French literature it was especially Belgium which came to the fore at a certain moment, producing more great names especially in symbolist literature—Maeterlinck, Verhaeren, Rodenbach and others—than the size of the small country would seem to warrant.

With regard to dialect literature, finally, particularly Italy and Switzerland seem to prevail: the former with Neapolitan (Di Giacomo) and Venetian (Gallina) dialect works, the latter with Simon Gfeller from Bern and Meinrad Lienert from Zürich. Compared to the impressive and oppressive unity and monotony during the Classical Age, when the voice of France alone lorded it over all Europe, modern European literature is of a richness and a variety that is enviable and encouraging indeed and that seems the best possible safeguard against the encroachments of a new totalitarian uniformity.

C. REALISM

Because the line between Romanticism and Realism can be more sharply drawn than that between Romanticism and Symbolism and because Symbolism developed in part as a reaction against Realism, we will examine the evolution of Realism first. This development can be studied as a series of impulses, each one carrying the practitioners further in the direction of extreme tendencies.

Phases of Development

For purposes of simplifying the examination, we might list the following five phases in the development of what, broadly speaking, is usually called Realism: Young Europe, Epigones, Artistic Realism, Naturalism, Impressionism.

First, there was the political reaction against the passivity of ever so many romanticists in the face of the oppressiveness of the Holy Alliance. We have seen that, in contrast to the militant patriotism of some romanticists (Pellico, Petöfi, Mickiewicz), others tended to be reactionary and acquiescent to the system of Metternich or of Napoleon III. Hence the political vehemence of the Young European writers who turned away from romantic day-dreaming to militant liberalism and who at times were apt to prostitute literature into a mere vehicle for political pamphleteering and journalism. Of them (Heine, Hugo and others) and of the renascence of the ideals of 1789 in the uprisings of 1830, 1848 and 1863 we have already spoken.

Second, there was a distinct return to classical inspiration—not only in fundamentally classical France, where the so-called "école du bon sens" after the failure of Hugo's *Les Burgraves* in 1843 managed to stage a short-lived revival of classical principles, but also in Germany (Platen) and in Italy (Carducci). Grillparzer's Greek-inspired tragedies (*Sappho, Das goldene Vlies, Des Meeres und der Liebe Wellen*) perhaps indicate best the desire of those who called themselves Epigones to "stand where Goethe and Schiller stood"; after the excesses of romantic haziness, literature again sought a concrete and plastic style. Though called Epigones in relation to the great classical masters preceding them, the quality of their works does not necessarily have an inferior connotation at all.

Out of these two preparatory tendencies, the greater emphasis on contemporary social and political affairs of the Young Europeans and the finer stylistic efforts of the Epigones, there developed, from 1850 to about 1890, the age of what we can best call Artistic Realism, which achieved its finest works especially in the novels of France and Russia.

The factors which affected the development of this third and most important phase of Realism are several. An important element was the new political climate which was a mixture of two not always compatible drives: the drive for democracy and the drive for national unity. The drive for democracy produced the 1848 Revolution in France which had great international repercussions, and the drive for national unity contributed to the establishment of modern Italy and Germany and to the *pax Britannica* imposed by the now dominant British Empire. Both of these drives compelled the public and the writers to remain ever conscious of political and social phenomena, and so it was only natural that the authors, no longer even wanting to pursue the elusive Blue Flower of Romanticism, should turn to the real world about them. Another extremely important factor in the development of Realism was science. While the best literary minds had reaped only disillusionment from their beautiful romantic attempts to change the world, scientists had methodically worked away and were now actually changing the world. It seems only natural that the authors should decide that they might find greater success if they should take over the methods of the scientists. Virtually all of the significant scientific developments were eventually reflected in literature, but three men in particular were especially important in the field of science and the social sciences for their influence on Realism: Auguste Comte, Charles Darwin, and Karl Marx.

In COMTE's Positivism (*Cours de philosophie positive*, 1830; *Système de philosophie positive*, 1851) many of the intellectual leaders of the century found expressed the foundation for a new literary aesthetic. Abstract visions, vague yearnings, Platonic ideals had no place in the positivistic world, for scientists working with demonstrable evidence could lead the way to the perfect world that had somehow escaped the romantic seekers. Because Positivism was linked with the evolving social sciences, the writers tended, particularly in the novel and the drama, to practice a kind of social science themselves—an exact, professedly scientific analysis and anatomization of society. Even those authors who were essentially artists rather than scientists were infected with the new fashion of regarding human society as something capable of exact scientific study, and this acceptance (as the belated popularity of Schopenhauer indicates) led to the pessimism which pervades most prose fiction and drama of Realism. If the world is just a meaningless mechanism, then the aspirations, ideals and hopes of the human beings living in this mechanism are rather pathetic phenomena to behold. The mechanistic view of the universe was given additional support by the Industrial Revolution which seemed effectively to be subordinating the human being to machines. Although Comte's positivist ideas are seldom reflected directly in the literature of the century, the spirit of Comte is, and this spirit was spread into England and America with the help of Stuart Mill and Herbert Spencer. Possibly another derivative of this trend is the science- and police-fiction which is very popular today, the former represented by Verne and Wells, the latter successful ever since Edgar Allan Poe and Conan Doyle.

Charles DARWIN supplied another startling influence on evolving Realism with his *The Origin of Species* (1859), which seemed to prove that the human race was just one of the many products which the machine of the universe turned out. The effect of Darwin's theories upon the late nineteenth century was comparable to the effect in the late sixteenth and seventeenth centuries of the Copernican heliocentric theory of the universe. The direct influence of Darwinism can be found in many works of the late nineteenth century, but its most important effect lay in the emphasis which it placed upon heredity and environment as controlling factors in the determination of human character and conduct. Later, Zola and Ibsen and their followers made the influence of heredity and/or environment one of their principal concerns in their representations of life in the modern world. In the field of philosophy, Darwin's influence was of course greatest upon Friedrich Nietzsche (*Also sprach Zarathustra,* 1883; *Jenseits von Gut und Böse,* 1886), the prophet of titanic vitality in a world which permits the survival only of the fittest, and the impact of Darwin remained potent also among such disciples of Nietzsche as Jack London (*The Call of the Wild,* 1903, *The Seawolf,* 1904, *Before Adam,* 1906, *Burning Daylight, The Valley of the Moon*). Darwin's work was frequently translated; among his best-known popularizers in Germany was Ernst Haeckel (*Die Welträtsel,* 1899).

Karl MARX did so much for the shaping, or unshaping, of the modern world that it seems hardly necessary to mention him for his influence upon literature. Although he and Engels had been active in their advocacy of socialism even before 1847, when the *Communist Manifesto* was issued, it was really not until after 1867, when the first volume of *Das Kapital* was published, that Marxian economic theory, given a kind of seeming ideological support by Darwinism, became an important factor in literature. Marx helped to give impetus to a trend that had been apparent as early as Hebbel's *Maria Magdalena,* the novels by Spielhagen or *La Dame aux Camélias* of Dumas fils to make of literature a means of social criticism and reform. Even the non-Marxist naturalists made a practice of holding the mirror up to nature (not in the way classical satirists had done, to improve human morality) in order to show the evils of political or social institutions so that these institutions could be reformed. With the spread of the Marxian doctrine of economic determinism, naturalists came to imply in their novels and plays that human suffering and human tragedy are the result not of any inherent tragic flaw in the character of the one who suffers, but of blind and ineluctable economic and political forces beyond the control of the individual. These authors were satisfied not merely with revealing how these forces worked, but went on to imply and even advocate reforms in the way society is organized which would establish a control over these forces. Eventually Marxist writers, in and out of Communist controlled countries, for the most part became propagandists rather than imaginative writers.

Those authors who were positively affected by the political developments of the century, by the seductions of science, and by the results which the social sciences promised, made principal use of three genres as the most appropriate media for the new literary concepts and purposes: the novel, the short story and the drama. The traditional poetic forms of verse satire, epistle, eclogue and so on were not only dead but now buried. Long narrative poetry was dying. The only poetic genre which was seriously cultivated during the period of Realism was the short lyric.

All these considerations have taken us further along the path of Realism into the very heart of the fourth phase to be mentioned here: Naturalism. The difference between Realism and Naturalism is necessarily one of degree rather than of kind. Naturalism is merely the logical extension and intensification of the fundamental principles of Realism. If, as is frequently done, Realism is compared with photography, then the difference between Realism and Naturalism would be the difference between a photograph made from the best possible aesthetic angle, with due attention to the patterns of light and shade and to the inherent aesthetic qualities of the objective being photographed, and a photograph of a scene essentially ugly with harsh flat lighting that reveals all of the distortions in the object. The realist photographs a house from the front, framing it in an attractive composition of trees and fine lawn, while the naturalist goes around back and photographs the same house through the wash hanging on the line with the garbage cans decorating the approaches. This analogy implies the extremes of Realism and Naturalism, but in practice it is often difficult and usually pointless to try to distinguish between the two. At any rate the naturalist is more concerned with presenting reality as it actually is, and so he engages in less selection than does the realist. He is much more of a social scientist who presents the world just as it is for the purpose of discerning social, political, economic, or psychological forces operating in that world. And because of the implied scientific impulse that lies beyond his aesthetic, the naturalist tends to regard society as a whole as more important than the individual members of it, and so he is usually more in favor of some collective modification of society than he is in any moral or psychological alteration of the individual. Since too his purpose is to expose social problems, he is inevitably concerned with the sordid, the ugly, the discordant aspects of society which create these problems. He is avowedly uninterested in producing something that might be described as "beautiful", for his purpose is to reproduce the world as it is, and if that world lacks beauty, then, according to him, it would be sentimental romanticizing to insist that he should make it seem beautiful.

Because Realism and Naturalism differ only in degree, it would be pedantic to try to establish a date at which one trend ended and another began. The best we can say is that sometime around 1880 sociological emphasis overcame the artistic, and the literature, of France and Germany at least, became naturalistic rather than realistic. The peak of Naturalism lasted from 1890 to the First World War when it was largely replaced by Expressionism; in America, however, where the whole movement began only with Jack London, Norris and Dreiser, Naturalism (occasionally interrupted by other stylistic principles, it is true) may be said to last until the present day. It should be emphasized, too, that Naturalism till 1914 was dominated by Zola, Ibsen, and their ideas of heredity, while Naturalism between the two World Wars was mostly dominated by Marxist ideas and was particularly productive in American literature. In other words, at first most of the emphasis in naturalistic literature was on the biological forces of heredity and appetite which control the lives of human beings. As Western society became ever more politically and economically conscious, the emphasis shifted to political and economic forces, and these forces controlled the action in most of the naturalistic works written between the two World Wars.

The characteristics of Naturalism are those implied by its theory: extreme verisimilitude of language, leading ultimately in the twentieth century to the inclusion not only of dialects (Hauptmann) but also of heretofore unprintably profane words (Hemingway) ; relative formlessness corresponding to the formlessness of life as it is lived; a bias in favor of the oppressed classes of society, that is to say in favor of members of the proletariat instead of the middle class which supplied the characters for Realism; a lack of faith in the individual's ability to control his own destiny; and usually an implied faith in the ability of some political or social panacea to ameliorate the unsatisfactory conditions represented. Most naturalistic works are tragic without being tragedies, for the sufferers are always the victims of forces beyond their control and their suffering seems both needless and meaningless because if society would only correct itself such suffering would never exist. We should add, too, that though Freud has served as a godfather especially to the symbolists, he has also contributed to naturalistic anatomizations of sexual problems and perversions.

Since Naturalism jettisoned the strict aesthetic control practiced by such realists as Gautier, Flaubert, Thackeray, Turgenev, Tolstoy, Meyer, Storm and Hebbel, it tended to restrict itself to the two genres of the novel and the drama. Although a considerable number of naturalistic poems have been written (Holz,

Schlaf, Edgar Lee Masters), they are historically unimportant because they have consisted mostly of political propaganda, written in such formlessly colloquial idioms as to limit their appeal to small segments of a single country's population and then only for a few years. While it might be interesting to study the development of Marxist and proletarian poetry, the interest attaching to such a study would be political rather than aesthetic.

While Naturalism represents a decline from the high artistic standards of Realism, the fifth and final phase of the entire realistic movement represents an extension of the artistic implications of Realism in the direction of Symbolism. This final phase—Impressionism—existed concurrently with Naturalism and maintains a kind of middle road between the extremes of Naturalism on the one hand and the extreme reactions against Naturalism on the other. Actually it is often impossible to distinguish definitively between the impressionist work and the symbolist work, just as it is sometimes impossible to distinguish definitively between the impressionist work and some of the achievements of artistic Realism. Impressionism might be defined as a refinement and sublimation of the artistic principles of Realism. In contrast to the common stylistic grossness of the naturalists and in contrast to the frequent, almost willful obscurity of the symbolists, the impressionist fuses the realities of the objective world with his own reactions, or impressions, of that world. The impressionist, while still describing the realities of nature, emphasizes not that which is seen, but the impression which the object observed makes upon him who sees. The impressionist gives a mental rather than a physical picture, he is not so objective as the naturalist, but not so excessively subjective as the symbolist. He may seem more irrational than the former, but closer to life and reality than the latter. As opposed to the vigor, the militant tone, and the somewhat monotonous tendency of the naturalists to preach, to distort and to exaggerate, the impressionist, tired of endless milieu descriptions, dwells again on the importance of the poet, the observer, the artist; he endeavors to record the finest fluctuations of his mood, his ego. Hence the great vogue of artists' novels or *Künstlerromane* among these impressionists, in which the authors analyze the reactions of their own sensitive nervous systems to the crude world without (Mann's *Tonio Kröger*, 1903;

Hesse's *Peter Camenzind,* 1904; Joyce's *Portrait of the Artist as a Young Man,* 1916).

Perhaps the distinction between Impressionism and Symbolism can best be explained in terms of style. The impressionist still tries to reduce the world to a tangible, palpable form, even though it is only the form of his impressions rather than of the world. For this reason his style is often lucid, musical, and even precisely imagistic at times. The symbolist, however, even though he may seek to appeal to the senses, is not concerned with a tangible form in nature, but rather with a symbolic form which can be apprehended by the senses *and* the total sensibility. He reduces reality to a form, but it is the form which his inner being imposes upon that reality, not the form which reality imposes upon his senses. The distinction may be further illuminated by remembering that the impressionists were often the friends of such impressionistic painters as Cézanne and Manet, while the symbolists in the early years of their movement sought to make poetry like music. Furthermore, since the impressionists were more immediately concerned with the concrete world than the symbolists, they more frequently expressed themselves in the novel, while the symbolists exploited the medium of poetry and developed the medium of the prose poem. At best the line between Impressionism and Symbolism is as difficult to draw sharply as the line between Realism and Naturalism. And many authors developed from the one into the other. For example, James Joyce's *Dubliners* and the early part of *Portrait of the Artist as a Young Man* are essentially impressionistic while the remainder of Joyce's work is clearly symbolistic.

The Novel and Short Story

The period from 1850 to 1950 might almost be called the Century of the Novel. No literary genre has been so popular, with the public and with authors, as the novel, and in no other genre have masterpieces been created comparable to those produced in novel form. The novel is the form best suited to the conceptions of the nature and purposes of imaginative writing held by the writers of Realism. Although the realistic novel and short story were developing indigenously in other countries about the same time they were being developed in France, it is notably the French, and a little later the Russian prose-fiction writers who contributed the most to the technique of the modern novel.

Henri Beyle, called STENDHAL, should be mentioned among the most important forerunners of Realism. Although he lived in the Romantic Period, he himself recognized that he was half a century ahead of his time. Perhaps some of his advanced qualities derived from his travels in Germany and Russia and his long residence in Italy. Whatever the source of his brilliantly subtle realism and perfectly controlled psychological analysis, his two great novels, *Le Rouge et le Noir* (1830) and *La Chartreuse de Parme* (1839), were not fully recognized until the end of the century, and his importance as a master of the realistic psychological novel and as a model for twentieth century novelists has been steadily growing ever since. The problem of Stendhal's influence on the novel is complicated by the fact that the kind of novel he wrote had to develop on its own before he became properly recognized. But English and American novelists in particular have studied him as a model, Arnold Bennett and Henry James being two notable examples. As one might expect, Stendhal's reputation in the Latin countries is also deserving of study, for example with Carducci in Italy and Valle-Inclán in Spain. In addition to Stendhal, Prosper Mérimée deserves mention as a late romantic whose purity of style and subtle irony anticipate Realism, as does George Sand, whose novels for a brief time during the forties mirrored the fashionable concern with sociological problems and humanitarian sympathies. Mérimée's *Chronique du règne de Charles IX* (1829) might be examined as a source for C. F. Meyer's *Das Amulett* (1873) ; his influence can also be studied in connection with such diverse figures as Thornton Wilder in America and Valle-Inclán in Spain. While George Sand was not one of the outstanding novelists of the nineteenth century, the force of her personality and her achievements, especially on behalf of the oppressed classes and of women, were such as to make her reputation and career abroad significant in literary history. In addition to the obvious parallel between England's George Eliot and George Sand, there are the problems of George Sand's possible influence on such writers as Heine, Gutzkow, Ibsen, Mrs. Browning, Walt Whitman, Mickiewicz, and Dostoevsky. Especially the Spanish novels of Galdós often mirror social, matrimonial or religious difficulties which the French authoress had earlier tried to face and to solve. George Sand's highly romantic life, emancipated in the best tradition of Young European mentality, has also supplied material for romantic fiction (*Lélie,* by André Maurois).

One of the very greatest French contributors to the European novel was Honoré de BALZAC (1799-1850). Though he, too, lived in what may still largely be called the Age of Romanticism, he was distinctly a representative of Realism in the meticulous detail of his descriptions and in the moving revelation of contemporary life which his novels contain. He may have begun his career as a novelist in imitation of Sir Walter Scott, but he very quickly transferred his interest to French, and especially Parisian, life as he saw it around him. In his ninety-six novels grouped together under the title of *Comédie humaine* (1833 ff.) he created one of the most amazing imaginative worlds in the history of literature. It has been suggested that no one, except for God and Shakespeare, has been so successful in creating human beings as was Balzac (*Le Curé de Tours,* 1832; *Eugénie Grandet,* 1834; *Le Père Goriot,* 1835; *César Birotteau,* 1837). Despite the weaknesses in his style and despite his too frequent use of rather cheap melodramatic plot devices and Gothic atmosphere, his *Comédie humaine* represents one of the great literary achievements of the last one hundred and twenty years. Balzac in effect invented the technique, which has since been used by Zola, Keller, Romains, Proust, Lewis, Faulkner and others, of creating in his own mind a complete world, so rich, so varied, and so verisimilar to the real world that it could furnish endless materials for a series of novels, all of which are interrelated because they all are based upon the same imaginative social framework. Also in his moving revelation of the power and savagery of basic human emotions Balzac succeeded in distilling from the fictional forms which had been the eighteenth century and the romantic novels the significant imitations of life which the modern novel has become. In many ways Balzac was the first truly modern novelist, and as such his influence on James, Dreiser, and Faulkner in America, on Thackeray, Trollope, and Lawrence in England, Anzengruber in Austria, Wassermann and Mann in Germany, Pereda and Galdós in Spain, Teixeira de Queiroz (*Comedia burgueza,* in seven volumes, 1879 ff.) in Portugal, and Dostoevski in Russia (who began his literary career by translating *Eugénie Grandet*) has been very significant. Balzac's enthusiasm for occult sciences and his frequent use in the plot structure of his novels of mysterious organizations and people who seem to have a kind of supernatural power made him a favorite among the symbolists, so that one can find evidence that such a novel as *Louis Lambert* contributed to the formulation of the occult and symbolic philosophical framework which W. B. Yeats used as the basis of so many of his finest poems. Starting with the France of Balzac, the interested student might follow up the modern predilection of writing great cyclic novels. Such an investigation would take us from Balzac, Zola, Rolland and Proust to *Les Hommes de bonne volonté* (*Men of Good Will*, 1932 ff.) by Jules Romains, and from there to the England of Galsworthy (*The Forsythe Saga*, 1906 ff.), the Spain of Pio Baroja (*La lucha por la vida*, 1904, *Memorias de un hombre de acción*, 1913 ff.), the Germany of Hans Friedrich Blunck (*Werdendes Volk*, 1923), Josef Ponten (*Volk auf dem Wege*, 1933), and Thomas Mann (*Joseph und seine Brüder*, 1933-44) and the America of John Dos Passos (*U.S.A.*, 1938).

Although the Goncourt brothers and especially Alphonse Daudet (in his relations with Henry James) contributed to the development of the modern European novel, it was Gustave FLAUBERT (1821-80) who did more than any other single man to define the values and establish the standards of Realism in the novel. Flaubert's cool, impersonal, analytical, and perfectly controlled point of view, his lucid, subtle, and infinitely polished style, and the incisive understanding of the problems facing the individual in an alien society mark his one great masterpiece, *Madame Bovary* (1857). It has been said that if there is a Platonic world of ideas, the idea of the perfect novel contained there must be *Madame Bovary*. Flaubert's masterpiece has all of the qualities which other realists have aspired to invest their works with: objectivity, but subtle analysis of the psychology of the characters; a style that makes every word contribute to the total effect for which the author strives; an irony that enables the reader to see the action from several points of view at once; a restraint and plasticity of imagery that recalls Classicism. Although Flaubert's output was relatively slight and although *Salammbô* (1862), *L'Education sentimentale* (1869) and *La Tentation de saint Antoine* (1874) are not the equals of *Madame Bovary*, Flaubert has remained one of the most important influences on modern artistic prose. His influence on the style and method of the novel has been most important, for it was from him principally that Turgenev and Henry James acquired the values which they sought to give their works. Apart from technical perfection, Flaubert has also contributed to the irony and the tone of the novel for the last eighty years. The marks of his influence can be found in almost any serious novel of the modern age: specific examples are almost too abundant, including, in addition to Turgenev and James, George Moore, Lafcadio Hearn, William Faulkner, and even Sinclair Lewis, the frustrated heroine of whose *Main Street* may indeed be called an American Madame Bovary. In Germany, Theodor Fontane came perhaps closest to the artistry and the deep psychological insight of Flaubert; indeed his *Effi Briest* (1895), the wife of a stern Prussian officer, is yet another incarnation of Madame Bovary.

With the exception of Zola and Maupassant, no French realistic writer prior to World War II has acquired outstanding international importance. Such authors as Jules Romains, Huysmans, Pierre Loti, François Mauriac and others have often been widely read, but they have contributed little that is new to the development of the modern novel. The most important among them was Anatole France, whose works reflect a skepticism and an impassivity which place him in the best tradition of Classicism and Realism. He floated midstream in the main current of that tradition, being the modern equivalent of Rabelais, Racine and Voltaire. In such novels as his *Thaïs* (1894), *La Rôtisserie de la Reine Pédauque, La Vie de Jeanne d'Arc*, and *Les Dieux ont soif* (*The Gods are Thirsty*, 1912), his urbane, acutely critical intelligence and his ever tolerant skepticism provided refreshing relief from the messianic trumpetings of the naturalists and the sometimes pathological inversions of the symbolists. The coolness and essential rationality of France's prose found admirers abroad, among them Willa Cather, Robert Nathan, Jacinto Benavente and others. Although the satire is much more bitter and the method much more naturalistic, the contempt for the modern world's retreat from basic human values expressed in Aldous Huxley's satiric novels also echoes Anatole France.

No comparative examination of modern literature is possible without the inclusion of the four great Russian masters

of the prose fiction of the nineteenth century. The fact that
the student may not be able to read Turgenev, Dostoevski,
Tolstoy, and Chekhov in the original should not bar him from
studying the impact which each of these men has had in the
West; for after all most of the authors whom they have influenced became acquainted with them through translations,
a fact which in itself attests to the power of their work. The
knowledge and influence abroad of Dante, Shakespeare, Cervantes, Racine and Goethe was based on relatively large numbers of men abroad who could read them in the original. But
the four Russian masters of prose fiction have become literary
giants of world-wide importance almost solely through translations of their works.

Ivan TURGENEV (1818-83) was, by his own admission,
more of a Western European than a Russian, for he spent the
last thirty years of his life abroad, mostly in Paris, and was
intimately acquainted with Flaubert, Daudet and Zola. His
fame and influence abroad have been based principally upon
those qualities which he shares with Flaubert: objectivity,
subtle irony, restraint and perfect control of his material. Perhaps one of his greatest contributions to the West was that he
became the first Russian author to be widely read in the West
and so opened the gates to knowledge of Russian literature. His
first important work was *Tales of a Hunter* (1847) in which he
was almost revolutionary in being the first to write about the
actual life and the problems of Russian peasantry. Even more
important was his *Fathers and Children* (1861)—a novel which
had something of a unique influence of its own in its dramatization of the Nihilist movement and its providing of one of the
earliest models for the artistic treatment in novel form of the
problems of the individual (Bazarov) who defines his world
politically. It also represents one of the early treatments of
the perennial modern theme of the spiritual emptiness of the
contemporary world. The same incipient struggle against Russian autocracy can be seen in Turgenev's last great novel,
Virgin Soil (1877), though it also points to the inability of many
a Russian idealist and intellectual (Nezhdanov) to put across
and fight for his revolutionary plans. Turgenev was rendered
into German and French by the Pushkin translators Bodenstedt
(1865) and Mérimée (1866).

The most dramatically powerful of Russia's great four is

Fedor DOSTOEVSKI (1821-81) and his influence, of a very
different kind than that of Flaubert or Turgenev, has been
considerable. Dostoevski's appeal has been the overwhelming
power of his narratives, which in turn has derived from his
profound and merciless probings of his principal characters.
His moving dramatizations of those human doubts and aspirations which always border on the pathological have contributed
to the increased emphasis placed upon abnormal psychological
behavior in the modern novel. His greatest novels, and the
ones which have been most influential abroad, are *Crime and
Punishment* (1866) which has endlessly fascinated Western
readers and authors alike, and *The Brothers Karamazov* (1880)
which poses more effectively than any other modern work the
crucial spiritual problems of the contemporary age. A book
could be written on the contributions of *Crime and Punishment*
to detective literature alone. The central character in this novel,
Raskolnikov, has become, along with Hamlet, the symbol of the
modern man who must determine upon a course of action and
then pursue that course, but who lacks the final conviction that
will give him sufficient strength to remain in his chosen path.
As symbol and as foil, Raskolnikov is influential in the works of
Eliot, Koestler, Gide, Kafka, and Proust. *The Brothers Karamazov*—the rake, the nihilist, the saint and the epileptic—is
again a sordid picture of vice and degradation, of murder and
of punishment; its allegory of the Grand Inquisitor and of his
condemnation of Christ is particularly famous and terrifyingly
pertinent to the modern world. Other works of Dostoevski's
include his *House of the Dead* (1861), an account of his four
horrible years in Siberia; *The Idiot* (1869) which represents
innate goodness in the person of an idiot, Prince Myshkin,
hardly a conventional saint; and *The Possessed* (1871), probably Dostoevski's most overtly political and melodramatic novel
which, among other things, is an attack upon Turgenev's con-
doning of Nihilism and of dangerous Western influences. While
Dostoevski was not the brilliant craftsman of the novel that
Flaubert or Tolstoy were, his endless psychological analyses or
dramatizations of his characters have contributed to the so-
called stream-of-consciousness technique used by the symbolist
novelists as a means of revealing the subconscious of their
heroes (for example by Joyce, Proust, Kafka, Döblin, Virginia
Woolf and others). Indeed, one could probably find the direct

or indirect influences of Dostoevski's subjective probings or of
his penetrating insights into the political motivations of modern
man in almost any serious modern novel, from Paul Ernst to
Thomas Mann, from Pio Baroja to Ignazio Silone, and from
D. H. Lawrence to Thomas Wolfe. In addition, he has contributed to the ideological and spiritual temperament of the
modern world by the appeal which he has had for such diverse
writers and thinkers as Hauptmann, Ortega y Gasset, Maupassant, Nietzsche, and so on; the entire lyrical poetry of Rainer
Maria Rilke is permeated by the Russian mysticism, the call
for man's inner regeneration and the "Bruder Mensch" theme
so richly encountered in Dostoevski.

It is customary to dwell upon the marked contrasts between
Dostoevski and his companion giant, Count Leo TOLSTOY
(1828-1910): the contrast of the plebeian and the aristocrat,
of the one's pride and the other's humility, of Dostoevski's
almost masochistic naturalism and Tolstoy's saint-like spirituali-
ty, of the former's chaotic, kaleidoscopic, and quite imperfect
organization and form and the latter's purer, systematized, almost geometric patterns of thought and development. Whatever validity may obtain in these contrasts, the impact of
Tolstoy upon the Western World has been quite different from
that of Dostoevski. Tolstoy's contribution to the West has been
dual: his technical contribution as a brilliant artist, and his
lofty spiritual contribution. As an artist he provided in *War
and Peace* (1868) and *Anna Karenina* (1877) two models for
the modern novel which are equalled in importance only by
Madame Bovary—and yet they are even more important than
Flaubert's masterpiece, for they attempt more and so their
success is the more awe-inspiring. *War and Peace* in particular
demonstrated to the modern world that the novel is an art form
comparable to that of the classical epic, for in this novel Tolstoy
has captured the complex flux of the life of an era and presented
it in such a way that the reader can at one and the same time
perceive all of the intricate cross currents of the flux and trace
individual currents through it and can understand the complete
character of each of dozens of individuals even while seeing
each character as a component of the flowing currents of history. Tolstoy's subtly indirect and objective method echoes
that of Stendhal and Flaubert and has inspired a greater desire
for emulation than the direct, subjective outpourings of the less

artful Dostoevski. The firm but delicate control of his genius
over the whole mass of his material established almost im-
possibly high standards for the intellectualized novel art of the
twentieth century. Among those who have undertaken, some
with considerable, others with very slight success, to equal
Tolstoy's artistic achievement have been Galsworthy, Hauptmann, Wassermann, Mann, Romains, Hemingway and Dos
Passos.

As a spiritual leader Tolstoy has found but a small following,
for the self-denial of his mystical Christianity has little appeal
to the pragmatic, industrialized modern world. But among some
of these who have been the most bitter critics of the modern
world, Tolstoy's solution to today's spiritual problems has often
had the quality of the light of salvation. His urgent demand for
a spiritual rebirth of man, for a return to patriarchal and idyllic
goodness in the manner of Rousseau and a Christ-like saintliness of man, is evident in *Anna Karenina*—not so much in the
character of the heroine, an adulteress who ends in suicide, but
especially in Levin, Tolstoy's noblest creation; it can also be
seen in his last great novel, *Resurrection* (1899). It has already been mentioned that one of the greatest spiritual leaders
of the twentieth century, Mohandas Gandhi, read Tolstoy as a
young man and then wrote to him. Emulations of Tolstoy's
spiritual message range from Galdós (*Nazarin y Halma,* 1895)
and Emilia Pardo Bazán (*La sirena negra,* 1908) to Hauptmann
(*Der Narr in Christo, Emanuel Quint*) and Wassermann (*Christian Wahnschaffe*) ; but if Tolstoy left a literary spiritual heir
in the West, that heir must be Rainer Maria Rilke, the greatest
of modern German poets and one of the greatest poets of
Symbolism. The English-speaking world first learned to know
the two Russian giants in the mid-eighties: *War and Peace* was
translated in 1884, *Crime and Punishment* in 1885, *Anna Karenina* in 1886.

The final great Russian influence emanating from the nineteenth century is that of Anton CHEKHOV (1860-1904), who,
although he comes somewhat later than the other prose writers
whom we are discussing, was still an artistic realist rather than
a naturalist. Along with Poe and Maupassant, Chekhov deserves credit for helping to create the modern short story (*Tales
of a Stranger,* 1893, *Three Years,* 1894, and others). The
question might be raised whether Chekhov's stories—and those

contemporary stories which he influenced so heavily—are short stories at all in the traditional sense of the Italian *novella* or the French *conte,* or whether they should not rather be called little vignettes or sketches. In his tales Chekhov gives us a character, lets us watch that character for a brief time, and then leaves us. His stories do not have regular plots; some readers complain that they do not move, that nothing really happens. But Chekhov does not really try to "tell a story" so much as he tries to reveal some aspect of human character in its relation to the world in which the individual lives. For this purpose he uses the utmost economy in his style and makes each detail carry a very heavy burden of meaning. In his technique he therefore often borders on Symbolism; in his philosophy of life he tends to dwell on the essential aloneness of every human being, though he permeates the frightening atmosphere of man's isolation with a warmth and a compassion of which Maupassant was never quite capable. In the superficially static, but subtly revealing and sympathetically pessimistic stories of Chekhov, modern short story writers, particularly English and American, have found models for their own work. Two of the greatest modern Anglo-American short story writers have been Katherine Mansfield and Sherwood Anderson, both of whom seem to write less in their native artistic traditions than in the tradition of Chekhov. Through these two writers and by direct influence Chekhov has contributed greatly to the pattern of the modern short story. One can read almost at random in the little magazines or *The New Yorker* and feel the presence of Chekhov in practically every story.

France and Russia contributed most during the period of Realism to the development of prose fiction, but even as the writers of these two countries were formulating and putting into practice the aesthetic of Realism, authors in other countries were working out independently a Realism of their own. Few of these authors acquired much international reputation, and so only brief mention need be made of them here. In England neither Carlyle (*Sartor Resartus,* 1838), Thackeray (*Vanity Fair,* 1848), George Eliot (*Adam Bede,* 1859), Meredith (*The Ordeal of Richard Feverel,* 1859) nor indeed Jane Austen (*Pride and Prejudice,* 1813) and Charlotte (*Jane Eyre,* 1847) and Emily Brontë (*Wuthering Heights,* 1847) became as influential abroad as they might have deserved; the only great exception was Charles Dickens who, perhaps because of the kindly humor which he spread over scenes of stark realism in London slums (*Oliver Twist*, 1838, *David Copperfield*, 1850, *Little Dorritt*, 1857), was avidly read all over Europe and imitated, among others, by Raabe and Reuter in Germany and Strindberg in Sweden. Mention should be made also of Robert Louis Stevenson—not so much because of the international success of his children's tales of adventure (*The Treasure Island*) but because tales of the type of *The Strange Case of Dr. Jekyll and Mr. Hyde* (1886) intensified the growing contemporary interest in the study of the abnormal and the macabre in men's souls. The expatriate Henry James forms the connection between America, England and France; he learned Realism from Flaubert and Turgenev in the company of Daudet and Bourget and his presentation of expatriate Americans of the type of *Daisy Miller* (1878) is particularly interesting. How much the current James revival may be duplicated abroad it is still too early to say, and whether James' rather Victorian qualities will contribute anything more to the development of the European novel seems rather doubtful.

It should, perhaps, be pointed out that the conscious aesthetic of Realism as it had been developing notably in France and practiced in France and Russia became the basis of literary Realism in America under the leadership of William Dean Howells. While Howells may have had something new to say to the America of his own day (*The Rise of Silas Lapham*, 1884), he said little that had not been said earlier in Europe and thus made no real contribution to European Realism. Indeed, even as he was advocating Realism for America, the United States was beginning to produce the novels of Naturalism which were soon to appeal to the whole world. Excellent in themselves, but equally unable to surpass their French and Russian masters and to achieve an international popularity abroad were the novelists of Germany (Raabe, Storm and especially Theodor Fontane). In Spain, Realism witnessed the development of the *novela costumbrista*, the novel of manners and customs of which *La Gaviota* (first written in French in 1849) by Fernán Caballero alias Cecilia Böhl de Faber was among the first and the best. Other Spanish realists were Juan Valera (*Pepita Jiménez*, 1874) and Pedro Antonio de Alarcón, author of novels (*El sombrero de tres picos*, 1874; *El escándalo*,

1875) as well as of short stories. With Pereda, Galdós and
Emilia Pardo Bazán in Spain and with Verga in Italy, the realistic novel often developed into regional literature or into Naturalism or both; but among the regular realists of Italy mention
should be made of the essayist Edmondo de Amicis (*Vita mili-
tare, Il cuore*) and especially of the pleasantly didactic Antonio
Fogazzaro, author of the well-known *Piccolo mondo antico* (*The
Small World of Our Fathers*, 1896). In the novels and the
poems of Gottfried Keller and Conrad Ferdinand Meyer German-Swiss literature produced its finest works—but neither the
beautiful *Leute von Seldwyla* (*People from Seldwyla*, 1856 and
1873) by Keller nor the historical novels by Meyer evoked a
great echo abroad.

In connection with Switzerland, however, we must refer to
the development of a new genre by Jeremias Gotthelf—though
that genre later developed rapidly and quite independently in
other literatures, too: the type of *Heimatliteratur* which is
usually called regional or provincial literature and which far
more than in lyrical poetry (Annette von Droste-Hülshoff in
Germany, Keller in Switzerland, Pascoli in Italy) found its finest
expression in the rustic novel. Gotthelf's *Bauernspiegel* (*Mirror of Peasants*, 1835), *Uli der Knecht* (*Ulrich the Farm Hand*,
1841) and *Uli der Pächter* (*Ulrich the Tenant*, 1849) are outstanding and early examples of this type of novel about the
sturdy peasants in the canton of Bern, with all their virtues and
their foibles. Keller likewise followed this genre in some of his
Seldwyla stories, especially in his *Romeo und Julia auf dem
Dorfe* (*A Village Romeo and Juliet*), often said to be the finest
rustic tale in the whole realm of German literature. Swiss
authors, in German (Federer) as well as in French Switzerland
(Ramuz), have continued to display this strong attachment to
their native soil to this very day. In France, Balzac wrote on
provincial characters and manners (*Le médicin de campagne,
Le curé de village, Les paysans*, 1841); so did George Sand (*La
mare au diable*, 1846, *La petite Fadette*, 1849) who should be
remembered for these as well as for her socialistic or pro-
feministic works. They were followed by minor French *Heimat*-
authors from Fabre up to Bazin; among better known works of
this type we might indeed include also the humorous *Les aven-
tures prodigieuses de Tartarin de Tarascon* (1872) by Alphonse
Daudet, *La Terre* (*Earth*, 1887) by Zola and perhaps even *Les*

pêcheurs d'Islande (*The Fishermen of Iceland,* 1886) by Loti. More important, in English literature, than *Lorna Doone* by Blackmore (1869) and the *Scottish Tales* by Barrie (1888) are the fourteen fine novels about Wessex by Thomas Hardy (*The Return of the Native,* 1878; *Wessex Tales,* 1888; *Tess of the d'Urbervilles,* 1891, and others). Italian regional novels range from Ippolito Nievo (*Il conte pecoraio,* 1857) to *Il paese di Cuccagna* (*The Land of Cockaigne*) and other tales by Matilde Serao which deal with the lower classes of Naples and especially with their great passion for gambling. The greatest of these Italian regionalists, however, was Giovanni Verga, whose tales of Sicilian life, poverty and iniquity often border on Naturalism (*Vita dei campi,* 1880, *Novelle rusticane,* 1883). One of these tales, *La Cavalleria rusticana* (*Rustic Chivalry*) was also dramatized by him (1884) and achieved international success in the opera by Mascagni. The Italian brand of regionalism, with its emphasis on peasant life and social problems among the laboring classes, is generally known by a term of its own, Verism. Spanish regionalism, like Verga's Verism, likewise borders on a naturalism which is quite native. Among its representatives should be named Pereda, whose tales deal with the peasants as well as with the fishermen of northern Spain (*Escenas montañesas,* 1864, *Sotileza,* 1884) ; Pérez Galdós, famous especially for his *Episodios nacionales* (1873 ff.) which blend the historical with the regional trends in Spanish fiction, and for social novels (*La desheredada,* 1890) which cause him to be compared to Balzac, George Sand and Dickens rather than to Zola; and Blasco Ibáñez, who began his career with novels about the peasants and the fishermen of Valencia (*Flor de Mayo,* 1895; *La barraca,* 1898; *Cañas y barro,* 1902).

Rather than allude to regional works from the Russia of Turgenev (*Tales of a Hunter,* 1847) to the Norway of Hamsun, we must stress that this type of novel produced its finest blossoms in Germany and in America. German *Heimat*-stories extend from Immermann's *Oberhof* (1838) about Westphalia, Storm's *Schimmelreiter* (*The Rider of the White Horse,* 1888) about the Frisian coast, Reuter's *Kein Hüsung* (*Homeless,* 1858) about Mecklenburg, and Auerbach's *Schwarzwälder Dorfgeschichten* (*Village Tales from the Black Forest,* 1843 ff.) about Swabia, to Stifter's *Nachsommer* (*The Indian Summer,* 1857) about Bohemia, Rosegger's *Geschichten aus Steiermark*

(*Tales from Styria,* 1871) and Anzengruber's *Der Schandfleck* (*The Stain,* 1876) about Austria. Anzengruber, it might be added, was also the author of several good peasant-tragedies and peasant-comedies. With Clara Viebig we witness the blending of regionalism and Naturalism (*Kinder der Eifel,* 1897, *Das schlafende Heer,* 1904), and the Alsatian Friedrich Lienhard should be noted as the author of a programmatic essay of importance for all regionalists (*Los von Berlin,* 1900). German regionalism of the twentieth century added a flavor not originally to be found in the beautiful descriptions of rustic landscapes and agrarian preoccupations: with Gustav Frenssen (*Jörn Uhl,* 1901) and Hermann Löns (*Der Werwolf,* 1910) it veered so much towards nationalistic exaltation and, with Hermann Stehr (*Der Heiligenhof,* 1917), towards mysticism that the final result, even before the National Socialist regime, was the *Blut und Boden* (Blood and Soil) literature of which Blunck, Ponten and Grimm were early and Vesper and Griese later representatives. American regionalism came to the fore after the Civil War; its novels and short stories ranged from the California of Bret Harte to the New England of Edith Wharton, from the Louisiana of George Washington Cable (*Old Creole Days,* 1879) to the Indiana of Edward Eggleston (*The Hoosier Schoolmaster,* 1871) and from the Missouri of Mark Twain to the somewhat later and naturalistic novels of Jack London about Alaska. The regional movement in America has also produced the earthy dialect tales and anecdotes of frontier life by such well-known American humorists as Artemus Ward, Josh Billings and Petroleum N. Nasby as well as the sordid, literally too earthy novel of Erskine Caldwell, *Tobacco Road* (1932). However limited they may seem, the regional novels of Europe and of the American East Coast produced some of the finest masterpieces of artistic Realism.

To turn from the novel of Realism to the novel of Naturalism, we should emphasize again that it went through two phases of development, each phase dominated by a different country. The first phase begins with Zola and indicates the development to its mature form of the naturalistic novel. The second phase is marked by American domination between the two World Wars and is characterized by the lost generation pessimism and the Marxist absorption of the authors of the period. Because the rapid means of international communication have been so very greatly improved during the last two or three generations, the problem of sorting out the international lines of development in the novel through these two phases becomes quite difficult.

The acknowledged founder of Naturalism in the novel is Emile ZOLA (1840-1902), who proudly thought of the modern novelist as an exact scientist. In the important programmatic preface to his *Thérèse Raquin* (1867) he proposed and tried to practice the theory that the author uses his novel as a scientist uses his test tube, carefully measuring into it the necessary elements to cause a reaction, controlling the conditions for the reaction, and then observing the results and inducing his hypotheses about the natural laws governing the reaction. By using this method the novelist-scientist must be scrupulously careful not to adulterate the substances he puts into his test tube by romanticizing, sentimentalizing, or moralizing. He must select life just as it is; otherwise his experiment becomes unreliable. Zola's own primary interest in using this experimental method was to study the "mechanism of passion" in order to determine the fixed natural laws which govern its operation. The basic assumption underlying Zola's theory has found few adherents, but his conception and technique of the novel have been the strongest single determinants of the modern naturalistic novel. The strength of Zola's influence has persisted in spite of the decline in respect for his works. It has frequently been pointed out that what remains of interest in his novels is the imperfect fulfillment of his naturalistic aims. Most of his novels belong to the cycle called *Les Rougon-Macquart, histoire naturelle et sociale d'une famille sous le Second Empire* (1871 ff.), for like Balzac he created a whole fictitious world for himself. *Nana* (1880) is Zola's best known novel, largely because of its notoriety, while *Germinal* (1885), a powerful story of the violent and desperate life of a coal miner, and *L'Assommoir*, the story of a Parisian laborer, are among his best works. These, along with the many other novels he wrote (*L'Oeuvre, La Bête humaine, La Débâcle*) provided the examples of his theory, and the examples did as much to bring on Naturalism as did his rather fantastic theories.

Zola's heirs are legion, including contemporary novelists who may never have read him at all. They include at a minimum Maupassant, Huysmans, Bordeaux, and Romains in France;

Kretzer, Clara Viebig, Sudermann and Hauptmann in Germany; George Moore, Gissing and Galsworthy in England; Frank Norris, Dreiser, Upton Sinclair, Dos Passos, Erskine Caldwell and James T. Farrell in the United States. In France, Paul Bourget wrote his famous novel *Le Disciple*, the tale of a carefully planned seduction, against the onesidedly biological interpretation of life in Zola, and Brunetière, who had begun to analyze *Le roman naturaliste* from 1883 on, proclaimed *La Banqueroute du naturalisme* (*The Bankruptcy of Naturalism*) as early as 1887. The same mixed reception can be seen in Germany: Arno Holz elaborated on the new trends in literature in his programmatic essay *Die Kunst, ihr Wesen und ihre Gesetze* (*Art, Its Nature and Laws*, 1891) and collaborated with Johannes Schlaf in the naturalistic sketches contained in *Papa Hamlet* (1889)—but at the very same time Hermann Bahr prophesied the downfall of Naturalism in two essays *Zur Kritik der Moderne* (*Criticism of Naturalism*, 1890) and *Die Überwindung des Naturalismus* (*The Displacement of Naturalism*, 1890), to be followed somewhat later by the three essays by Samuel Lublinski *Die Bilanz der Moderne* (*The Balance of Naturalism*, 1904), *Ausgang der Moderne* (*The Decline of Naturalism*, 1909) and *Holz und Schlaf* (with the subtitle "A painful chapter of literary history"). Victorian England reacted not so much against the imitators of Zola or those who adapted his novels to the stage (Charles Reade's *Drink* of 1877 is based upon *Assommoir*), but against the publishers of the translations of Zola's works who, amidst a general literary uproar, were condemned to imprisonment (1889). In Spain, where Zola's theories competed with strong native traditions of Naturalism, Emilia Pardo Bazán was especially important, not so much for the preface to her naturalistic novel *Un viaje de novios* (*A Journey of the Betrothed*, 1881) but because of her basically important essay *La cuestión palpitante* (*The Actual Problem*, 1883), with a preface by Zola. Conflicting opinions about native Spanish traditions or new French influences are especially frequent in connection with the famous novels by Blasco Ibáñez (*La Catedral*, 1903; *El intruso, La bodega, La horda*). In Italy, Zola's influences became tinged with native Verism in Verga and his friend Luigi Capuana; among scholarly investigators of the new trend was de Sanctis who wrote a series of eleven articles on Zola (1877 ff.), and among his later disciples can be named Silone. Elsewhere in Eu-

rope the influence of Zola was powerful from the Sweden of
Strindberg to the Portugal of Eça de Queiroz and the Russia of
Gorki. Indeed, Zola's influence on the modern novel is comparable with that of Rousseau upon Romanticism—everywhere one
looks he sees the shadow of Zola.

Next to Zola, even the importance of the exquisite artist
Guy de MAUPASSANT (1850-93) seems slight. Although
Maupassant first published in a collection prepared by Zola, it
was really Flaubert who was his master, he having been a
nephew of a good friend of Flaubert's and having received instruction from the great stylist. It does not seem strange,
therefore, that Maupassant is much more of an artist than Zola
and that his achievement, even though it consists primarily of
short stories, should seem much greater today. Maupassant,
like Flaubert, was a master of the precisely correct word and of
perfect economy of narration and description. In his finely
contrived short stories, his restrained and classically objective
presentation of character provides subtle insights into the inner
workings of the people he gives us to know. Among his collections of short stories are *Mlle. Fifi* (1883), *Contes du jour et
de la nuit* (1885), *La Main gauche* (1889), while his novels
include such titles as *Une Vie* (*A Life,* 1883), *Bel Ami* (1885)
and *Mont-Oriol* (1887). While Chekhov was one of the major
formative influences on the modern Anglo-American short story,
Maupassant perfected the traditional European *novella* or *conte*
and his influence is evident in such authors as d'Annunzio and
Schnitzler. He was introduced into the United States by Lafcadio Hearn and had some influence on Ambrose Bierce. The
excessively popular O'Henry, by coming to be known as the
"Yankee de Maupassant", probably did as much to discredit the
French author as he did to perpetuate his influence.

It has already been indicated that Realism developed indigenously in the United States in the form of local color stories
before the theories and more artistic practices of European
Realism became widely known. But once the influx of French
prose and poetry began in earnest during the nineties, America
caught up with Europe rapidly. The native tradition of local
color had continued without much help from Europe in the work
of Hearn, Craddock and others, and has never really spent itself with the twentieth century perpetuators of that tradition
such as Ellen Glasgow, Elizabeth Madox Roberts, and Ring

Lardner. Around the turn of the century the European brand of Realism, imported largely through the efforts of James and Howells, and local color began to fuse, so that from this time on there is not much point in trying to trace two separate lines of development. And with the exception of Henry James and the never very successful novels of Howells, there was in America no substantial crop of realistic novels comparable in method and intent to, say, those of Flaubert, Turgenev or Meyer. All of the various influences upon prose fiction which had been doing their work in Europe (Darwin, Comte, Marx), plus the products of these influences from Europe, plus the native tradition were lumped into the melting pot with a result—Naturalism —which eventually was poured back to Europe before World War II.

Among the earliest naturalistic novelists in America were Frank Norris, (*The Octopus*, 1901), Upton Sinclair, (*King Coal, The Jungle*), Jack London (*The Iron Heel*), and Theodore Dreiser (*An American Tragedy*). A little later came the gentler Naturalism, reminiscent in quality of Flaubert, of Edith Wharton (*Ethan Frome*) and Willa Cather (*Death Comes to the Archbishop*). As diverse as all of these authors are, they share at least the reaction against sentimentality, a willingness and usually a desire to see the world as it is, and a hardening of style with often a greatly increased awareness of the possibilities for subtlety through style. None of them became widely known abroad until after World War I, and then often the muckraking works of Norris, Sinclair, and Dreiser were read to support the desire to believe that America was nothing but a land of mercenary, heartless, bloodsucking robber-barons—as attested by the amazing popularity of Jack London and also of Dreiser in Bolshevik Russia.

It was only during the between-wars period that American Naturalism began really to bear its unique fruit and that it exported back to Europe the new product which it had made from its own resources and from the imports which it had received from Europe. The new quality of American prose fiction—its hardness, incisiveness, often fine understanding of character, and oblique revelations of emotions—appeared probably first in 1919 with Sherwood Anderson's *Winesburg*, which, as has been mentioned, owed considerably to Chekhov. Anderson contributed more to the development of American prose fiction than he did to Europe, for his book was hailed by the younger writers in the early twenties as a masterpiece and a guide. Foremost among the tragic topics ready to be exploited by left wing naturalists was the execution of Sacco and Vanzetti: it was treated, among others, in Upton Sinclair's *Boston,* Dos Passos' *Big Money* and, indirectly at least, in Maxwell Anderson's *Winterset.* Also the Spanish Civil War, the eagerness to fight for a cause, the awareness of what was at stake, and a blind faith in the motives of Russia, was treated over and over again, from Hemingway's *Fifth Column* and Dos Passos' *Adventures of a Young Man* to Granville Hicks' *Only One Storm* and Maxwell Anderson's *Key Largo.*

Of the many American novelists of the period who did become known abroad, we can mention only four. First there was Sinclair LEWIS with his bitter, brassy, and not always very subtle satiric novels which mocked the most cherished virtues of the American middle class (*Main Street,* 1920, *Babbitt,* 1922, *Arrowsmith,* 1925, *Elmer Gantry,* 1927). The quality and intent of Lewis' novels are such as to defy European emulation, for they are too completely rooted in the American culture to be transplanted. But Lewis has been widely read and honored abroad, perhaps for the same reason as Norris and Sinclair— to support the illusions about the typical American, illusions which were unfortunately proved to be realities in the form of many American tourists. Ernest HEMINGWAY, for a while one of the expatriates and still a constant traveller, is that author most frequently referred to as representative of the Lost Generation. His favorite subject has been the American out of his own culture—the American in Italy during World War I (*Farewell to Arms,* 1929), the American in the Carribean (*To Have and Have Not,* 1937), the American in Spain during the Spanish Revolution (*For Whom The Bell Tolls,* 1940), the American on a safari in Africa (*The Short, Happy Life of Francis Macomber*) and so on. Hemingway is typically American himself, but he seems to be a writer without cultural roots, one who would subconsciously like to be an integral part of a strong and coherent culture but who could never accept one however much he was fascinated by its traditions and institutions. Hemingway's style, which has been endlessly imitated, almost always without success, is deceptively simple, a kind of reduction to perfection of the realists' insistence upon economy and purity.

John STEINBECK is a kind of archetype of modern Naturalism. His *Of Mice and Men* (1937) seems to have sought the most unaesthetic subject matter possible and to have treated it in as brutal a way as possible, nevertheless suggesting a tenderness and sensitivity in the social derelicts who form its characters. *The Grapes of Wrath* (1939) is the finest example of American sociological Naturalism in the novel, the story of the overwhelming and brutalizing catastrophes which befall a family of displaced American farm workers who are the victims both of nature and of an economic system. His *In Dubious Battle* (1936) gives us a fine study of labor problems, strikes, lockouts and social strife, while *The Moon is Down* (1942) with equal compassion sketches the self-defeating stupidity and futility of the oppression of a subjugated nation by militaristic dictatorships. The fourth significant novelist to be mentioned here, William FAULKNER, received the supreme mark of European recognition when he, like Lewis, was awarded the Nobel prize for his novels, which lie somewhere between Naturalism and Symbolism. At times the grossness, grotesqueness, and violence of his stories seem to constitute a burlesque of Naturalism, while at other times his stream-of-consciousness method (for example, in *The Sound and the Fury*, 1929, part of which is narrated as a kind of interior monologue by an idiot) seems to burlesque the avant-garde novels of Symbolism. Always in Faulkner there is violence and brutality, sometimes presented directly, sometimes only lying beneath the action, and usually there is abnormality of some kind—nymphomania, religious fanaticism, sadism, rape, necrophilia, pyromania. Despite his preoccupation with the fantastically abnormal and the grotesquely violent and an apparent compulsion to include a corpse as one of the complicating factors in his stories, Faulkner has a kind of Dostoevskian power without his ever resorting to the impassioned exposition of the Russian. Faulkner's unique genius rests in his ability to be a modern baroque novelist without ever abandoning completely classical objectivity, restraint and detachment. For all of the complexity of his often fantastically involuted style, he is able to make every detail obliquely contribute to the total effect.

Naturalism had its practitioners in other countries, but none of these practitioners gave to all of Europe anything like as much as he received from France, Russia, and eventually the United States. It would seem that Spain, which had perfected a kind of Naturalism as early as the *Celestina* and which had given to Europe the picaresque novel (a very real antecedent of such an example of modern Naturalism as Farrell's unsavory *Studs Lonigan*), would have contributed rather than received in the recent development of the naturalistic novel. She has been heavily touched by Naturalism, as her social and regional novelists demonstrate; but with the exception of Blasco Ibáñez (*Sangre y arena*, 1908; *Los cuatro jinetes del Apocalipsis*, 1916) even her best novelists are little known outside Spanish speaking countries. At the very end of the nineteenth century there arose a movement in Spain, commonly called *La generación de 1898*, which, in the finely polished language of Impressionism, opposed most of the destructive influences that had come in mainly from or through France, from the *Encyclopédie* to Comte and Zola, and which strove for a moral regeneration of Spain and for a spiritual rebirth of Catholicism. Among the representatives of the Generation of 1898, philosophers and essayists rather than novelists, we should name Azorín (*Alma castellana*, 1900, *Las confesiones de un pequeño filosofo*, 1904), Miguel de Unamuno (*Andanzas y visiones españolas*, 1902; *Comentarios a la vida de Don Quijote y Sancho*, 1906; *La agonía del Cristianismo*) and perhaps even José Ortega y Gasset (*España invertebrada*, 1923; *La deshumanización del arte, Ideas sobre la novela*, 1925).

Though Germany produced quite a few naturalistic novels and short stories, as evidenced by Max Kretzer's *Die Betrogenen* (*The Deceived*, 1882) and *Die Verkommenen* (*The Degenerated*, 1883), Hauptmann's *Bahnwärter Thiel* (*Flagman Thiel*, 1887), Sudermann's *Frau Sorge* (*Dame Care*, 1887), Clara Viebig's *Das Weiberdorf* (*The Women's Village*, 1900) and *Das schlafende Heer* (*The Sleeping Army*, 1904), it should be emphasized that she is far more noted for her Impressionism—the novels in which artists, at times with naturalistic thoroughness, finely delineate the milieu in which the sensitive hero, more likely than not, succumbs in his struggle against a harsh outer world. Thus, for instance, Ricarda Huch's *Erinnerungen von Ludolf Ursleu dem Jüngeren* (*Recollections of Ludolf Ursleu the Younger*, 1893) and Thomas Mann's *Die Buddenbrooks*

(1901) which deal with the decay of formerly vigorous patrician families. Mann's *Der Zauberberg* (*The Magic Mountain,* 1924) with its analytical presentation of sophistication and shallowness in a Swiss sanitorium likewise shows a society doomed to death, just as the characters in Hauptmann's *Atlantis* (1912), the story of a shipwreck, were doomed to death. Mann's novels are frequently in the form of the German apprenticeship novels, borrowing from the techniques of Naturalism at one time and from those of Symbolism at another. While Mann has enjoyed a somewhat excessive popularity, especially in America, there is little evidence that he has exerted any influence on those who came after him—although the theme of the *Buddenbrooks* has recurred frequently, particularly in American novels and plays about the decline of the Old South (Paul Green's *The House of Connelly,* 1932). Later, as a reaction against the irrational exaggerations of Symbolism and Expressionism, there developed, in the 1920's, a return to a new form of Realism called *Neue Sachlichkeit* (New Matter-of-Factness), of which Lion Feuchtwanger (*Erfolg,* 1931), Hans Carossa (*Der Arzt Gion,* 1931), Erich Maria Remarque (*Der Weg zurück,* 1931) and Hans Fallada (*Kleiner Mann, was nun?* 1932) may be said to be the outstanding representatives.

The Drama

The period of Realism produced little lastingly significant drama; the work prior to 1870 was important, however, in preparing the ground for Naturalism. The application to the drama of the aesthetic theories of Realism was made first and most strikingly in France and Germany, with significant influences emanating only from a few plays of the period.

Following the unsuccessful attempts of the *école du bon sens* in France to effect a lasting classical revival in the drama, the new democratic, bourgeois and commercial influences which had helped to encourage Realism in the novel led Dumas fils, Augier and Scribe to modify the comedy of manners until it became in effect social commentary. Such plays as *La Dame aux Camélias* (as novel in 1848, as drama in 1852), *Le Demi-Monde,* and *La Question d'Argent* (the title alone is symptomatic of the new type of drama) by Alexandre Dumas fils and *Le Gendre de Monsieur Poirier* (*The Son-in-Law of Mr. Poirier,* 1854) and *Le Mariage de l'Olympe* by Augier were concerned with typical problems of the newly dominant bourgeois class: problems of money, of social position, of ruinous love-affairs, of ambition to join the aristocracy, and so on. Almost all of the problems (and this is characteristic of the dramas of the period, that they should be *pièces à thèse*) are problems which confronted the newly prosperous bourgeoisie. To a certain extent the treatment of these problems is romantic, particularly in the tendency to glorify the traditional outcasts of society, as for example Marguerite in *La Dame aux Camélias*, the demie-mondaine whose love for Duval forced her to sacrifice herself. Dumas fils was the only one of the French realistic dramatists who had any significant influence abroad. His advocacy of the *pièce à thèse* and his later proposal for the establishment of the *théâtre utile* anticipated Ibsen and Hauptmann and defined in its ultimate form the drama of Naturalism. Dumas fils in theory and practice presented contemporary life on the stage, in the language and idiom of his days, for the purpose of analyzing some social problem or the relationship between the individual and society. Thus he can legitimately be studied for his contributions not only to Ibsen and Hauptmann, but also to Oscar Wilde, G. B. Shaw, and others in the school of naturalistic drama. And, of course, his *La Dame aux Camélias*, for its Romanticism rather than its Realism, has been a recurringly popular story, having been used as the basis for *La Traviata* by Verdi and having proven very popular as a novel, a drama as well as an opera and a film.

By far the most important realistic dramatist in Germany was Friedrich HEBBEL (1813-63). His *Maria Magdalena* (1844) was one of the striking examples of nineteenth century realistic drama, satisfying most of the requirements for the bourgeois problem tragedy and yet achieving a universality which made it somewhat better than most of the rather sordid and sentimental bourgeois plays written in the manner of Lillo and Kotzebue. Hebbel's conception of the drama was not, however, the same as that of Dumas fils or of the later naturalists. In spite of the realism in this play, in spite of Hebbel's pessimism which has more in common with the pessimism of Realism than of Romanticism, Hebbel's historical tragedies such as *Judith* (1840), *Herodes und Mariamne* (1848), *Agnes Bernauer* (1850), *Gyges und sein Ring* (1854) are based on a philosophical conception of the relationship between man and society, and between the individual and the forces of history rather than upon a sociological conception or the traditional guilt-punishment sequence. Hebbel was less concerned with social problems as problems which needed to be solved than he was with the struggles of the individual who tried to retard or accelerate the ineluctable march of history. He was therefore a much more significant dramatist than Dumas fils and although he may not seem as close to Ibsen as does Dumas fils, he undoubtedly contributed just as much, if not more, to the evolution of Ibsen's dramatic conceptions. If one analyzes *An Enemy of the People, The Wild Duck,* or *Hedda Gabler,* he can see at work in the conflicts of the play the Hegelian dialectic of man's place in the historical evolution of humanity which Hebbel used as the basis for his theory of tragedy.

No other country produced drama of international significance during this period, with the isolated exception of a few plays from Russia. Only Gogol's political satire, *The Inspector General* (1836), which is closer to eighteenth century comedy than to nineteenth century Realism, and Chekhov's *The Cherry Orchard, Uncle Vanya* (1899), and *The Three Sisters,* which are among the finest representatives of Realism in the drama, have become internationally famous. The problem of Chekhov's influence upon the drama is one that deserves study, for his plays are like his short stories in that they abandon much of the traditional emphasis upon plot and action in favor of emphasis upon character analysis through the association of a group of characters. Although few modern dramatists have followed Chekhov in dispensing so completely with clearly defined plots, the tendency to subordinate action to character presentation can be detected. Whether this is a natural evolution in the direction of greater verismilitude, whether it results from the influence of the short story and the novel, whether it is the result of conscious efforts to emulate Chekhov, or whether this tendency results from a combination of all of these factors is a problem which merits investigation.

In discussing the development of the naturalistic drama, one can dwell at length on the *Théâtre Libre* in France and the *Freie Bühne* in Germany as very important in its establishment. But, just as Zola dominates the development of the naturalistic novel, so Henrik IBSEN (1828-1906) dominates the naturalistic drama. Norway's greatest dramatist has acquired not only international fame but a commanding position as the father of the naturalistic drama—some would even say the father of modern drama. Ibsen did not, of course, invent the naturalistic drama out of thin air: he had the examples of earlier Realism of Hebbel, Dumas fils, and Augier to help him, and the theories of Realism which were part of the aesthetic climate led inevitably to the kind of drama which Ibsen developed. Nevertheless, his skill in giving his naturalistic materials and themes brilliantly effective dramatic form made him the leader of European dramatists and his plays the models for European drama for a number of years. Part of Ibsen's superior craftsmanship undoubtedly came from his many years of working in the theatre as a stage manager and director. During the decades of his greatest successes he resided almost continuously abroad, mainly in Germany and Italy. He was known slightly abroad before 1880, but it was only with the appearance of *A Doll's House* in late 1879 that he almost overnight became internationally prominent, if not notorious. For the next seventy years few tragedies were written in the Western World that do not reflect in one way or another the tremendous contribution which Ibsen made to the drama. Problem plays had been written before *A Doll's House,* but Ibsen's treatment of a woman's efforts to establish her independence and moral freedom and dignity (foreshadowed in Halm's *Griseldis* and in Hebbel's *Herodes und Mariamne*) proved so very effective as drama that it seemed, and indeed was, something entirely new.

A *Doll's House* was performed all over Europe and its message caused considerable discussion, but Ibsen's next play, *Ghosts* (1881), became a *cause célèbre*. *Ghosts* picks up a theme that was hinted at in *A Doll's House*—the tragedy of a man whose heredity dooms him to destruction. The drama caused such a great furor because one of the principal forces leading to the ultimate destruction of Oswald, the hero, was venereal disease. Ibsen was reviled everywhere for his sensationalism and his play was refused performance until finally it was produced in Norwegian in Chicago. The challenge to dramatic producers and playwrights who saw in *Ghosts* the drama of the future gave impetus to the establishment of the *Théâtre Libre* in Paris and the *Freie Bühne* in Berlin. Meanwhile Ibsen lashed back at the public and his enemies among the critics with *An Enemy of the People* (1882), a thinly disguised dramatization of his own fate at the hands of the conservative, provincial moralists. This play, along with *Ghosts* and *A Doll's House,* provided the repertory for the new kind of theatre which was springing up—a theatre which would unashamedly and boldy tear away the mask of hypocrisy from society and emancipate the individual from every kind of social tyranny.

It is curious that Ibsen himself, as soon as an army of supporters had gathered around him and as soon as his plays became widely performed, turned away from what had come to be known as "Ibsenism" and moved in the direction of Symbolism, for which his Faustian *Peer Gynt* of 1867 had prepared the ground. His very next play, *The Wild Duck* (1884), shows that mere emancipation from social tyranny can also lead to destruction, that the individual, if he is to have any kind of satisfactory life, must be a part of society and must accept some of the responsibilities and restrictions which society demands of him. After *The Wild Duck,* Ibsen wrote less and less in the fashion which was now being imitated everywhere; no longer was the pressure of society a major factor in the dramatic problem, but some inner distortion of the personality—something approaching the classical tragic flaw—which compels the character to destroy himself. Of his later plays, which became increasingly obscure, only *Hedda Gabler* (1890) is regularly produced internationally.

Since what Ibsen did was not startlingly new, the question remains of why he became the "Father of Modern Drama". The answer probably is that he was the first of a number of dramatists who were groping toward the kind of problem play which Naturalism produced who had the superior intelligence and dramatic skill to take an essentially topical social problem and develop it in a play as exciting, significant drama. Actually, he was the final straw which broke the back of traditionalism in the selection of subject matter and theme for the drama. But also Ibsen's contribution to dramatic technique was something entirely new, and his influence on the form and development of the drama has been of even greater significance than his influence upon the subjects which modern drama treats. He showed later dramatists how to pace the action of their tragedies, how to develop a character chosen from contemporary society and formed by the pressures operating in that society without encumbering his plays with unnecessary commentary, and how to make each of the characters of his plays dramatically significant and appealing both to the actors and the audience.

The study of Ibsen's influence on the modern drama is the study of naturalistic drama itself. Specific problems of the influence of Ibsen on individual later dramatists are so numerous as almost to deny their value; they include at least the French dramatists who developed out of the *Théâtre Libre,* such as Becque, Brieux, and Hervieu; the German dramatists who developed out of the *Freie Bühne,* such as Gerhart Hauptmann, Max Halbe and Sudermann; such English dramatists as Shaw, Galsworthy and George Moore, such Spanish dramatists as Echegarary (*El hijo de Don Juan,* 1892) and Galdós (*La de San Quintin,* 1894), such Italian dramatists as Roberto Bracco (*Tragedie dell'anima, Maternità*) Enrico Butti (*Gli atei*), and such American dramatists as Anderson and O'Neill. There is little point in trying to trace Ibsenism through the works of these authors, but it should be understood that in the discussion of the naturalistic drama in these countries Ibsen's contributions are pervasive. A complete German translation of Ibsen began to appear in 1898; among the earliest English translators was William Archer (*A Doll's House,* 1889, *Peer Gynt,* 1892, etc.).

One other Scandinavian author deserves to be mentioned, although his importance in the development of modern drama is overshadowed by that of Ibsen. The tragic, paranoiac August Strindberg (1849-1912) of Sweden, a bitter misogynist and disciple of Nietzsche, wrote violent and powerful plays which contributed an emotional intensity to Naturalism beyond that of the other early naturalists. *The Father* (1887), translated almost immediately into French, is expressive of Strindberg's pathological distrust and hatred of women, while *Miss Julie* (1888) is a naturalistic experimental play, written in a single long act in an effort to achieve greater verisimilitude. Strindberg soon became known in France (his *Plaidoyer d'un Fou* was first written in French in 1887), Germany, England and America and led the way for later naturalists who were interested in the investigation of the violence produced by sex and passion—for example Wedekind in Germany.

The development of Naturalism in France has already been suggested. The *Théâtre Libre* was established by André Antoine in 1887 for the purpose of guaranteeing performances for the

new kind of drama which Ibsen had introduced.   He was given
particular encouragement to establish his experimental theatre
by the controversy which had been aroused by *Les Corbeaux*
(*The Ravens*, 1882) of Henri Becque, that French play which
marks the transition from Realism to Naturalism.   Becque,
like Ibsen in *A Doll's House*, was interested less in entertaining
his audience than he was in transferring real life to the stage
and arousing his audience's interest in social problems.   Becque
was followed by Brieux and Hervieu who helped to establish
Naturalism in the French theatre.   It should be mentioned in
connection with the *Théâtre Libre* that Antoine also encouraged
the performance of foreign plays which other theatres would
not produce, including Leo Tolstoy's *Power of Darkness* (1887)
and Hauptmann's *Die Weber* (*The Weavers*, 1892).   The tradition of Naturalism has been continued in the French drama
and is especially evident in some of the great French films.

In Germany, the development of Naturalism in the drama
parallels its development in France.   In 1889 Otto Brahm did
what Antoine had done in Paris by establishing *Die freie Bühne*
(*The Free Stage*) to guarantee the production of the plays of
the new devotees of Naturalism and to provide an opportunity
for seeing on the stage plays by such foreign authors as Ibsen,
Strindberg, and Tolstoy.   While Germany produced a number
of naturalistic dramatists, one towers above the rest—Gerhart
HAUPTMANN (1862-1946), whose *Vor Sonnenaufgang* (*Before Dawn*, 1889) precipitated the same kind of outraged controversy as had Ibsen's *Ghosts* throughout Europe and Becque's
Les Corbeaux in France.   Hauptmann imitated Ibsen by treating the theme of the hereditary curse of alcoholism, but he also
pointed out that those who may cry loudest about emancipation
from social curses often contributed to tragedies through their
own weakness and cowardice.   *Vor Sonnenaufgang* established
Hauptmann as the leader of German naturalistic drama and for
the next five or six years he produced some of the masterpieces
in this field: *Das Friedensfest* (*The Reconciliation*, 1890),
Einsame Menschen (*Lonely Lives*, 1891) and notably his famous
Die Weber (*The Weavers*, 1892).   Written partly in Silesian
dialect, it is a socialist plea about the exploitation of weavers by
capitalistic sweatshop methods in which the masses rather than
one individual and rebellious proletarian constitute the hero of
the tragedy.   He should be noted, too, as the rare author of two

of the best naturalistic comedies: *Kollege Crampton* (*Colleague Crampton*, 1892), about a lovable drunk, and *Der Biberpelz* (*The Beaver Coat*, 1893), about a thieving washerwoman. Hauptmann became known especially in France, England and America and contributed to the development of Naturalism, but he, like Ibsen, turned away from Naturalism and as early as 1893 began writing symbolist plays (such as the impressive mixture of naturalistic sordidness and Christian exaltation in his *Hanneles Himmelfahrt* and also his famous *Die versunkene Glocke* of 1896) which probably had considerably more influence, especially in France, than did his naturalistic plays.

Second only to Hauptmann in the effectiveness of his technique and the hard-striking quality of his themes was Hermann Sudermann, author of *Heimat* (*Magda,* 1893), a play of the emancipation of the new woman in which actresses like Sarah Bernhardt and Eleonore Duse excelled—and of *Die Ehre* (*Honor,* 1889) about sexual morality among capitalists and proletarians. One other German naturalist, Frank Wedekind, is important for continuing the kind of Naturalism mixed with expressionistic emotionalism developed by Strindberg. Wedekind's concern was not with social problems as such, but with the problems arising from the power of sexual urges which are frustrated and repressed by an unenlightened society (*Frühlings Erwachen,* 1891).

The theatre in England has been dominated for the last fifty years by both the personality and works of one man, George Bernard SHAW (1856-1950). Although his plays reflect the influence of Ibsen (as indicated also by his essay *The Quintessence of Ibsenism,* 1891) and of Shaw's own theoretical socialism, they are much too individual to be included in the general stream of Ibsenism. Their unique flavor derives from the puckish character of the author. Shaw's achievement in the drama was a very great one and what he did was indeed individual and new, but the coloration of his own personality over every one of his plays makes them inimitable (*Candida,* 1895; *Mrs. Warren's Profession,* 1898; and others). More typical of Naturalism, and perhaps therefore much less successful as a dramatist, is John Galsworthy whose plays dealing with social problems are poured into the mould developed by the continental naturalists (*The Silver Box,* 1906; *Justice,* 1910).

In America, the naturalistic drama flourished with a number

of plays, such as *What Price Glory?* by Maxwell Anderson and Laurence Stallings, *The Front Page* by Ben Hecht and Charles MacArthur, *Dead End* by Sidney Kingsley, *The Little Foxes* by Lillian Hellman, and so on.   The native tradition of local color was fused with Naturalism in the folk dramas of Dubose Heyward (*Porgy*) and Paul Green.   Probably the most notable development in the drama in America has been the violent kind of Naturalism which Hollywood has occasionally succeeded in converting into fine movies, such as *Little Caesar, I was a Fugitive from a Chain Gang,* and the movies of such directors as John Ford, John Huston, and Billy Wilder.   But of all of these examples of Naturalism in the American drama, the most significant writer for the theatre between the wars and the greatest dramatist America ever had was Eugene O'Neill, who wrote both naturalistic (*Desire under the Elms, Gold, Anna Christie, The Hairy Ape*) and symbolistic plays (*Strange Interlude*). His last play, *The Iceman Cometh,* is the most naturalistic of any.

Spain and Italy again reflect but do not contribute to the growth of Naturalism in the drama.   With his social satires, Jacinto Benavente is only partially in the stream of Ibsenism (*Los intereses creados,* 1909).   In Italy, Naturalism flourished with Antona-Traversi (*I martiri del lavoro*), but it did not produce its most significant results until after World War II, when such strikingly and freshly naturalistic movies as *Open City* and *Bicycle Thief* taught a world that had become jaded with Naturalism that the method still could produce movingly artistic results.

Summing up these aspects of Naturalism, we might say that before World War II Naturalism tended to assume too readily and too easily that the mere representation of evil conditions in the world and the advocacy of sweeping social reforms would eliminate the evils.   But if any post-war trends can be discerned at all, they seem to be in the direction of a more fundamental and sympathetic understanding of the relationship between the individual and society.   Naturalism has tended to merge with Symbolism by taking over more subjective revelation of character and some of the technical perfection of the symbolists.   Certainly the plays and novels of our contemporary naturalists are a far cry from Zola's "bleeding slice of life".   They recognize the essential dignity and humanity of man and seem to recognize that despite overwhelming social and economic forces and despite the biological conditions of human existence, the hero with his individual morality can still do something with his own life.

Poetry

While prose fiction and the drama were the natural media for the realists, poets could not help but be touched on the one hand by the reaction against Romanticism and on the other by the forces which were contributing to the formulation of the doctrine of Realism. Poetry, which is so patently unrealistic by its very nature, followed the lead of the novel and the drama mostly by reverting to classical objectivity, technical perfection, and intellectuality. Just as the realists in prose and drama sought to eliminate the subjective intrusion of the author upon his material, to perfect the style so that every word contributed to the final effect, and to discipline the form so that it would become an almost scientifically accurate instrument for measuring out the content, so the poets transliterated these values in their theories of verse.

The most notable and most influential example of Realism in poetry can be found in the French poets of the group known as *Le Parnasse*. The earliest representative of this group was Théophile GAUTIER, author of such collections of poems as *Emaux et Camées* (1852), who formulated the poetics for the parnassian poets in his famous *L'Art* (1857). The principal precepts as practiced by Gautier, Leconte de Lisle, José-Maria de Heredia, Sully-Prudhomme, and the other parnassians were these: the "moi" should be purged from poetry; the poet should never reveal his own heart, but should imply what he wishes the reader to feel through his imagery; the poem should be hard and cold, like a statue; the poem should be highly polished, with every detail presented with sharp and plastic clarity. In short, the aesthetic of the parnassians was the poetic equivalent of the aesthetic of the realistic novelists and dramatists. One significant characteristic of the parnassians, however, is the interest which many of them had in non-European cultures and in their going back to older ages in their own cultures for material and verse forms. Thus Leconte de Lisle was drawn to Antiquity and to India (*Poèmes antiques*, 1852; *Poèmes barbares*, 1857); Heredia, who was born in Cuba, to the Carribbean (*Les trophées*, 1893); Gautier, to the impassivity of the African desert which he thought he saw mirrored in Spain (*España*, 1845). The major international importance of the parnassians lies in their perfecting the style, chiseling off the sentimental incrustations of Romanticism, and sharpening and hardening the poetic idiom for the symbolists. Indeed, it is difficult to draw the line between the parnassians and the symbolists, for the method of the latter is very close to the method of the former: to use to the utmost a precise imagery to evoke symbolically the inner experiences of the poet.

One of the especially interesting international relationships of the whole period lies in the parallel development of French and American poetry from Realism to Symbolism. When the Anglo-American poetic revolution against Romanticism finally occurred around 1912, the imagists, influenced considerably by the parnassians, especially Gautier, formulated a new poetics which is essentially the same as the parnassian poetics: poetry should be clear, cool, chiselled, objective and should use as its principal device sharp and evocative images. But because the imagists had not only the parnassians, but also the symbolists to draw upon for ideas and methods, they very quickly developed beyond pure Imagism into full-blown Symbolism. Even so late as Archibald MacLeish's *Ars Poetica* ("A poem should be palpable and mute"), one can hear the echo of Gautier's *L'Art*. Gautier in particular among the parnassians exerted important general and specific influences upon such twentieth century poets as Ezra Pound, T. S. Eliot, W. B. Yeats, MacLeish, Auden, and a virtual army of lesser Anglo-American poets. In addition, the purity, coldness and technical perfection of the Rhinelander Stefan George suggest that his antecedents include the parnassians, while Rilke's own interest in the French symbolists extended back to the parnassians. Spanish poetry reflected the influence of Parnassianism first in South America (Nájera of Mexico and Rubén Darío of Nicaragua) and then later in Spain, when the combined effects of Parnassianism and Symbolism produced the *modernistas*.

In Germany, August Graf von Platen provides a very early example of the attempt to escape the softness, sentimentality and vagueness of Romanticism (*Sonette aus Venedig*, 1825; *Gedichte*, 1828). His artistry as one of the great masters of the sonnet in Germany makes him an aesthetic peer of the parnassians, and his interest in classical Antiquity and his love for

Italy make him a nineteenth century classicist living among romantics. Perhaps because he spent his last years in Italy, Platen contributed also to Carducci's poetry. Among the Italians, CARDUCCI's vigorous personality, his carefully chiselled language and strong ethical struggle against all forms of oppression and in favor of the cultural greatness of other ages (*Odi barbare,* 1877 ff.) make him far more admirable and inspiring than the shallow and bombastic aestheticism of Gabriele d'Annunzio (*Piacere, L'Innocente, Le laudi*). In Switzerland, Conrad Ferdinand Meyer, whose cool and plastic *Novellen* include some of the finest representatives of German realistic historical fiction, was a contemporary of the parnassians, and the economy, clarity, and perfection of his lyrics place him alongside Gautier and Leconte de Lisle (*Zwanzig Balladen,* 1864; *Gedichte,* 1882).

The literature of nineteenth century England reveals all of the current problems, the spiritual, economic, political, and scientific issues which contributed to the development of poetic Realism in Germany and France—but in spite of this, English poetry, as represented by Tennyson, Browning and Arnold, was still fundamentally romantic in style and method. Tennyson and Arnold grappled with spiritual doubt and Browning was aware of the effects of industrialism, but none of them developed any really new idiom, each being satisfied to adapt the traditional verse to his own purposes. Even so, the French symbolists, led by the early example of Baudelaire and by Mallarmé's study and teaching of English literature, were quite interested in English poetry and included Tennyson among their readings, so that one can speak of definite contributions which Tennyson made to them and to Francis Jammes. New trends comparable to the parnassians' began to appear in English lyrical poetry only with the Pre-Raphaelites, with men like D. G. Rossetti, Morris and especially Swinburne.

America produced a poet comparable to the realistic poets of France and Germany and another who, in part because he is uniquely American, made a very great contribution to the development of modern European poetry. The first, Emily Dickinson, developed in the seclusion of her isolated life a poetic idiom which, in its precision and hardness, compares with the best of the parnassian poetry and which, in its subtlety, subjective insight, and psychological perceptivity, places it alongside the best in symbolist poetry (*Poems,* 1890 ff.). Miss Dickin-

son's reputation has grown very gradually and only in recent
years has knowledge of her poetry begun to spread, not simply
beyond the borders of the United States, but through the United
States itself.   The second American poet of importance of this
period is Walt WHITMAN (1819-92), whose romantic impulses,
dressed in a style and idiom that approach Naturalism, gave
something new and unique to America and to the rest of the
world.   After generations of absorbing European literary values,
America, through Whitman, was now ready to give back ideals
and styles of her own (*Leaves of Grass*, 1855; *Drum Taps*, 1867).
Whitman's importance derives primarily from his free verse
style and his unrestricted poetic vocabulary and idiom.   He was
soon translated into almost every European language and became known throughout Europe and South America.   He was a
major contributor to the development of *vers libre* among the
French symbolists, Laforgue translating ten of his poems in the
1880's.   Since Laforgue wrote some of the earliest French poems
in *vers libre*, his debt and therefore France's debt to Whitman is
significant.   Additional translators of and borrowers from
Whitman include André Gide, Valéry Larbaud, Francis Vielé-
Griffin, Verhaeren, and Jammes as well as others.   Echoes of
Whitman's genius in Germany extend from Young Germans
like Freiligrath, realists like Dehmel, and naturalists like Holz
and Schlaf to the twentieth century of George, Lerch and Werfel.   Whitman's reputation abroad provides another example
of that frequent American practice (evident also in the case of
Poe) of holding in considerable disrepute an author who is widely acclaimed elsewhere.

Little need be said about the lyrical poetry of Naturalism,
for this genre had only a limited appeal to the naturalists and
the poets of the various countries did not mutually inspire one
another.   Among them we can mention Arno Holz (*Das Buch
der Zeit*, 1885; *Phantasus*, 1899) and to some extent also
Richard Dehmel (*Predigt an das Grosstadtvolk*) in Germany,
Ada Negri (*Fatalità, Tempeste*) in Italy, and Edgar Lee Masters
(*Spoon River Anthology*, 1915) in America.

D. SYMBOLISM

General Observations

While the development of Realism over the last one hundred years seems naturally to fall into five phases, the development of Symbolism has moved in a fairly steady line, from the symbolists of the 1880's to the contemporary practitioners. We have defined Symbolism as that body of contemporary literature which represents in part a continuation of Romanticism by virtue of its conception of the nature of literature as the projection of the inner vision of the author by means of symbolic language. Any attempt to classify this type of literature of the last century by narrower definitions would create the problem of sorting out the various -isms which the symbolists have delighted in inventing: Fantasism, Expressionism, Imagism, Futurism, Cubism, Dadaism, Surrealism, and so on. However much this chaotic assortment of "schools" may profess to differ among themselves, they share the fundamental proposition that art is the projection of the consciousness (or subconsciousness) of the artist. And so, rather than confound the chaos, we will discuss this whole body of writing under the generic heading of Symbolism.

The same factors which contributed to the development of Naturalism contributed inversely to the development of Symbolism. The increased social and economic pressures of the contemporary world revolted some authors and led them to retreat within themselves to seek a means of reconciliation or escape from the materialistic, mercenary, and mechanistic realities of society. The discoveries in the physical sciences inspired the naturalists to emulate the scientists, but these same discoveries indicated to the symbolists that science was determined to make of man a mere bio-chemical organism essentially no different from a guinea pig, and so they tended to abandon the rationalistic method of seeking knowledge which the scientists had appropriated in favor of an intuitive quest for some higher kind of knowledge that would demonstrate that man is unique and perhaps divine. Indeed, the tendency among the symbolists was to retreat ever further from reason and beyond intuition back into the subconscious as a possible source for knowledge and poetic inspiration and method. The political events which had served as a stimulus to the naturalists served further to disillusion the symbolists and encouraged them to band together in small, exclusive and esoteric little groups (for instance the circle of Stefan George), writing for one another and proud that the vulgar middle class could not understand what they were saying. In their opposition primarily to the bourgeoisie the symbolists completed the rift that had appeared between some romanticists and the public, and proudly and militantly they worked to widen the gap. But in spite of their pride in their isolation from the middle class, one of their favorite themes became the lonely struggle of the sensitive individual to find some means of adjusting himself to society.

Certain baroque authors like Góngora and John Donne and certain German romanticists like Hölderlin, Novalis, Hoffmann and Wagner belong to the most significant forerunners of European Symbolism, along with Blake in England and Gérard de Nerval in France. E. T. A. HOFFMANN (1776-1822) is important primarily for his influence upon Poe and Baudelaire, and after Symbolism had developed he began to exert additional influence on such writers as Villiers de l'Isle-Adam. Hoffmann's fantastic tales of mystery and the mysterious (*Fantasiestücke*, 1814; *Nachtstücke*, 1817) contributed to the belief that the world of appearances conceals a strange, sometimes sinister world of mystery which lies behind the appearance and which influences men's lives. Baudelaire in particular was drawn to the doctrine of "correspondences" which he found expressed in Hoffmann's *Kreisleriana*— the doctrine that perceptions are interchangeable among the senses, that one can hear the "colors" of music, smell the "textures" of perfume, and see the aural harmonies of a visual scene. This doctrine implies, of course, that the world of sensual appearance is merely a world of symbols which stand for the real world beyond. Hoffmann's impact in Russia was felt even earlier than in France; it extended from Pushkin's *Queen of Spades* and Gogol's *The Portrait* to Dostoevski's *The Double*.

Edgar Allan POE (1809-49) has proven one of the strongest single influences upon Symbolism, particularly in Europe. His stories of mystery (*Tales of the Arabesque and Grotesque*, 1840) appealed to the symbolists as indicative of the evanescent, imperfect, and finally meaningless nature of the world of appearance. The real world, of meaning and truth at least, is only faintly suggested in the world which we see, and the only means of experiencing the real world of truth is by retreating into one's imagination. His important French translator Baudelaire, it has often been pointed out, mentioned that in reading Poe he frequently found Poe expressing his own thoughts and convictions, just as he would like to have them expressed. Poe's theory of poetry (*Philosophy of Composition*, 1846; *The Poetic Principle*, 1848) and his poetry itself (*Tamerlane and Other Poems*, 1827; *The Raven and Other Poems*, 1845) also appealed to the symbolists. Poe's conviction that beauty must be defined as effect and his statement that no poem which has a beautiful effect can be a long poem, have obviously inspired modern poetry, for with a few, usually unsuccessful, exceptions, no symbolist poet has undertaken to write a long poem. Poe's poetry, however poorly regarded it may be by some modern American critics, has been perennially popular in Europe. The highly musical, sometimes excessively rhythmic quality of Poe's metrics and the consciously harmonic assonances of his language provided early symbolists such as Verlaine and Mallarmé with models for their own attempts to make poetry approach music in effect. Rimbaud, Laforgue, Villiers de l'Isle-Adam are only a few of the other symbolists influenced by Poe. Nor was Poe's influence restricted to the symbolists, for others who are in his debt include Rossetti, Dostoevski, Gautier, Banville, Maupassant, and Valéry. Among his French translators, Baudelaire (*Histoires extraordinaires*, 1856) and Mallarmé (who translated *The Raven* in 1875 and other poems in 1888) should be particularly noted.

There were a number of writers outside the field of literature who likewise exerted significant influences on Symbolism, but we can mention only two: Nietzsche and Freud. Friedrich NIETZSCHE (1844-1900), because of his vigorous rejection of the materialistic, shallow, and sentimental values which he saw all around him in nineteenth century society, inevitably appealed to those symbolists who found nothing in their contemporary world that did not revolt them. His teaching (*Unzeitgemässe Betrachtungen*, 1873; *Also sprach Zarathustra*, 1883; *Jenseits von Gut und Böse*, 1886) that men are different and therefore unequal and that those who are superior should develop their superiority and not allow it to become chained and atrophied by the petty restrictions which the unwashed

masses want to place upon them gave philosophic justification
to the symbolists for their rejection of society and their independence in living and writing. Nietzsche's insistence that the
superior intelligence can remain superior and exert its superiority only by constant discipline and education gave comfort to
the symbolists who economically and physically were obviously
inferior to their bourgeois fellows, but who felt proudly that
they were intellectually as far above the bourgeoisie as man is
the justification for the whole way of life cultivated by many of
above the amoeba. The philosophical support for the doctrine
of rebellious individualism and intellectual superiority, combined with an essentially mystical theory of knowledge (deriving in many ways from Swedenborg and Kierkegaard), provided the essential assumptions for the symbolist aesthetic and
the symbolists. Nietzsche's works were translated into English
from 1896 and into French from 1898 on; in Scandinavia his
significance was underscored especially by the famous Danish
critic Brandes.

One or more aspects of Nietzsche's philosophy can be seen in
such diverse symbolists as Wagner, Hauptmann, George, Rimbaud, Gide, Valéry, Unamuno, Ortega y Gasset, Shaw, Crane,
and Pound, to mention only a few. On the other hand it should
be emphasized that Nietzsche was also apt to inspire unbridled
physical prowess among titanic men who acted as though they
theories of human psychology and whose methods of psycho-
were beyond good and evil (for instance Jack London's *The Sea
Wolf*, and *Burning Daylight*). Instead of these various influences, one may also wish to investigate certain predecessors
of Nietzsche, for instance the fine shadings of different intellectual, physical or spiritual emphases in Emerson (*Oversoul*)
and Whitman (*Leaves of Grass*) in America and Spitteler
(*Prometheus und Epimetheus* and *Conrad der Leutnant*) in
Switzerland.

Had Symbolism appeared only after 1900, most literary his-

torians would probably have given complete credit (or blame)
for its emergence to Sigmund FREUD (1856-1939), whose
analysis not only lent tremendous support to the theory of
Symbolism but even provided a framework of symbols to take
the place of the worn out symbols of classical mythology.
Freud's teaching that the subconscious element in the human
mind exercises a fundamental and controlling influence over

the personality and the (sexual) behavior of the human being gave scientific justification for the symbolist reliance upon intuition. But it was even more important that his method of psychoanalysis (in which the free association of ideas and of unconscious dream symbols became a means of penetrating to the subconscious) provided support for and addition to the poetic method of Symbolism. His theories gave a meaningful pattern of symbolism which could be generally understood. Freud's influence on literature has been so great that it can be seen in practically all modern authors, and it was especially strong on the dadaist and surrealist writers of the twenties. Not only has his influence extended down to the present, but it has reached into the past so that it is now fashionable to attempt a kind of psychoanalysis of the great poets of the past.

Rather than elaborate on other contributors to the tenets of Symbolism such as Wagner in Germany and Bergson in France we should allude to the relationship between the literature of Symbolism and the other arts. At no time in the history of Western literature, with the possible exception of the Renaissance, have all arts been so closely inter-related. Symbolist poets have regularly been the close friends and fellow manifesto-writers of painters, and very often painters have undertaken to write poetry and poets to do paintings. In their rebellion against tradition and against their contemporary culture, poets, painters, and musicians alike have sought new media, new forms, and new techniques by means of which they might communicate their subjective visions. It is no accident that many of the literary -isms of the modern age are terms borrowed from painting, such as Impressionism, Expressionism, Cubism. For both the modernist painters and the modernist poets have tried not only to alter the forms of the past, but to destroy the old media and create entirely new ones. Comparable to the various kinds of abstractionism in painting and sculpture are the various attempts made during the last thirty years to find a new syntax and even a new language for poetry. And the relationship between poetry and music is also deserving of study, for the attempts to discover new idioms and new harmonies beyond the traditional ones on the part of such composers as Schönberg and Bartok are quite comparable to the experimentations of the symbolist poets.

Among foreign countries particularly popular among the

delicate delineators of modern sensitivities is again Italy, the land rediscovered by the scores of travellers during the Age of Romanticism. Italy had fascinated realistic novelists like Henry James who, in *Roderick Hudson* (1876), wrote about an American sculptor in Rome; like Isolde Kurz, authoress of *Florentiner Novellen* and *Italienische Erzählungen* (*Italian Stories*, 1895) ; and like Ricarda Huch, who in *Menschen und Schicksale aus dem Risorgimento* (*Men and Destinies during the Risorgimento*, 1908) delved into Italian history and in *Aus der Triumphgasse* (*The Street of Triumph*, 1902) into the greatness and decline of Italian cities. Italy was even more alluring to those who in a finely chiselled style wanted to analyze the quivering nervous system of men (Hofmannsthal's *Der Tod des Tizian*, 1892), their inclination towards eroticism (Schnitzler's two *Casanovas* of 1918 and *Der Schleier der Beatrice*, 1899), sexual aberrations (Thomas Mann's *Der Tod in Venedig*, 1913) and frenzied criminology (Heinrich Mann's *Die Göttinnen oder die drei Romane der Herzogin von Assy*, 1903). Ever since Paul Heyse's *Die Kinder der Welt* (*The Children of the World*, 1873), Swinburne and Walter Pater's *Marius, the Epicurean* (1885), the air seemed filled with unrestrained sensualism; later authors like Oscar Wilde, d'Annunzio and Hofmannsthal added an atmosphere of elegant decadence, of a *fin du siècle* fatigue, a *blasé* aestheticism and a disdain of all but sensual pleasures—and to these poets Italy seemed particularly attractive, especially since Burckhardt had so boldly sketched the colossal amorality of the Italian Renaissance and since C. F. Meyer had made that period the center of his finely observed historical tales.

The Italian Renaissance was not the only source of inspiration for the symbolists. The Pléiade, the Elizabethans and Stuardians and the Spanish *Siglo de Oro* likewise held a new fascination for modern poets, as indicated by Hofmannsthal's modernizations of Otway's *Venice Preserved* and Calderón's *Grosses Welttheater*, Beer-Hofmann's adaptation of Massinger and Field's *The Fatal Dowry* (under the title of *Der Graf von Charolais*) and Stefan Zweig's and Jules Romains' modernizations of Ben Jonson's *Volpone*. In lyrical poetry one should note the reawakening of interest in Villon, Ronsard and du Bellay and the translations of Louise Labé and Michelangelo by Rilke, of Dante and Shakespeare's sonnets by George, and a general

revival of interest in Petrarchism and in the baroque style of
Donne and Góngora.

Poetry

The comparative history of Symbolism in modern poetry is
difficult to recount because one of the strongest characterizations
of the symbolist poet is that he seeks consciously to find a new
and often individual pattern in which to write. The symbolists
of every country have been notable for their explorations into
the past of their own and other countries and even into the
literature of heretofore unknown cultures. But the modern
nation which gave most to twentieth century symbolist poetry
was France.

Charles BAUDELAIRE (1821-67) is to modern poetry what
Flaubert is to the modern novel. He perfected the technique,
he implied the principles, and he provided examples approaching
perfection. However much they try, few modern poets are able
to match the perfect style of Baudelaire's *Les Fleurs du mal*
(*The Flowers of Evil*, 1857), few are able to convey as simply
and yet as richly the spiritual and moral *ennui* which the sensitive individual feels in the modern world, few are able so deftly
to unify the discordant and warring emotions and aspirations
into single experiences, and few are able to convey so profound
a sense of religious yearning by means of such passionate and
compellingly sensual imagery. In form Baudelaire was conservative, but in language and style he was a deft innovator.
His imagery never seems daring or harsh, but it has the organic
complexity which makes it carry the burden of the poem and
never serves merely as decoration. Baudelaire is in part responsible for the characteristic method of modern poetry to use
imagery functionally as a means of communicating the complexity of experience. Both for his sensibility and his style
Baudelaire has appealed profoundly to twentieth century symbolists, few of whom do not reflect in their poetry the results
of their reading in *Les Fleurs du mal*. Baudelaire's influence is
not, however, restricted to the symbolists: any list of his debtors
would include at least Carducci, Swinburne, Pater, George,
Rilke, Eliot, Pound, Stevens, Yeats, Auden, and Tate, plus
practically every serious French poet who has written since
1870.

With the exception of Baudelaire, French poetry between the

end of Romanticism and 1870 was written largely under the influence of Realism, under the banner of Parnassianism, as we have already discussed. Then around 1870 a strong reaction set in—induced in part by the disillusionment of the Franco-Prussian War, which had proved that the bourgeois culture of the Second Empire was weak as well as gaudy and superficial, and in part by a natural aversion to the growing excesses of Realism which led to outright Naturalism. Two symbolists anticipated the formal movement of 1885 (when the term Symbolism was first used): Arthur RIMBAUD and Tristan Corbière. Rimbaud in particular, for his strange, associational, obscure poetry with its startling imagery, daring linguistic usage, and supralogical development (*Le Bâteau ivre*, 1871; *Poésies complètes*, 1895) has remained for fifty years one of the fountainheads of Symbolism. He contributed particularly to the evolving styles of George, Rilke, Lorca, Pound, Williams, MacLeish, and even the young Aldous Huxley. The affinity between Rimbaud and the American Hart Crane is one of the most striking examples of literary and psychological parallels in literary history. Rimbaud's prose poem *Une Saison en enfer* (*A Season in Hell*, 1873) and his set of mystical jottings, *Illuminations* (1886), have been equally popular, contributing not only to the poetry of this century, but to the merger of poetry and prose which has been developing since the end of the nineteenth century. Two notable examples of relatively modern prose poems comparable to Rimbaud's are W. C. Williams' *Kora in Hell* and García Lorca's *Poeta en Nueva York*. While Tristan Corbière is less widely known and comparably less influential (*Les Amours jaunes*, 1873), he was one of the many symbolists whom Ezra Pound praised, and he contributed to the evolution of the Anglo-American symbolist idiom.

Practically all of the symbolists of the 1885 group were influential abroad, especially in Germany, England and America, but we can discuss only a few. Paul VERLAINE's musical but clear style and his almost romantic pessimism (*Sagesse*, 1881; *Jadis et Naguère*, 1884; *Amour*, 1888) brought him immediate international fame, while the other symbolists were not acclaimed until the second and third decades of this century. While Verlaine inspired some very ineffective imitations in America and England even before 1900, his prestige in this century has declined slightly. Even so, he has contributed a delicacy and grace to much twentieth century poetry which it desperately needs. Where one finds, as in Yeats, Stevens, Eugenio de Castro or Rilke, genuine lyric grace, one can expect to find an admirer of Verlaine. Jules LAFORGUE's adolescent pessimism (*Les Complaintes*, 1885) has caused his poetry to decline in popularity, but his daringly original imagery and his fantastic use of language, including the boldest neologisms, guarantee that he will remain a text for fledgling symbolist poets for some time. In addition to his contributions to the style and technique of Symbolism, we should recall the Laforguian irony which was mentioned in connection with Heine and which is one of the distinguishing features of modern poetry —that irony which allows the poet to reveal his innermost thoughts and feelings while at the same time examining them objectively and critically. The classic example of Laforguian irony is contained in T. S. Eliot's *Prufrock* (1917), the most notable result of Eliot's tutelage under Laforgue. Eliot's own domination of Anglo-American poetry has been largely responsible for the great influence Laforgue has had during the last thirty years. Not only has the latter been imitated by Wallace Stevens, Archibald MacLeish, Ezra Pound, and influenced almost every younger poet, but the Laforguian fashion became so strong that even such a poet as Hart Crane, who was temperamentally opposed to the Laforguian sensibility, attempted imitations of his poetry. Stéphane MALLARMÉ, finally, was the subtlest and most sophisticated of the symbolists. An urbane and highly intelligent professor of English, he served as the intellectual leader of Symbolism, and in his poetry (*L'Après-midi d'un faune*, 1876; *Les Poésies*, 1887) and prose (*Pages*, 1891; *Divagations*, 1897) he cultivated an idiom that is comparable to the parnassian in its technical perfection and polish, but which is unique in its subtle evocativeness and exotic richness. Mallarmé's particular contribution to twentieth century poetry lies in his insistence upon technical perfection and the highly intellectualized way he goes about capturing evanescent and irrational feelings and experiences. While Rimbaud and Laforgue were working away at language itself in an effort to extort useful meanings from it, Mallarmé accepted the language but worked toward a supralogical syntax which utilized the connotations rather than the denotations of words. He has had an especial appeal to the most sophisticated and subtly refined of the moderns, including Eugenio de Castro, Wallace Stevens, and Rainer Maria Rilke.

Aside from these four, the remaining symbolists must be treated in bulk, although the investigation of individual influences of any one of them would prove profitable: the expatriate Americans, Stuart Merrill and Francis Vielé-Griffin, the Belgians Verhaeren and Maeterlinck, the Greek Moréas, and so on. In the field of symbolist theory we should note the manifesto by Moréas; in the same year 1886 the Belgian symbolists began to publish their journal *La Wallonie* (to be followed by the *Blätter für die Kunst*, 1890 ff. by Stefan George). Among the younger poets who came mostly after the 1885 phase of Symbolism were Francis Jammes and Paul Fort, both especially appealing to Amy Lowell and John Gould Fletcher; Paul Claudel, particularly interesting because of his later diplomatic career which took him to Tokyo and Washington as full ambassador; Rémy de Gourmont, an important influence on Eliot and the later school of "New Criticism"; and Paul Valéry, the twentieth century Mallarmé, whose brilliant, philosophical criticism and technically perfect poetry have gained him world-wide respect among the most intellectual of the symbolists. During the second and third decades of our century, Symbolism produced an off-shoot of extremists who went under various labels, including North-Southists and Dadaists, but who belong to the movement of Surrealism. This movement cannot be dismissed too readily, for it contributed fundamentally to the poetic revolution of the last thirty years. Notable among its practitioners are Guillaume Apollinaire, who is currently being revived in America, and that jack-of-all-arts, Jean Cocteau. Among the Americans who were on the fringes of this movement and who reflect its influence are Hart Crane and E. E. Cummings, while the brilliant young English poet Dylan Thomas could hardly have cultivated his highly individual style had not the surrealists prepared the way.

The development of Symbolism in Anglo-American poetry has succeeded effectively in making the division between American and English literature appear rather artificial. Just before the first World War young English and American poets banded together to conduct their poetic revolution, and the developments in poetry in English since then have made it impossible to disentangle the two bodies of poetry. Symbolic of this poetic

"union now" has been the expatriation of Eliot to England and
of Auden to the United States. About 1912, a group of young
men and women from America and England adopted the label
of Imagism, and from this movement have developed most of
the significant features of modern Anglo-American poetry. The
group included Ezra Pound, Richard Aldington, Amy Lowell,
W. C. Williams, and James Joyce, among others. Particularly
under the guidance of that tireless intermediary Ezra POUND
they sought in the poetry of all lands and all times models for
their new writing. We have mentioned the major sources of
their poetry earlier, but the principal single source was France
—first the parnassians, especially Gautier, and second the symbolists. Developing out of their study and imitation of the
symbolistes and out of their investigations of other forms
emerged the modern Anglo-American symbolist poetry which is
so very similar to the French. Ezra Pound, although not the
best poet produced by this movement, was the most important
influence on it, primarily because of his indefatigable search
for new forms and his militant advocacy of daring new techniques. His major work, *The Cantos,* is a hodgepodge of many
languages, classical and modern. Indeed, Pound's poetry, for
all of its occasional brilliance, is a congeries of borrowings from
everywhere in the world of literature. Thomas Stearns ELIOT,
the outstanding modern Anglo-American poet, is the Valéry
of England. His poetry has been determined in part by his
readings in the French and Italian, especially Dante, but is an
individual and original poetry which has inspired but defied
dozens of imitators. William Butler YEATS, whom some regard
as the greatest English poet of our age, began as a romantic
pre-Raphaelite and, partially through his study of the symbolists
and partially as a result of his personal mysticism, developed
one of the most powerful poetic styles in English since the Renaissance. Others among the important Anglo-American poets
are Wallace Stevens, William Carlos Williams, E. E. Cummings,
John Crowe Ransom, W. H. Auden, Stephen Spender, and Dylan
Thomas.

The wide range of modern German lyrical poetry is encom-
passed by the two names of Rainer Maria RILKE (1875-1926)
and Stefan George (1868-1933), the former born in Bohemia
and an extensive traveller in Russia, France (where he lived
with and was inspired by the sculptor Rodin), Dalmatia, and

Spain, the latter born in the Rhineland, and both buried in southern Switzerland. Rilke was a mystic, a humanitarian, a poet dreaming of man's regeneration not in terms of Nietzschean supermen and blond demigods, but in terms of humility, compassion and brotherhood (*Das Stundenbuch*, 1905; *Neue Gedichte*, 1907; *Sonette an Orpheus*, 1923; *Die Duineser Elegien*, 1923). This *Wandlung* of the individual, the complete obliteration of foolish bourgeois pride and egotism, meant everything to him. Not the plastic gods of Greece, not the amoral characters of the Italian Renaissance, but the half-Oriental mysticism, the endless plains, the figures of Dostoevski and Tolstoy, the communistic dreams of old Russia inspired him most deeply. Every human being is created in the image of God; like Buddha and Christ, we must go out among the sick and the poor if we want to find again the nobility of our souls. Though Rilke was an accomplished artist, he cannot be called merely a decadent aesthete and symbolist; his message is too earnest, his convictions are too strong and too pure. By contrast to Rilke, Stefan GEORGE seems quite Nietzschean in his quest for self-perfection and high ethical convictions. Both poets extensively translated from their French contemporaries; yet George, surrounded by a small circle of disciples, kept aloof from the follies and weaknesses of the world and strove above all after a form that was pure, cold and perfect (*Das Jahr der Seele*, 1897; *Der siebente Ring*, 1911; *Der Stern des Bundes*, 1914; *Das neue Reich*, 1929). The poet, according to him, is a seer, a prophet, who speaks for the chosen few only and inspires them with Apollonian restraint and with a stern will to quality. Rilke and George dominate the field of German symbolist lyricism so much that the names of minor poets can be omitted—though the beautiful Rilke-inspired expressionistic poems of Franz Werfel (*Der Weltfreund*, 1911; *Wir sind*, 1913; *Einander*, 1915; *Der Gerichtstag*, 1919) and the tragic *Moabiter Sonette* of Albrecht Haushofer should at least be mentioned.

In Italy, reference can be made to the cult of form and the decadence of Gabriele d'Annunzio; yet while his flamboyant personality gave him international fame during much of his life, he contributed little to European literature but a legend—if one excepts isolated examples of his influence such as that on the prose of Ramón María del Valle-Inclán (*Sonata de Primavera*). The Spanish poets of the Generation of 1898 stood deeply under the spell of French Symbolism as well as of the preceding Parnassianism; among them should be named the Sevillan Antonio Machado y Ruiz (*Soledades*, 1903) and, with regard to South America, the Nicaraguan Rubén DARÍO, who led a tragic and restless life comparable to Verlaine's and whose finely chiselled poems with their frequent praise of the Spanish race (*Cantos de vida y esperanza*, 1905) inspired emulation from the Pyrenees to the Andes. The loss of Cuba and of the Philippines and the disappearance of the Spanish Empire explain the patriotism as well as the pessimism, the decadence as well as the call for a spiritual regeneration, which are so typical for the *modernistas* of '98.

The Novel

Although Symbolism would naturally find its best medium of expression in poetry, it has adapted the novel to its purposes and produced a considerable body of long prose works of great subtlety, intelligence, and often obscurity. The origins of the symbolist novel go back through one channel to the self-revelations of Rousseau's *Confessions*, through another to the technical and stylistic perfection of Flaubert, and through another to the attempts of the symbolist poets to abandon the restrictions of form in an effort to express the inexpressible within themselves.

Rather than refer to an early example of symbolist prose in *Sixtine, roman de la vie cérébrale* by Rémy de Gourmont (1890) we should point to the real greatness of Romain ROLLAND, who quite in the tradition of the German apprenticeship novel produced in the ten volumes of his *Jean-Christophe* (1904-12) a magnificent and powerful record of the inner struggles of his hero to find his place in society. For the technique and even more for the earnest message of his novel, Rolland was hailed by the sincere pacifists of Europe who, together with all other men of good will, will always consider a Franco-German reconciliation the very cornerstone of the peace and the strength of Europe—and he who himself had written biographies of Goethe and Beethoven (1903 and 1930) was in turn the object of an admirable study by Stefan Zweig (*Romain Rolland*, 1921). But two more recent French writers rather than Rolland have contributed the most to the subjectively motivated novel—Proust and Gide. Marcel PROUST, who isolated himself from the society of his day and who in this isolation spun out of himself a penetrating picture of that society in decay, produced in the twelve volumes of his *A la recherche du temps perdu* (*In Quest of Lost Time*, 1913 ff.) one of the seminal books of modern imaginative prose. The central character, Marcel, observing life around him, finds small details in his environment evoking by a process of slow, involuntary stream-of-consciousness the whole of his past experience. Proust's method reveals the inner workings of the human mind by virtue of his ability to project by means of delicately handled details the evanescent experiences which are often the most complex; his profound insight into relationships in society contributes to make him one of the major figures in the modern novel. André GIDE, whose life was a rebellion against the moral strictures of society, endlessly explored his own inner being and boldly revealed everything there. His *Les faux monnayeurs* (*The Counterfeiters*, 1926) is concerned with the relationships among a group of adolescents and between them and the adult society. He subtly weaves together three strands, embracing the problem of individual morality, the problem of the literary artist, and the problem of society's relationship to the individual. His keen insights, his frank treatment of sexual perversion, and his pervading irony combine to make this one of the outstanding and most influential of modern novels, having been imitated in the very successful *Point Counter Point* of Aldous Huxley. Gide and Proust dominate the modern French symbolist novel and leave little room for others of the group of very competent novelists that France has produced, such as Valéry Larbaud, Georges Duhamel, and André Maurois. Since the war, such existentialists as Sartre and Camus have effectively combined Naturalism and Symbolism in novels which have become internationally known.

Like France, America and England have produced a number of sensitive and competent novelists, adept in deep psychological probings and symbolical technique. Among earlier novelists whose importance seems to continue to grow, mention should be made of Nathaniel Hawthorne, whose preoccupation with the problem of evil and sin (*The Scarlet Letter*, 1850; *The House of Seven Gables*, 1851; *The Marble Faun*, 1860) and whose explorations of human psychology under darkly repressive conditions make him seem quite modern. Also Herman Melville, particularly because of the symbolism of his *Moby Dick* (1851) and the mysticism of his *Mardi* (1849), has gradually emerged as one of the great figures of American literature. Thomas WOLFE is one of the outstanding later novelists (*Look Homeward, Angel*, 1929), who is particularly important for his popularity in Germany (where his works, often resembling a typical German apprenticeship novel, are greatly appreciated) and in the rest of Europe. And finally, of course, William Faulkner, who has been discussed as a naturalist, is perhaps the greatest American symbolist novelist.

In England, D. H. Lawrence, with his almost Nietzschean individualism and Virginia Woolf, with her delicate stream-of-consciousness, are both major figures in the modern novel; preceding them were Samuel Butler (*The Way of all Flesh*. 1903) and Oscar Wilde, author of that masterpiece of *fin du siècle* aestheticism and amorality, *The Picture of Dorian Gray* (1891). But among the Anglo-Saxon symbolists there is above all one man who dominates the period: James JOYCE. In his *Portrait of an Artist as a Young Man*, Joyce introduced a stream-of-consciousness style which he developed further in *Ulysses* (1922) and then perfected, in his own terms, in *Finnegans Wake*. His method was to project the subconsciousness of his hero in an effort to capture the constant and complex flux of his thought, feelings and unrealized perceptions. In developing this method, Joyce felt compelled to dispense with the traditional syntax of language and ultimately to dispense with the traditional vocabulary itself. The final result in *Finnegans Wake* is a book of forbidding difficulty, one about which even sympathetic critics raise the question of whether the difficulty is sufficiently rewarded by the results. In addition to his violent modifications of the language, Joyce has constructed his two long novels on patterns of complexly interrelated symbols, each symbol having values on several levels of meaning. Regardless of Joyce's final position in literary history, he has been a profound influence on the modern novel, having done more than any other man to make the novel a means of communication comparable to poetry. Joyce's international life and, one might say, the international language which he invented in *Finnegans Wake*, make his work a storehouse of Western culture and himself an intimate of many of the leading European figures in literature of the last fifty years.

Although we mentioned Dostoevski in connection with the

naturalistic novel, it should be recalled that his searching portrayals of pathological psychology helped to prepare the way also for the symbolist novel. Italy and Spain are less noted for this type of novel; the Italian Italo Svevo, for instance, an early friend of and influence on James Joyce, has only recently begun to become widely known, while the Spaniards of the Generation of 1898 displayed a certain racial exaltation appealing to the *hispanidad* on either side of the Atlantic Ocean (*Los Argonautas* by Blasco Ibáñez, 1914) which might be compared to a similar Catholic exaltation in such French authors as Barrès and Maurras. Much richer, however, was the output in Germany—in minor authors like Klabund (*Krankheit*, 1916) and Max Brod (*Tycho Brahes Weg zu Gott*, 1916) as well as in major authors like Alfred Döblin who in *Berlin Alexanderplatz* (1929) emulated the stream-of-consciousness technique of James Joyce. Jakob WASSERMANN excelled in this type of novel in *Der Fall Maurizius* (*The Maurizius Case*, 1928) and *Etzel Andergast*, and, better still, in *Caspar Hauser* and *Das Gänsemännchen* (*The Goose Man*, 1915); his *Christian Wahnschaffe* (*The World's Illusion*, 1919) is one of the most deeply searching and rewarding German apprenticeship novels about the *Wandlung* of a young capitalist who forewent the wealth of his family in order to go, a new Christ and a new Buddha, to the outcasts of society who were in greatest need of his compassion. Equally valuable in their deeper implications are the expressionistic novels of Franz WERFEL—for instance the novel with the telling title *Nicht der Mörder, der Ermordete ist schuldig* (*Not the Murderer, But the Murdered Man is Guilty*, 1920). Symbolism can also be found in the novels of others like Thomas Mann—but the major contribution of German literature in that field can no doubt be found in the work of Franz KAFKA, whose *Der Prozess* (*The Trial*) and *Das Schloss* (*The Castle*) and short stories (all published posthumously by Max Brod in 1935 ff.) present in the sharp and visually precise language of the best realistic prose a symbolic world of terrifying and nightmarish inner experiences. Kafka's deep religious probings and his merciless exploitation of doubt and spiritual fear make him one of the most moving and provocative of the twentieth century novelists. He, like Joyce and Proust, has contributed fundamentally to the European novel of recent decades. But Kafka's strange blend of realism and spiritual exploration, of psychological terror

and grotesque humor make him, rather like America's Faulkner, a novelist who inspires but defies imitation.

The Drama

Off-hand it would seem that the drama is the least suitable of all the major literary genres for the purposes and methods of Symbolism. The drama's insistence upon objectivity and visual presentation of action provides inadequate opportunities for the symbolist, but the steady development of the symbolist technique of revealing subjective experience obliquely, by means of clusters of visual symbols which suggest the complexity of meaning, has encouraged more and more authors to attempt subduing the drama to the symbolist aesthetic. We have already mentioned that both Ibsen (in *Peer Gynt*) and Hauptmann (in *Hanneles Himmelfahrt* and *Die versunkene Glocke*) turned from Naturalism to Symbolism; so did Eugene O'Neill in America. Germany between the two World Wars was no doubt the leader in this field—not only because of truly outstanding and ingenious theatre directors (Max Reinhardt, Erwin Piscator) able to express the hallucinative visions of the symbolists, but also because of many leading dramatists in this field—men like Walter Hasenclever (*Der Sohn*, 1914), Fritz von Unruh (*Ein Geschlecht*, 1917, *Der Platz*, 1920), Anton Wildgans (*Dies irae*, 1919), Franz Werfel (*Der Spiegelmensch*, 1920), and above all, Georg KAISER and Ernst Toller. Kaiser excelled in plays like *Die Bürger von Calais* (*The Citizens of Calais*, 1914), *Von Morgens bis Mitternachts* (*From Morn till Midnight*, 1916), *Die Koralle* (1917), *Gas* (1918 and 1920)—all dramas preaching the necessity of man's inner regeneration in a mechanized and brutalized world; in *Die jüdische Witwe* (*The Jewish Widow*, 1911) he modernized the story of Judith, and in *König Hahnrei* (*King Cuckold*, 1913) the adultery of Tristan and Isolde. Even more radical in their political implications were the tragedies by TOLLER, written against war (*Der deutsche Hinkemann, Feuer aus den Kesseln!*), against machines (*Die Maschinenstürmer*, 1922) and for the coming revolution (*Die Wandlung, Masse Mensch*, 1920). Especially this latter play is significant because the nameless masses rather than single individuals have become the real heroes of the action—and the impressive and unique staging by men like Max Reinhardt made these plays doubly effective.

While no author has yet succeeded in writing a symbolist play that will compare with, say, *Der Prozess* among the novels, dramatists have continued their attempts. One of the earliest to strike out in this direction was Maurice Maeterlinck in Belgium with his *La Princesse Maleine* and *L'oiseau bleu* (*The Blue Bird,* 1909). In Italy, Luigi Pirandello has made notable contributions to the modern theatre, especially with his *Sei personaggi in cerca d'autore* (*Six Characters in Search of an Author*). Spain's García Lorca made a number of dramatic experiments (*Yerma, Bodas de sangre, La casa de Bernarda Alba*) which began to become known abroad only after his tragic execution during the Spanish Civil War. With his *R.U.R.*, Karel Capek in Czechoslovakia combined again the social commentary of Naturalism with the imaginative fantasy of Symbolism to give an exciting and disturbing play which has become internationally known. Jean Cocteau has remained one of the most daringly experimental dramatists in France and has also experimented with movies in an effort to produce symbolist plays by this means. Sartre's existentialist dramas have been among the more theatrically successful of recent attempts at Symbolism— *Les Mouches,* for instance, having been a subtle means of expressing his resistance to German occupation. In England T. S. Eliot has written several plays in his own idiom, one of the most recent of which, *The Cocktail Party,* surprised even the author by becoming a Broadway sensation. And recently also Christopher Fry captivated English and American audiences with his symbolist dramatic poetry (*Venus Observed,* 1949, *The Lady's Not for Burning, A Sleep of Prisoners*).

We conclude this rapid survey by referring to some of the significant American authors, for instance to Maxwell Anderson with his lyrical *Winterset* (1935) and his historical tragedies about Joan of Arc, Ann Boleyn, Elizabeth and Mary Stuart (1933); Robert Sherwood, author, among other things, of *Idiot's Delight*; and Sidney Kingsley, who transformed Koestler's *Darkness at Noon* into a gripping and fearful drama. But the greatest of all American dramatists, of course, was Eugene O'NEILL, author of such symbolist plays as *Emperor Jones* (1920), *The Fountain, The Great God Brown, Lazarus Laughed, Strange Interlude,* and *Mourning Becomes Electra* (1931), in which he occasionally used the daring innovation of introducing masks in order to make clear the deep meaning of his symbolical presentation of men's lives and passions.

Index